# Google App Engine Java and GWT Application Development

Build powerful, scalable, and interactive
web applications in the cloud

**Daniel Guermeur**

**Amy Unruh**

PUBLISHING

BIRMINGHAM - MUMBAI

# Google App Engine Java and GWT Application Development

First published: November 2010

Production Reference: 1161110

Published by Packt Publishing Ltd.
32 Lincoln Road
Olton
Birmingham, B27 6PA, UK.

ISBN 978-1-849690-44-7

www.packtpub.com

Cover Image by Sujay Gawand (sujay0000@gmail.com)

# Credits

**Authors**

Daniel Guermeur

Amy Unruh

**Reviewers**

Dom Derrien

Yağız Erkan

Samuel Goebert

Ravi Sharma

**Acquisition Editor**

David Barnes

**Development Editor**

Hyacintha D'Souza

**Technical Editors**

Paramanand N.Bhat

Namita Sahni

**Copy Editor**

Laxmi  Subramanian

**Editorial Team Leader**

Aditya Belpathak

**Project Team Leader**

Lata Basantani

**Project Coordinator**

Vincila Colaco

**Indexers**

Monica Ajmera Mehta

Rekha Nair

**Proofreader**

Kevin McGowan

**Graphics**

Geetanjali Sawant

**Production Coordinator**

Arvindkumar Gupta

**Cover Work**

Arvindkumar Gupta

# About the Authors

**Daniel Guermeur** is the founder and CEO of Metadot Corporation. He holds a Diplome d'Ingenieur of Informatique from University of Technology of Compiegne (France) as well as a Master in Photonics from Ecole Nationale Superieure de Physique of Strasbourg (France). Before starting Metadot in 2000, he worked for oil services companies including giant Schlumberger Ltd where he was in charge of improving the worldwide IT infrastructure.

He has been developing large scale database-backed web applications since the very beginning of the democratization of the Internet in 1995, including an open source software content management system Metadot Portal Server, Mojo Helpdesk, a web-based customer support application and Montastic, a popular website monitor service.

> Thank you to my daughter Alexandra Guermeur and Cheryl Ridall for their love and continuous support while writing this book. This meant a lot to me. Cheryl, I miss you.

**Amy Unruh** currently does technology training and course development, with a focus on web technologies. Previously, she has been a Research Fellow at the University of Melbourne, where she taught web technologies and researched robust distributed agent systems. She has worked at several startups, building web applications using a variety of languages; served as adjunct faculty at the University of Texas; and was a member of the Distributed Agents Program at MCC. She received her Ph.D. in CS/AI from Stanford University, in the area of AI planning, and has a BS degree in CS from UCSB. She has numerous publications, and has co-edited a book on Safety and Security in Multiagent Systems.

> Thanks to Moon, and to Wesley and Eleanor Unruh, without whose love and support this book would not have been possible. And thanks also to Daniel, for getting us started!

# About the Reviewers

**Dom Derrien** joined **AnotherSocialEconomy.com** (**ASE**) as co-founder after having worked for more than 15 years in the software development area.

Dom's responsibilities in ASE cover the architecture definition of its communication engine and respective connectors enabling its multi-channel interfaces like e-mail, Twitter, Facebook, Android, Adobe AIR, and others. Dom is also in charge of defining the ASE public API (REST-based). He produces the vast majority of code and corresponding tests for the implementation ported on Google App Engine. Dom also coordinates the work of other contributors working on specific connectors as well as reviewing web materials and contributing to pre-sales consulting, the internal community site and business decision-making.

Prior to ASE, Dom worked for Compuware Corporation as Technical Consultant in the Web application and Mobile application domains, to bootstrap new projects in the Vantage product line. Before joining Compuware, as a Software Architect, he worked on the development of a Web 2.0 client for Rational Portfolio Manager enterprise project management server, at IBM Canada. Dom also worked at Oracle Canada, as a Senior Developer, in the Oracle Collaboration Suite team, to build its first Web 2.0 client, just at the time the corresponding technology was emerging.

Aside from his protected work for ASE, Dom shares some projects on github.com to give back materials to the open source community (like a library for Amazon FPS on GAE, utilities for internationalized Web applications, and others) and publishes his own blog at domderrien.blogspot.com.

Dom is also active in the Diku Dilenga organization which aims to bring microfinance services to the poorest in the Democratic Republic of the Congo. His dream is to connect ASE to Diku Dilenga, to use modern communication technologies at the service of microentrepreneurs.

Also important in his life is his family – his wife and two sons. They all enjoy their peaceful life in Montreal, Quebec, Canada, and their practice of karate, Chito-Ryu style.

**Yağız Erkan** is the Chief Technical Architect with DeCare Systems Ireland, an Ireland-based software development company building highly-scalable, large enterprise systems and retail sites. Before taking on an architectural role, he worked as a software engineer for various companies in France.

Yağız studied in Galatasaray High School in Istanbul, Turkey, then he obtained his MSc in Computer Science in Université Claude Bernard in Lyon, France. After working several years as a software engineer in Lyon, he moved to Ireland and joined DeCare Systems Ireland as a Technical Architect in 2000. He currently leads a team of hands-on architects who ensure the most up-to-date and suitable practices, technologies and tools are utilized, leading to the delivery of high quality applications and solutions.

Even though Yağız's background is mainly Java and Web technologies, he has worked on Microsoft .NET and mobile (iPhone and Android) projects. He has already been mentioned in various books as a reviewer and he keeps an on-line presence through blogging and social networking.

**Samuel Goebert** is a computer science master student at the University of Applied Sciences Darmstadt, Germany. Goebert has over 7 years of experience in web related development and associated technologies.

In his role as technology consultant for bigcurl (`http://www.bigcurl.de`) Goebert is responsible for the overall design and execution of various products from conception to launch including web applications, mobile applications, intranet tools and custom API's.

He wrote his award winning bachelor thesis about scalable data delivery in local area networks at Apple Inc. in California, which also awarded him with a students scholarship from 2006 until 2009.

Goebert holds a Diploma from the School of Audio Engineering and received a bachelors degree from the University of Applied Sciences Darmstadt, Germany in Computer Science.

He is currently working on receiving his master degree in Computer Science in the field of restoring communications for the population of post disaster areas with autonomously deploying cell phone towers.

**Ravi Sharma** has a B.Tech (Computer Science) from Y.M.C.A Institute of Engineering, Faridabad and has worked in banking and higher studies. He has 8 years of experience in java especially low latency applications.He runs his own company, NextInfotech (`www.nextinfotech.com`) and also works as a consultant.

# Table of Contents

# Preface

This book is designed to give developers the tools they need to build their own Google App Engine (GAE) with Google Web Toolkit (GWT) applications, with a particular focus on some of the technologies useful for building social-media-oriented applications. The book is centered on a GAE + GWT Java application called *Connectr*, which is developed throughout the chapters and demonstrates, by example, the use of the technologies described in the book. The application includes social-media information gathering and aggregation activities and incorporates the use of many App Engine services and APIs, as well as GWT design patterns and widget examples.

Several stages of the *Connectr* application are used throughout the book as features are added to the app. Code is included with the book for all application stages, and each chapter indicates the stage used.

## What this book covers

*Chapter 1, Introduction,* introduces the approaches and technology covered in the book, and discusses what lies ahead.

*Chapter 2, Using Eclipse and the Google Plugin,* describes the basics of setting up a project using the Eclipse IDE and Google's GWT/GAE plugin. Topics include defining, compiling and running an Eclipse GWT/GAE project, and using the GWT developer browser plugin with the interactive debugger. The chapter also covers how to set up an App Engine account and create applications, and how to deploy an app to App Engine and access its Admin Console.

*Chapter 3, Building The Connectr User Interface with GWT,* focuses on GWT, and building the first iteration of the *Connectr* application's frontend. The chapter looks at how to specify widgets, with a focus on declarative specification using GWT's UIBinder and using the GWT RPC API for server-side communication.

*Chapter 4, Persisting Data: The App Engine Datastore*, covers Datastore basics. In the process, the first iteration of *Connectr's* server-side functionality is built. The chapter looks at how the Datastore works, and the implications of its design for your data models and code development. It covers how to use Java Data Objects (JDO) as an interface to the Datastore and how to persist and retrieve Datastore entities.

*Chapter 5, JDO Object Relationships and Queries*, builds on the topics of *Chapter 4*. It describes how to build and manage JDO objects that have relationships to each other, such as one-to-many and one-to-one parent-child relationships. It also covers how to query the Datastore, and the important role that Datastore indexes play in this process.

*Chapter 6, Implementing MVP, an Event Bus and Other GWT Patterns*, builds on the client-side code of *Chapter 3*, and shows how to make the frontend code modular and extensible. It accomplishes this via use of the MVP (Model-View-Presenter) and Event Bus design patterns, history/bookmark management, and an RPC abstraction, which supports call retries and progress indicators.

*Chapter 7, Background Processing and Feed Management*, centers on defining and running decoupled backend asynchronous tasks. In the process, the chapter introduces several App Engine services, including URLFetch and Task Queues, shows the use of Query Cursors to distribute Datastore-related processing across multiple Tasks, and introduces the use of Java Servlets and the incorporation of third-party libraries in a deployed application.

*Chapter 8, Authentication using Twitter and Facebook OAuth and Google Accounts*, adds authentication, login, and account functionality to *Connectr*, allowing it to support multiple users. The chapter demonstrates the use of both the Google Accounts API and the OAuth protocol for creating user accounts.

*Chapter 9, Robustness and Scalability: Transactions, Memcache, and Datastore Design*, delves into more advanced Datastore-related topics. The chapter investigates Datastore-related means of increasing the robustness, speed, and scalability of an App Engine app, including several ways to design data classes for scalability and to support efficient join-like queries. The chapter also introduces App Engine transactions and Transactional Tasks and the use of Memcache, App Engine's volatile-memory key-value store.

*Chapter 10, Pushing fresh content to clients with the Channel API*, covers the implementation of a message push system using the App Engine Channel API, used by *Connectr* to keep application data streams current. The chapter describes how to open back-end channels connected to client-side socket listeners, and presents a strategy for preventing the server from pushing messages to unattended web clients.

*Chapter 11, Managing and Backing Up Your App Engine Application*, focuses on useful App Engine deployment strategies, and admin and tuning tools. It includes ways to quickly upload configuration files without redeploying your entire application and describes how to do bulk uploads and downloads of application data. The chapter also discusses tools to analyze and tune your application's behavior, and the App Engine billing model.

*Chapter 12, Asynchronous Processing with Cron, Task Queue, and XMPP*, finishes building the server-side part of the *Connectr* app. The chapter introduces the use of App Engine Cron jobs, configuration of customized Task Queues, and App Engine's XMPP service and API, which supports push notifications. The chapter shows the benefits of proactive and asynchronous updating—the behind-the scenes work that keeps *Connectr's* data stream fresh—and looks at how App Engine apps can both send and receive XMPP messages.

*Chapter 13, Conclusion*, summarizes some of the approaches and technology covered in the book, and discusses what might lie ahead.

# What you need for this book

The book assumes some previous exposure to the basics of using Google Web Toolkit (GWT). "Recommended GWT Background" in *Chapter 1* lists the basic GWT concepts that will be useful for you to know, and points to the online GWT documentation that covers these concepts. The book does not assume prior Google App Engine exposure.

# Who this book is for

This is an intermediate-level book. It is designed for readers with some prior programming experience, and previous experience with Java development and object-oriented programming. It also assumes a general understanding of web technologies and concepts, and how to build web applications.

# Conventions

In this book you will find a number of styles of text that distinguish between different kinds of information. Here are some examples of these styles, and an explanation of their meaning.

Code words in text are shown as follows: "We can include other contexts through the use of the `include` directive."

A block of code is set as follows:

```
package com.metadot.book.connectr.client;
// Imports omitted

public class ConnectrApp implements EntryPoint {

...
  public void onModuleLoad() {
...
    getLoggedInUser();
  }
```

When we wish to draw your attention to a particular part of a code block, the relevant lines or items are set in bold:

```
UserAccount u =
  new UserAccount(sid, AuthenticationProvider. TWITTER);
u.setName(user.getName());
UserAccount connectr =
  new LoginHelper().loginStarts(request.getSession(), u);
```

Any command-line input or output is written as follows:

```
# cp /usr/src/asterisk-addons/configs/cdr_mysql.conf.sample
/etc/asterisk/cdr_mysql.conf
```

**New terms** and **important words** are shown in bold. Words that you see on the screen, in menus or dialog boxes for example, appear in the text like this: "clicking the **Next** button moves you to the next screen".

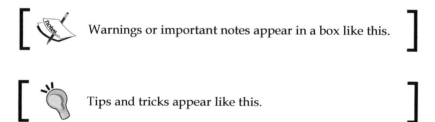

Warnings or important notes appear in a box like this.

Tips and tricks appear like this.

# Reader feedback

Feedback from our readers is always welcome. Let us know what you think about this book—what you liked or may have disliked. Reader feedback is important for us to develop titles that you really get the most out of.

To send us general feedback, simply send an e-mail to feedback@packtpub.com, and mention the book title via the subject of your message.

If there is a book that you need and would like to see us publish, please send us a note in the **SUGGEST A TITLE** form on www.packtpub.com or e-mail suggest@packtpub.com.

If there is a topic that you have expertise in and you are interested in either writing or contributing to a book, see our author guide on www.packtpub.com/authors.

# Customer support

Now that you are the proud owner of a Packt book, we have a number of things to help you to get the most from your purchase.

**Downloading the example code for this book**

You can download the example code files for all Packt books you have purchased from your account at http://www.PacktPub.com. If you purchased this book elsewhere, you can visit http://www.PacktPub.com/support and register to have the files e-mailed directly to you.

# Errata

Although we have taken every care to ensure the accuracy of our content, mistakes do happen. If you find a mistake in one of our books—maybe a mistake in the text or the code—we would be grateful if you would report this to us. By doing so, you can save other readers from frustration and help us improve subsequent versions of this book. If you find any errata, please report them by visiting http://www.packtpub.com/support, selecting your book, clicking on the **errata submission form** link, and entering the details of your errata. Once your errata are verified, your submission will be accepted and the errata will be uploaded on our website, or added to any list of existing errata, under the Errata section of that title. Any existing errata can be viewed by selecting your title from http://www.packtpub.com/support.

# Piracy

Piracy of copyright material on the Internet is an ongoing problem across all media. At Packt, we take the protection of our copyright and licenses very seriously. If you come across any illegal copies of our works, in any form, on the Internet, please provide us with the location address or website name immediately so that we can pursue a remedy.

Please contact us at copyright@packtpub.com with a link to the suspected pirated material.

We appreciate your help in protecting our authors, and our ability to bring you valuable content.

# Questions

You can contact us at questions@packtpub.com if you are having a problem with any aspect of the book, and we will do our best to address it.

# 1
# Introduction

**Google App Engine (GAE)** is a platform and SDK for developing and hosting web applications, using Google's servers and infrastructure. **Google Web Toolkit (GWT)** is a development toolkit for building complex AJAX-based web applications using Java, which is then compiled to optimized JavaScript. Used together, GAE/Java and GWT provide an end-to-end Java solution for AJAX web applications, which can solve many of the problems that arise in developing, maintaining, and scaling web applications.

GAE and GWT together provide:

- State-of-the-art AJAX web apps with optimized JavaScript and no worries about browser compatibility: all major browsers are supported automatically
- A powerful widget library enabling you to build complex UIs quickly
- Interactive debugging and compile-time checking of frontend Java code, prior to its compilation to JavaScript
- Almost unlimited scalability: App Engine applications are scaled and load-balanced automatically for you as the demand for your application as well as your data storage needs increase
- Freedom from application administration: app server and data storage administration is handled by the platform
- "One-click" deployment of an application to App Engine's hosting platform, with all of the GWT compilation and deployment details managed for you
- Access to powerful and scalable App Engine *services* that provide support for asynchronous computation and a range of communications APIs

This book is designed to give developers the tools they need to build their own GAE+GWT applications with a particular focus on some of the technologies useful for building social-media-oriented applications. The book is centered on a GAE+GWT Java application called *Connectr* that is developed throughout the chapters and demonstrates by example the use of the technologies described.

# Overview of the chapter

The remainder of this chapter will introduce the features of Google App Engine and Google Web Toolkit in more detail. Then we describe the *Connectr* application whose development provides a running example throughout the chapters, and highlight some of the technologies and approaches used by the application.

The final section of the chapter gives pointers to some useful online resources.

# Introduction to Google App Engine

Google App Engine (GAE) is a platform and SDK for developing and hosting web applications using Google's servers and infrastructure. The most current version of GAE at the time of writing is 1.3.7. App Engine supports both Java and Python runtime environments and SDKs, with each environment supporting standard protocols and technologies for web application development. This book focuses on the Java runtime.

Google App Engine as a platform is designed for scalability, robustness, and performance. App Engine allows you to build applications that are scaled and load-balanced automatically for you as the demand for your application and your data storage needs increase. With App Engine applications, you do not need to perform any server or database maintenance yourself—you just upload and run your app. Google's infrastructure offers reliable performance even under a heavy load and when using very large amounts of data.

A request to an App Engine app is routed to a selected app server, and the application is started on the server if necessary. No state on the server is saved between requests. (Instead, GAE has other means to persist data between requests). There is no guarantee that the same server will handle two subsequent requests, even if the time period between them is very short. Thus, a runtime instance often comes into existence when a request handler begins, and is terminated when it ends—though the instance may sometimes be retained, depending upon app traffic.

By making no assumption that a runtime will be maintained on a given server between requests, App Engine can distribute request traffic across as many servers as necessary, and target requests at servers that it expects will provide the fastest response.

It is useful to view App Engine in terms of the several facets of its functionality—the **App Engine Datastore**, its scalable services, and its runtime environments.

# The Datastore

App Engine's **Datastore** is based on Google's BigTable technology (`http://labs.google.com/papers/bigtable.html`). It is a non-centralized, persistent store, designed specifically to be distributed and to scale as it grows.

The Datastore is not a "join-query" relational database. Rather, it is essentially a property-value store, holding *entities*—each of a given *kind*—that contain property-value sets.

App Engine's Datastore is designed so that the request time is *linear in the size of the results*, not the size of the data stored. This is accomplished in part by the way in which Datastore builds indexes at write-time, and App Engine's imposition of constraints on the types of queries supported, resulting in extremely efficient reads over large distributed datasets.

The Datastore supports **transactions** and uses *optimistic concurrency control*. The transactional model is specific to how App Engine works: the allowed transactions are determined by how entities are defined and grouped in the Datastore.

# App Engine's scalable services

App Engine supports a number of useful capabilities and services, all designed to scale with the size of your app. The Datastore is in fact one such service. Other services include:

- APIs for **authentication** via both Google Accounts and OAuth
- An API for sending and receiving **e-mail**
- An API for sending and receiving **XMPP** messages
- Support for **Task Queues**, allowing work to be performed asynchronously outside the scope of a web request
- Support for running scheduled tasks at specified times or intervals: **Cron** jobs
- Support for image processing
- Integration with Google Apps

Both the Python and Java App Engine runtimes support the above-mentioned capabilities, and many discussions of App Engine capabilities and design approaches can be largely runtime-environment agnostic. In a few cases, the Python features or development tools, which have a head start on the Java version, are currently more capable, but in future their respective capabilities are intended to equalize.

Both runtime environments have some "sandbox" restrictions, imposed to allow App Engine to use any server for a new incoming request, and to control server responsiveness and security. For example, application code cannot access the server on which it is running, in the traditional sense.

SDKs are provided for both the Python and Java runtimes, along with tools for uploading and downloading app information, including bulk data uploads and downloads.

# Java App Engine runtime and the application development environment

This book uses Google App Engine's Java platform, with the exception of a few forays into Python in order to access some administrative tools.

The **Google App Engine Java (GAE/J)** runtime includes the **Java SE Runtime Environment (JRE)** 6 platform and libraries (with some sandbox restrictions implemented in the JVM). The Java Servlet standard is supported, and is a basis for how your app interacts with its environment.

The App Engine Java SDK currently supports developing apps using either Java 5 or 6. However, support in the SDK for Java 1.5 is now deprecated. Languages that use a JVM-based interpreter or compiler (and do not violate the sandbox restrictions), such as JRuby, can be run on App Engine as well.

# GAE/J and the Eclipse IDE

For most people, the easiest way to develop Java App Engine apps is via the Eclipse IDE (http://www.eclipse.org/). Eclipse has sophisticated general support for Java development. Google provides a plugin that supports development of GWT+GAE apps, and adds many additional capabilities. The plugin helps to generate the necessary directories for a GAE (and GWT) project, creates key files, sets up classpaths, and can do some code generation. The plugin also allows "push-button" uploading and deployment of an App Engine application, including automatic compilation of the GWT Java code to JavaScript as required, and copying and packaging of all the necessary files for the deployment.

Furthermore, the plugin integrates the SDK's development support for simulating GAE on your local computer, giving you the ability to set breakpoints and use an interactive debugger.

This book will use Eclipse for development.

# App Engine application hosting

GAE apps are hosted at `http://appspot.com` (you can map the apps to your own domain names as well, if you like). You can host multiple apps, and multiple versions of each app. You can host apps for free, with relatively limited resource quotas, or enable *billing* for an app in order to increase its available resources. The App Engine billing model is tied to the resources actually used by an app so if you enable billing you will be charged more only as your app becomes busier— up to fixed thresholds that you specify. An application will still have some resource quotas, even with billing enabled; if you are running up against these thresholds, you can request to have them raised.

To administer your app versions, track their resource usage and statistics and view their logs, manage app billing, and so on, an App Engine Admin Console web application is provided.

## Google App Engine for Business

Google has announced a new platform—Google App Engine for Business (`http://code.google.com/appengine/business/`). Its features include a **Service Level Agreement (SLA)**, a per-user-per-app pricing structure (up to a maximum threshold), and support for SQL and dedicated relational databases in addition to the Datastore.

At the time of writing, App Engine for Business has not been rolled out, its details are still subject to change, and it will not be covered in this book.

# App Engine "surprises" for new developers

Some aspects of the GAE model and App Engine development can be surprising to developers who are new to the platform. They stem in part from the constraints imposed by App Engine in order to ensure scalability and reliability. We will list some of these aspects here, and discuss all of them in more detail, later in the book.

- Not all core Java methods and networking capabilities are supported—so, not all third-party Java libraries port to App Engine. Many do, however, and we will use some in this book.

- There is no file system in the usual sense. Dynamic data must be persisted by other means; however, it is possible to read static files associated with an app.

- Datastore is not a "join-query" relational database. It does not support joins in the traditional sense, nor text search. So different approaches to data modeling and query construction may be required with App Engine apps.

- There are a number of usage limitations, including limits on the size of the data chunks that can be transferred and stored.

- There is a 30-second request limit; this includes background processes. Typically, long-running activities are split up, often using App Engine's Task Queue.

- When a new app server is allocated for a request, "spin-up time" is required to load the app instance, increasing both request CPU usage and response time. Low-traffic apps are often *evicted* from their server, and thus such apps may see the spin-up time reflected in a large percentage of requests to the app. (In future, it may be possible to address this by paying to retain a *warm* instance for a given app).

# Introduction to GWT

GWT is a development toolkit for building complex AJAX-based web applications using Java, which is then compiled to highly optimized JavaScript. The current version as of this writing is 2.0.4.

GWT allows you to write your application frontend in Java, and then compile the source to highly optimized JavaScript that runs across all major browsers. It allows you to debug applications in an IDE as you would debug a "regular" Java app, interactively setting breakpoints, while at the same time you can access the app in the browser as if it were generated JavaScript. It does this via a browser developer plugin, which spans the gap between Java bytecode in the debugger and the browser's JavaScript.

Once you are ready to deploy, the GWT Java code is compiled to JavaScript. More exactly, a compiled application frontend consists of JavaScript, HTML, and XML.

There are several advantages to this compilation process in terms of *efficiency*, *security*, and *browser compatibility*. The compiled JavaScript is highly efficient and optimized, and helps protect against **Cross-site scripting (XSS)** attacks. (The GWT documentation provides more detail on the specifics of this; essentially, you are well protected as long as you do not add your own JavaScript, use the JSON API to parse untrusted strings, or write code to set "innerHTML" in GWT widgets).

In addition, compatible JavaScript is generated for all major browsers (a current list of supported browsers is here: `http://code.google.com/webtoolkit/doc/latest/FAQ_GettingStarted.html#What_browsers_does_GWT_support?`). Every web browser has its own idiosyncrasies, and GWT allows you to work at a level of abstraction above these differences. When the Java app is compiled into JavaScript, a different, efficient version is generated for each browser type. However, only the JavaScript required by a given client is downloaded when a request is made to the app. GWT uses a technique called **deferred binding** to accomplish this. A bootstrapping process at runtime loads the right version for the client.

GWT doesn't require you to write your app using any JavaScript—you can stick to Java, with its strict typing and powerful compile-time checks, to build your app. However, you can integrate raw JavaScript with a GWT app if you like, as when calling other native code using JNI. You can define an entire application frontend to use GWT, or you can integrate small amounts of GWT with an existing app.

GWT also allows developer-guided code splitting. **Code splitting** is useful when your application's compiled JavaScript code base is large enough to require significant startup time while downloading it. In this case, you can indicate places in your GWT program where you want the program to pause and download more code. Code will always be loaded automatically on initial download if it is part of a dependency chain for the application's initial entry point. So, code splitting can require some consideration of program design, using patterns that allow control of "modules" of functionality and their access. However, the process can provide a large payoff in terms of efficiency.

## GWT UI support

GWT provides many pre-defined **widgets** and **panels** that you can use as UI building blocks and also allows you to build your own widgets, either as composites or from scratch. It allows both programmatic and declarative definition of UIs, or a combination of both, and allows use of CSS for formatting and layout.

We will make use of many of the GWT widgets and panels in this book. For a full list of the GWT-provided widgets, see the GWT gallery: `http://code.google.com/webtoolkit/doc/latest/RefWidgetGallery.html`.

# Other GWT features

The GWT toolkit includes other support for building AJAX-based applications. It addresses the "browser back button" issue by providing support for **history management**. This issue stems from the fact that with AJAX web apps, it is possible for the page content to change without a change in the URL. In such cases, the back button won't work as the user expects; nor will bookmarking the URL necessarily return them to the UI state that they expect. GWT's history management provides a way to rewrite the URL upon important state changes, so that the back button and bookmarking work as expected.

GWT also provides strong support for **event handling** — both low-level browser events, and more abstract application-level events.

# GWT's RPC API

GWT has a **Remote Procedure Call (RPC)** API and framework that supports client-server communication. It allows you to pass objects between the client and server, instantiated from shared data classes, in a straightforward manner.

The RPC package runs on App Engine, making it easy to build GWT frontends to App Engine apps — exactly as we will do in this book. (The RPC package can also be used with other Servlet containers, such as Tomcat).

The RPC calls are all *asynchronous*, that is, non-blocking. They return immediately, and use a callback method, defined by the user, to handle the results later returned from the server.

GWT supports client-server communication via other means as well (for example, using JSON), but this book focuses on the RPC API.

# GWT with GAE

GWT does not need to be paired with GAE/Java as the backend, but they are designed to be integrated, and work very effectively together. One goal of this book is to show how GWT combined with App Engine synergistically simplifies development and deployment in many ways.

A typical GWT+GAE code base will include `client`, `server`, and `shared` packages. The `shared` package includes classes that must be accessible to both the client GWT and server GAE code. Data Transfer Objects (those objects passed over GWT RPC) must be in the `shared` package and must not use any Java methods unavailable to GAE or GWT.

Third-party Java libraries cannot be used from client-side Java code unless their source code is available to the GWT compiler and this code uses only the supported subset of Java.

## The GWT/GAE Eclipse plugin

As indicated earlier, Google provides a GWT+GAE plugin for the Eclipse IDE, which provides a number of useful capabilities. The plugin includes the SDKs for both App Engine and GWT. The Eclipse plugin allows integrated use of the GWT SDK's **developer browser plugin**, letting you set Eclipse breakpoints in your frontend GWT Java code and debug and inspect interactively while accessing the app in the browser—a powerful development aid.

The Eclipse plugin also fully manages app deployment for you. It allows "push-button" uploading of an App Engine app, including automatic compilation of the GWT Java code, and copying and packaging of all the necessary files for the deployment.

## GWT support for Java

GWT supports most but not all core Java capabilities and language semantics. Its scope is constrained by its purpose—the Java code must be compilable into JavaScript. As an example, Java threading is not supported by GWT. In some cases, the GWT emulation differs from the standard Java runtime, or provides a subset of the JRE functionality.

In general, GWT's JRE emulation supports the following packages (sometimes with only a subset of the methods): `java.lang`, `java.lang.annotation`, `java.util`, `java.io`, and `java.sql`. Use of an IDE such as Eclipse is helpful in indicating when a given Java method is not supported. The GWT documentation (`http://code.google.com/webtoolkit/doc/latest/DevGuideCodingBasicsCompatibility.html`, `http://code.google.com/webtoolkit/doc/latest/RefJreEmulation.html`) provides specifics on supported classes.

# Recommended GWT background

There are many online resources and books that introduce GWT. This book assumes some basic prior knowledge about how to use GWT. In particular, it would be helpful for you to be familiar with the following concepts when reading this book:

- Have an understanding of the different types of files that are generated by the GWT compiler and what their purpose is. Similarly, have a general understanding of the "bootstrapping" process by which an application is loaded in a browser, and the files involved. (The Eclipse plugin will manage generation and uploading of these files for you on deployment of your App Engine app).

- Have an understanding of GWT modules, be familiar with the definition of gwt.xml files and what they can contain, understand how to define and use app entry point classes, and the role of the Root panel.

- Understand the basics of building widgets and panels programmatically. The GWT API Reference (http://google-web-toolkit.googlecode.com/svn/javadoc/2.1/index.html) can help with the details.

- Understand how to define and register GWT event handlers.

- Be familiar with the general concept of making Remote Procedure Calls, and be comfortable defining callbacks and anonymous Java subclasses.

All of these topics are covered in Google's online GWT documentation (http://code.google.com/webtoolkit/).

# Example application: *Connectr*

This book is centered on a GWT + Google App Engine application, designed to show the power of combining these two technologies. The app is also designed to explore many of the important features and capabilities of both GAE/J and GWT, which will likely be used in building your own apps, and demonstrates a number of useful design patterns.

The example application is a social-media-oriented app named *Connectr*. The application includes social-media information gathering and aggregation activities, and incorporates the use of App Engine's services and APIs.

*Connectr* allows a user to create an account and log in by authenticating via the Google Accounts API (for example, with their Gmail account), or via OAuth using a Twitter or Facebook account.

Once logged in, the user can maintain and edit contact information for a set of friends, and can display a stream aggregating the friends' updates. *Connectr* supports login authentication via either the Google Accounts API (App Engine's support for authentication via a Google login), or via Twitter or Facebook using OAuth.

A user's customized information stream is based on an aggregation of feed data. As part of the information associated with each friend, a user can add any number of RSS or Atom feed URLs for that friend, for example, from services such as Twitter, Flickr, and blogs. Figure 1 shows the editing of a friend's details in *Connectr*, with the friend's associated URLs specified.

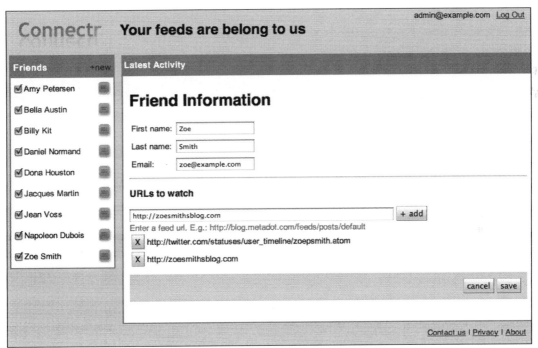

Figure 1: Editing Friend information in *Connectr*.

The feed data is fetched and integrated into a chronologically sorted and auto-updating "activity stream", supported by push from the App Engine's recently-introduced Channel API.

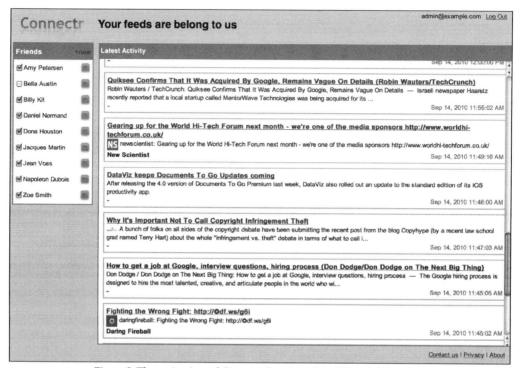

Figure 2: The main view of *Connctr*, showing a list of friends for a user, and a stream of items for selected friends.

The stream can show information from all of the user's friends' feeds, or be filtered to show the feeds for only a subset of friends. A user's activity stream can also be configured to include insertion of breaking news notifications, delivered to the app via XMPP.

Figure 2 shows a typical view of the main page of *Connectr*, with a user's friends listed on the left, and the activity stream for the selected users' associated feeds to the right (in this figure the feeds, for the purposes of the example, look suspiciously like news feeds).

Our use of the phrase "activity stream" is not to be confused with its more technical reference to an extension of the Atom feed format (http://activitystrea.ms/)—though use of Activity Stream-formatted feeds would certainly be consistent with the semantics of *Connectr's* stream.

Behind the scenes, the application makes use of App Engine services such as Cron jobs and Task Queues to update feeds asynchronously in the background, to push new content to the client, and to perform other administrative tasks.

# A look ahead

The *Connectr* application serves as a running example throughout the book. It is introduced in several progressive stages, with simpler versions of the application introduced in the first few chapters, and subsequent chapters further developing the app as functionality is added. One of the goals of this book is to be a resource for a number of design patterns, approaches, and idioms, as developed within *Connectr*.

As we introduce the various features of *Connectr*, we will develop these patterns and approaches both for GWT and App Engine, as well as for communication between the client and server components of an app.

For GWT, we introduce a number of design patterns for keeping code modular and manageable, including the MVP, Event Bus, and related patterns; and describe the use of GWT's UI Binder for declarative layout specification.

For App Engine, *Connectr* illustrates a number of approaches for data class design and querying, including design to get around the lack of a relational database, instead leveraging the Datastore's features. We describe models for decoupled and asynchronous processing and task design, in order to make an application more robust and scalable, including use of Task Queues and Cron Jobs to support background processing; show how to use *query cursors* to break data access into manageable chunks; and introduce some useful Memcache patterns.

Additionally, *Connectr* illustrates some useful patterns in client-server communication, including use of App Engine's recently developed Channel API to push content from the server to the client, and use of OAuth and Google accounts to support multiple login methods, so that the app need not store user passwords.

# Online resources

Much GAE and GWT information is available online. Some of the most useful resources are listed in the following sections.

# GAE and GWT galleries

Google maintains galleries of sites using GAE and GWT, both independently and together. The GWT galleries in particular can be useful in providing UI design inspiration and demonstrating the different ways in which GWT widgets can be used.

- App Engine: `http://appgallery.appspot.com/`
- GWT: `http://GWTgallery.appspot.com/`
- Google Wave (`http://wave.google.com`) uses GWT as well

# Documentation, blogs, and discussion groups

Google's associated documentation sites and blogs may be the first sites you bookmark:

- GWT documentation: `http://code.google.com/webtoolkit/`, as well as a series of articles and tutorials: `http://code.google.com/webtoolkit/articles.html`
- GAE documentation: `http://code.google.com/appengine/`, and articles: `http://code.google.com/appengine/articles/`
- GAE/Java documentation: `http://code.google.com/appengine/docs/java/overview.html`
- The official GAE blog: `http://googleappengine.blogspot.com/`
- The official GWT blog: `http://googlewebtoolkit.blogspot.com/`
- The Google Code blog: `http://googlecode.blogspot.com/`

If you are a Twitter user, Google's Twitter accounts (for example, `@app_engine`, `@GoogleCode`) are good sources for announcements as well.

The Google Groups lists for GWT and App Engine are monitored by Google employees:

- The GWT Google Group: `http://groups.google.com/group/google-web-toolkit/topics`
- The general GAE Google Group: `http://groups.google.com/group/google-appengine/topics`
- The GAE/Java Google Group: `http://groups.google.com/group/google-appengine-java/topics`

Many other blogs are good resources as well. For example:

`http://gae-java-persistence.blogspot.com/`, written by Google employee Max Ross, is an excellent source of GAE/Java Datastore-related information and tips.

# Summary

In this chapter, we have introduced Google App Engine and GWT, and given a preview of how these two technologies combine in a powerful and useful manner.

We have also described the social-media-oriented application, *Connectr*, which we will develop in stages as a running example throughout the book, and taken a look ahead at some of the primary approaches and patterns that the application will be used to illustrate.

In *Chapter 2, Using Eclipse and the Google Plugin*, we will describe how to use the Eclipse IDE and the Google Plugin for easy Google App Engine plus GWT development and deployment, and become familiar with the different components of a GAE+GWT project.

# 2
# Using Eclipse and the Google Plugin

**Eclipse** is an open source IDE written in Java. It employs **plugins** to provide support for development in various languages and frameworks, and provides particularly strong support for Java-based development.

Google makes an Eclipse plugin that provides highly useful support for Google App Engine Java (GAE/J) and Google Web Toolkit (GWT) development. When you use Eclipse and the Google plugin, you can take advantage of a number of features that make all of the stages of application development easier:

- The plugin organizes the files that make up your project and application. It creates the necessary project directory structure, adds the correct libraries, and generates a number of useful templates and defaults, including required configuration files.

- It provides a number of useful GWT and GAE-specific code assists, template editors, and wizards while you are developing your application, and provides as-you-type validation and refactoring support.

- It supports **Development Mode** debugging, which allows you to launch a local server to view and debug your applications locally, and browse your debugging logs.

- It manages the build process required for deployment, including various post-compilation enhancements, and compilation and packaging of the GWT-generated JavaScript code, so that you do not need to run any additional build scripts.

- It provides a useful interface to the App Engine deployment process, leading you through each step, and providing links to your online App Engine **Admin Console**.

- The Google Eclipse plugin will install the GAE and GWT SDKs for you, and track updates to them, so you do not need to do so separately.

In this chapter, we will first describe the process of installing the Google Eclipse plugin, and installing its required supporting software—Java and Eclipse.

Then we'll generate a sample application, and take a first look at the anatomy of an App Engine application with GWT—what files are created where. Then, we'll explore the process of running and debugging your app locally.

Finally, we will describe the process of application deployment to the Google App Engine servers, and see how to access the App Engine Admin Console in order to manage your deployed app.

# Installing the plugin and supporting software

This section first describes the process of installing Java and Eclipse. Then, we will walk through the installation of the Google plugin for Eclipse, which provides support for GAE and GWT.

## Installing the Java SDK

Google App Engine and GWT, as well as Eclipse itself, require Java. Both versions 5 and 6 of the Java Development Kit (JDK) will work with the App Engine and GWT SDKs. However, you may find that some of the example code you encounter online assumes Java 6.

If you already have a version of Java installed, then from the command line, you can type:

```
javac -version
```

to check the version number. If you have Java 6 JDK installed, this will output a version number similar to "1.6.0". If you have Java 5 installed, you will see a version number like "1.5.0". The details depend upon the version that you have installed.

# Installing Java on Mac OS X

Macs should already have Java and its JDK installed. However, the specifics of what is installed depends upon your OS version and your machine hardware—in particular, whether you have a 32-bit or 64-bit processor.

Snow Leopard (OS X 10.6.x) includes both 32- and 64-bit versions of Java 6; your processor determines which it uses as the default. If you have a 64-bit processor, you will be using 64-bit Java by default. Leopard (OS X 10.5.x) only supports Java 6 with 64-bit processors. However, Leopard includes Java 5 as well. Thus, if you are running OS X 10.5 on a 32-bit machine, you must use Java 5.

If you want to change the version of Java that you are using by default, open the Java Preferences application, which you will find in the /Applications/Utilities directory. In the **Java Applications** window of this utility, drag your preferred version to the top of the list. The next screenshot shows the OS X Java Preferences Utility, with the default set in this example to be 64-bit Java 6.

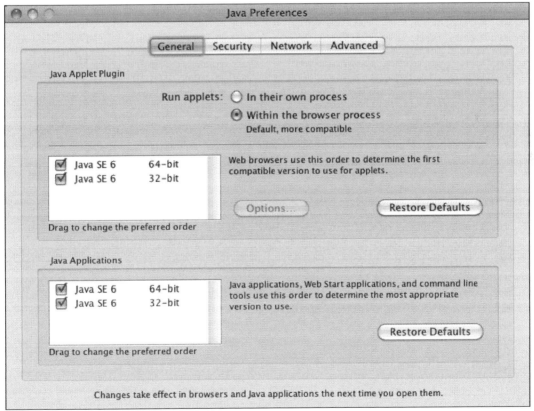

Figure 1: Setting the default Java version in Mac OS X.

As we will see in the next section, you must make sure that you install the version of Eclipse that matches your processor.

## Installing Java on other platforms

For platforms other than Mac OS X, you can obtain the Java 6 JDK from Oracle's website: `http://www.oracle.com/technetwork/java/javase/downloads/index.html`. Again, if you are not sure whether you already have the Java JDK installed, you can run `javac -version` from the command line as a check.

# Installing Eclipse

Once you have installed Java, you can download and install the Eclipse IDE, which is itself written in Java and provides strong support for Java code development.

Download the latest version of Eclipse from: `http://www.eclipse.org/downloads`. With App Engine, it is suggested that you download **Eclipse IDE for Java EE Developers**, which includes the Web Tools Platform (WTP) plugins. WTP includes useful editing modes for JSP and HTML files.

 Be sure to select the appropriate 32-bit or 64-bit version of Eclipse for your machine and OS.

This book does not cover generic use of Eclipse outside the capabilities provided by the Google plugin. However, there are many useful Eclipse tutorials online. The Eclipse Getting Started guide is a good place to start: `http://help.eclipse.org/ganymede/index.jsp?nav=/1_1`.

Eclipse provides much help with general Java development in addition to that supported by the Google plugin, including code completion, refactoring help, management of your imports, debugging, and class definition browsing. There are a number of Eclipse and Java tutorials as well. A good resource is: `http://eclipsetutorial.sourceforge.net/`.

# Installing the Google plugin

The final step in our installation process is to install the Google plugin for Eclipse. Eclipse makes it straightforward to install and update your plugins.

These instructions assume the use of Eclipse 3.6 (Helios), which is the current version at the time of writing; the process is similar for other versions.

See http://code.google.com/eclipse/docs/download.html for instructions on installing the plugin with other versions of Eclipse.

1. To install the Google plugin with Eclipse 3.6, select **Help | Install New Software** from the Eclipse menu.

2. In the **Work with** field of the dialog that pops up, type: http://dl.google.com/eclipse/plugin/3.6, then click on **Add**.

3. It is not necessary to supply a name. Click on **OK**.

4. In the resultant dialog, select (check) both the **Plugin** and the **SDKs**, as shown in the next screenshot. (The version numbers displayed may be different from the version number in the screenshot, as they indicate the current version).

5. Click on **Next** and follow the prompts.

 A bug may cause the wizard to get stuck at the **Review Licenses** section with the **Next** and **Finish** buttons disabled (https://bugs.eclipse.org/bugs/show_bug.cgi?id=277265). Clicking on **Cancel** and restarting the installation should solve the problem.

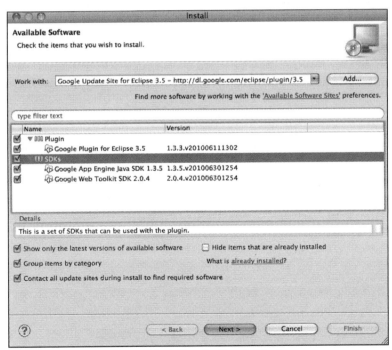

Figure 2: Installing the Google Plugin

After installation, you should see three new buttons in your top toolbar, as shown in the next screenshot. The first (the blue globe) creates a new Web Application project. The second (the red toolbox) will perform a compilation of your GWT code into JavaScript. The third deploys your application to Google App Engine.

Figure 3: The Google plugin toolbar buttons

The functionality provided by these buttons will be described in the following sections.

# Updating the Google plugin

To update an installed Eclipse plugin, including the Google Plugin, select **Help | Check for Updates** from the Eclipse menu. Eclipse will notify you if there are updates for any of your plugins.

In your Eclipse preferences, you can indicate that you wish to be notified automatically about updates to the Google plugin or SDKs. Eclipse preferences are accessed via **Eclipse>Preferences** on Mac OS X, or **Window>Preferences** on a PC. Select **Google**, then ensure the **Notify me** box is checked, as shown in the next screenshot.

Figure 4: The Google pane of the Eclipse preferences

# Developing your application in Eclipse

In this section, we'll explore many of the capabilities of the Google Eclipse plugin, in the context of a sample GAE and GWT application. We'll go through the process of generating the application, examine the project directories that are created, and take a look at some of the configuration and support files.

Then we'll walk through running and debugging the application locally, using a very useful feature called **Development Mode**.

# Creating a new web application project in Eclipse

1. To create a **New Google Web Application Project**, click on the small blue globe, shown in the next screenshot, which appears in your menu bar when you install the plugin. You can also select **File | New | Web Application Project** from the menu.

Figure 5: Begin the process of creating a Web Application project

2. A **New Web Application Project** dialog will be displayed. Name your new project and assign it a package name.

3. In the next screenshot , the project is named SampleApp, and it is indicated that it will be in the sampleapp package.

4. Checking the boxes indicates that you will use both the **Google Web Toolkit** and **Google App Engine**, as shown in the next screenshot. (The default SDKs shown are the current ones at the time of writing; you will want to use the most recent versions available to you).

5. Then click on **Finish**.

This will create a small sample application that uses GWT and is deployable to App Engine.

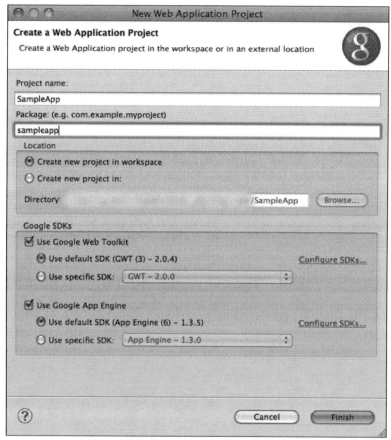

Figure 6: Creating a new Web Application Project

In general, you can use GAE and/or GWT. In our examples and applications throughout this book, we will be using both together.

# First look: The anatomy of a web application project

When you create a new web application project, such as the SampleApp project, a project directory structure is created for you, with a number of files and configuration defaults auto-generated, and a set of jar files installed. The specifics depend upon whether you are creating an application that will use GAE, GWT, or both. In our case, it is both.

We will take a brief tour of some of the more important components of the project directory, and some of the files that were generated for us. Subsequent chapters will cover them in more detail.

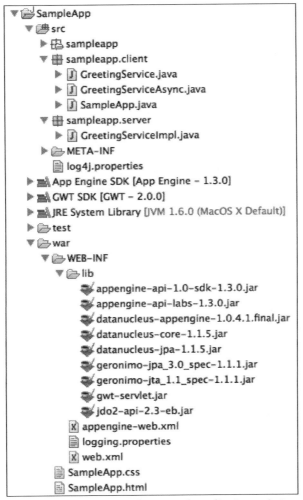

Figure 7: The structure of a new web application project

Expand your new project in the Eclipse **Package Explorer** view. It should look similar to the structure shown previously. The top-level project directory (here, SampleApp) contains three sub-directories, src, war, and test. It also shows the Java libraries that have been added to your build path; in this case both the **App Engine SDK** and **GWT SDK**, as well as the **JRE System Library**.

Under the **src** directory, the sampleapp package contains **client** and **server** subpackages (subdirectories). You may add other packages as well. Because we have generated a sample app, which includes the use of GWT, the application includes an example implementation of both the client and server sides of the GWT RPC service — which we will cover in the next chapter — with the GreetingService* files in the client and server subdirectories. The client package contains the code that will be compiled to JavaScript for deployment.

Java App Engine applications use Java Servlets for interacting with the application server. Thus, your application will always contain one or more classes that extend a base Servlet class.

You will notice a SampleApp.gwt.xml file under the sampleapp package root (if you named your project SampleApp). This is a **GWT module** configuration file. Modules are the GWT units of configuration. Each module must have a defined **entry point** class, and the onModuleLoad() method of that class will be called when a module is loaded. For our example application, the class sampleapp.client. SampleApp is the entry point class. A GWT project must always include one or more module definitions.

The src/META-INF directory includes a jdoconfig.xml file. This file contains configuration information for an application's use of **App Engine's Java Data Objects (JDOs)**, which will be introduced in *Chapter 4*. The file is copied into the war directory during Eclipse's build process.

All of the files that constitute a compiled and deployable Java application are organized under the war directory. This includes the compiled Java class files, the compiled JavaScript that will be generated from your GWT code, static files such as images and stylesheets, configuration files, and necessary library files. You can see that a number of App Engine and GWT-related library files have been added by the Web Application Project creation wizard to war/WEB-INF/lib. If your application uses any other third-party .jar files, they must be added to this directory as well; otherwise they will not be included during app deployment.

Two files of particular note under war/WEB-INF are appengine-web.xml and web. xml. The appengine-web.xml file contains App Engine-specific configuration information for your application, including information about the **application id** and version number, which is required for deployment. The web.xml file includes the specification of how incoming request URLs are mapped to your application's Servlets, security constraints on requests, Servlet filters, and other related definitions.

You will also find a file called <YourProject>.html (for example, SampleApp.html) under the war directory. This is an HTML **host page** used to load one or more GWT modules when the application is launched, in our case, the SampleApp module.

A multi-step build process is necessary to make a `war` directory ready for App Engine deployment (for example, post-compilation data object enhancement is often required). When you use Eclipse, this build process is handled for you. (Outside Eclipse, Apache Ant or Apache Maven is often used to manage the build process).

# The Google plugin wizards and helpers

The Google plugin includes a number of **wizards** and helpers to make your web application development process easier. We will describe them in detail in subsequent chapters. However, we will illustrate some of them now so that you become familiar with them in the IDE.

Under **File | New**, you will find a number of GWT-related wizards. Look for the toolbox icon. The following image shows how GWT wizards can help you build your client-side code.

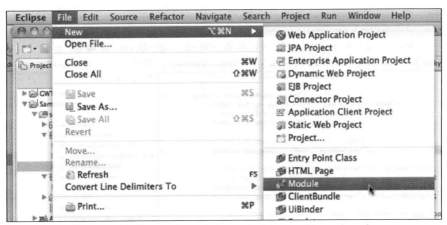

Figure 8: GWT wizards can help you build your client-side code.

These wizards help you construct the different components of your GWT-based application. For example, the Module wizard generates a `*.gwt.xml` module definition file for you, and helps you specify which modules your new module will inherit from.

The plugin also provides coding assists such as you-type validation and auto completion. It also has a "RPC helper", which will assist in generating your GWT RPC interfaces.

# Running and debugging your application

In this section, we'll look at how to run and debug your application locally, and how to configure its startup parameters. There are two modes in which you can run a web application—the first is Development Mode, which uses the Java version of your GWT code and allows client-side debugging via Eclipse as your application runs. The second, Production Mode, uses the compiled-to-JavaScript version of your GWT code, as in the deployed version of your application.

Before we describe them, let's first take a quick look at how the automatically-generated sample application behaves. This application is a simple example which shows the use of a few GWT UI components—buttons, text fields, and dialog panels—and illustrates how to make an asynchronous call to the server, generate a response on the server, and process that response client-side.

On the client side, the user enters their name into a text field and clicks on **Send** to initiate the asynchronous request. The server responds with information about the type of web browser that made the request. This information is displayed to the user in a popup dialog panel, as shown in the next screenshot:

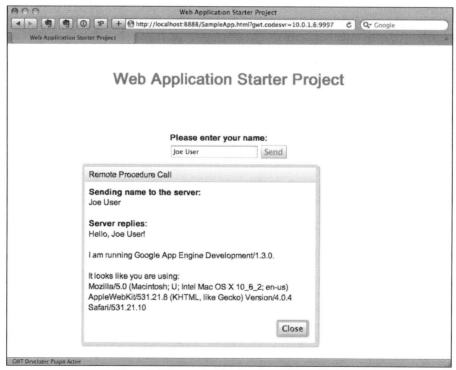

Figure 9: The sample Web Application in action.

# Running your application in Development Mode

**Development Mode** allows you to view and interact with your running GWT-based application in a web browser, prior to compiling the client-side code to JavaScript. You can edit and see the result of your changes without restarting the server, and debug and step through your Java GWT code within Eclipse. This is a powerful and useful feature. The Eclipse Google plugin manages initiation of this mode automatically for you, and displays output specific to it in a **Development Mode** view tab.

Eclipse starts applications using **launch configurations**. You can launch your application in either **Run** or **Debug** launch mode. (When we created our application via the Web Application Wizard, default launch configurations were generated). In either case, you will be running within Development Mode.

One simple way to launch your application is to right-click on the project name, and select **Debug As | Web Application** or **Run As | Web Application**. You can also select the project, and then click on the **Run** or **Debug** icon in the top toolbar, as shown in the next screenshot, to launch in Run or Debug mode, respectively. Additionally, you can select **Run | Debug As | Web Application** (or **Run | Run As | Web Application**) from the top menubar.

## Developing the application in debug mode

Debug launch mode allows you to set breakpoints and step through your code while it is running. Furthermore, in Debug mode, the running server will automatically reload to reflect most of the changes you make to the code. (**App Engine Datastore**-related changes are an exception, and require a server restart. We will introduce the Datastore in *Chapter 4*).

So, for the most part, it is preferable to stay in Debug mode while you're developing. However, the basic process of launching your application is the same for both Debug and Run modes. The first screenshot below shows the **Debug** toolbar icon, and the second shows the **Run** toolbar icon.

Figure 10: The Debug toolbar icon launches the application in Debug mode.

Figure 11: The Run toolbar icon launches the selected application in Run mode

The "Debug" and "Run" toolbar icons launch the selected application in Debug or Run mode respectively.

The launch process starts up a local server, by default on port 8888. In the case of GWT-based applications, a second development mode code server is started as well. You'll see the output of the primary server startup in the **Console** view, which by default is in the bottom pane of your Eclipse Java perspective. Then, once the application is started, Eclipse will switch to the Development Mode view in the bottom pane. It will display a URL for you to copy. The URL will look something like this:

`http://localhost:8888/SampleApp.html?gwt.codesvr=<your-local-ip>:9997` (where "`<your-local-ip>` is replaced with your address on your local network), as shown in the next screenshot:

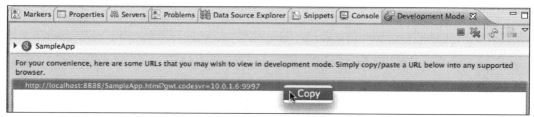

Figure 12: Copy the generated Development Mode URL

Paste the previous URL in your browser to bring up the running web application. On the URL request, the GWT module will be loaded. You will see some additional messages in the **Development Mode** view pane when this occurs.

# Development Mode and the GWT browser plugin

When you start a GWT-based web application as described previously, you are running the application in Development Mode. Development Mode functionality is supported via a **GWT Developer browser plugin**, new to GWT 2.0, which spans the gap between the Java bytecode and what is viewed in the browser. The "`gwt.codesvr`" parameter in the URL triggers the use of this plugin (and specifies the GWT code server's address).

So, the first time you bring up a GWT-based app in your browser, you will need to install the GWT Developer plugin in order to run your application in Development Mode. An install link will be provided in your browser window. After installation, a browser restart may be required.

 When installing the GWT Developer plugin on Windows 7, some configurations may require you to explicitly save the installer as a file and then **Run as Administrator**.

Once you have the GWT plugin installed and the application running, you can interact with your application in your browser. It should behave just as its compiled-JavaScript and deployed version will (albeit perhaps a bit more slowly).

 If you get a "plugin failed to connect to hosted mode server at 127.0.0.1:9997" error, try adding "-bindAddress 0.0.0.0" to the arguments tab of your configuration, via **Debug | Debug Configurations** or **Run | Run Configurations**.

Changes to the GWT client code while in Development Mode do not require a server restart. Simply refresh your browser window.

At the time of writing, the browser plugins are available for Firefox (all platforms), Windows IE, Mac Safari, and Chrome for Windows. You must use a supported browser when running your application in Development Mode. (As we will see shortly, you can alternately run your application in **Production Mode** when you do not require GWT debugging capabilities; Production Mode does not require that the browser plugin be supported).

In fact, it is possible to connect via more than one supported browser during a given session. This allows you to see how your application looks in different browsers. You can even connect using a browser running on a different networked machine (you will need to edit the URL generated by Eclipse). The browser on the remote machine will of course need to use the GWT Developer plugin too.

Figure 13: The red box icon terminates a running application server.

Experiment with making small changes to the application code. For example, make a server-side change to the message returned by the `greetServer()` method of `GreetingServiceImpl`. Then make a client-side change in the text created for the dialog panel in the `onModuleLoad()` method of `SampleApp`. You'll see that Eclipse automatically compiles your changes for you, and will indicate where it encounters any problems.

If you make client code changes, simply reload the application's URL in your browser to see them. If you are running in Debug mode, your server-side changes should be automatically reflected, with no need to restart the server. In Run mode, click on the yellow **Reload web server** icon (to the right of the **Terminate** icon) in the **Development Mode** view to see server-side changes reflected.

To terminate a running application server, select the **Console** or **Development Mode** tab, then click on the small red box, as shown in the previous image.

## Defining a run or debug configuration

You may want to change the default run configuration for your application. For example, you may wish to change what port the server starts on, or set environment variables. To do this, select **Run | Run Configurations** from the top menu. You can also right-click on your project, and select **Run As | Run Configurations**.

This brings up a dialog window showing the settings you can define. Make sure that the correct application is selected under **Web Applications** in the left-hand sidebar's list of configurations. After you've made any desired changes to the setting, click on **Run**. In future, when you select **Run As | Web Application,** or click on the green **Run** button in the top toolbar, this configuration will be used as the default for the given app.

Analogous to the Run Configuration dialog, there is a Debug Configuration dialog, which lets you change the default debug mode settings for an application.

The amount of information displayed in the **Console** and **Development Mode** tabs depends upon the log levels set for the application. You can change the GWT log level by clicking on the **GWT** pane in the **Debug Configuration** or **Run Configuration** dialog. Select **Debug** as the log level. After the relaunch, you will notice that much more information about your application is now displayed in both the **Development Mode** view and the **Console**.

# Debugging

Now that we have the sample application launched and running successfully, we will explore the Debug launch mode features.

First, launch your application in Debug mode. (If your application is currently running in Run mode, terminate it first by clicking on the red **Terminate** icon). Right-click on the project name, and select **Debug As | Web Application**, or select **Run > Debug As | Web Application** from the top menubar. Alternately, select the project name, then click on the Debug icon in the top toolbar.

Next, set one or more breakpoints in the code. Open a source file, then double-click on the left-hand side of the line of code for which you wish to set the breakpoint. As shown in the next screenshot, a blue dot should appear, indicating that the breakpoint is set. Double-click again on an existing breakpoint to remove it.

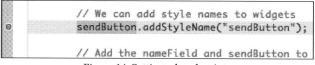

Figure 14: Setting a breakpoint.

You can interact with the running application in your browser using the given URL, as done previously. However, now you will see a difference. When the application hits a breakpoint, the app will pause (suspend) in your browser, and Eclipse will switch into its **Debug perspective**, showing you the breakpoint in your code. (The first time this happens, Eclipse will check with you first about switching perspectives; you can indicate that it is OK to do without checking from then on). The default Debug perspective layout is as shown in the next screenshot.

The Eclipse Debug perspective will indicate the line of code where the debugger has stopped. It provides a set of controls for stepping 'into' and 'through' your code, resuming, suspending, terminating, and a number of other features. You may find it useful to mouse over the controls to see what each icon does. You can access much of the same functionality from the Run menu. The Debug Perspective also allows you to view the run stack and examine variable values as you step through your code.

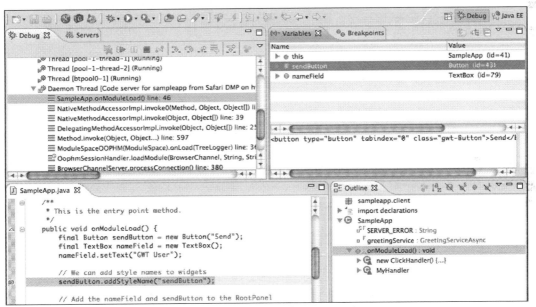

Figure 15: The Eclipse Debug Perspective

You may wish to experiment with setting breakpoints in both the client- and server-side code in our sample application. For example, try setting a breakpoint in the onModuleLoad() method in sampleapp.client.SampleApp. The GWT browser plugin lets you interact with your application as you step through the Java bytecode version of its client-side code.

Then, try setting a breakpoint in the greetServer() method of the sampleapp.server.GreetingServiceImpl class.

If you wish to return to your original Java EE perspective, click on the **Java EE** icon in the top right-hand side corner of the Eclipse window. (You can leave the application running in Debug mode while you switch back and forth). The next screenshot shows the two perspective icons. If you want to temporarily disable your breakpoints without removing them, select **Skip All Breakpoints** from the **Run** menu. (You can enlarge the **Perspectives** tab by dragging it towards the left-hand side if some of the perspectives are obscured).

You can leave the breakpoints in your code as you switch between launch modes; if you launch your app in Run mode, they will not be triggered.

Figure 16: Toggle between the Eclipse Debug and Java perspectives

# Compiling your GWT code for production mode

The GWT client-side Java code that you write will be compiled to optimized, stand-alone JavaScript for use by your deployed application. However, you do not need to compile your GWT code to JavaScript prior to running and debugging your application locally, in fact, Development Mode specifically uses the GWT Java code.

During the process of deploying an application, your Java code will be compiled to JavaScript, and the result placed under the war directory in a subdirectory whose name is based on your GWT module name.

You do not necessarily need to compile the GWT code prior to initiating the deployment process. However, it is a good idea to locally check the pure JavaScript version of your client-side code before deploying, in all your target browsers. To do this, click on the red toolbox icon on the top Eclipse toolbar, as shown in the next screenshot. This will bring up a modal window in which you can set various properties, then click on the **Compile** button. You can follow the process of compilation in the Console view.

Figure 17: The 'toolbox' icon compiles your GWT code to JavaScript

Then, launch your application (for example, by selecting **Run As | Web Application**), but this time remove the `gwt.codesvr` parameter from the URL generated in the **Development Mode** view, before loading the application in your browser. For example, if your local server is running on the default port 8888, just use `http://localhost:8888/SampleApp.html`. This causes your application to run in **Production Mode**, which means that it is now using actual JavaScript client-side, as it will when it is deployed. Thus, in Production Mode, you cannot debug your client-side code. However, you can still do server-side debugging if you like.

Production Mode does not use the GWT browser plugin, so you can load the production-mode URL in any browser, and are not restricted to those that support the plugin. As before, you can access the server via a networked machine (you will need to edit the URL first), and thus can try your application on browsers outside your development platform.

# Deploying your application

In this section, we'll describe how to deploy your application to Google App Engine, with the attendant benefits of scalability, data replication, and fault-tolerance.

In the process, we'll first take a look at some of the administrative capabilities provided by your App Engine **Admin Console**.

# Registering and setting an application ID for your application

Once you have created an application in Eclipse, the first step in deploying it is to register an **application ID** for it. This requires that you create a Google developer account. This developer account will be tied to your mobile phone number: when you first start registering application IDs, Google will send an SMS to your phone with a confirmation code, which you must enter to finish registration. You can tie only one account to your mobile number, so if you have multiple Google accounts, be sure to use the one that you intend to use with App Engine in future.

To start the process of registering an application ID, follow this link: `https://appengine.google.com`. If you have a Google Apps account that you would like to use, use this link instead: `https://appengine.google.com/a/<YOURDOMAIN.COM>/`, where `<YOURDOMAIN.COM>` is replaced with your actual Google Apps domain name. Google is in the process of changing how Google Apps accounts are handled, so in future this separate URL should not be neccessary

(If you do not yet have a Google Account, you can follow the link on the page to create one).

If you do not have a mobile phone, you can apply to Google via a web form for account confirmation. At the time of writing, this URL is: `https://appengine.google.com/waitlist/sms_issues`.

Once signed in, click on **Create an Application**, as shown in the next screenshot, to start the process of registering a new application ID.

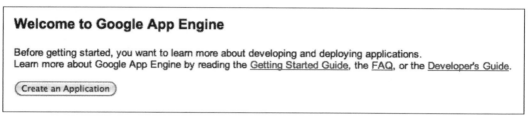

Figure 18: The first step in creating an App Engine application.

This will lead to a page where you can create an application ID and a corresponding application title, as shown in the next screenshot. You can have as many as 10 active application IDs associated with a given developer account. You can later disable and then delete an existing app ID and its associated application, in order to free one of your 10 available IDs. (after your application is deleted, its app ID will remain reserved).

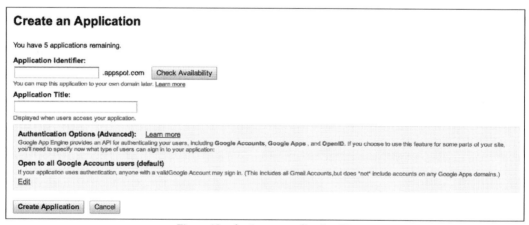

Figure 19: selecting an application ID

Choose an ID for your sample app. You will need to pick an application ID that no one else has already used. If you are stuck, an ID that includes your name or initials might be a good bet. (The ID can be any not yet used; it does not need to reflect the name of your project). Then, enter an application title. For now, leave the authentication and access options as the defaults; we will return to these features in a later chapter. Click on **Save** to register your app.

A given app ID is not automatically associated with any particular application project; we do that when we deploy an app. In fact, after you register the app ID, if you return to `http://appengine.google.com/`, you will see that your new ID is listed as not deployed. So, make note of the application ID that you just created; we will use it next to deploy our sample application from Eclipse.

# How to set the application ID and version for a project

After we have registered an application ID for our example app, the next step in deployment is to tell Eclipse that we wish to associate that app ID and an application **version number**, with our application.

An easy way to do this is to click on the **App Engine** icon (the one that looks like a jet engine) on Eclipse's top toolbar, as shown in the next screenshot. This starts the deployment process.

Figure 20: Initiating app engine project deployment in Eclipse.

Clicking on the icon will launch a dialog like the one shown in the next screenshot. The dialog notification tells us that we haven't associated our project with an app ID yet. Click on the **App Engine project settings** link to set it. This will take us to the project dialog window for the Google plugin. You can reach this same dialog by bringing up the project Properties, then expanding the **Google** entry and selecting **App Engine**.

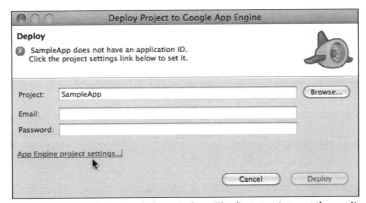

Figure 21: App Engine deployment dialog window. The first step is to set the application ID.

In the project dialog window, enter the new application ID that you just created, and leave the version number as 1, indicating that this is the first version of our deployed application. Click on **OK** to return to the **Deploy Project** dialog.

# Uploading and deploying your application

After you have configured the app ID and version number for your project, the **Deploy Project** dialog should now indicate that we are ready to deploy.

Figure 22: After the application ID is set, enter your Google Account credentials to start deployment.

Enter your Google development account **Email** and **Password**, and click on **Deploy**, as shown in previous the image. That's it! Eclipse takes care of the build processing required to turn your project code into an app-engine-deployable WAR, and then uploads and deploys it. (If you were not using Eclipse, you might run an Ant build script instead). During this process, the GWT code will be compiled to JavaScript.

Go check out your live application! It will be running at:

```
<your-app-id>.appspot.com
```

where `<your-app-id>` is replaced with the application ID you chose. The application should behave just as you observed when you were running it locally via Eclipse.

After you've deployed your app, take a look at the project file `war/WEB-INF/appengine-web.xml`. You will see that it has been updated to contain the information that you just specified:

```
<application>your-app-id</application>
<version>1</version>
```

You can edit `appengine-web.xml` directly to change your application's associated app ID and version, rather than changing it via the project **Properties** dialog as we did previously. Changes to `appengine-web.xml` will be reflected in the **Properties** dialog settings.

We will discuss application versions further in a later chapter. It is possible to deploy more than one version of an application, with one version designated as the default.

# Your App Engine Admin Console

Now that we've deployed the application, we can examine its settings, logs, and stats via the App Engine Admin Console.

Go to `http://appengine.google.com/` and log in. You should see a listing of your application(s), and now your new app ID should indicate **Current Version** as **1**. If you click on the version number, it will open the live version of the app you just deployed in a new browser window.

Next, click on the application ID link. This will take you to the application's dashboard, where you can manage and inspect the application. You can view the application's logs, browse its data, control access to the application, and look at its usage statistics. You should see something similar to the display in the next image. (At the moment, there shouldn't be much going on). As you can see from your dashboard, App Engine apps have quotas associated with them which are reset every 24 hours. The quotas can be increased if you upgrade from a free account to a paid account.

The Admin Console is the "control center" for managing your deployed applications and their administrative access. We will further explore Admin Console functionality and discuss quota management in later chapters.

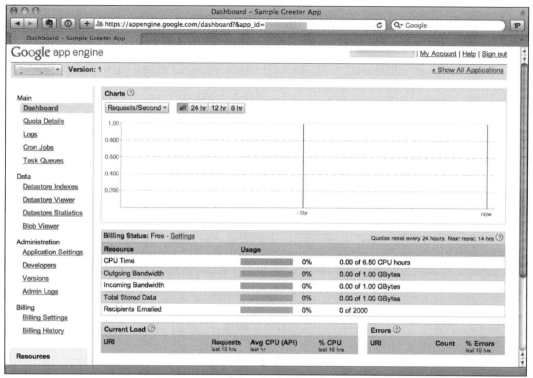

Figure 23: The Dashboard of the App Engine Admin Console

# Importing an existing application

If you want to import existing code into your Eclipse workspace, there are several ways to go about it. If your existing code is already organized as an Eclipse project, and includes a `.project` file, you can pull the project into your workspace via **File | Import | General**, then select **Existing Projects into Workspace**. *Chapter 3* will provide details on how to do this for the *Connectr* application. If your pre-existing project was built for earlier versions of the Google SDKs, you may need to upgrade your project to use the latest versions. Check the GWT and GAE release notes for more information. (See below to use older versions of the SDK with an older project).

Otherwise, the easiest way to import is to create a new Web Application project, using the package name of the source you will import. Remove the automatically-generated example source files, then select the src folder and select **File | Import** to pull in your own existing source code. This will set up your build path and basic directory structure properly, but you will need to modify the auto-generated configuration files, such as the war/WEB-INF/web.xml file, and the HTML "host" page under the war directory, to reflect your imported project.

Alternately, you can select **File | New | Java Project**. Then choose **Create project from existing source**, and pull in your existing source files. If you do this, you will need to create your war directory to support the GAE application. You will also need to add the GAE and GWT SDKs to your build path.

# Adding the Google SDKs to your project's build path

To add the App Engine SDK to your project's build path,

1. Right-click on your project, and select **Google | App Engine Settings**.

2. Check the **Use Google App Engine** box and click on **OK**.

3. Similarly, to add the GWT SDK to your project, right-click on your project, and select **Google | Web Toolkit Settings**, then check **Use Google Web Toolkit**.

# Adding third-party JAR files

If your application requires third-party libraries, add their JAR files to war/WEB-INF/lib, then add the JAR files to the build path. (Right-click on a JAR file, and select **Build Path | Add to Build Path**).

If your application includes libraries that you know are not required at runtime (such as testing libraries), you can simply add them to the project build path without copying them into war/WEB-INF/lib. Only libraries under the war directory will be deployed to App Engine. However, if you see a warning in your Eclipse **Problems** view indicating that there is a JAR on the build path that will not be available at runtime, it needs to be copied in to war/WEB-INF/lib. You can click on the warning for a 'quick fix' action to copy the file.

# Managing multiple Google SDKs

At times, you may want to delay updating an app to the current GWT or GAE SDK and continue to use an older version. Perhaps you are importing an older project and do not want to bring it up to date just yet. Eclipse can manage multiple versions of the SDKs for you, allow you to specify a default version of an SDK, and support deployment based on a specific version.

To add an additional version of an SDK, launch **Preferences**, and expand the Google entry to show **App Engine** and **Web Toolkit**. Click on either of them, click on **Add** to add an additional SDK, then browse to the directory where the other version is located.

If you have multiple versions of an SDK installed, click on the checkbox of the one you wish to use as the default. If you switch the SDK used by a project, the relevant SDK libraries for the old version will be removed from the `war/WEB-INF/lib` folder, and the new libraries will be copied in.

# Running Google's demo apps in Eclipse

Once you feel that you are confident on the basics of using Eclipse and running |GAE- and GWT-based web applications, you may explore some Google demo apps within Eclipse. For example, a number of demos are included as part of the App Engine SDK. You will find them under `<eclipse>/plugins/com.google.appengine.eclipse.sdkbundle.*`, in the `demos` subdirectory, where `<eclipse>` is the location of your Eclipse install.

Check the `README` files for each demo for more information. The scripts that generate Eclipse-ready project directories from the demo code require Apache Ant, which can be found at (`http://ant.apache.org/`).

# Summary

In this chapter, we've explored the Eclipse IDE and its use with the Google plugin to develop and manage GAE and GWT-based Java applications. The plugin provides support for all stages of the application's life cycle, including the creation of the project directory structure, development, debugging, and deployment.

We've made a brief survey of some of the different components of a Web Application project, and have shown how to run and debug an application locally in **Development Mode** via use of a browser plugin. Then, we walked through the steps required to deploy your project as an App Engine application.

In the following chapters, as we further explore GWT and Google App Engine development, we'll take a closer look at some of the plugin's helpers and wizards, and will return to look at the App Engine Admin Console in more detail.

# 3

# Building the *Connectr* User Interface with GWT

In *Chapter 2*, we saw how to build an example application using the Google Web Toolkit (GWT) plugin for Eclipse, as well as how to run the application in debug mode (recall that this is the preferred mode), and how to deploy it on App Engine.

In this chapter, we are going to build the *Connectr* application user interface, enable it to get its data from the server-side, and discuss some high-level notions that are important to understand when building scalable applications. While diving into the implementation details, we will also introduce key concepts of modern AJAX/GWT-based web applications. Here are the topics covered in this chapter:

- We will describe the anatomy of an AJAX/GWT-based web application and discuss what makes it scalable

- We will show how GWT works as an AJAX framework, and why it makes you more productive as a developer

- We'll construct the *Connectr* user interface elements with UiBinder so that we can separate the user interface from its logic

- We'll explain how to get data from the backend using Remote Procedure Calls

This chapter and subsequent GWT-focused chapters in the book assume some basic prior knowledge about how to use GWT. In particular, it would be helpful for you to be familiar with the following concepts:

- Have an understanding of the different types of files that are generated by the GWT compiler and what their purpose is. Similarly, have a general understanding of the **bootstrapping** process by which an application is loaded in a browser, and the files involved. (The Eclipse plugin will manage the generation and uploading of these files for you on deployment of your App Engine app).

- Have an understanding of GWT modules, be familiar with the definition of .gwt.xml files and what they can contain, understand how to define and use app entry point classes, and the role of the Root panel.

- Understand the basics of building widgets and panels programmatically. The GWT API Reference (http://google-web- toolkit.googlecode.com/ svn/javadoc/2.1/index.html) can help with the details.

- Understand how to define and register GWT event handlers.

- Be familiar with the general concept of making Remote Procedure Calls, and be comfortable defining callbacks and anonymous Java subclasses.

All of these topics are covered in Google's online GWT documentation (http://code.google.com/webtoolkit/). In addition, there are many online resources and books that introduce GWT.

# Installing the (first version of) the *Connectr* project in Eclipse

In *Chapter 2*, we explored the basics of using Eclipse via a sample GWT/Google App Engine application generated automatically by the Google plugin.

In this chapter, we begin working with the application, *Connectr*, which we will develop throughout the book. In this chapter and the next two, we will start with a simpler version of the application, which does not yet include its full functionality. Then, in subsequent chapters, we will reference more complete versions of *Connectr*. To distinguish the initial version of this chapter from its successor, we will name its Eclipse project, **ConnectrStage1**.

1. The **ConnectrStage1** code is packaged as an Eclipse project. To install it, first download the ConnectrStage1.zip file from the Packt website.

2. Then, choose **File | Import** from the Eclipse menu.

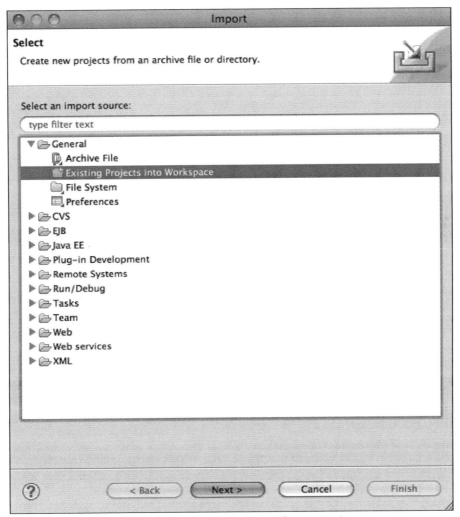

Figure 1: Importing project into Eclipse – step 1

3.  From the **Import** modal window, choose **Existing Projects into Workspace**. As shown in the following screenshot, this brings up a modal window that allows you to indicate how to do the import.

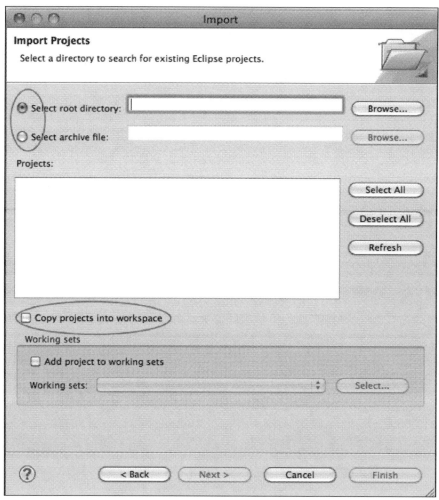

Figure 2: Importing project into Eclipse – step 2

If you like, you can unzip the ConnectrStage1.zip file into a location convenient to you and then browse to select its root directory, ConnectrStage1. With this option, you do not have to (though you may) copy the project files into the workspace. If you leave the **Copy projects into workspace** box unchecked, you will be accessing the project files in their current location.

Alternately, you can import the downloaded `ConnectrStage1.zip` file directly, by selecting the **Archive** option. This will unpack it and copy its contents into your Eclipse workspace.

The import will create a new project called **ConnectrStage1**. From this project, you can run the app and explore the files referenced in this chapter.

4. When you first import the **ConnectrStage1** project, the App Engine and GWT jars will be specified in your classpath, but will not yet be added to the `war/WEB-INF/lib` directory. Until that occurs, the app will not run. The jars should be added automatically if you restart Eclipse. If they are not, then edit the properties of **ConnectrStage1**, for example, by right-clicking on the project name in the **Project Explorer** tab, and selecting **Properties** from the context menu. In the modal window that launches, under **Google**, first select **App Engine**.

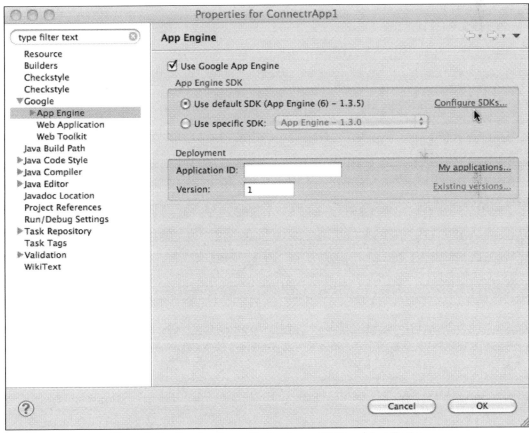

Figure 3: Configuring the application to use GWT and App Engine

5. Click on the **Configure SDKs** link. This will bring up a modal window that lets you select your preferred default version of the SDK. Make sure that the version you want as default is selected (typically the most recent version), then click on **OK**. This will populate war\WEB-INF\lib with the correct jar files for that SDK. Next, follow the same procedure for **Web Toolkit** under **Google**. Click on its **Configure SDKs** link, then click on **OK** in the modal window to add its jar file to the lib directory.

# AJAX and its benefits

AJAX-based applications are relatively new in the Web landscape. **AJAX** (which stands for **Asynchronous JavaScript and XML**) refers to a set of techniques including the use of JavaScript, CSS, and asynchronous HTML requests, which can bring a desktop-like experience to the client-side of a web application. The use of the term "AJAX" has grown to include any applications built with open standards and asynchronous communications.

AJAX applications make the Web a better place to live. They run in web browsers and are designed to be responsive, and feel like an application running on your desktop. AJAX applications have richer user interfaces and implement more complex treatments of user input, than do traditional HTML-based web applications. At the same time, AJAX's use of open standards and its ability to support accessibility guidelines often make AJAX applications preferable to those that use technologies such as Flash.

# Why AJAX apps are the way forward

At AJAX's heart is JavaScript—a lightweight, interpreted, dynamic, and loosely typed language. JavaScript should not be confused with Java. They are not related, the only commonality between the two is in their name. JavaScript was developed by Brendan Eich from Netscape in 1995, in order to be integrated in Netscape Navigator 2.0.

Because AJAX is a programming technique, other languages besides JavaScript can be used to perform the job. Even though JavaScript is supported by most modern web browsers and is by far the most used language, there are others such as VBScript (short for Visual Basic Scripting Edition), and JScript—both developed by Microsoft, and ActionScript used by Adobe Flash Player. They can do a similar job but have a smaller share of the market.

# AJAX apps minimize traffic and workload both on the client and the server

In sharp contrast with non-AJAX web apps, which synchronously request whole web pages from their servers, AJAX apps minimize the traffic and the server load by asynchronously requesting only the necessary information from a server.

As an example, let's imagine users trying to log in to their e-mail application. Assuming the username and password are correct, the only real job of the app is to replace a login link by a message such as **Welcome back, Daniel, not Daniel? Logout**. The following figure depicts in a naïve fashion the sequence of events and the web traffic happening for an AJAX and a HTML-only non-AJAX app:

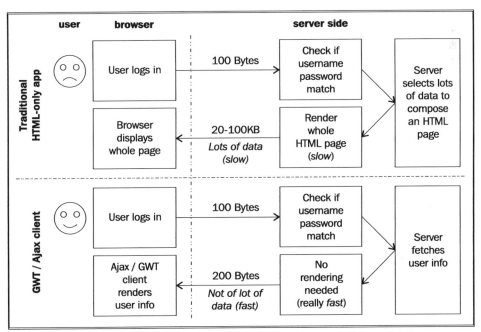

Figure 4: Comparing AJAX light traffic needs versus legacy HTML applications

In the upper half of the diagram, a person using a non-AJAX app enters his/her username and password and clicks on **login**. Here is what happens:

1. The web browser sends the username and password to the server.

2. The server checks for a match: match found.

3. The server gathers all the data needed to construct the whole web page.

4. The server creates a web page by rendering a template with the data needed for the page.

5.  The server sends back a substantial (for example, 20-100 kilobyte) web page to the web browser.

6.  The browser starts processing the server response and requests images and CSS files that are not in the browser cache. For example, if there are ten images on the web page and two CSS files, this makes a potential 12 extra HTTP requests.

7.  The server responds with the appropriate content.

8.  The browser loads the images and the CSS files from the server responses and the browser cache.

9.  The browser displays the web page.

In sharp contrast, the person using an AJAX app will trigger a sequence like this:

1.  The AJAX client (via the web browser) sends the username and password to the server.

2.  The server checks for a match: match found.

3.  The server gathers user information such as name and e-mail address.

4.  The server sends a small response—for example 200 bytes, back to the AJAX client.

5.  The AJAX client receives the response and replaces the **login** link with **Welcome back Daniel**.

6.  The AJAX app displays any additional images by loading them from memory as they are preloaded.

Thus, AJAX apps can often cut down the amount of traffic by 1000 and the number of HTTP requests by 10. This may vary depending on the application, but it gives us a general idea of why an AJAX app is more efficient. Multiply these savings by the number of users your app has and by how many times they click on it per day and the numbers will show that the AJAX app is incredibly more efficient. Therefore, this is the way to go when it comes to scalability and great user experience.

However, the development of AJAX apps can be challenging, as explained in the following section.

# Challenges associated with AJAX programming and how GWT solves them

In this section, we describe some of the ways in which GWT makes it easier to build AJAX-based applications.

# JavaScript browser's implementation is not consistent

JavaScript implementations differ across browsers—this means that if the users of an app use Firefox, the app may potentially behave one way, and if they use Internet Explorer or Google Chrome, it could behave another way. There are also differences in the extent to which a browser supports standards for CSS, DOM events and so on, again resulting in rendering and behavioral differences across browsers.

In an effort to standardize these implementations, the Web Standards Project provides tests that can be applied to browsers to see how compliant to standards their implementation is. The **Acid3 test** can be run by visiting `http://acid3.acidtests.org`.

Here is an example running the test with Internet Explorer 8 and Safari 4, both on a Windows 7 computer:

Figure 5: The Acid 3 JavaScript online browser compliance test failed by IE8

The previous screenshot depicts Microsoft Internet Explorer 8 failing the ACID3 tests at test # 20.

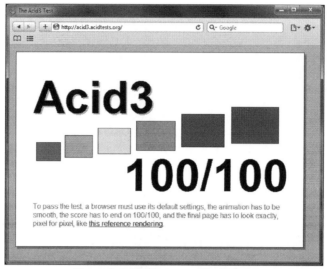

Figure 6: Acid 3 test passed by Safari.

This screenshot shows Safari 4 successfully passing all the 100 ACID3 tests.

This disparity creates a lot of extra work for web developers because they need to code their JavaScript and CSS against specific browsers, making tests to handle special cases. Therefore, they may often need to write checks like this (in pseudo-code):

```
if(browser is IE)
    implement IE bug #343 workaround
else
    take normal action
```

# Mastering JavaScript—an uphill battle

Most web application developers know a language such as PHP, Java, or Python. Developing AJAX web applications would require them to learn yet another language: JavaScript. Even though JavaScript is not a complex language, becoming proficient at it requires a long learning curve because developers need to know browser-specific implementation caveats and issues. Furthermore, switching back and forth between JavaScript and the backend language makes programmers' neurons go berserk during the change of context.

Learning JavaScript is only the first challenge. A programmer will also have to learn about various technical concepts and techniques such as security (to avoid cross-site scripting attacks), and memory management (to avoid leaks — JavaScript is notorious for this).

# How GWT comes to the rescue to make developers more efficient

Google Web Toolkit, or GWT, allows programmers to write the client-side code in Java. GWT compiles the Java code to generate JavaScript that the browser will load. In practice, a GWT developer will rarely encounter any JavaScript. This means that there is a minimal GWT learning curve for Java developers because they can write their AJAX clients in Java.

One key issue to be aware of as a Java developer is that not all of the Java libraries that you are familiar with are available in GWT. This is because the GWT Java code must be compilable to JavaScript.

GWT supports most of the core Java language syntax and semantics, but with a few small differences. It supports only a subset of the classes available in the Java 2 Standard and Enterprise Edition libraries, as these libraries are quite large and rely on functionality that is unavailable within web browsers.

The GWT documentation, in particular that at `http://code.google.com/webtoolkit/doc/latest/DevGuideCodingBasicsCompatibility.html` provides specifics.

To help you identify problems early, your GWT code will be checked against the JRE emulation library whenever you run it in development mode. As a result, most unsupported library usage will be caught right away when you attempt to run your application locally.

The following table summarizes some of the ways in which GWT helps in building AJAX applications.

| Challenge with AJAX apps | How GWT helps |
| --- | --- |
| JavaScript is yet another language to learn. | GWT uses Java to develop AJAX apps. |
| JavaScript apps leak memory easily. | GWT generates optimized JavaScript that limits or eliminates this issue. |
| AJAX apps are difficult to bookmark. | GWT provides full support to browser history allowing bookmarking. |

| Challenge with AJAX apps | How GWT helps |
|---|---|
| AJAX apps are vulnerable to cross-site scripting and requests forging. | GWT limits these issues by generating clean JavaScript. |
| AJAX apps are hard to debug. | Developers write their app in Java and therefore can use the help of a Java debugger such as the one provided by Eclipse with the Google Eclipse plugin. |
| JavaScript apps are huge and the startup time can be too long. | GWT code splitting cuts AJAX apps into small pieces that are downloaded by the client only as needed. |
| JavaScript syntax errors are caught only at runtime. | As GWT is in Java, the compiler won't allow any syntax errors. |
| Each browser has specific CSS and JavaScript implementation details. | GWT knows about browser differences, and generates different source code for mainstream browsers. Only the version for a given browser is loaded on request. |

Now that we have seen how GWT can save developers' time and make their apps more efficient, let's see how GWT can help us build rich user interfaces.

# Google Web Toolkit overview—modern tools for modern developers

This book focuses on building an application with GWT and GAE and (as discussed earlier) presupposes that readers have some basic knowledge of GWT. However, it is useful to review various Google Web Toolkit features, many of which will be used by the *Connectr* application.

GWT includes a complete suite of tools that developers can use for their AJAX projects. These tools help with different aspects of the development cycle and can be grouped into the following categories:

- **Building interfaces**: GWT provides cross-browser support and comes with built-in widgets, tables, and panels that can be used to create a rich user interface.

- **Event handling**: GWT provides facilities to handle keyboard and mouse events and also allows developers to create an unlimited number of timers.

- **Internationalization**: GWT provides tools to handle different languages, including languages written right to left.

- **Accessibility**: GWT helps developers create interfaces that are compatible with screen readers.

- **Testing**: Automated testing increases software quality—GWT supports **JUnit** and provides support for testing remote systems.

- **Optimization**: Here lies the secret of GWT's lightning fast applications—`ClientBundle` allows the grouping of JavaScript, images, and CSS files into bundles that can be downloaded by the client more efficiently. Code Splitting can cut big apps into smaller chunks to reduce application startup time. The **Lightweight Metrics System** and the compile report provide inquisitive developers with in-depth information that can be used for optimization.

- **Remote Procedure Calls (RPC)**: GWT provides the plumbing that makes communicating with a backend server a breeze.

# GWT user interface building blocks

Before we dive into building the *Connectr* application, let's have a high-level look at GWT user interface capabilities.

From a somewhat simplistic point of view, we can consider a GWT user interface to have two primary aspects: the visual artifacts called **widgets**, of which a web page is composed, and the **event handlers** that are defined to process the events associated with the widgets—both lower-level events such as user mouse clicks, and application-defined events such as a user login event.

Widgets themselves can be grouped into two categories: panels and widgets:

- **Panels** exist in order to contain widgets and other panels. They don't usually have logic associated with them. Examples of panels are `VerticalPanel`, `VerticalSplitPanel`, `DockLayoutPanel`, `FlowPanel`, `HorizontalPanel`, `PopupPanel`, and `TabPanel`. There are many more variations but the concept remains the same: they are containers.

- **Widgets** can be seen as standalone elements. They often have logic associated with them and can include numerous other elements such as panels and more widgets. GWT provides a fair set of widgets such as buttons, labels, and calendars. Developers can also build their own widgets. The following figure shows examples of widgets.

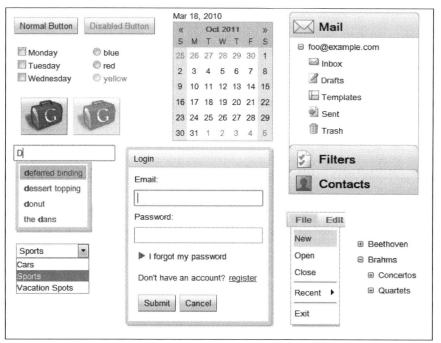

Figure 7: Examples of widgets created with GWT

Now that we are familiar with the basic building blocks of a GWT user interface, let's get started with the *Connectr* user interface.

# Building the *Connectr* application—the user interface

As we build *Connectr* throughout the course of this book, its features will include:

- The ability to add and edit contact information about friends, including their associated RSS or ATOM feeds (Twitter and blog feeds, and so on).

- The ability to display a "loading" indicator, indicating that the app is waiting for the backend to send back data.

- The ability to log in and log out of the application with the choice of several different authentication mechanisms.

- The ability to display a fresh and automatically updating stream of status items based on the associated feeds of a selected subset of friends.

- In this and the next few chapters, we will first focus on creating and modifying "friend" information. Then in subsequent chapters, we will add additional functionality.

Now that we have summarized the requirements of the *Connectr* application, let's look at a high-level user interface design.

# User interface design elements of *Connectr*

As indicated in the following figure, *Connectr* uses a standard two-column layout along with a header and footer. The header contains the logo and the app name on the left and the login information on the right. The footer provides a place for the usual suspects such as links to **Privacy**, **About**, and **Contact us** information.

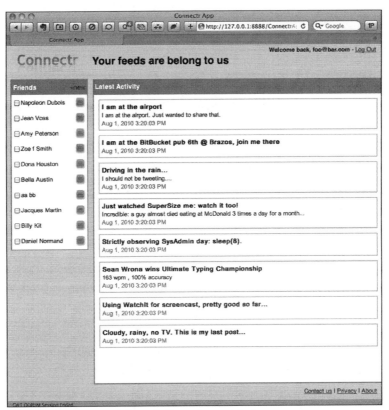

Figure 8: *Connectr* user interface

A list of friends will be displayed on the left along with a **+new** button to add new friends. The main content will be located at the center of the app and will show feeds based on friend selection. The main area will also be used to display other information such as friend information, when adding and editing friends. It will be equipped with a scroll bar.

The activity indicator, located in the upper-left corner, will be visible only when the app is waiting for the backend to respond.

Now that we know how the app should look, let's get to work and begin to code the user interface.

# Coding the *Connectr* user interface

GWT provides two ways of creating user interfaces:

- Declaratively using `UiBinder`
- Procedurally in pure Java

The *Connectr* user interface uses both methods. As we will discuss in the next section, it can often be preferable to use `UiBinder`, but because it is still a young product, it sometimes lacks the power provided by coding widgets directly in Java.

Let's now introduce `UiBinder` and see how it helps programmers become more productive.

# Introducing UiBinder to increase productivity

`UiBinder` is a GWT framework that allows developers to create user interfaces by declaring XML elements in a template. Think of it as HTML on steroids. CSS styles can be embedded in the code very much like when coding HTML.

`UiBinder` allows developers to position their widget into a HTML document using tags, which is a common way of creating user interfaces. Here are some advantages of using `UiBinder`:

- It separates the UI from the Java code: This makes the code clearer and separates UI from its logic. Having a clear UI/logic separation enables easier collaboration between UI designers and developers. The `UiBinder` code is easier to read than its equivalent in Java. Building interfaces in Java is straightforward, but the result can be hard to read, and it can be difficult to mentally visualize what the output will be without actually running the code.

- It provides compile-time syntax checking, thus preventing errors.
- It provides compile-time CSS validation. This ensures that the declared CSS style actually exists.

However, `UiBinder` is different from a templating language such as PHP or JSP—it has no `for` loops, no variables, and no logic at all. It is simply a user interface description language.

Let's compare `UiBinder` implementation to a pure Java one using a simple example.

## Declarative UiBinder versus procedural Java—let's compare

To compare the two approaches, we are going to create an application that displays a login box widget as shown in the following figure.

First, we create a version of the widget in pure Java and then by declaratively using `UiBinder`. For each implementation, the **login** button can receive click events.

Figure 9: login box to be created with UiBinder and in Java

The only job of the entry point class is to instantiate the `LoginWidget` and then to add it to the HTML `div` element `login`:

```
package com.metadot.book.chap3.client;

import com.google.gwt.core.client.EntryPoint;
import com.google.gwt.user.client.ui.HTML;
import com.google.gwt.user.client.ui.RootPanel;

public class Chap3LoginBox implements EntryPoint
{
  public void onModuleLoad() {

    RootPanel.get("login").add(new LoginWidget());

  }
}
```

Here is the procedural Java implementation of `LoginWidget`:

```java
package com.metadot.book.connectr.client;

import …

public class LoginWidget extends Composite {
  Button login = new Button("Login");
  Button cancel = new Button("Cancel");

  public LoginWidget(){
    final DialogBox dialogBox = new DialogBox();
    dialogBox.setText("Please login");
    initWidget(dialogBox);
    VerticalPanel container = new VerticalPanel();
    container.setSpacing(4);
    container.add(new Label("Username:"));
    container.add(new TextBox());
    container.add(new Label("Password:"));
    container.add(new PasswordTextBox());

    HorizontalPanel buttons = new HorizontalPanel();
    buttons.setSpacing(12);
    buttons.add(login);
    buttons.add(cancel);
    container.add(buttons);

    // add user click handler
    login.addClickHandler(new ClickHandler()
    {
      @Override
      public void onClick(ClickEvent event) {
          onLoginClick();
      }

    });

    dialogBox.setWidget(container);

  }

  void onLoginClick()
  {
      Window.alert("You are logged in!");
  }
}
```

The procedural approach shows how to build a widget in Java by adding dialog elements such as labels, fields, and buttons to panels; then adding the panels to the `DialogBox` object. Note the way the **Cancel** and **Login** buttons align horizontally. It is achieved by adding them to a `HorizontalPanel`. Furthermore, handling user clicks involves writing some boilerplate code that calls the `onLoginClick()` method.

Let's now implement the same widget using `UiBinder`.

1. First, we create a `UiBinder` XML template containing the user interface elements as follows:

```
<!DOCTYPE ui:UiBinder SYSTEM "http://dl.google.com/gwt/DTD/xhtml.
ent">
<ui:UiBinder xmlns:ui="urn:ui:com.google.gwt.uibinder"
    xmlns:g="urn:import:com.google.gwt.user.client.ui">
    <ui:style>
      buttonsDiv {
        float: right;
        margin-top: 5px;
      }
    </ui:style>

    <g:DialogBox text="Please login">
      <g:HTMLPanel>
        <g:Label>Username:</g:Label>
        <g:TextBox></g:TextBox>
        <g:Label>Password:</g:Label>
        <g:PasswordTextBox></g:PasswordTextBox>

        <g:HTMLPanel styleName='buttonsDiv'>
          <g:Button ui:field="loginButton">Login</g:Button>
          <g:Button>Cancel</g:Button>
        </g:HTMLPanel>

      </g:HTMLPanel>
    </g:DialogBox>
</ui:UiBinder>
```

2. Then we bind the widget template in Java. The following code instantiates the template (we say *bind* in GWT lingo) and attaches the click event:

```
import ...

public class LoginWidget extends Composite
{
    private static LoginWidgetUiBinder uiBinder =
      GWT.create(LoginWidgetUiBinder.class);

    interface LoginWidgetUBUiBinder extends UiBinder
      <Widget, LoginWidget> {    }
    public LoginWidget() {
```

```
        initWidget(uiBinder.createAndBindUi(this));
    }
    @UiHandler("loginButton")
    void onLoginClick(ClickEvent e)
    {
        Window.alert("You are logged in!");
    }
}
```

As seen in the previous code, creating a login box using `UiBinder` involves two steps: first we create a `UiBinder` template, and then bind it in Java. The XML looks very much like HTML but also has widget tags such as buttons and text fields.

Experienced web developers will be able to visualize the widget resulting from a `UiBinder` template more easily than when reading the equivalent procedural implementation in Java.

Furthermore, the way user interface elements align is specified by the HTML elements that they are placed into, and their associated CSS styles. For example, the **Login** and **Cancel** buttons are located inside a `div` with the CSS style `float: right` that forces the buttons to align horizontally. With `UiBinder`, there is little or no need to use vertical or horizontal panels as seen in the Java implementation.

Additionally, event handling for `UiBinder` widgets is much simpler than when the widget is created in Java: adding the annotation `@UiHandler("loginButton")` to the `onLoginClick()` method does the trick.

To summarize, `UiBinder` uses template files and CSS styles that decouple the interface presentation from its logic. This separation of concerns tends to make user interface building more efficient, allows different teams to work more easily on different parts of an application, and makes maintenance more straightforward.

# Implementing the application layout with UiBinder

It is easy to create a `UiBinder` template using the Eclipse GWT plugin by right-clicking on the directory where the template should be created and selecting `UiBinder` in the new menu as depicted in the following figure:

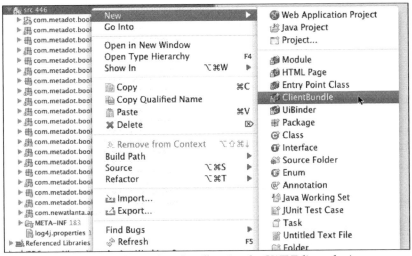

Figure 10: Adding a client bundle using the GWT Eclipse plugin

Once selected, the GWT plugin opens a dialog box where the developer can specify the name and location of the template file, as well as whether the plugin should generate some default content to help developers get started.

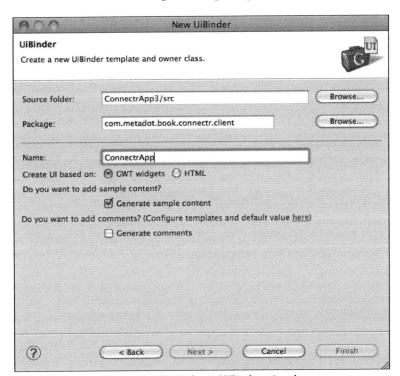

Figure 11: GWT plugin UiBinder wizard

Our *Connectr* UI will take up the entire browser area. Our app needs to maintain its general layout when the user resizes the browser window: in that case, we want only the main content area to resize. This can be achieved using a DockLayoutPanel. The DockLayoutPanel allows a developer to specify component places using geographical directions such as north, south, west, and east.

Here is the UiBinder code that implements the application layout:

The following code is added in the ConnectrApp.ui.xml file.

```
<!DOCTYPE ui:UiBinder SYSTEM "http://dl.google.com/gwt/DTD/xhtml.ent">
<ui:UiBinder xmlns:ui="urn:ui:com.google.gwt.uibinder"
    xmlns:g="urn:import:com.google.gwt.user.client.ui"
    xmlns:app='urn:import:com.metadot.book.connectr.client'
    xmlns:connectr='urn:import:com.metadot.book.connectr.client'>

  <ui:style src="Resources/GlobalStyles.css" />

  <g:DockLayoutPanel unit='EM' styleName='{style.outer}'>

    <g:north size='5'>
      <app:HeaderPanel ui:field='headerPanel' />
    </g:north>

    <g:west size='14'>
      <connectr:FriendList ui:field='friendList' />
    </g:west>

    <g:center>
      <g:HTMLPanel styleName='{style.boxPadding}'>

        <div class="{style.titleBar}">Latest Activity</div>
        <g:ScrollPanel ui:field='mainPanel'
          styleName='{style.mainPanel}' />
      </g:HTMLPanel>
    </g:center>

    <g:south size="3">
      <g:HTMLPanel styleName='{style.footerPanel}'>
        <div>
          <a href="#">Contact us</a>
          |
          <a href="#">Privacy</a>
          |
          <a href="#">About</a>
```

```
        </div>
      </g:HTMLPanel>
    </g:south>

  </g:DockLayoutPanel>

</ui:UiBinder>
```

As shown in the previous code and the following figure, the header widget called `HeaderPanel` is positioned using a north panel. Then we proceed by adding our "friend list" widget `FriendList` in a panel on the west side of the layout. The center panel will hold the stream of feed items from the friends' associated feeds. We place the main panel area called `mainPanel` in the center using a `ScrollPanel`. This will allow scrolling up and down the list of feed items. Because the footer has no logic associated to it, it is implemented in pure HTML using a south panel.

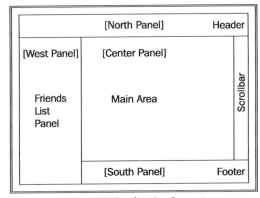

Figure 12: Application Layout

# Tying the view to the Java code

1. Once the layout is ready, the developer needs to tell the application to use it. Here is how it is done:

   The following code is added in the `ConnectrApp.java` file.

   ...

   ```
   @UiField
   HeaderPanel headerPanel;
   @UiField
   ScrollPanel mainPanel;
   @UiField
   FriendList friendList;
   interface ConnectrAppUiBinder extends UiBinder<DockLayoutPanel,
   ConnectrApp> {}
   ```

```
private static final ConnectrAppUiBinder binder =
  GWT.create(ConnectrAppUiBinder.class);

public void onModuleLoad() {
  ...
   DockLayoutPanel outer = binder.createAndBindUi(this);
   root = RootLayoutPanel.get();
   root.add(outer);
   ...
}
```

2. As shown in the previous code, first we instantiate the *Connectr* headerPanel, mainPanel, and messagePanel classes and map them with their respective UiBinder equivalent using the GWT @uiField directive. We then need to create an interface called ConnectrAppUiBinder:

```
interface ConnectrAppUiBinder extends UiBinder<DockLayoutPanel,
ConnectrApp> {}
```

> **Note:** UiBinder<DockLayoutPanel, ConnectrApp> **declares two parameters. One is the root** *element* **container of the template, here** DockLayoutPanel, **and the second,** ConnectrApp—**the class that uses this** UiBinder **template.**

3. Then it needs to be instantiated:

```
private static final ConnectrAppUiBinder binder =
  GWT.create(ConnectrAppUiBinder.class);
```

4. Finally, we access it from our Java code and add it to the root container of our HTML document:

```
DockLayoutPanel outer = binder.createAndBindUi(this);
root.add(outer);
```

# Adding custom widgets to UiBinder

Developers can easily make their application widgets available inside UiBinder. As seen in the application layout previously shown, the XML document needs to be augmented so that it can know about the application widgets:

```
...
<ui:UiBinder xmlns:ui="urn:ui:com.google.gwt.uibinder"
   xmlns:g="urn:import:com.google.gwt.user.client.ui"
   xmlns:app='urn:import:com.metadot.book.connectr.client'
   xmlns:connectr='urn:import:com.metadot.book.connectr.client'>
...
```

Then the application's `FriendList` widget is declared like this:

```
<connectr:FriendList ui:field='friendList' />
```

The `ui:field` attribute is optional. It is used here because we need this `FriendList` widget to be available from inside our Java code.

Then, in the Java code, `friendList` needs to be declared like this:

```
@UiField
FriendList friendList;
```

And voila, the application layout is assembled with its widgets. Now it needs to be polished up with some CSS styles.

# Adding CSS styles to the application

There are basically two choices when it comes to implementing CSS styles. A style can either be declared inside the widget XML code or centralized into a global CSS file. Here is an example taken from the *Connectr* application header, where we implemented the styles directly in the XML template.

The following code is added in the `HeaderPanel.ui.xml` file.

```
<!DOCTYPE ui:UiBinder SYSTEM "http://dl.google.com/gwt/DTD/xhtml.ent">
<ui:UiBinder xmlns:ui='urn:ui:com.google.gwt.uibinder'
    xmlns:g='urn:import:com.google.gwt.user.client.ui'>

  <ui:image field='logo' src='logo_small.png' />

  <ui:style>
    .headerContainer {
      padding: 0 11px;
    }
    .welcomeDiv {
      float: right;
      margin-top: 5px;
    }
    @sprite .logo_small {
      margin-left: 10px;
      gwt-image: 'logo';
      position: absolute;
    }
    .tagLine {
      margin-left: 180px;
      padding-top: 22px;
```

```
                font-size: 1.8em;
                font-weight: bold;
            }
    </ui:style>

    <g:HTMLPanel>
        <div class='{style.headerContainer}'>
            <div class='{style.logo_small}' />
            <div>
                <div class="{style.welcomeDiv}">
                    <b>Welcome back, foo@bar.com</b>
                    -

                    <g:Anchor href='javascript:;' ui:field='signOutLink'>
                    Log Out</g:Anchor>
                </div>
                <div class='{style.tagLine}'>Your feeds are belong to us</div>
            </div>
        </div>
    </g:HTMLPanel>
</ui:UiBinder>
```

As shown in the previous code, once a CSS style is declared within a `<ui:style>` element it can be accessed in the `UiBinder` template, using the `class` keyword if it is an HTML element or the `styleName` keyword if it is a widget that implements the `setStyleName` function. If a style is used without being declared, the compiler will generate an error. This compile-time check is a great safety feature as well as a time saver when working with complex user interfaces that may have hundreds of CSS classes associated to them.

Spelling mistakes are easy to make and the compiler will catch them before deployment. Here is an example of the compiler complaining about a misspelled `contentColumn` CSS style accidentally written as `contentColumnz`.

```
The following obfuscated style classes were missing from the source CSS
file:
    [ERROR] contentColumn: Fix by adding .contentColumn{}
    [ERROR] The following unobfuscated classes were present in a strict
CssResource:
    [ERROR] contentColumn
Fix by adding String accessor method(s) to the CssResource interface for
obfuscated classes, or using an @external declaration for unobfuscated
classes.
    [ERROR] Unable to process CSS
```

However, rather than declaring styles within a widget template, most programmers like to implement them into a global CSS file that is to be used across the entire application (as we are going to see in the next section).

# Implementing CSS styles in a global CSS file

As previously shown in the application layout template, `ConnectrApp.ui.xml`, CSS styles can be imported easily by declaring the source file in the `UiBinder` XML template as follows:

```
<ui:style src="Resources/GlobalStyles.css" />
```

The advantages of having all of the styles in one file are ease of maintenance and separation of concerns, which means that designers can provide programmers a CSS file that can drop in the application easily.

# Adding a logo to the application

Let's add the *Connectr* logo to the header. Adding an image to the application requires only a few lines of code in `HeaderPanel.ui.xml`, as shown here:

```
<ui:image field='logo' src='Resources/logo_small.png' />
<ui:style>
  @sprite .logo_small
  {
    margin-left: 10px;
    gwt-image: 'logo';
    position: absolute;
  }
  ...
</ui:style>
```

Then the `UiBinder` XML in `HeaderPanel.ui.xml` can use:

```
<div class='{style.logo_small}'/>
```

# Catching mouse and keyboard events

Coding keyboard and mouse event handlers can be tedious because it involves writing a lot of boilerplate code. As an example, let's have a look at the *Connectr* **Friends** pop-up window shown in the following screenshot:

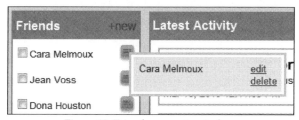

Figure 13: Friends property window

To catch user clicks, the **edit** link could have been coded "the old-fashioned way" directly in Java in the following manner:

```
...
Label editLink = new Label("Edit");
editLink.addClickHandler(new ClickHandler() {
    @Override
    public void onClick(ClickEvent event) {
        onEditClick(ClickEvent e);
    }
});
...

void onEditClick(ClickEvent e) {
    // handle click
// handle click
}
...
```

Luckily, UiBinder provides a useful facility allowing programmers to tie an interface widget to a Java method just by adding a single Java annotation, @UiHandler:

```
@UiHandler("edit")
void onEditClick(ClickEvent e) {
// handle click ...
}
```

The preceding code from `client.FriendList` shows the `@UiHandler` annotation binding the `onEditClick` method to the widget that declared its `ui:field` to be `edit`. Then, the following `UiBinder` code from `client/FriendPopup.ui.xml` shows the widget declaration:

```
<g:Hyperlink ui:field='edit' styleName='{style.link}' >edit</
g:Hyperlink>
```

# Grouping CSS files and images for faster speed with ClientBundle

Resources such as CSS files, logos, icons, and files used by the application need to be downloaded by the client at some point. If there are many items to fetch, even if they are tiny icons, it can impact the user experience negatively because users will have to wait for those resources to be retrieved.

A significant part of an application loading time is spent making multiple connections to the server in order to download this myriad of small images and files. Once the app is loaded, consequent network communication with the server is needed by the browser to check if a resource has changed and needs to be reloaded. These checks are mostly unnecessary because logos, icons, CSS files, and JavaScript resources don't change if they are part of the app. Therefore, such resources are prime candidates for optimization so that they download quickly and can be cached by the browser using aggressive caching policies. This can be tricky to achieve manually.

Enter `ClientBundle`: one HTTP request and the job is done.

GWT comes to the rescue by providing `ClientBundle`—a facility that assembles resources into a big compressed blob and sends it over the wire to the client during the initial HTTP connection at loading time. Once the bundle is received, it will be unpacked and cached by the client forever, thus suppressing the need to periodically check if it needs to be updated. This decreases the number of HTTP requests from "a lot" to only one.

# Creating a ClientBundle

*Connectr* uses a `ClientBundle` to group images and its CSS file. To create a `ClientBundle`, developers can use the Eclipse GWT plugin from **File | New | ClientBundle**, as shown in the following screenshot:

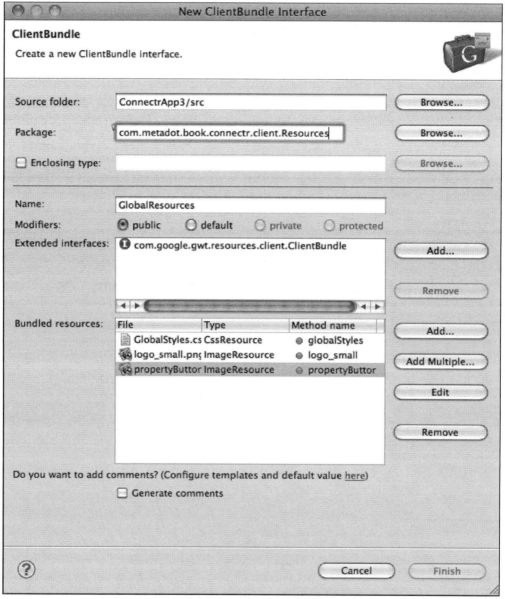

Figure 14: Adding a client bundle in Eclipse

The GWT plugin generates two files—one named `GlobalResources.java` containing the list of resources, which we added in the wizard window, and `GlobalStylesheet.java`, containing a list of CSS classes. This file is automatically named after the CSS file we added, namely `GlobalStylesheet.css`.

The following file shows the resources we added to the bundle.

The following code is added in the `client\Resources\GlobalResources.java` file.

```
...
public interface GlobalResources extends ClientBundle {
    @Source("com/metadot/book/connectr/client/Resources/
      logo_small.png")
    ImageResource logo_small();

    @Source("com/metadot/book/connectr/client/Resources/
      propertyButton.png")
    ImageResource propertyButton();

    @Source("com/metadot/book/connectr/client/Resources/
      GlobalStyles.css")
    GlobalStylesheet globalStyles();
}
```

# Using image resources in *Connectr*

Images can be declared either in `UiBinder` templates as seen previously for the application logo or directly in the Java code. Here is how to get access to the resource bundle programmatically.

First, in the resource bundle interface declaration, instantiate the resource class with `GWT.create()` as follows:

The following code is added in the `client/Resources/GlobalResources.java` file.

```
public interface GlobalResources extends ClientBundle {
    public static final GlobalResources RESOURCE =
      GWT.create(GlobalResources.class);
    . . .
```

Then it is easy to access the bundle items from your application.

```
Image propertyButton = new Image(GlobalResources.RESOURCE.
propertyButton());
panel.add(propertyButton);
```

# Automatically checking CSS styles at compile time with CssResource

When adding a CSS file to a `ClientBundle`, GWT will generate a CSS resource automatically. A **CSS resource** has a Java interface that provides methods named after their corresponding CSS styles. The CSS resource provides plenty of features including (but not limited to) syntax validation and support for conditional CSS styles based on browser type or end-user language. *Connectr* uses a CSS resource to access centralized CSS information and to have support for syntax checking. More detailed information can be found on the GWT website at `http://code.google.com/webtoolkit/doc/latest/DevGuideClientBundle.html#CssResource`.

Looking at `GlobalStyles.java`, we see that the GWT Eclipse plugin has generated the Java CSS accessor methods corresponding to the CSS class selectors:

The following code is added in the `client/Resources/GlobalStylesheet.java` file.

```
...
public interface GlobalStylesheet extends CssResource {
    String addFriendBox();

    String addFriendLink();

    String alignTextRight();

    String boxBorder();

    String boxPadding();

    ...
}
```

`UiBinder` elements can now use styles located in this CSS file.

# Getting data from the server using GWT RPC

When traditional non-AJAX application clients need to get data, they make calls to a server and block the interface till they receive a response. This forces users to wait until clients receive the data and update the interface. These blocking calls are known as **synchronous calls** because things happen only in chronological sequence, one step at a time.

GWT does not allow synchronous calls to the server and forces developers to use **asynchronous calls**, which are non-blocking. This means that many things can happen in parallel. In the GWT world, a call to the server is called a **Remote Procedure Call (RPC)**. A primary advantage of using asynchronous calls is that they provide a much better user experience, as the user interface remains responsive and it can do other tasks while waiting for the server to answer. When the server sends the response back to the client, the client receives it in a method called **callback function**.

Another perk of using GWT RPC is that it is possible to share data classes between the client and the server. For example, a developer could choose to tell the server-side to send a user object to the client and the client would receive it as a user object.

However, asynchronous calls are harder to implement than synchronous ones. Luckily for us, GWT makes it easy to provide great end-user experience with minimum work by following a few simple steps. This section shows a step-by-step implementation of the *Connectr* login service using GWT RPC as an example.

# Creating the login service

First, we need to create an interface that extends GWT `RemoteService` and lists `login()` as a service.

The following code is added in the `client/UserAccountService.java` file.

```
package com.metadot.book.connectr.client;

import com.google.gwt.user.client.rpc.RemoteService;
import com.google.gwt.user.client.rpc.RemoteServiceRelativePath;
import com.metadot.book.connectr.shared.UserAccountDTO;


@RemoteServiceRelativePath("userAccountService")
public interface UserAccountService extends RemoteService {

    public UserAccountDTO login(String email, String password);

}
```

The preceding code shows that the login service requires two parameters—an `email` address and a `password`. The login service returns a `UserAccountDTO` object.

# Implementing the server-side login service

GWT server-side services are based on Java Servlet. Therefore, our implementation, `server.UserAccountServiceImpl`, needs to extend `RemoteServiceServlet` and implements the login service interface that we just created:

```
package com.metadot.book.connectr.server;

import com.metadot.book.connectr.client.UserAccountService;
import ...

...
public class UserAccountServiceImpl extends RemoteServiceServlet
implements UserAccountService {

    public UserAccountDTO login(String email, String password) {
        new AppMisc().populateDataStoreOnce();
        return UserAccount.toDTO(UserAccount.getDefaultUser());
    }
}
```

Once this server-side code is implemented, we need to inform the compiler of its existence by adding it into the `web.xml` file:

The following code is added in the `war\WEB-INF\Web.xml` file.

```
...
<servlet>
  <servlet-name>userAccountService</servlet-name>
  <servlet-class>
    com.metadot.book.connectr.server.UserAccountServiceImpl
  </servlet-class>
</servlet>

<servlet-mapping>
  <servlet-name>userAccountService</servlet-name>
  <url-pattern>/connectr/userAccountService</url-pattern>
</servlet-mapping>
...
```

# Creating the asynchronous interface

The last step of creating a GWT RPC is to create the asynchronous login interface. It must have the same name as the synchronous service, but with an `Async` suffix. To continue our example, the filename must be `UserAccountServiceAsync.java`. Failure to use this naming convention will generate a compiler error:

The following code is added in the `client/UserAccountServiceAsync.java` file

```
package com.metadot.book.connectr.client;

import com.google.gwt.user.client.rpc.AsyncCallback;
import com.metadot.book.connectr.shared.UserAccountDTO;

public interface UserAccountServiceAsync {
  void login(String email, String password,
    AsyncCallback<UserAccountDTO>
    callback);
}
```

The preceding code snippet shows that the `login` function has three parameters: `email`, `password`, and `callback`.

The `callback` parameter is an implementation of the `AsyncCallback` interface that the client must implement, and `<UserAccountDTO>` is the type of the return value.

Now that the login RPC is ready, let's see how we implement it on the client side.

# Invoking the login service

In the client code, we need to call the asynchronous `login` method with the three parameters discussed previously: `email`, `password`, and `callback`. The callback parameter must implement the `AsyncCallback` interface, that is, it needs to implement two methods—`onSuccess()` and `onFailure()`. The astute programmer will infer that the `onSuccess()` method is called in case of a successful call and `onFailure()` is called in case of an error:

The following code is added in the `client/ConnectrApp.java` file.

```
private void login()
{
  userService.login("email", "password",
    new AsyncCallback<UserAccountDTO>()
    {
      public void onFailure(Throwable caught) {
        Window.alert("An error occurred");
```

```
        }
    public void onSuccess(UserAccountDTO user) {
        currentUser = user;
        displayFriendsAndMessages();
    }
    });
}
```

As shown in the previous code, in case of success, the client will save the result object user as the currentUser and update the user interface by displaying the user list of friends and messages. In case of error, the client will simply display the error message: **An error occurred**.

Additionally, because the result of the login call, user is sent over the wire from the server to the client, it needs to be serialized. This is accomplished by having the shared.UserAccountDTO class implement the Serializable interface as shown in the following code snippet:

The following code is added in the shared/UserAccountDTO.java file

```
package com.metadot.book.connectr.shared;

import java.io.Serializable;
...


@SuppressWarnings("serial")
public class UserAccountDTO implements Serializable {
... // more code here
```

# Catching exceptions

When a client requests data from a server, a number of things can go wrong. Whether it is a network failure or a server issue, the client-side can catch an error via the transmission of an exception and respond accordingly based on its type.

There are two types of exceptions. The first type is called **checked exceptions**; they are generated by the application itself on the server-side. An example of a checked exception would be **user needs to login first** or **insufficient privilege** when a user tries to access sensitive information.

The other type is called **unexpected exceptions**, which cover errors such as network transmission errors, crashes, and timeouts.

As part of *Chapter 6, Implementing MVP, an Event Bus, and Other GWT Patterns*, we will extend *Connectr* to handle both types of exceptions. We will implement a global RPC class that will manage *Connectr* application exceptions as well as display a user interface **loading indicator**.

# Summary

In this chapter, we began to implement the *Connectr* user interface using `UiBinder`. We will continue this implementation in later chapters.

- We have discussed the integration of CSS styles and visual artifacts such as images, into the UI. Additionally, we have seen how to tie XML elements to the Java code using the `@UiField` annotation and how to catch user actions using `@UiHandler`.

- We also made the initial download of the application images and CSS files more efficient by grouping them into a bundle via `ResourceBundle`.

- We added a `CSSResource` that makes sure that the CSS styles we use in our application are declared in our CSS stylesheet.

- Finally, we introduced the **Remote Procedure Call (RPC)** concept to populate the user interface with data coming from the server. We have seen that RPCs are asynchronous and that they need to implement two method. `onSuccess()` is called in case of successful completion of the call, and `onFailure()` in case of error. Finally, we have learned that the objects sent between client and server need to be serialized.

Now that we have the UI elements in place and the capability to request data from the server, we will explore data storage and retrieval with Google Datastore.

# 4

# Persisting Data: The App Engine Datastore

## Introduction

*Chapter 3* introduced GWT and RPCs, using the initial version of our developing *Connectr* application. However, *Chapter 3* did not examine how the server-side of the application works nor how data objects are persisted and retrieved.

In this chapter, we start looking at the application's server-side operations, and how to use the **App Engine Datastore** to provide persistence.

In the process, we will explore the following topics:

- How the Datastore works, and the implications of its design for your data models and code development. The Datastore model provides scalability and robustness. However, as we will see, it is different from a relational model, and this sometimes requires a different way of thinking about your data modeling.

- How to use Java Data Objects (JDO)— a standard interface for working with data objects— with the Datastore.

- How to make data classes persistable, and the constraints on the construction of those classes.

- How to create, retrieve, and delete objects from the Datastore.

# The *Connectr* server-side object model

*Connectr's* initial server-side object model is shown in the next image (it will be extended in later chapters). The dotted-line classes, FriendSummaryDTO and FriendDTO, are non-persistence-capable classes. They are used as Data Transfer Objects (DTOs), which support communication over RPC to the client-side of the application.

The persistence-capable classes, whose instances may be saved in the Datastore, are UserAccount, Friend, and FriendDetails. A UserAccount instance has a collection of associated Friends, and each Friend has a FriendDetails child object. (As you might expect, a Friend object contains basic information about the friend, and the FriendDetails object contains more detailed data). Instances of such classes are often termed Data Access Objects (DAOs).

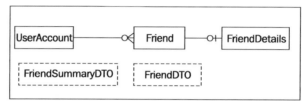

Figure 1: The initial *Connectr* server-side object model. The classes outlined with dotted lines are transient, and the solid-line classes are persistence-capable.

In this chapter and the next, while describing the Datastore's features, we will explore how we might represent this domain model in a JDO-fronted Datastore.

The code examples in this chapter show one approach to support object relationships, in which parent-child relationships are managed at the application level.

The application code used for this chapter is ConnectrStage1_alt.

*Chapter 5* will demonstrate a different approach to modeling object relationships using JDO's support for *owned relationships*. The application code for *Chapter 5* is ConnectrStage1.

Both approaches have their advantages, and the most appropriate tactic depends upon context. In subsequent chapters we will continue to develop the application based on the ConnectrStage1 version.

# The Datastore

The **Datastore** provides Google App Engine's support for data persistence.

The Datastore's design and implementation are a key part of the App Engine's provision of scalability and reliability for its apps. It provides a query engine and supports atomic transactions. It is based on Google's BigTable design.

The Datastore's design makes it easy to distribute and optimize how data is distributed. You, as an end-user of the Datastore, do not need to manage redundancy and data replication, or worry about connectivity to specific servers.

Its design has a focus on scalability, with the goal that query performance should scale linearly with the size of the result set (not the size of the data set). This has implications for the kinds of queries you can perform.

The Datastore is not a relational database, and thus its features may seem a bit non-intuitive at first, if you are used to interacting with RDBMSs. You can think of it loosely as an object database, one in which objects of the same type need not have the same schema. In a sense, it is more like a distributed, sorted hash table than an RDBMS.

The Datastore's design allows its data to be partitioned, or sharded, and it is distributed in a way that makes partitioning data and performing queries extremely efficient. It accomplishes this by building and organizing its distributed indexes, by restricting the types of queries that you may perform over those indexes, and by building indexes when data is written, not when read.

Because of the way the Datastore is designed, you may find that you need to rethink the way you approach data modeling. For example, your data organization will probably become more de-normalized.

# Datastore entities and their properties

The Datastore holds data objects called **entities**, which are the basic unit of storage. An entity has a **key**, and one or more **properties**, where data is stored. After creation, the key cannot be changed.

The Datastore supports a number of **property data types**, and the property values must be of those types. We will list the mapping of these supported data types to Java classes when we introduce the JDO (Java Data Objects) API.

A given property can have one or more values (multiple values). At the Datastore entity level, multiple values of a property can be of different types. However, the JDO interface, which we will be using, supports multiple property values of the same type only.

An important aspect of an entity is its **kind**. An entity's kind allows the entities to be organized so that queries on them may be efficiently performed. The kind is reflected in (is part of) the entity's key, so that you can always tell the kind of an entity given its key.

For example, an entity of kind Friend appears as shown in the next table with *firstName*, *lastName*, and *tags* as the entity's properties. In this example, *tags* is a multi-valued property, with two values, *colleague* and *sports*.

| Kind | Friend |
|---|---|
| (Entity ID portion of) Key | 12345 |
| firstName | Bob |
| lastName | Smith |
| tags | colleague, sports |

A Friend entity.

It may be helpful to loosely view kinds as tables, entities as table rows, and properties as table fields or columns. However this is not entirely accurate.

Entities have a soft schema, meaning that entities of the same kind need not have the same properties. It is perfectly fine from the point of view of the Datastore to create one entity of kind X that has a given property, and another which does not.

For example, in the following table, the Friend entity with *firstName* Joe has no *lastName* property. It's not set to null—the lastName property does not exist at all for that entity. But, Joe does have an *emailAddress* property.

| Kind | Friend |
|---|---|
| (Entity ID portion of) Key | 44 |
| firstName | Joe |
| tags | coffee-drinker |
| emailAddress | joe@joe.com |

A second Friend entity with a different "schema".

Another way to think about this is that if you were to view all Datastore entities of the kind Friend in a matrix, the information for both Bob and Joe would have a missing cell, as shown in the next table, and this is perfectly legal.

| Kind | Friend | Friend |
|---|---|---|
| (Entity ID portion of) Key | 12345 | 44 |
| firstName | Bob | Joe |
| lastName | Smith | |
| tags | colleague, sports | coffee-drinker |
| emailAddress | | joe@joe.com |

Entities of the same kind but with different sets of properties.

This means that schema consistency—to the extent that it is required for application semantics—must be managed at the application level. We will see how the use of JDO helps us to do that in our application.

 Datastore entities can be at most 1MB in size. Because entities can contain references to other entities, it's possible to split up a large file across multiple entities, and reconstruct the file when it is requested (several third-party libraries are available which support this). However, the App Engine also supports a Blobstore service in addition to its entity Datastore, with which you can store files of up to 50MB that have been directly uploaded, and serve these files back to apps. The Blobstore may be more appropriate for large-file storage.

# Entity keys

An entity's **key** identifies it across the entire App Engine system, and cannot be changed once created. Your application ID is automatically included in the key.

A key includes several pieces of information including the application ID, the entity's kind (for example, we will define a kind "friend"), and an **entity ID**. The entity ID part of the key can be either auto-generated by the system or set by the application.

The key determines an entity's **entity group**, which relates to how entities can be used in *transactions*. We will discuss transactions and entity groups in more detail in *Chapter 9*.

The JDO API abstracts away from the details of the entity keys' structure, but still lets you access and manipulate them.

# Datastore queries and indexes

Entities in the Datastore can be fetched either by key or by a query on the entity's properties. A JDO query operates on all entities of a given kind. The query can specify various filters on property values and specify sort orders. Queries can limit the number of results returned.

Entities are returned as query results when all filter criteria are met, and the entity has value(s), possibly null, for every property mentioned in the query. For example, suppose we constructed a query over the *Friend* kind, and the query specified that the results should be ordered by the lastName property. If there were Friend entities without a lastName property—such as Joe in the previous examples of the *A second Friend entity with a different "schema"* table—those entities would not be returned in the query result. However, entities with a lastName property set to null would be returned.

## Queries are supported by indexes

Every query accesses an **index**, which is essentially an ordered table of possible answers for the query. An application has an index for each combination of kind, filter property and operator, and sort order used in some query for that app. (More precisely, an index is maintained for a set of queries that use the same filters and sort orders, allowing different values for the filters).

The indexes are built and maintained at write time, when data is created or modified, and they are kept sorted. So if you make a change to an entity, say, a change to one of its property values, and then update the entity, its associated indexes will be updated as well before the call returns. The relevant rows in the index tables will be added or modified, and the indexes re-sorted as necessary.

Certain simple index tables are always built automatically, regardless of the queries performed by your application, and these tables support a set of simple queries. For other more complex queries, indexes must be specifically built. It would be intractable to build index tables for all possible queries that might arise, and the indexes required by your application will be a tiny subset of these. So, indexes are built only for the queries actually used by your application.

Because of the way in which queries are based upon index traversal, you cannot construct queries of arbitrary structure. To meet the Datastore's scalability requirements, the query mechanism generally requires all results for a query to be adjacent to one another in the index table, to avoid having to scan the entire table for results, or having to perform multiple scans. This has the implication that certain types of queries are not allowed because of the retrieval combinatorics that they would trigger.

*Chapter 5* will describe queries and indexes in more detail.

# App Engine queries are fast

App Engine queries are fast, even with a large number of entities in the Datastore—the speed of a query is nearly independent of the size of the data set. By building large index tables at the write time, and updating them when property values change, queries are not computationally expensive. Because indexes are sorted, it is not expensive to find the relevant part of the index for a given query.

Furthermore, entities and indexes may be distributed across a number of machines. In parallel, each machine will scan its index, and return its results to App Engine, which will organize the result components and deliver the aggregate result to the app as if it had been drawn from one large index.

# The Datastore versus a relational database

As can be seen from the previous discussion, the Datastore is different from a relational database. It has no fixed schema. Another way of looking at this is that the application layer is in charge of managing the schemas for the entities. A soft schema can have an advantage in supporting much faster application iterations. As noted previously, it may be helpful to loosely view kinds as tables, entities as table rows, and properties as table fields or columns; but remember that it is misleading to carry this analogy too far.

An RDBMS has relatively cheap writes but its queries can be expensive. In contrast, the Datastore performs more complex writes (as its index tables are updated in the process) but its reads are quick and cheap. Furthermore, because of the way the entities are stored, direct entity lookups by key can be much faster than performing a query to find an object. As we will see, JDO supports both direct lookups and queries.

The Datastore does not generally support natural, inner, or outer joins, as these joins are difficult to scale within the Datastore model. We will return to this topic in *Chapter 9* and discuss some approaches for mapping relational models to Datastore models. As we will see, one effective approach is to use multi-valued entity properties instead of joins across different tables—essentially, denormalizing your model.

 Google is researching algorithms to make some types of join operations more scalable but at the time of writing they are not production-ready.

The Datastore supports atomic transactions, though its model is different from that of a relational database. Entities can belong to entity groups, determined by how the entities' keys are constructed, and transaction semantics depend upon the entity groups. We will describe the Datastore's transactional model in more detail in *Chapter 9*.

# JDO

The App Engine includes support for two standard interfaces for storing objects containing data into a database: Java Data Objects (**JDO**) and the Java Persistence API (**JPA**). Both allow you to describe data structures in terms of Java classes, with Java's advantage of type-safety. Both allow you to enforce a stronger schema than required by just the Datastore entities—as long as your class definitions do not change. Thus, these interfaces can serve as a portability and data-modeling layer.

JDO is an Apache-run project, being developed as a Java Specification Request under the Java Community Process. The JDO standard uses annotations on Java objects to describe how instances of objects should be stored in a database. JDO also supports a query language for retrieving objects and has support for specifying transactions. Google App Engine uses a specific implementation of the JDO interface specification, the DataNucleus Data Access Platform, which is an open source reference implementation for App Engine. At the time of writing, the implementation is of JDO 2.3. It specifies how the instances of your annotated Java classes are mapped to entities in the Datastore, and supports queries and transactions over those entities.

There are several advantages to using JDO (or JPA). These interfaces abstract from the database specifics, thus making your code more portable. An application that uses the JDO interface can work with different kinds of databases (not just the Datastore) including object, relational, and hierarchical databases, without using database-specific code.

JDO and JPA also support management of relationships between objects in the Datastore. This is a useful feature, as we shall see in *Chapter 5*. You can define one-to-one or many-to-one relationships between objects or object collections, and allow JDO to implement the details of defining the objects, performing the necessary bookkeeping to support the relationships, so that your defined object relationships "just work". This can simplify code significantly over what would be required using the lower-level API.

However, at times, there may be a Datastore feature that is not exposed by JDO (or JPA). There also exists a direct, lower-level App Engine Datastore API. This API exposes all of the features of the Datastore.

We will use JDO for the applications and examples in this book; however, JPA is acceptable too, and the application could have been written using JPA instead. See the Resources section for links to the JDO API, for information about JPA, and a DataNucleus discussion of JDO versus JPA, as well as links to documentation for the lower-level App Engine API.

In the next sections, we will first look at data modeling using JDO, then describe how to construct and execute queries, and work with the Datastore indexes.

# Setting up JDO

Since we are using Eclipse, it is easy to use JDO—the setup is taken care of for you. First, the necessary JDO and DataNucleus JAR files are installed under `war/WEB-INF/lib`. This is done when you create a project that uses Google App Engine. Then, a default JDO configuration file is created for you, called `jdoconfig.xml`. You will find it under `src/META-INF`, and it will be copied to the `war` directory during the build process. Finally, post-compilation **enhancement** must be performed on your compiled data classes, during the build process, to associate them with the JDO. This too is taken care of by Eclipse.

> The DataNucleus site contains more information about the enhancement process. Check out the examples at:
>
> `http://www.datanucleus.org/products/accessplatform/enhancer.html`.
>
> If you were not using Eclipse, then typically you would run an Apache Ant task or similar to perform the post-compilation enhancement. More information is available in the Google documentation.

As you write your Datastore-related code, you will be importing from two libraries:

- `javax.jdo.*`: The JDO libraries
- `com.google.appengine.api.datastore.*`: At times you may be directly manipulating App Engine Datastore classes.

# Creating *Connectr's* data models

Once we've confirmed that our project is set up to use JDO, we can begin the process of defining persistence-capable data models for *Connectr* using the JDO API. In this section, we focus on specifying the data models, then in the next section we describe how to query the Datastore for them.

When we make a Java class persistent, we are mapping its instances to Datastore entities, where an entity's kind is derived from the class name. This is accomplished in JDO by adding class and field annotations and by deciding how we want to map the class fields to the Java analogues of the **property data types** supported by the Datastore.

We also have some decisions to make about how we want to represent the relationships between our data objects. Our application includes object relationships such as one-to-one or one-to-many relationships, that we wish to model. There are various ways to represent these relationships and the right approach depends upon how the data objects will be used. We will take a look at some of these design decisions in this chapter and the next, in the context of persisting the Friend and User Account models.

 The first step in implementing JDO-based persistence is to define access to a PersistenceManager, which supports Datastore interaction.

# The PersistenceManager and the PersistenceManagerFactory

In JDO, you interact with the Datastore via a PersistenceManager instance, both to persist and update objects, and to fetch and query over them. The PersistenceManager instance is provided by a PersistenceManagerFactory object. Since the PersistenceManagerFactory is time-consuming to create, typically the Singleton pattern is used to ensure that only one is created per application. In our application, a class named server.PMF, as shown in the following code, serves this purpose:

```
import javax.jdo.JDOHelper;
import javax.jdo.PersistenceManagerFactory;

public final class PMF {
  private static final PersistenceManagerFactory pmfInstance =
    JDOHelper.getPersistenceManagerFactory("transactions-optional");

  private PMF() {}

  public static PersistenceManagerFactory get() {
    return pmfInstance;
  }
}
```

The `PersistenceManagerFactory` instance is accessed via the `PMF` class when a `PersistenceManager` is required:

```
import javax.jdo.JDOHelper;
import javax.jdo.PersistenceManager;
import javax.jdo.PersistenceManagerFactory;

import PMF;

// ...
    PersistenceManager pm = PMF.get().getPersistenceManager();
```

Typically, a `PersistenceManager` instance is retained for the life of a web request (though it may be for a shorter period). It is not expensive to create a `PersistenceManager`, in contrast to the creation of the `PersistenceManagerFactory`.

You must always close a given `PersistenceManager` instance when you are done with it, by calling its `close()` method. Thus, it is good practice to use the returned `PersistenceManager` instance within a `try` block and put the `close()` call within the `finally` clause. This will ensure that the instance is always closed properly even if an exception is thrown:

```
PersistenceManager pm = PMF.get().getPersistenceManager();
try {
    // create or modify entities via the pm
} finally {
    pm.close(); // be sure to close the pm
}
```

If you close a `PersistenceManager` and then attempt to use it to save an object associated with it after it is closed, it generates an error.

# Making data classes persistable

Now that we are able to generate a `PersistenceManager` instance on demand, we will look at how to map Java classes to Datastore entities using JDO.

## Class and field annotations

To indicate that the instances of a given class should be persisted to the Datastore, add a `@PersistenceCapable` annotation to the class, using the 'identityType' attribute as shown in the following lines of code. As an organizational convention, *Connectr* places all persistence-capable classes in the `server.domain` subpackage.

We start by defining a new persistence-capable `server.domain.Friend` class:

```
import javax.jdo.annotations.IdentityType;
import javax.jdo.annotations.PersistenceCapable;
... other imports...

@PersistenceCapable(identityType = IdentityType.APPLICATION)
public class Friend {
   ...
 } // end class
```

Then, you must indicate which fields of the class are to be made persistent and stored as part of the Datastore entity. JDO is the only persistence standard whose API allows definition of which class fields are persisted. So, you do not necessarily need to persist all fields of a persistence-capable class to the Datastore. You can indicate that specific fields (for example, those which hold transient data) should not be persisted.

Indicate a persistent field by using the `@Persistent` annotation. If you specifically do not want a field persisted, give it the `@NotPersistent` annotation instead. Some data types are persisted by default, but this is done not entirely consistently with the JDO specification, so to be on the safe side, be explicit about which fields you do and do not want persisted.

```
import javax.jdo.annotations.IdentityType;
import javax.jdo.annotations.PersistenceCapable;
import javax.jdo.annotations.Persistent;
... other imports...

PersistenceCapable(identityType = IdentityType.APPLICATION,
detachable="true")
public class Friend   {

   ...
   @Persistent
   private String firstName;

   ...

} //end class
```

In the previous code, from `server.domain.Friend`, we are defining the `firstName` field of the `Friend` class to be persistent. When an instance of type `Friend` is persisted, this will result in a Datastore entity of kind Friend, with a `firstName` property of type String.

Be sure to make all of your persistent fields private and create accessors for them. In addition to all the usual good reasons for encapsulation, if a persistent object field is accessed directly from another object, this may circumvent the JDO class enhancement post-processing.

Of course, this is not yet the full story. Remember that Datastore entity properties may hold values from a specific set of 'core' data types, and properties may be multi-valued. Further recall that all entities have keys which are composed of multiple parts. Key creation occurs when an object is persisted, after which its key may not be changed.

Next we will look at how these Datastore features are mapped to Java and JDO.

# Persistable field types

For a class field to be made persistent, it must meet one of the following requirements:

- Its type is mapped to one of the core value types supported by the Datastore or it is a Collection or an array of values of a core Datastore type.

- The field is declared as `serialized` and references a serializable object or a Collection of instances of a serializable class. The object (or Collection) referenced by the field will be serialized and stored as a Blob, not as an entity.

- The field references a class declared as an *embedded* class. The fields of embedded classes are stored as additional properties on the enclosing entity, not as an additional entity.

- The field references an instance or Collection of instances of a class annotated as `@PersistenceCapable`. This means that the instances of the referenced class are also persisted in the Datastore.

We will discuss each of these cases in turn. For most of them, additional annotations and/or attributes are required to indicate to JDO how to handle the field.

# Core value types

The table below—drawn from the Google documentation—describes the mapping between Datastore core value types and Java data types. This means that using JDO, a class field of a Java type listed in the table can be persisted directly, and will correspond to a property value in the resultant Datastore entity. You will see that some of the listed Java data types are from the `com.google.appengine.api` library.

| Type | Java class | Sort order | Notes |
|---|---|---|---|
| short text string, < 500 bytes | `java.lang.String` | Unicode | A value longer than 500 bytes throws a JDOFatalUserException. |
| short byte string, < 500 bytes | `com.google.appengine.api.datastore.ShortBlob` | byte order | A value longer than 500 bytes throws a JDOFatalUserException. |
| Boolean value | `boolean` or `java.lang.Boolean` | `false < true` | |
| integer | `short`, `java.lang.Short`, `int`, `java.lang.Integer`, `long`, `java.lang.Long` | Numeric | Stored as long integer, then converted to the field type. Out-of-range values overflow. |
| floating point number | `float`, `java.lang.Float`, `double`, `java.lang.Double` | Numeric | Stored as double-width float, then converted to the field type. Out-of-range values overflow. |
| date-time | `java.util.Date` | Chronological | |
| Google account | `com.google.appengine.api.users.User` | By e-mail address (Unicode) | |
| long text string | `com.google.appengine.api.datastore.Text` | (not orderable) | Not indexed. |
| long byte string | `com.google.appengine.api.datastore.Blob` | (not orderable) | Not indexed. |
| entity key | `com.google.appengine.api.datastore.Key`, or the referenced object (as a child) | By path elements (kind, ID or name) | |
| a category | `com.google.appengine.api.datastore.Category` | Unicode | |

| Type | Java class | Sort order | Notes |
|------|-----------|-----------|-------|
| an e-mail address | `com.google.appengine.api.datastore.Email` | Unicode | |
| a geographical point | `com.google.appengine.api.datastore.GeoPt` | By latitude, then longitude | |
| an instant messaging handle | `com.google.appengine.api.datastore.IMHandle` | Unicode | |
| a URL | `com.google.appengine.api.datastore.Link` | Unicode | |
| a phone number | `com.google.appengine.api.datastore.PhoneNumber` | Unicode | |
| a postal address | `com.google.appengine.api.datastore.PostalAddress` | Unicode | |
| a user-provided rating, an integer between 0 to 100 | `com.google.appengine.api.datastore.Rating` | Numeric | |

Note that the `Text` and `Blob` types are indicated as not indexed — that is, index tables are never built for fields of this type. This means that you cannot use `Text` or `Blob` fields in a query, in contrast to the `String` field, which is indexed.

# Collections and multi-valued properties

A Datastore entity property can have more than one value — these are termed *multi-valued* properties.

Using JDO, you can express a multi-valued property as either a Collection field of a core data type or as an array field of a core value type. Note that in contrast to the raw Datastore properties, with JDO you cannot define a multi-valued field that contains more than one data type. For example, you cannot build a JDO list that includes both `String` and `int`, though the Datastore itself allows a mix. The order of the values is preserved for a multi-valued property, and thus preserved by JDO when using ordered Collection types or arrays.

In *Chapter 7*, we will use multi-valued properties to store a set of URLs, as part of our Friend data. For each Friend that the user defines, the user will be able to add a set of RSS/Atom feed URLs associated with that friend (for example, feeds for their blog or Twitter timeline). We will store these `urls` as a persisted Set of Strings, as shown in the following lines of code:

```
@PersistenceCapable(identityType = IdentityType.APPLICATION,
detachable="true")
public class FriendDetails  {
   ...
  @Persistent
  private Set<String> urls;
   ...
  }
```

Then, we can add feed URLs to the list:

```
...
urls = new HashSet<String>();
...
urls.add("http://xyz.com/feed.xml");
urls.add("http://twitter.com/statuses/user_timeline/xyz.atom");
```

In the corresponding Datastore entity, the list of URLs will be stored as a multi-valued property, similar to the tags example in *A second Friend entity with a different "schema"* table. As we will introduce in *Chapter 5*, queries over multi-valued fields like `urls` have an interesting and useful behavior, which we will make use of for *Connectr*.

The following collection types are supported by JDO:

- `java.util.ArrayList<...>`
- `java.util.HashSet<...>`
- `java.util.LinkedHashSet<...>`
- `java.util.LinkedList<...>`
- `java.util.List<...>`
- `java.util.Set<...>`
- `java.util.SortedSet<...>`
- `java.util.Stack<...>`
- `java.util.TreeSet<...>`
- `java.util.Vector<...>`

In addition to holding a collection of a core value type, as shown previously, collection fields can also be used to support a collection of serializable objects (stored as a serialized field), or to indicate a one-to-many relationship between persistence-capable objects. We will discuss these cases later in this chapter as well as in *Chapter 5*.

# Datastore keys and JDO key fields

Every entity in the Datastore has a unique key. The key includes the App Engine application ID and is unique over all App Engine entities. The key also includes the entity kind, tied to the Java class (for example, `Friend`), and an entity ID. This is not quite the full picture if the key includes path information, which specifies its membership in an entity group—we'll return to this in *Chapter 9*. Remember that once created, the key of a Datastore entity cannot be changed.

JDO provides support for key creation and can generate keys for new objects automatically. Any persistence-capable class must have a key field, annotated to indicate that the field is the `@PrimaryKey`.

JDO supports four types of `@PrimaryKey` fields: *unencoded String, Long, Key,* and *encoded String*.

The String and Long fields access the object key's entity ID part. The application must set the String variant; the Long variant is auto-populated by the system.

The Key and encoded String variants allow the primary key field to include key path information. This allows the entity to be defined as part of a Datastore entity group, as will be described in *Chapter 9*. Under the hood, JDO uses key paths and entity groups to support its owned relationships. As a consequence, only the Key and encoded String key types can be used for child objects in an owned relationship, as we'll see in *Chapter 5*.

The Key type cannot be used in objects that will be sent via RPC to the client side of your application. This is because the client code will not have access to the App Engine libraries. Thus, if you want to transfer an object over RPC, and its key field must include path information, use the encoded String.

Next, we look at each primary key field type in more detail.

## Unencoded String key field

An *unencoded* key field of type `String` (`java.lang.String`) allows the application to set the key name (entity ID) for an object's key before it is persisted. It does not allow path information to be specified for the key.

Once such an object is persisted, you can fetch it from the Datastore using the value of its key field. For example, you might define a set of Personnel objects to use employee ID Strings as primary keys. You could later retrieve a Personnel object via employee ID.

A String key is specified as follows, using the `@PrimaryKey` annotation:

```
import javax.jdo.annotations.PrimaryKey;

// ...
    @PrimaryKey
    private String nameID;
```

When an instance contains an unencoded String key, the application must set the key before persisting the instance. The value of the key field—`nameID` in this example—must be unique across all entities of that kind (that is, object class). If it is not, the new entity will overwrite the existing entity with the same `nameID` in the Datastore, without complaint. You can use a Transaction, which we will discuss in *Chapter 9*, to first check for the existence of an object with that key, then persist the new object.

The unencoded String key type is not used in this initial version of the *Connectr* application, but we will see it in upcoming chapters.

## Long key field

Similar to the unencoded String type above, a Long key field holds the entity ID part of the object's key, but in this case it is a system-generated numeric value. That is, the application code does not explicitly set the key field. Rather, once the object has been persisted, the key field is populated and its value may be accessed.

You can retrieve a persisted object from the Datastore using its Long key field value.

We will use a Long key for our `server.domain.UserAccount` class.

```
import javax.jdo.annotations.IdGeneratorStrategy;
import javax.jdo.annotations.Persistent;
import javax.jdo.annotations.PrimaryKey;

@PersistenceCapable(identityType =
  IdentityType.APPLICATION, detachable="true")
public class UserAccount {

  @PrimaryKey
```

```
@Persistent(valueStrategy = IdGeneratorStrategy.IDENTITY)
private Long id;
    ...
}
```

Again the `@PrimaryKey` annotation is used. The `valueStrategy` annotation indicates that the value is system-generated. Once an object is persisted you can access its key field — id in this example — to obtain the key that was assigned to the object when it was saved. You can use that value later to fetch the object from the Datastore.

The last two types of key fields, Key and encoded String, in contrast to the two above, do allow path information to be encoded in the key. Thus, you must use one of these two latter types for a child in a JDO *owned relationship*.

# Key

A key field of type Key is defined as follows:

```
import javax.jdo.annotations.IdGeneratorStrategy;
import javax.jdo.annotations.Persistent;
import javax.jdo.annotations.PrimaryKey;
import com.google.appengine.api.datastore.Key;

// ...
    @PrimaryKey
    @Persistent(valueStrategy = IdGeneratorStrategy.IDENTITY)
    private Key key;
```

A Key includes an entity ID component. You can either let the system automatically generate the entity ID portion of a Key field, or have the application set it. If you want to let the system generate the entity ID part of the key, do not set the key. It will be automatically created when the object is persisted. This is the approach shown above.

Alternately, you may want to create a key with an application-assigned entity ID (key name) component. To assign an application string ID to the key before creating it, and if your key does not need to be defined as part of an entity group, you can use the `KeyFactory.createKey()` method as follows:

```
Key key = KeyFactory.createKey(<your_class>.class.getSimpleName(),
"your_string_id");
```

where <your_class> is replaced with the name of your object class, for example, Friend. Set the key field of your object with the result before persisting the object.

If you need to create a key that includes path information, this is possible as well. *Chapter 9* provides more information.

For objects that you will pass via RPC, do not use the Key type, as your client code cannot access the App Engine libraries; use of the Key type will fail at runtime.

## Key as encoded string

If an object includes a Key field, it cannot be passed to the client side of your application— that is, it is not portable. The key as encoded string form provides a way around this. The encoded String acts similarly to Key, and can encode path information, but as it is a String, it can be sent over RPC and used by GWT.

We will use an encoded String key for our server.domain.Friend class. The encoded String key is defined as follows. The id field, which holds the key, will be set by the system, not by the *Connectr* application code. Note the @Extension annotation, which requires an additional import.

```
import javax.jdo.annotations.Extension;
import javax.jdo.annotations.IdGeneratorStrategy;
import javax.jdo.annotations.Persistent;
import javax.jdo.annotations.PrimaryKey;

...

@PersistenceCapable(identityType = IdentityType.APPLICATION,
detachable="true")
  public class Friend  {

  @PrimaryKey
  @Persistent(valueStrategy = IdGeneratorStrategy.IDENTITY)
  @Extension(vendorName="datanucleus", key="gae.encoded-pk",
value="true")
  private String id;
  ...
}
```

There exist KeyFactory utility methods keyToString and stringToKey, to convert back and forth between the Key and encoded String formats. For example:

```
String enk = KeyFactory.keyToString(key);
```

You will need to import com.google.appengine.api.datastore.KeyFactory to use these methods.

If you are using a key encoded as a String, you can declare an additional field in the class that holds the object's string (application-assigned) or numeric (system-generated) entity ID. Do this via one of the following forms of the @Extension annotation on the additional field:

```
@Persistent
@Extension(vendorName="datanucleus", key="gae.pk-id",
  value="true")
private Long keyId;
```

or

```
@Persistent
@Extension(vendorName="datanucleus", key="gae.pk-name",
  value="true")
private String keyName;
```

If using a gae.pk-name field (here, keyName), set the field before saving your object. This will define the 'key name' portion of the key.

The 'gae.pk-id' field should not be set, but will be populated when your object is persisted, and can be accessed.

## Defining keys and core value type fields for Friend and UserAccount

In this section, we'll begin to define persistable Friend and UserAccount classes, using core value types for our persistent fields. We will refine these initial definitions in the following sections. As noted in *Introduction*, the examples in this chapter are from the ConnectrStage1_alt application code.

Friend contains String fields for firstName and lastName. As introduced previously, we'll define the server.domain.Friend primary key field, id, to be an encoded String. This is because later we will require the Friend key to encode entity group information. The id field will be set by the system. The following code shows this definition.

```
import javax.jdo.annotations.IdGeneratorStrategy;
import javax.jdo.annotations.IdentityType;
import javax.jdo.annotations.PersistenceCapable;
import javax.jdo.annotations.Persistent;
import javax.jdo.annotations.PrimaryKey;
import javax.jdo.annotations.Extension;
```

```
// .. other imports


@PersistenceCapable(identityType = IdentityType.APPLICATION,
detachable="true")
public class Friend  {

  @PrimaryKey
  @Persistent(valueStrategy = IdGeneratorStrategy.IDENTITY)
  @Extension(vendorName="datanucleus", key="gae.encoded-pk",
value="true")
  private String id;

  ...

  @Persistent
  private String firstName;

  @Persistent
  private String lastName;
  ...
  // constructor, setters, getters, and other methods.
  // No setter for the id field.
  // We will not explicitly set the id field,
  // but instead let the system generate it.
}
```

Next, we will define a persistence-capable `server.domain.UserAccount` class, as shown in the following code. The `UserAccount` primary key will not need to encode entity group information, so here we will use Long as the key `id`, which the system will set. `UserAccount` also holds Strings for the user's `name` and `emailAddress`. We also define a `friends` field of type `List<String>`. We will use this list to hold the keys, represented as encoded Strings, of the `Friend` objects associated with the given `UserAccount` object. This `friends` list is mapped to a multi-valued property in the Datastore.

```
import javax.jdo.annotations.IdGeneratorStrategy;
import javax.jdo.annotations.IdentityType;
import javax.jdo.annotations.PersistenceCapable;
import javax.jdo.annotations.Persistent;
import javax.jdo.annotations.PrimaryKey;

// ... other imports...
```

```
@PersistenceCapable(identityType = IdentityType.APPLICATION,
detachable="true")
public class UserAccount {

  @PrimaryKey
  @Persistent(valueStrategy = IdGeneratorStrategy.IDENTITY)
  private Long id;

  @Persistent
  private String name;
  @Persistent
  private String emailAddress;

  // this field will hold the list of keys from the associated Friend
  // data objects
  List<String> friends;
  ...
  // ... constructor, getters, setters, and other methods.
  // Again, there is no setter for the id
  ...
  public List<String> getFriendsList() {
    return friends;
  }
}
```

You may have noticed that the UserAccount and Friend classes are annotated with the "detachable" attribute. This means that they can be detached from their PersistenceManager, modified after that PersistenceManager is closed, and "re-attached" to a different PersistenceManager later. We will describe detachable in more detail in an upcoming section.

# Referencing complex objects

We have described how a field can hold a Datastore core value type or a collection of a core value type. However, you will often want the fields in your persistence-capable classes to reference more complex objects. This is necessary to model object relationships.

With JDO, there are several ways to do this:

- Create a serializable class, and then define a **serialized field** to reference that type, which indicates to JDO that the referenced object (or collection of serializable objects) should be serialized and stored as a Blob type. This approach is quite straightforward, but we cannot inspect or query over the Blob contents in the Datastore. In many cases this may not be an issue.

- Create an **embedded** class. This lets you model a field value using a class, then instructs JDO to implement the inclusion of the embedded class fields by adding those fields as properties of the containing entity. So no additional entity kinds are created, but the fields from the embedded object can be accessed as part of the enclosing entity.

- Define additional **persistence-capable** classes and store their corresponding entities in the Datastore as well. Then we must be able to reference one object from another.

There are two approaches to "connecting up" Datastore entities that reference each other.

One way is to explicitly manage the connections between objects at the application level by having objects store the primary keys of other objects, essentially providing pointers to them. This is what we will show in this chapter, with the ConnectrStage1_alt version of our application. A UserAccount object stores a list of Friend keys.

Or, we can let the JDO framework handle the object relationships for us, via its owned relationship mechanism. This is what we will do in *Chapter 5*, with the ConnectrStage1 version of the application. This is usually easier to build, and works well for our application, but is not supportable for all types of object relationships.

# Serializable objects and serialized fields

A Java class may be defined as serializable, by declaring that it "implements Serializable". If its fields reference objects from other classes, these classes must be serializable as well. See the Java documentation for further details on serializability.

If a class is serializable, then we can indicate to JDO that a given object of that type (or a collection containing that type) should be stored in its serialized form. This is called a **serialized field**.

The serialized instance is stored as a com.google.appengine.api.datastore. Blob, one of the Datastore core data types. When a data object with a serialized field is retrieved from the Datastore, the Blob is de-serialized, with all original references intact, and the field is set to the reconstituted result.

It is not difficult to manage serialized fields. However, Blob fields are not indexed, and their contents are not queryable, so you cannot inspect serialized objects in the Datastore.

To declare a serialized field, add a `serialized` attribute to the field's `@Persistent` annotation as follows:

```
@Persistent(serialized = "true")
```

## Using a serialized field to hold friend details

As an example of using a serialized field, we will define a `FriendDetails` class, containing an `emailAddress` field. We will add a `details` field of type `FriendDetails` to the `Friend` class.

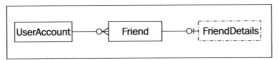

Figure 2: In the application *Connectr*Stage1_alt, a FriendDetails instance is stored as a serialized field— indicated by the dotted lines— in a persisted Friend object.

In `ConnectrStage1_alt`, we define the `details` field to be a 'serialized' field. This means that the `FriendDetails` object will be serialized as a `Blob` property of `Friend`. Figure 2 suggests this structure. Because the `details` data will be serialized, we will not be able to query for e-mail strings in the Datastore, but we decide for now that this is okay.

The new field declaration for the `server.domain.Friend` class is shown in the following code. The `details` field holds a value of type `FriendDetails` and is annotated to be a serialized persistent field.

```
@PersistenceCapable(identityType = IdentityType.APPLICATION,
  detachable="true")
public class Friend  {

  @PrimaryKey
  @Persistent(valueStrategy = IdGeneratorStrategy.IDENTITY)
  @Extension(vendorName="datanucleus", key="gae.encoded-pk",
    value="true")
  private String id;

  @Persistent(serialized = "true")
  private FriendDetails details;

  @Persistent
  private String firstName;

  @Persistent
  private String lastName;
  ...
}
```

We must define a `server.domain.FriendDetails` class as well, as shown next. We are not modeling it as a Datastore class, so it does not need to be persistence-capable. However, it does need to be serializable, and so the `FriendDetails` class must declare that it "`implements Serializable`". Thus, all of its field values must be serializable too.

```
public class FriendDetails
    implements Serializable {

    private String emailAddress;
    ...
    // Constructor, setters, and getters

}
```

This is all that is required to support a serialized field. When we persist a `Friend` object, its `details` field will store the serialized `FriendDetails` object.

## Changing the value of a serialized field

With an object that has a serialized field, JDO uses the field reference to determine whether or not the field contents have changed and need to be re-persisted. Only when the reference changes is the field's corresponding `Blob` updated in the Datastore entity. If you have a serialized field pointing to an object, and you change one of the object's fields, this will not change the actual reference to the serializable object. Thus its changed content will not be updated in the Datastore.

This means that to update a serialized field in the Datastore, you must set the corresponding instance's field to a *new* object. It is easy to forget to do this, so pay particular attention when you are using serialized fields.

It is also possible to use the `JDOHelper.makeDirty()` method to indicate that a field needs to be re-persisted, but this is less preferable.

This issue is addressed in the `server.domain.Friend.updateFromDTO()` method in the following code (this method is called when new Friend data comes back from the client over RPC). We are updating an existing `Friend` object with new information. So we will create a new `FriendDetails` sub-object, set it with the client `emailAddress` information, and set the `details` field of `Friend` to the new object. If we had instead set the fields of the existing `FriendDetails` sub-object, this would not have had the desired effect—the `details` `Blob` would not have been changed in the Datastore.

```
@PersistenceCapable(identityType = IdentityType.APPLICATION,
detachable="true")
public class Friend  {
  ...
  public void updateFromDTO (FriendDTO fr) {

    this.details = new FriendDetails();
    this.firstName = friendDTO.getFirstName();
    this.lastName = friendDTO.getLastName();
    this.setEmailAddress(friendDTO.getEmailAddress());
  }
```

# Embedded classes

At times you may want to insert the fields of one class into another to produce one big entity in the Datastore. You can use a JDO embedded class to accomplish this. Embedding a class allows you to construct queries that access both the embedded and non-embedded fields together, since in the Datastore they are stored in one combined entity. This can be very useful. If you had instead generated two separate entities, you could not query over the properties of both together, since the App Engine does not support "join" queries.

To create an embedded class you must first annotate the class that you wish to "embed" as `@PersistenceCapable`. You may also annotate it as `@EmbeddedOnly`; if you do this, then the class cannot be used to create entities on its own, but can only be used embedded. It is not required, but is useful, to declare your embedded class as an inner class of its "enclosing" class.

Then create a field of that embedded class type in your enclosing class and annotate that field as both `@Persistent` and `@Embedded`. Set the field to an instance of the embedded class before persisting the enclosing object.

For example, suppose that instead of the serialized details field of the previous section, we had decided to define an embedded EFriendDetails class containing the emailAddress of our Friends, and an @Embedded edetails field to hold it. We could do this as shown in the following example (not included in the application code):

```
import javax.jdo.annotations.Embedded;
import javax.jdo.annotations.EmbeddedOnly;
// ... other imports ...

@PersistenceCapable(identityType = IdentityType.APPLICATION)
public class Friend {
    @PrimaryKey
    @Persistent(valueStrategy = IdGeneratorStrategy.IDENTITY)
    @Extension(vendorName="datanucleus", key="gae.encoded-pk",
value="true")
    private String id;

    @PersistenceCapable
    @EmbeddedOnly
    public static class EFriendDetails {
        @Persistent
        private String emailAddress;

        // ...
    }

    @Persistent
    @Embedded
    private EFriendDetails edetails;

    // .. Other Friend fields and methods
}
```

The edetails field of Friend can then be set to an instance of the embedded object:

```
this.edetails = new EFriendDetails();
```

When you persist an instance of the enclosing class (Friend), its corresponding entity in the Datastore will include the properties of the embedded class (EFriendDetails), named as per the embedded class field(s), here emailAddress. It is possible to change the names of the embedded properties; consult the App Engine documentation for more information. No entities of kind EFriendDetails will be created.

When you retrieve an object of the enclosing class from the Datastore, the embedded field(s) of that object (for example, the `edetails` field) will be set with a correctly-populated instance of the embedded class, which you access normally.

In defining JDO queries that include the embedded fields, use dot notation to refer to the embedded field names. In the previous example, you would query on the e-mail field with: `edetails.emailAddress`.

# Data class inheritance

With JDO, it is possible to specify that one data class **inherits** from another. The App Engine implementation does not cover the full JDO specification, but it does support two types of inheritance: "subclass-table" and "complete-table".

"Subclass-table" indicates that the subclass entity will 'inherit' the fields of the superclass, and this will be reflected in the Datastore: JDO will store all persistent fields of the superclass in the Datastore entities of the subclass. There will be no entities of the superclass type in the Datastore.

"Subclass-table" inheritance is specified by adding the following annotation to the superclass:

```
@Inheritance(strategy = InheritanceStrategy.SUBCLASS_TABLE)
```

The superclass should be defined as `abstract`: if a class has an `@Inheritance` strategy of type `SUBCLASS_TABLE`, you may not persist instances of it. Then, declare that the subclass `extends` the superclass. Any persistent fields defined in the superclass will be reflected in the Datastore objects of the subclass kind.

For example, suppose that we were to create a persistable class `Name`, which holds name information and inherits from a superclass called `AbsName`. As shown in the following code, `AbsName` declares a primary key field as well as a persistent field named 'species'. `AbsName` must be persistence-capable and must be declared as abstract. It must also declare that it uses "subclass-table" inheritance.

```
// ... Other imports ...
import javax.jdo.annotations.Inheritance;
import javax.jdo.annotations.InheritanceStrategy;

@PersistenceCapable(identityType = IdentityType.APPLICATION,
detachable="true")
@Inheritance(strategy = InheritanceStrategy.SUBCLASS_TABLE)
public abstract class AbsName {

    @PrimaryKey
```

```
@Persistent(valueStrategy = IdGeneratorStrategy.IDENTITY)
@Extension(vendorName="datanucleus", key="gae.encoded-pk",
value="true")
private String id;

@Persistent
private String species;

// ...Constructor, setters and getters.  Includes getId() accessor,
// but no setId()

} // end class
```

Then, we would define the Name class to extend AbsName. It too must be defined as persistence-capable. Name does not need to declare a primary key—this, and the getId() method, is inherited from AbsName, along with the field and accessors for species. We declare two Name fields, firstName and lastName.

```
@PersistenceCapable(identityType = IdentityType.APPLICATION,
detachable="true")
public class Name extends AbsName {

@Persistent
private String firstName;
@Persistent
private String lastName;
...
}
```

When we persist a Name instance to the Datastore an entity will be created of kind Name. It will have three properties: firstName, lastName, and species. No AbsName entities will be created.

 One thing to be aware of when defining inheritance on persisted classes is that *polymorphism in JDO owned relationships is not supported by App Engine* (JDO-owned relationships are described in *Chapter 5*). This restriction means that if we were to define JDO relationships involving Name objects, we could not reference objects of type AbsName in our code. Instead, we would have to refer to objects of the specific non-abstract class, Name.

A "*complete-table*" variant of JDO inheritance is available as well. This requires an annotation on the sub-class (not the superclass) of the following form:

```
@Inheritance(customStrategy = "complete-table")
```

This tells JDO to store all persistent fields of the subclass and its superclasses in Datastore subclass entities. See the App Engine JDO documentation for more information.

# Saving, updating, and deleting data objects

In the previous section, we looked at how to define persistence-capable classes. In this section, we will describe how to save instances of these classes to the Datastore, modify them, and delete them. Often such objects are termed **Data Access Objects** (**DAOs**). We will, at times, refer to them in this way to distinguish them from instances of non-persistence-capable classes.

## Persisting an object

To save an instance of a persistence-capable class to the Datastore, call the `makePersistent()` method of your `PersistenceManager` instance:

```
PersistenceManager pm = PMF.get().getPersistenceManager();
Friend f = new Friend(…);
try {
  pm.makePersistent(f);
} finally {
  pm.close();
}
```

Recall that earlier we defined a Singleton class, `server.PMF`, to hold a `PersistenceManagerFactory` object. It is important to do this. While it is not expensive to generate a `PersistenceManager`, it is expensive to create a `PersistenceManagerFactory`, so you should only do so once per application.

When you call `makePersistent()` on a persistence-capable object it is persisted as a Datastore entity. `makePersistent()` is synchronous. The method call will not return until the object is saved in the Datastore and all relevant Datastore indexes are updated as necessary.

There also exists a `makePersistentAll` method of `PersistenceManager`. This method takes as an argument an array of objects to persist, essentially performing a batch save on them. This is more efficient if you have a number of objects to save at once.

Once you have made an object persistent, then any subsequent changes to the object within the same `PersistenceManager` context are persisted automatically when the `PersistenceManager` is closed (or if you call `makePersistent()` on the object again). Similarly, if you fetch an existing Datastore object using a `PersistenceManager`, and then update the object, those updates are persisted when that `PersistenceManager` is closed.

# Fetching a persisted object by its key

As described in *Datastore Keys and JDO Key Fields*, you can define the primary key for a persistence-capable JDO class to be either system-assigned or app-assigned. If system-assigned, then you do not set the key field and the key is generated when the object is first persisted via the `makePersistent` method. Once that has occurred, you can access the object to get its generated key.

Given an object's key, you can then fetch the object from the Datastore using the `getObjectById` method of the `PersistenceManager`. The first argument of the method is the class of the object that you are fetching (which maps to its entity 'kind'), and the second argument is its key. The key argument can be any of the supported key field types: string ID, numeric ID, Key value, or encoded key string.

In the following example, we create and persist a new `UserAccount` object and grab its system-generated `id` once the object has been persisted. We can later use the key to fetch that object from the Datastore.

```
UserAccount usr = new UserAccount();
...
pm1 = PMF.get().getPersistenceManager();
pm1.makePersistent(usr);
Long uid = usr.getId(); // hold on to the generated id
...
pm1.close();
// ... later ...
pm2 = PMF.get().getPersistenceManager();


UserAccount usr2 =
  pm2.getObjectById(UserAccount.class, uid);
...
```

It is also possible to fetch objects via a *query* as well as by their IDs, as described in *Chapter 5*. However, **key lookups are much faster than general queries**. Google has stated that direct Datastore key lookups return on average four to five times faster than query executions. It is worth thinking about how to design your application to exploit the faster key-based retrievals when possible.

# Deleting a persisted object

You can delete a persisted object by calling the `deletePersistence` method of a `PersistenceManager` instance. The method takes as its argument an object that has been fetched by the `PersistenceManager`. For example, if we know the ID of a `Friend` object, we can use the following code to delete it:

```
Friend f = pm.getObjectById(Friend.class, friendID);
 pm.deletePersistent(f);
```

If the `PersistenceManager` has not yet fetched the object, you can combine the calls as follows:

```
pm.deletePersistent(pm.getObjectById(Friend.class,
    friendID));
```

You can also pass `deletePersistent` a Collection or array of persisted objects.

# An object has an associated PersistenceManager

A persistent object can only be managed by one `PersistenceManager` at a time. Once a `PersistenceManager` has been closed, it is an error to use that manager to try to persist an object. It is also an error to call `makePersistent()` from one `PersistenceManager` on an object being managed by a different `PersistenceManager`. Similarly, if you try to delete an object not associated with the given `PersistenceManager`, you will get an error. If you are seeing errors that indicate that this is an issue, you can call `JDOHelper.getPersistenceManager(obj)` to see which persistence manager a given object is associated with.

It is possible to detach an object from one `PersistenceManager`, close that manager, and then later re-attach the object to another manager, as we will describe next in *Detached Objects*. A caveat is that object re-attachment is not supported over RPC to GWT and back (recall that on the client side, your objects are translated to JavaScript).

# Fetch groups

When an object is retrieved from the Datastore by JDO, not all object fields are necessarily retrieved immediately. For efficiency, only a subset of fields may be retrieved in the initial access of the object, and then any other field values are retrieved when accessed. This is called *lazy loading*. If a field is lazily loaded, then before you've accessed it, it will not appear properly set when inspecting the object in the debugger.

The group of fields that are initially loaded is called the object's **fetch group**. After the `PersistenceManager` associated with an object is closed, any unfetched fields are inaccessible.

JDO defines a 'default fetch group'. Unindexed properties, including `Text` and `Blob` data types, are not retrieved by default. This means that 'serialized field' values, including the `details` field of our `Friend` class, will not be retrieved by default. Fields that support JDO 'owned relationships'by serving as references to other persistable objects, as described in *Chapter 5*, are also not retrieved by default.

You can pull in an unfetched field simply by accessing it while the `PersistenceManager` is open. For example:

```
Friend f = pm.getObjectById(Friend.class, friendID);

FriendDetails deets = f.getDetails();
// fetches the serialized field
// …
// pm.close();
```

In many cases you can indicate that a persistent field should be part of the default fetch group by annotating it accordingly:

```
@Persistent(defaultFetchGroup = "true")
```

However, you should not do this for every field; lazy loading is more efficient when you will not always need access. Additionally, you cannot specify that owned relationship fields be part of the fetch group; those annotations will be ignored with a warning. See the DataNucleus documentation for more information on Fetch Groups as supported by the DataNucleus JDO implementation.

In general, it is easier to work on an object (or set of related objects) within a single PersistenceManager context until you are done, then close the PersistenceManager and persist any updates. That way you do not have to worry about pre-fetching any of the object's fields— you simply access them when they are needed. Typically, a PersistenceManager instance is retained for the life of a web request, or less.

# *Connectr* example: creating and modifying UserAccount and Friend data objects

In *Defining Keys and Core Value Type Fields for Friend and UserAccount*, we defined a UserAccount object to hold a list of Friend keys, in the friends field. This list is used to model the one-to-many relationship of Figure 1, between a UserAccount object and its Friend. In this section, we look at how that list is created and maintained.

Our data model requires that we add a key to the UserAccount friends list when a new Friend associated with that user is created, delete the appropriate key when a Friend is deleted, and fetch a list of Friend objects based on their keys. Then, when we modify a Friend object, we must pay particular attention to our handling of its details serialized field.

We'll look at each of these activities in turn. Throughout this chapter, the examples are from the ConnectrStage1_alt code.

Note that in this initial version of *Connectr*, we have not yet implemented support for a multi-user model (that is added in *Chapter 8*). So, for now, the app creates just one default UserAccount instance as necessary at load time and accesses it as the "current user" using a hardwired getDefaultUser method. This method will be replaced when multi-user functionality is added.

In this chapter, we're showing naïve code that doesn't yet include the use of transactions. When we introduce App Engine Transactions in *Chapter 9* we will wrap transactional control around many of the code fragments in this chapter. For now, we will make the simple (and unrealistic) assumption that our app runs as a single process and its code completes without interruption.

# Creating new Friend objects

Let's first look at what's necessary to create and persist new `Friend` objects.

We can see this in the code from `server.AppMisc.populateDataStoreOnce()`, as shown next. This method creates sample data consisting of a 'default' `UserAccount` object and a set of associated `Friend` objects. If a default user object already exists the method just returns. We will create the sample data within the context of a single `PersistenceManager` and wrap the initialization activity in a `try` or `finally` block to ensure that the `PersistenceManager` is closed even if we generate an exception.

```
public class AppMisc {
  ...
  static void populateDataStoreOnce() {
    UserAccount defaultUser = UserAccount.getDefaultUser();
    if (defaultUser != null)
    return; // already populated

    PersistenceManager pm =
        PMF.get().getPersistenceManager();
    Friend friend = null;
    try {
      defaultUser = new UserAccount();
      defaultUser.setBasicInfo("bob",
        "default@default.com");
      // give our user some friends
      for (int i = 0; i < friendsFirstNameData.length; ++i) {
      friend = new Friend();
      friend.setBasicInfo(friendsFirstNameData[i],
      friendsLastNameData[i],
      friendsEmailData[i]);
      pm.makePersistent(friend);
      // now the friend's id is set
      defaultUser.addFriendKey(friend.getId());
      } // end for
      pm.makePersistent(defaultUser);
    } // end try
    catch (Exception e) {
      e.printStackTrace();
    }
    finally {
      pm.close();
    }
  }
}
```

We persist each `Friend` object after we populate it with test data. This sets its system-generated ID. Once the `id` is created, we can add it to the list of friend keys for the `defaultUser`. We must wait to add its `id` to this list until after the `Friend` object is persisted—prior to that, the key won't exist. Then `defaultUser` is persisted as well.

The same approach is seen in `server.FriendsServiceImpl.addFriend()`, as follows. This method is called when new friend data is created client-side and the information is passed via RPC to the server in the form of a `FriendDTO` object. The `addFriend` method creates a new persistable `Friend` object from the client-side data. The new Friend object must be persisted before adding its ID to the `friends` list of the `currentUser`. The new Friend object must be persisted before adding its ID to the friends list of the currentUser. When we close the `PersistenceManager`, the `currentUser` changes are saved to the Datastore.

```
public class FriendsServiceImpl extends RemoteServiceServlet
implements
    FriendsService {
...
  // create new Friend object in Datastore
  private Friend addFriend(FriendDTO friendDTO) {

    PersistenceManager pm = PMF.get().getPersistenceManager();
    Friend friend = null;
    try {
      // for now, just get 'default' user
      UserAccount currentUser =
         UserAccount.getDefaultUser(pm);
      friend = new Friend(friendDTO);
      pm.makePersistent(friend);
      currentUser.addFriendKey(friend.getId());
    } finally {
      pm.close();
    }
    return friend;
  }
  ...
}
```

# Deleting a Friend object

Deleting a `Friend` object requires two steps. We must first delete the `Friend` object from the Datastore, and then remove the `Friend` key from the associated `UserAccount` object's `friends` list.

The `deleteFriend()` method of `server.FriendsServiceImpl`, which follows, shows this process. We are passed the ID of the `Friend` to delete. We fetch the `Friend` object using `getObjectById()`, then use the `PersistenceManager` `deletePersistent()` method to delete it. Then, we remove the `id` from the `friends` list of the associated `UserAccount` object.

```
public class FriendsServiceImpl extends RemoteServiceServlet
implements
    FriendsService {
  ...
  public Boolean deleteFriend(String id) {
    PersistenceManager pm = PMF.get().getPersistenceManager();
    try {
      Friend friend = pm.getObjectById(Friend.class, id);
      if (friend != null) {
        pm.deletePersistent(friend);
        // then delete from associated user's friend list
        UserAccount currentUser =
            UserAccount.getDefaultUser(pm);
        List<String> fidList = currentUser.getFriendsList();
        fidList.remove(id);
      }
    } finally {
      pm.close();
    }
    return true;
  }
  ...
}
```

# Fetching a list of Friend objects using the key list

Finally, let's take a quick preview of how we can use the list of `friend` keys to fetch the corresponding `Friend` objects, as used in the `getFriendSummaries()` method of `server.FriendsServiceImpl`. This is achieved by using a `Query`; the syntax used here will be described in *Chapter 5*.

```
public ArrayList<FriendSummaryDTO> getFriendSummaries() {

  ArrayList<FriendSummaryDTO> friendsSummaries =
    new ArrayList<FriendSummaryDTO>();
```

```
PersistenceManager pm = PMF.get().getPersistenceManager();

try {
  UserAccount user = UserAccount.getDefaultUser(pm);
  List<String> fidList = user.getFriendsList();
  // if the list contains at least one friend ID
  if (fidList.size() > 0) {
    Query q = pm.newQuery("select from " +
      Friend.class.getName() + " where id == :keys");
    List<Friend> friends =
      (List<Friend>) q.execute(fidList);
  ...
  }
}
...
}
```

The query in this example returns a list of the `Friend` that match the list of keys from the `UserAccount` object `user`.

# Detached objects

By default, JDO objects are only updatable when the `PersistenceManager` that created them is open. That is, if you close the `PersistenceManager` for the object, you can't do further work on the object and update it in the Datastore later.

However, it is possible to **detach** a copy of an object from one `PersistenceManager` and then re-attach the detached copy to another `PersistenceManager` later. If you do this then you can update the re-attached object.

To detach a data object, you must first add the "detachable" attribute to the `@PersistenceCapable` annotation of your class:

```
@PersistenceCapable(identityType = IdentityType.APPLICATION,
detachable="true")
```

Recall that we have added this annotation for our `UserAccount` and `Friend` classes.

Then, get a detached copy of the object before closing the `PersistenceManager` that it is associated with, by calling `detachedCopy()`. If you want your detached copy to include an instantiated field that is not in the object's default fetch group, you must fetch it explicitly before detaching. For example, if we were to detach a `Friend` object, we would likely want to fetch the `details` field before we did so. Otherwise, we would not be able to access the `Friend`'s `emailAddress` in the detached copy.

Once detached, you can access and modify the detached object. Then you can later attach it to another `PersistenceManager` and persist it.

The following `server.domain.UserAccount.getDefaultUser()` method shows how an object is detached, and the detached copy returned (*Chapter 5* will describe the query process shown in the method).

```
@PersistenceCapable(identityType = IdentityType.APPLICATION,
detachable="true")
public class UserAccount {

  ...
   public static UserAccount getDefaultUser() {

    String defaultEmail = "default@default.com";

    PersistenceManager pm = PMF.get().getPersistenceManager();
    UserAccount oneResult = null, detached = null;
    Query q = pm.newQuery(UserAccount.class,
      "emailAddress == :email");
    q.setUnique(true);
    try {
      oneResult = (UserAccount) q.execute(defaultEmail);
      if (oneResult != null) {
        detached = pm.detachCopy(oneResult);
      }
    } catch (Exception e) {
      e.printStackTrace();
    } finally {
      pm.close();
      q.closeAll();
    }
    return detached;
  }
  ...
}
```

Note that if the `UserAccount` object had fields that were not part of the default fetch group, we may have needed to pre-fetch them before detaching. However, in this case both String fields, as well as Collections of String—a core value type—are fetched by default.

The previous method is not actually required for *Connectr* (it is more efficient to use an alternate version, which works within the enclosing `PersistenceManager` context), but it is included as an example.

Call `makePersistent()` on a detached object from within a new `PersistenceManager` instance to "re-attach" the object and associate it with the new `PersistenceManager`. This will attach fields that were originally detached as well as fields that were modified while detached.

The following code shows this process. A detached `UserAccount` object `user` is re-attached and modified. When the `PersistenceManager pm` is closed, the changes to `user` will be saved.

```
try {
  // detached object returned from method call..
  UserAccount user = UserAccount.getDefaultUser();
  user = pm.makePersistent(user); // attach
  // …
  user.addFriendKey(friendId);
}
finally {
  pm.close();
}
```

# Detached Data Access Objects and Data Transfer Objects

The objects returned from Datastore queries can be viewed as Data Access Objects (DAOs). Detached copies of these objects can in many cases be sent via RPC to your app's client side, as long as the data class does not import any App Engine libraries. Also note that a data class must implement the `Serializable` interface if you plan to send it over RPC.

It is important to send only detached copies of Datastore objects over RPC, not the directly retrieved instances. The detachment process converts DataNucleus SCO data types (such as `org.datanucleus.sco.backed.ArrayList`) to core Java types (such as `java.util.ArrayList`). Be sure to explicitly fetch any necessary fields that are not part of your object's default fetch group before detaching. If you do not, then these fields will not be included in the detached copy. Detachment bookkeeping is not preserved across RPC, so you cannot "re-attach" objects sent from the client.

If your data class imports any App Engine libraries, you will not be able to pass instances of that class to the GWT RPC, as your client-side code does not have access to these libraries. Furthermore, in many cases you may not want to pass the full Datastore object through RPC, for both efficiency and security reasons. Your client-side code may not need to access all of the information stored in your Datastore entities, at least not in every context. It is more efficient to send smaller data objects via RPC. In addition, your data objects may include sensitive information that you have no need to send over the wire.

For these reasons it is often useful to employ **Data Transfer Objects** (DTOs) to communicate with the client, where the DTOs include only the DAO information needed by the client-side code. The pertinent information from a Datastore object is copied to—or summarized in—its corresponding DTO and the DTO is sent over RPC instead. This is the approach taken in *Connectr*.

A common design pattern places the logic for mapping to or from the DTO class in the DAO class itself. We use this pattern in *Connectr*. When an object needs to be sent to the client the DAO generates its corresponding DTO. When a DTO comes back it is handed to the DAO class, which knows how to create or update the Datastore objects appropriately.

A given DAO may potentially utilize more than one DTO class. For example, you may often find it useful to generate DTO variants that encapsulate differing amounts of information. Often a "summary" class is used to send initial information over RPC, and only if the client wants to inspect the object in more detail is a fuller version requested. We will see this pattern used in *Connectr*. This can greatly reduce data transmission if the more detailed versions are only requested for a subset of the objects.

 If your code copies sub-objects from a persistent object to a DTO, create a detached copy of the Datastore object before copying, to avoid type conversion issues.

## DTOs in the *Connectr* application

The `Friend` data class uses the DTO pattern described previously. Two Friend DTO classes are defined: `shared.FriendSummaryDTO` and `shared.FriendDTO`. Note that both of these DTO classes reside in the `shared` package, this is because they are used both by the client and the server sides of the application.

`FriendSummaryDTO` contains a lightweight or summarized version of the `Friend` information. It contains only the `Friend` id and a `fullName`, which concatenates the `Friend` first and last name, and does not include the e-mail address. `FriendDTO` contains first and last names, and e-mail address. In later chapters, as we further develop *Connectr*, `FriendDTO` will hold more information.

The `server.domain.Friend` class knows how to generate these DTOs on request via the `toLightWeightDTO` and `toDTO` methods, as shown in the following code:

```
@PersistenceCapable(identityType = IdentityType.APPLICATION,
detachable="true")
public class Friend {

    ...
```

```
   public FriendSummaryDTO toLightWeightDTO() {
     return new FriendSummaryDTO(id, getFullName());
   }

   public FriendDTO toDTO() {
     FriendDTO friendDTO = new FriendDTO(this.getFirstName(),
       this.getLastName(), this.getEmailAddress());
     friendDTO.setId(this.getId());
     return friendDTO;
   }
   ...
 }
```

Note that both DTOs include the Friend key, id. Because the key is an encoded String, it can pass back and forth via RPC. This is a crucial inclusion, as it will allow us to identify and fetch the corresponding objects when client-side modifications are passed back over the wire.

The getFriend method of server.FriendsServiceImpl sends a FriendDTO—corresponding to the requested friend ID—over RPC to the client. The method first retrieves the Friend associated with the ID and detaches it after fetching its FriendDetails (if this fetch is not done first, then the e-mail address will not be available in the detached copy). Then, fields from the detached object are copied to the DTO. If the data object is not first detached, as described above, incompatible DataNucleus SCO data types may be copied to the DTO, generating runtime serialization errors during the RPC call. In this version of the app this is not an issue, but it is necessary for subsequent versions. This process is as follows:

```
public class FriendsServiceImpl extends RemoteServiceServlet
implements
    FriendsService {
  ...
  public FriendDTO getFriend(String id) {

    PersistenceManager pm = PMF.get().getPersistenceManager();
    Friend dsFriend, detached;

    try {
      dsFriend = pm.getObjectById(Friend.class, id);
      dsFriend.getDetails();
      detached = pm.detachCopy(dsFriend);
    } finally {
      pm.close();
    }

    return detached.toDTO();
  }
  ...
}
```

The `FriendsServiceImpl.getFriendSummaries()` method (not shown) similarly builds and sends a list of lighter-weight `FriendSummaryDTO` objects over RPC.

In the converse scenario, when a DTO is sent from the client-side code, its contents need to be reflected back into Datastore modifications. Thus, the DTOs must be designed so that they allow their corresponding Datastore entity to be identified and fetched. We do this by preserving entity ID information in the client-side objects.

The `server.domain.Friend.updateFromDTO()` method implements an update to an existing `Friend` object, as shown in the following code:

```
@PersistenceCapable(identityType = IdentityType.APPLICATION,
detachable="true")
public class Friend {
  ...
  public void updateFromDTO (FriendDTO fr) {
    // create new serialized field reference
    this.details = new FriendDetails();
    this.firstName = friendDTO.getFirstName();
    this.lastName = friendDTO.getLastName();
    this.setEmailAddress(friendDTO.getEmailAddress());
  }
  ...
}
```

A DTO from the client has retained the `id` of its corresponding `Friend` object. In `server.FriendsServiceImpl.updateFriend()`, we use that ID to fetch its object from the Datastore as shown in the following code, then update the object with the DTO information, using the `Friend.updateFromDTO()` method.

```
public class FriendsServiceImpl extends RemoteServiceServlet
implements
    FriendsService {
  ...
  public FriendDTO updateFriend(FriendDTO friendDTO) {
    if (friendDTO.getId() == null){ // create new
      Friend newFriend = addFriend(friendDTO);
      return newFriend.toDTO();
    }

    PersistenceManager pm = PMF.get().getPersistenceManager();
    Friend friend = null;
    try {
      friend = pm.getObjectById(Friend.class,
        friendDTO.getId());
      friend.updateFromDTO(friendDTO);
```

```
  } catch (Exception e) {
    e.printStackTrace();
  } finally {
    pm.close();
  }
  return friendDTO;
}  ...
}
```

The `server.FriendsServiceImpl.addFriend()` method implements the creation of a new `Friend` object from a `FriendDTO`. As shown below, we create a new `Friend` using the information contained in the passed-in `FriendDTO` object, persist the `Friend`, then update the default `currentUser` friend key list accordingly. When we close the `PersistenceManager`, `currentUser` is updated.

```
public class FriendsServiceImpl extends RemoteServiceServlet
  implements FriendsService {

  ...
  // create new Friend object in Datastore
  private Friend addFriend(FriendDTO friendDTO) {

    PersistenceManager pm = PMF.get().getPersistenceManager();
    Friend friend = null;
    try {
      UserAccount currentUser = UserAccount.getDefaultUser(pm);
      friend = new Friend(friendDTO);
      pm.makePersistent(friend);
      currentUser.addFriendKey(friend.getId());
    } finally {
      pm.close();
    }
    return friend;
  }
  ...
}
```

# Inspecting the Datastore

So far we've looked at how to create, modify, and delete Datastore entities, but have not yet discussed how to inspect the Datastore itself.

It is possible to browse a local development copy of the Datastore while you are developing your application and to delete entities from it. This is supported by a development console which you can access when your development server is running.

The App Engine Admin Console allows access to the Datastore of your deployed application. You can browse the App Engine Datastore, query it, add and delete items from it, and view your Datastore usage statistics.

In this section, we'll look at both of these services.

# The local development console

A local Datastore service is supported as part of the App Engine's development web server's features. It contains the data entities that you have generated programmatically while you run your application locally. The App Engine development web server includes a development console which provides an interface for inspecting the local Datastore. It does not reflect the full capabilities of the "real" App Engine Datastore viewer. Nevertheless, it allows you to browse and delete local entities and can be a very useful debugging tool.

When the development server is running you can find the admin console at:
`http://localhost:8888/_ah/admin`

Launch it from the previous URL and then select `Datastore Viewer` from the sidebar. As indicated by the links in the sidebar, the development console also allows limited local access to other App Engine services, such as the Task Queue. We will return to these other capabilities in later chapters.

You can view your local Datastore contents, sorted by kind. For example, Figure 3 shows a listing of the `Friend` entities currently in the local Datastore. Figure 4 shows a listing of the `UserAccount` entities.

 In contrast to the actual App Engine console, this local view does not indicate fields of type `Blob`.

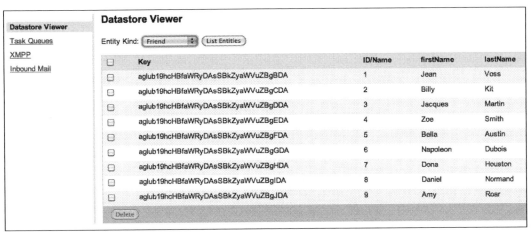

Figure 3: Friend entities in the local version of the Datastore.

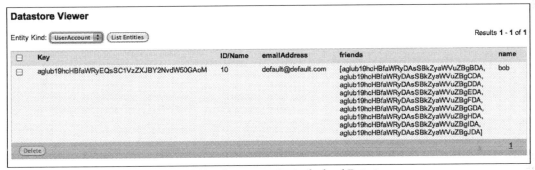

Figure 4: A UserAccount entity in the local Datastore.

The local Datastore is kept in the file war/WEB-INF/appengine-generated/ local_db.bin. (You will not see this file until you have generated some data). The development console thus supports an interface for browsing the contents of this file.

local_db.bin persists between launches of your local development server. If you want to unceremoniously remove your entire local Datastore, just shut down your local server, and then delete the file. It is often useful to do this when you change a data class in order to ensure that you are testing with the entities of the "correct" schema. local_db.bin is not uploaded to App Engine when you deploy an application.

You may notice another file in your appengine-generated directory, the datastore-indexes-auto.xml file. This file holds information about any custom indexes required by your application, as determined by the queries performed when you run your application. We will discuss this file in *Chapter 5*.

# The App Engine Datastore

Once you've deployed your application, you can access its hosted Datastore via the App Engine Admin Console. Here you can browse and delete entities as well as generate queries over them, create new entities, and view their statistics.

 If you have deployed multiple versions of a given application, all versions share the same Datastore.

## Browsing the App Engine Datastore

To view the data generated by your deployed application, connect to the App Engine Admin Console as described in *Chapter 2* (visit `https://appengine.google.com/`, and log in as necessary). You will see a number of links in the left sidebar of your Dashboard view. Click on the Datastore Viewer link. This allows you to view your Datastore entities by kind.

 The Blob Viewer link that you see in the left sidebar does not indicate the core Blob type, but something different called the Blobstore, which allows uploading and storage of large files.

| Main | Query the Datastore | Create an Entity |
| --- | --- |
| Dashboard | ● Kind ○ Query (using GQL) |
| Quota Details | Friend ⬍ |
| Logs | kinds as of 0:00:37 ago |
| Cron Jobs | **Friend Entities** |
| Task Queues | |
| Blacklist | ‹ Prev 20 **1-9** Next 20 › |

| ☐ ID/Name | details | firstName | lastName |
| --- | --- | --- | --- |
| ☐ id=14001 | 202 bytes, SHA-1 = 2dc8ee7ad832822f765aeff68192b9e4615379be | Jean | Voss |
| ☐ id=15001 | 202 bytes, SHA-1 = b16762523dc5820bb9bffa835488982424628600 | Billy | Kit |
| ☐ id=16001 | 204 bytes, SHA-1 = 471761f439fa3be7aeaadc340552b4801861069e | Jacques | Martin |
| ☐ id=17001 | 200 bytes, SHA-1 = e6e4709541d3f1390317315d4e6a5e890e7a142b | Zoe | Smith |
| ☐ id=18001 | 202 bytes, SHA-1 = f424481597f3a41210a10866c11353952fdaaede | Bella | Austin |
| ☐ id=19001 | 205 bytes, SHA-1 = f2f8ad987715b14544caa2ec9b0ef731492e2da6 | Napoleon | Dubois |
| ☐ id=20001 | 201 bytes, SHA-1 = c33bcae94e861b94e9e8415cee1e8ee6514a7e62 | Dona | Houston |
| ☐ id=21001 | 203 bytes, SHA-1 = 331890ecbbf19abffecbb7167d2919655d007923 | Daniel | Normand |
| ☐ id=22001 | 200 bytes, SHA-1 = b9db6f1456c39bdb339cbeb03bb5c7947c5cb557 | Amy | Peterson |

Data
Datastore Indexes
**Datastore Viewer**
Datastore Statistics
Blob Viewer

Administration
Application Settings
Developers
Versions
Admin Logs
Billing

Delete

Figure 5: Friend entities in the App Engine Datastore.

The screenshot of Figure 5 shows a list of `Friend` entities. The "details" Blob property (holding a serialized `FriendDetails` object) is listed, though you can't inspect it.

Note that the interface allows you to delete entities. Be careful doing this, as you can affect the consistency of your application data. If you click on the ID link for an individual entity, you may edit it to some extent.

## Edit Entity: Friend

Decoded entity key: <u>Friend: id=14001</u>

Entity key: agZhbXktam9yDQsSBkZyaWVuZBixbQw

Enter information for the entity below. If you'd like to change a property's type, set it t
change the type.

**details**
   value:   202 bytes, SHA-1 = 2dc8ee7ad832822f765aeff68192b9e4615379be
   type:   blob

**firstName**
   value:   Jeanne
   type:   string ⬍

**lastName**
   value:   Voss
   type:   string ⬍

Figure 6: The App Engine Datastore allows some web-based entity edits.

Note the **Query** option at the top right-hand side of Figure 5. This query functionality does not use the JDO query syntax that we will be using in our code, but rather uses an App Engine query language called **GQL**.

See the GQL documentation for more information:
`http://code.google.com/appengine/docs/`
`python/datastore/gqlreference.html`.

# Viewing application data statistics

The Datastore keeps statistics about the data stored for an application. It tracks information such as how many entities there are of a given kind, how much space is used by each kind and for a given kind, and how much space is used for each property or property type. You can view these statistics by clicking on **Datastore Statistics** at the left-hand side navigation bar of the App Engine Admin Console.

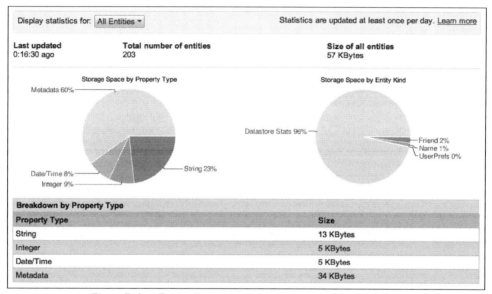

Figure 7: App Engine Datastore statistics summary for all entities.

Use the pull-down menu to select the information that you wish to view. You can view statistics across all entities or you can view information specific to a particular entity, as shown in the next figure. The "Metadata" property type represents space used by the Datastore to store information about the entities.

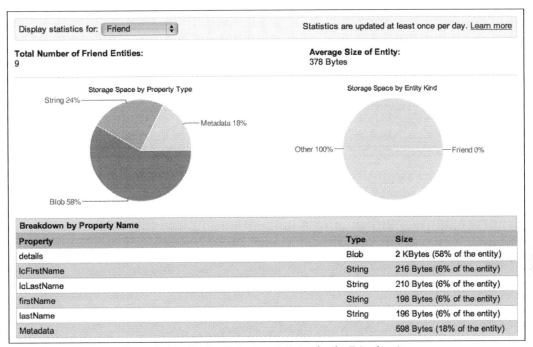

Figure8: App Engine Datastore statistics for the Friend entity.

The statistics data itself is stored in your app's Datastore. To make sure that there is room for your application's data, Google App Engine will only store statistics if they consume less than 1MB (if your application's statistics go over the 1MB limit, any previously reported statistics may remain undisplayed).

# Resources

The following links provide further resources on some of the topics mentioned in this chapter:

- A paper on Google's BigTable, on which the Datastore is based: http://labs.google.com/papers/bigtable.html.

- More information about JDO: http://www.datanucleus.org/products/ accessplatform_1_1/jdo/index.html, http://www.datanucleus.org/ products/accessplatform_1_1/jdo/api.html, and http://java.sun. com/jdo/index.jsp.

- Information about the JPA (Java Persistence API): http://code.google. com/appengine/docs/java/datastore/usingjpa.html, http://java. sun.com/developer/technicalArticles/J2EE/jpa/.

- The "low-level" Java Datastore API, accessed via the `com.google.appengine.api.datastore` **libraries:** `http://code.google.com/appengine/docs/java/javadoc/com/google/appengine/api/datastore/package-summary.html`.

- The App Engine Python SDK: `http://code.google.com/appengine/downloads.html#Google_App_Engine_SDK_for_Python`.

# Summary

In this chapter, we continued our development of the *Connectr* application that we'll build throughout the book, by introducing the use of the App Engine Datastore to persist the application's data objects.

For our example application we are using the App Engine/DataNucleus implementation of the JDO (Java Data Objects) standard interface. This chapter showed how JDO serves as a data modeling layer, handling mapping from Java classes and fields to Datastore entities and properties, and providing application-level support for enforcement of "schema" consistency.

We looked at how to persist, update, and delete Datastore entities via JDO, and how to fetch objects based on their IDs.

Next, *Chapter 5* continues our look at Datastore fundamentals. It describes how to query for Datastore entities, define JDO one-to-one and one-to-many owned relationships, and takes a closer look at how Datastore indexes are generated and used.

# 5

# JDO Object Relationships and Queries

This chapter continues the exploration of the Datastore begun in *Chapter 4*. It shows:

- How to build and manage objects that have relationships to each other such as one-to-many and one-to-one parent-child relationships, using **JDO (Java Data Objects)** support for owned relationships

- How to query for objects and the role that Datastore indexes play in this process

- How to browse your data objects both locally and when your application is deployed to the App Engine, and to view statistics about their use

- How to use callbacks to support population of data object fields when the objects are persisted

This chapter uses the ConnectrStage1 version of the *Connectr* application for its examples. This version differs from the ConnectrStage1_alt version of *Chapter 4* in that it uses JDO-owned relationships to model the relationships between its data objects.

## Modeling relationships between objects

The examples of *Chapter 4* supported object parent-child relationships in two different ways. The UserAccount object maintained a collection of the *keys* of its child Friend objects. In addition, the Friend object used a *serialized field* to hold its child FriendDetails object so that the FriendDetails were not stored as actual Datastore entities, but rather Blob properties.

It is always possible to use object primary keys to express the relationship between Datastore objects, as we did with UserAccount and Friend in *Chapter 4*. However, the collection of keys must be managed at the application level with this approach. For example, we saw that if a Friend object is added or deleted, the corresponding key must be added or deleted from the UserAccount key list in the application code.

We can instead use JDO to push the relationship bookkeeping "below" the application level so that you as the application developer do not need to explicitly manage it.

The JDO framework supports both one-to-one and many-to-one owned relationships. In an **owned relationship**, one of the objects in the relationship (the "child") cannot exist without the other (the "parent"). For example, we can consider the *UserAccount:Friend* relationship an owned one as the Friend objects are defined in the context of a particular user's account and cannot "belong" to more than one user.

Using JDO-owned relationships, your application-level code simply needs to set parent object fields to their child objects (or collections of child objects) as appropriate, just as if you were building an in-memory object tree. The underlying entity relationship bookkeeping is managed by JDO and is transparent to the application. Relationship field values are lazily fetched.

In this chapter, we use the ConnectrStage1 application code, which uses JDO-owned relationships to implement its data model, and which we will continue to develop throughout this book.

The use of JDO (or JPA) owned relationships can make the life of the application developer easier in a number of ways. However, for one-to-many relationships with a very large number of children, you may find that for performance reasons you need more explicit control over when and how the children are fetched from the Datastore. In such cases, it may be more efficient to do explicit application-level key-based relationship management, as was illustrated in *Chapter 4*.

JDO-owned relationships can be **uni-directional** or **bi-directional**. A **uni-directional relationship** means that the parent has a reference to the child (or children), but the child does not link back to the parent. **Bi-directional relationships** allow both parent and child to reference each other. For example, it makes sense for our *UserAccount:Friend* relationship to be an owned one-to-many bidirectional relationship as at times it will be useful for a *Friend* to be able to reference its associated *UserAccount*.

# Owned relationships and entity groups

The JDO framework creates owned relationship parent and child objects so that they are in the same **entity group** (more specifically, as we will see in *Chapter 9, Robustness and Scalability: Transactions, Memcache, and Datastore Design*, the child key is created so that the key of its parent object is specified as the parent key part of its key *path*. This not only supports the relationship but also allows the objects to be used within the same *transaction*).

Thus, you must define the key of the child in the relationship to be of a type that supports encoding of this information. As described in *Chapter 4*, this means that it must be either of type Key or an encoded String.

You must allow JDO to perform child object creation for you, as shown in the following part of this chapter.

 Do not persist child objects before associating them with the parent.

If you do not allow JDO to perform child object creation, the children will not be created as part of the same entity group as the parent, and keys cannot be changed after object creation. Instead, build or modify the parent-child object tree, then persist only the parent. If the parent has already been persisted (that is, if it already exists in the Datastore), then you only need to close the PersistenceManager (or commit an enclosing transaction, as described in *Chapter 9*). Any new children of that parent will be automatically persisted by JDO, and under the hood, their keys will be constructed so that the children belong to the same entity group as the parent. We'll illustrate this process below.

 JDO manages the owned relationships via entity key construction so you will not see owned relationship fields listed as properties of your application domain entities when you browse them in the Datastore viewer.

# Uni-directional owned relationships

JDO makes it very straightforward to create uni-directional owned relationships. With uni-directional relationships, the children do not refer back to the parent.

Simply define your child class to be `@PersistenceCapable`. Then, in the parent, define a field of the child type, or a `Collection` of that type. Setting a single child value creates a one-to-one owned relationship, and setting a `Collection` creates a one-to-many relationship. You must use a `Collection`, not an array, to create a one-to-many relationship.

As discussed earlier, be sure that you do not explicitly persist the child object(s) before adding them to the parent. If you do so, they will not be created in the same *entity group* as the parent. Persist only the parent, and allow the JDO framework to create the children as necessary.

## Supporting uni-directional owned relationships in *Connectr*

Figure 1: In the `ConnectrStage1` version of the application, `FriendDetails` objects are now persisted as entities, not serialized.

In this section, we'll define the *Connectr* server-side data classes to support uni-directional owned relationships (we will add bi-directional support later on.)

We will create a **uni-directional owned one-to-one** relationship between `Friend` and `FriendDetails`. This means that we no longer want the `FriendDetails` object to be serialized into a `Blob` (as we did in *Chapter 4*); instead we want it to be a persistent object, stored as a first-class entity in the Datastore, as suggested in Figure 1. We need two small code changes to make this happen.

First, as shown in the `server.domain.Friend` code below, the `details` field remains persistent, but no longer serialized. Additionally, we define the field to have a dependent attribute (discussed shortly).

```
@PersistenceCapable(identityType = IdentityType.APPLICATION,
    detachable="true")
public class Friend implements StoreCallback {

  @PrimaryKey
  @Persistent(valueStrategy = IdGeneratorStrategy.IDENTITY)
```

```
@Extension(vendorName="datanucleus", key="gae.encoded-pk",
   value="true")
private String id;

@Persistent(dependent = "true")
private FriendDetails details;
  ...

}
```

Second, we will define the `server.domain.FriendDetails` class to be persistence-capable, as shown in the following code. We will annotate its fields to be `@Persistent`. Then, we will define a primary key for the class, called `id`. We will use an encoded `String` key so that its generated key can support entity group information, as required for its child relationship.

```
@PersistenceCapable(identityType = IdentityType.APPLICATION,
    detachable="true")
public class FriendDetails implements Serializable {

  @PrimaryKey
  @Persistent(valueStrategy = IdGeneratorStrategy.IDENTITY)
  @Extension(vendorName="datanucleus", key="gae.encoded-pk",
      value="true")
  private String id;

  @Persistent
  private String emailAddress;
  @Persistent
  private Set<String> urls;
  ...
}
```

That's all that is required.

When a new `Friend` is created, its constructor creates and populates a `FriendDetails` object, and sets the `Friend.details` field with it. The `FriendDetails` object is not explicitly persisted in the application code. When the `Friend` object is persisted, its child `FriendDetails` is persisted as well and thus a one-to-one unidirectional relationship is defined between them.

Similarly, we will create a **uni-directional owned one-to-many** relationship between `server.domain.UserAccount` and `Friend`. Instead of maintaining a list of `Friend` keys (as in *Chapter 4*), we can create a field in `UserAccount` that holds a `Collection` of `Friends`.

```
@PersistenceCapable(identityType = IdentityType.APPLICATION,
   detachable="true")
public class UserAccount {

  @PrimaryKey
  @Persistent(valueStrategy = IdGeneratorStrategy.IDENTITY)
  private Long id;

  ...

  @Element(dependent = "true")
  private Set<Friend> friends = new HashSet();

  ...
}
```

Now we no longer need to explicitly manage the `Friend` keys, we can just access the `Friend` objects in the collection. *We no longer explicitly persist the child* `Friend` *objects (as we did with the list-of-keys version).* Instead, as shown in the `server.FriendsServiceImpl.addFriend()` method, we assign the `Friend` instances to the `UserAccount` collection.

```
public class FriendsServiceImpl extends RemoteServiceServlet
implements FriendsService {
...
// create new Friend object in Datastore
  private Friend addFriend(FriendDTO friendDTO) {

    PersistenceManager pm = PMF.get().getPersistenceManager();
    Friend friend = null;
    try {
      UserAccount currentUser = UserAccount.getDefaultUser(pm);
      friend = new Friend(friendDTO);
      currentUser.getFriends().add(friend);
    } finally {
      pm.close();
    }
    return friend;
  }
    ...
}
```

The modified `UserAccount` object is updated when the `PersistenceManager` is closed, and the new `Friend` that we have added to its `friend` set is implicitly persisted as well by the JDO framework. Once the parent `UserAccount` object has been updated—triggering the save of the child `Friend`—the child's `id` field will be populated with its key created such that it is in the same entity group as its parent.

# Dependent children

It is often appropriate to define your child objects to be **dependent** upon their parent objects. This means that the child cannot exist without the parent. If a dependent relationship is defined, then if the parent is deleted, the child is deleted too.

This semantics makes sense for *Connectr*. So, we have defined child dependency for both the *UserAccount:Friend* and *Friend:FriendDetails* relationships. In both cases, if we delete a parent, we want the children to be automatically deleted along with them.

To define a one-to-one relationship to be dependent, import the `Persistent` class:

```
import javax.jdo.annotations.Persistent;
```

and add a `@Persistent(dependent = "true")` annotation to the child field in the parent object. We have done this for the `details` field of the `Friend` class (as was shown earlier):

```
@Persistent(dependent = "true")
private FriendDetails details;
```

To define a one-to-many relationship to be dependent, import the `Element` class:

```
import javax.jdo.annotations.Element;
```

and add a `@Element(dependent = "true")` annotation to the field that holds the collection of children in the parent object. We have done this in the `UserAccount` class by annotating the `friends` field, as was shown earlier:

```
@Element(dependent = "true")
private Set<Friend> friends = new HashSet();
```

This dependency model is supported by the JDO relationship framework. This means that the JDO implementation manages the dependency deletions, not the Datastore. So, if you delete a parent entity using the low-level Datastore API (or the admin console) rather than via JDO, the dependent child objects will not be deleted.

# Bi-directional owned relationships

Thus far, we've constructed *uni-directional* relationships between a UserAccount and its Friend children, and between a Friend and its FriendDetails child. In a uni-directional relationship, the parent points to the child, but not vice versa.

However, the JDO relationship framework supports *bi-directional* relationships as well. With bi-directional relationships, the child or children have a reference to the parent, in addition to the parent's reference to the children.

It is straightforward to support bi-directional relationships in JDO. However, to do so requires that you create an additional field in the child class to support the reference to the parent, and requires a new field annotation. The placement of the annotation depends upon whether you want to support a one-to-one or one-to-many bi-directional relationship.

We will look at how to modify both of the uni-directional relationships of the previous section so that they become bi-directional relationships.

## Bi-directional one-to-one relationship

To support a bi-directional one-to-one relationship, place the following annotation

```
@Persistent(mappedBy = "<parent_class_field_name>")
```

before the field in the child class that should contain a reference to its parent, where <parent_field_name> is replaced with the name of the field in the parent class that points to the child object.

To create a one-to-one bi-directional relationship between Friend and its child server.domain.FriendDetails, we add a Friend field in the FriendDetails class, and annotate it using the mappedBy attribute. The attribute value is details, indicating the name of the field in the parent class that points to the FriendDetails child.

```
@PersistenceCapable(identityType =
  IdentityType.APPLICATION, detachable="true")

public class FriendDetails  {
  ...
  @Persistent(mappedBy = "details")
  private Friend friend;
```

# Bi-directional one-to-many relationship

To support a bi-directional one-to-many relationship, place the following annotation

```
@Persistent(mappedBy = "<child_class_field_name>")
```

before the field in the parent class that references the child collection, where `<child_class_field_name>` is replaced with the name of the field in the child class that points to the parent object.

We will modify our one-to-many relationship between a `UserAccount` object and its child `Friend` objects to make it bi-directional, allowing the `Friend` objects to maintain a pointer to their associated `UserAccount` parent.

To do this, we annotate the fields as shown in the following example. In `server.domain.UserAccount`, the `friends` set is given a `mappedBy` attribute. The value of this attribute, `userAccount`, must be the name of the field in the `Friend` class that points to the `UserAccount` object.

```
@PersistenceCapable(identityType =
  IdentityType.APPLICATION, detachable="true")
public class UserAccount {

  ...
  @Persistent(mappedBy = "userAccount")
  @Element(dependent = "true")
  private Set<Friend> friends = new HashSet();
...
```

Then, in the `server.domain.Friend` class, we add that new field, of type `UserAccount`, and name it `userAccount` to match the annotation in the parent class.

```
@PersistenceCapable(identityType = IdentityType.APPLICATION,
    detachable="true")
public class Friend implements StoreCallback{

    ...
  // pointer back to UserAccount object with which
  // this friend is associated
  @Persistent
  private UserAccount userAccount;
```

 Do not explicitly set the new `userAccount` field in the child `Friend` class. The JDO framework populates this field in your retrieved instances. The `userAccount` field value is lazily fetched.

# One-to-many Collection ordering

When you represent one-to-many relationships by a `Collection`, JDO must do some extra work if the collection is *ordered* (for example, if it is a `List`). Under the hood, JDO needs to maintain the ordering of the child entities and operations on this list can cause a fair bit of work at the framework level.

If you do not need to maintain a specific order in your collection, make it an unordered collection (for example, a `Set`). We did this for the *UserAccount:Friend* relationship.

If you want to use an ordered collection, it is most efficient to specify that the collection order should be maintained based on entity properties (data class fields). Do this by using the `@Order` annotation, which allows you to specify one or more fields and the sort order to use on them. The following code shows an example of specifying a one-to-many collection order.

```
import java.util.List;
import javax.jdo.annotations.Extension;
import javax.jdo.annotations.Order;
import javax.jdo.annotations.Persistent;

// ...
    @Persistent
    @Order(extensions = @Extension(vendorName="datanucleus",
        key="list-ordering", value="fieldA asc, fieldB asc"))
    private List<DomainObject> obj = new List<DomainObject>();
```

The sort order is supported by Datastore indexes on the given entity kind and properties. Just as with queries (as we will see in the next section), if your `@Order` annotation includes a sort on more than one property then a **custom index** will be required for it.

# Unowned relationships

Sometimes, domain semantics may dictate that a relationship is **unowned** — that is, a child can potentially belong to more than one parent. This can be the case for both one-to-many and one-to-one relationships. For example, in an application where users listed their favorite books, multiple users could have the same favorite. Additionally, your domain may contain many-to-many relationships. For example, in a "books" domain, you can have more than one *Author* associated with a given *Book*, and an *Author* can write more than one *Book*.

You cannot implement such an unowned relationship via the JDO relationship framework. In these situations, you must support the unowned relationship by using object keys as references. This is the approach we took in *Chapter 4*, when we stored a list of `Friend` keys in a `UserAccount` object. With this approach, the application-level logic must manage the relationship references (rather than relying on JDO to do so), and must modify the key information as appropriate when objects are added and deleted. In *Chapter 7*, we will see an example of an unowned many-to-many relationship.

# Finding objects—queries and indexes

In the previous chapter, we described how to retrieve an object from the Datastore given its ID via the `getObjectById()` method of the `PersistenceManager`. In this section, we'll look at how to query the Datastore using JDO and its query language, **JDOQL**. JDOQL looks somewhat similar to SQL in syntax but has a more object-oriented bias.

To effectively query the Datastore via JDOQL, it's useful not only to understand the JDOQL syntax, how to execute queries, and iterate over the results, but also to understand how the Datastore index works, and the constraints its operation places on the queries that you can perform. JDO is a standard interface, but its implementation on top of the Datastore must respect how the App Engine is implemented. Certain classes of queries that are allowable with respect to JDOQL syntax are disallowed by App Engine because they do not scale. So, after describing the query syntax, we will also take a high-level look at the index and some of the underlying reasons for the App Engine JDOQL restrictions.

## Constructing JDOQL queries

A JDOQL query can have four parts:

- The entity kind (the data class name) that you are querying over
- Entity property (field) filters
- Sort orders on properties
- The range of results to be returned

You must always define the entity *kind* when constructing a query. The other components may be optionally specified. Once a query is constructed, it is executed on the Datastore, and returns the entities that match it, sorted as indicated.

JDO Object Relationships and Queries

You can build a query in different ways, including the following:

- You can specify a `select` statement, including the kind, as a (parameterized) string.

- You can specify the select *kind* by indicating its class, then specify query clauses as a string.

- You can add filter, sort order, and range constraints to a query by method calls, which are added in the order called.

As we will see, you can combine these approaches by constructing a string for part of the query, and calling methods to add additional clauses.

Strings may be parameterized. There are two ways of indicating parameterization—explicit and implicit. With **explicit** parameters, you define the parameter type explicitly. With **implicit** parameters, the parameter type is inferred from the context.

## Query examples

We'll first list some query examples using the `Friend` class, and then delve into the details of `query` construction. In the following examples, we will use two `Friend` fields that we have not explicitly discussed yet, although you may have noticed them in the `ConnectrStage1` code—`lcFirstName` and `lcLastName`. These fields will be populated automatically with lowercased versions of the corresponding name field values. In the *Pre-persist callbacks — normalizing the name information* section of this chapter, we'll see how that is done. For now, just assume that they have been populated appropriately.

To build a query, call the `newQuery` method of a `PersistenceManager` instance. This returns an object of the type `javax.jdo.Query`. You can pass this method in one of the following ways:

- The data class (kind) to query over

- The data class and a `where` clause string that includes filter and ordering clauses

- A `select` query string that includes the kind

Then, you can make additional method calls on the query object to refine the query further. When the query construction is finished, call the `execute()` method of `Query`. The method's arguments are the values of any parameterizations that you have indicated.

The following examples assume that the `PersistenceManager` instance pm is being created and closed elsewhere.

# Example 1:

```
import javax.jdo.Query;

Query query = pm.newQuery("select from
    packagepath.server.domain.Friend where lcFirstName == 'bob'");
List<Friend> res = (List<Friend>)query.execute();
```

In Example 1, we have defined the query via a non-parameterized string. The kind is specified as the fully qualified name of the data class (here, packagepath.server. domain.Friend; replace packagepath with your package path). To dynamically generate the kind instead, use the getName() method of the class, for example, Friend.class.getName(). We do not pass any arguments to the execute() method as we have not defined any parameters.

# Example 2:

```
Query query = pm.newQuery(Friend.class,
    "lcFirstName == :fn order by lcLastName desc");
List<Friend> res = (List<Friend>)query.execute("bob");
```

In Example 2, we've passed newQuery the class of the *kind,* and specified query conditions—corresponding to the where clause—via a string (note that with this variant, the word where is not included in the conditions string). The :fn construct indicates an implicit parameter. We will then pass the parameter value to be associated with :fn to the execute() method—in this case, the String bob. The Query object's execute() method is called with the values to substitute in the query, in the order in which their associated parameters are listed.

# Example 3:

```
Query query = pm.newQuery(Friend.class, "lcFirstName == :fn");
query.setOrdering("lcLastName desc");
List<Friend> res = (List<Friend>)query.execute("bob");
```

In Example 3, we've called the setOrdering method on the query object to specify a query sort order. Again, we use an implicit parameter, :fn, and pass the parameter value to the execute() method.

# Example 4:

```
Query query = pm.newQuery(Friend.class);
query.setFilter("lcFirstName == :fn &&
    emailAddress == 'bob@bob.com'");
query.setOrdering("lcLastName asc");
List<Friend> res = (List<Friend>)query.execute("bob");
```

In Example 4, we've passed only the class of the Friend kind to `newQuery`, and then specified query conditions separately via the `setFilter` and `setOrdering` methods on the query object. Again, we use an implicit parameter `:fn`, and pass the parameter value to the `execute()` method. We could have alternately used two successive `setFilter()` calls to indicate the same semantics, as follows:

```
query.setFilter("lcFirstName == :fn");
query.setFilter("emailAddress == 'bob@bob.com'");
```

## Example 5:

```
Query query = pm.newQuery(Friend.class);
query.setFilter("lcFirstName == :fn && emailAddress == :em");
List<Friend> res = (List<Friend>)query.execute("bob", "bob@bob.com");
```

Example 5 uses two implicit parameters. We pass two arguments to the `execute()` method, which are matched in the order indicated. So, `bob` is substituted for `:fn`, and `bob@bob.com` is substituted for `:em`.

## Example 6:

```
Query query = pm.newQuery("select from " + Friend.class.getName() +
    " where lcFirstName == fname order by lcLastName desc");
query.declareParameters("String fname");
List<Friend> res = (List<Friend>)query.execute("bob");
```

Example 6 uses an *explicit* parameter `fname` rather than an implicit parameter. With an explicit parameter, we must indicate via the `declareParameters` method that `fname` is a parameter of type `String`. Once declared, we then pass the parameter values to `execute()` as before.

With JDOQL, conditional AND is indicated by `&&` and conditional OR is indicated by `||`.

Now that we've looked at some examples, we will take a closer look at query construction.

# Query filter operators

As the preceding examples show, you can specify a query filter via a string passed to the `newQuery` method and/or by calling the `setFilter` method of `Query`. You may make multiple `setFilter` calls (as seen in Example 4 earlier); they will be handled as a conjunction.

Query filters must specify a *field name*, an *operator*, and a *value*. To specify embedded field names in a query, use dot notation. For example, with the embedded `EFriendDetails` class model of *Chapter 4*, we would access its `emailAddress` subfield as so:

```
"select from " + Friend.class.getName() +
    " where edetails.emailAddress == 'bob@xyz.com'"
```

You may filter on the key field of an object. You cannot use the field of a child entity in a filter when performing a query on the parent kind, this would be a "join" query, which is not supported by App Engine. The filter operator can be any of the following:

- `==` [equal to]
- `<` [less than]
- `<=` [less than or equal to]
- `>` [greater than]
- `>=` [greater than or equal to]
- `!=` [not equal to]
- `contains()` filters [like "IN" filters in SQL]

 A query filter can't match patterns within a string value, and string queries are *case-sensitive*.

Inequality filters return results according to the sort order of the given property type, as listed in the *Core Value Types* table in *Chapter 4*. Strings have a Unicode sort order. So, for example, you could use the filter `lcLastName >= 'Z'` to access all strings starting with z (or greater).

The `!=` and `contains()` queries are not directly supported by the Datastore indexes but are implemented via a series of subqueries using other operators.

## Constraints on using inequality filters

The nature of the App Engine query mechanism imposes some restrictions on how queries can be formed, in order to ensure that they remain scalable.

There are important constraints on how you can use inequality filters.

A query may only use inequality filters (`<, <=, >=, >, !=`) on one field (property) across all of its filters. Multiple inequality filters on the same field are allowed (thus supporting queries over a range of values on a given field).

For example, suppose we have User objects with height and age fields. It is not legal to perform a query like this:

```
select User where height > 3  && age < 10 // wrong
```

because it uses inequality filters on two different fields.

However, this query is legal because both filters are on the same field:

```
select User where age > 3  && age < 10
```

It is allowed to use multiple equality filters for different fields in the same query, as long as any inequality filters are all on the same property. For example, this query is allowed:

```
select User where name == 'Bob' && age == 10 && height > 3
```

If a query has both a filter with an inequality comparison and one or more sort orders, the query must include a sort order for the property used in the inequality, and the sort order must appear before sort orders on other properties.

For example, the following query is allowed:

```
select from User where height > 3 order by height, age
```

However, the following query is illegal as it does not order by the field with the inequality filter:

```
select from User where height > 3 order by age //wrong
```

The next query is also illegal as it does not order by the field with the inequality filter first:

```
select from User where height > 3 order by age, height //wrong
```

These constraints stem from the way in which the Datastore indexes work and the App Engine scalability requirements. In the next section, which describes how the Datastore indexes are built and used, we will look at the rationale behind these requirements.

# The contains() operator and ||

The `contains()` operator allows you to express the analog of an SQL "IN" query. Define a query parameter that calls `contains` on a field, as shown in the following code. Then pass an array of the values to match with `execute()`. The following example looks for `Friends` with a last name "smith" and a first name "bob", "tom", or "mary":

```
Query q = pm.newQuery("select from "  + Friend.class.getName() +
   " where lcLastName == 'smith' && :p1.contains(lcFirstName)");
List<Friend> results =
   (List<Friend>)q.execute(Arrays.asList("bob", "tom", "mary"));
```

The conditional OR (||) can be used only when the filters in its disjuncts all use the same field name—that is, only when its clauses can be mapped to a single `contains()` filter. So, the following is not legal:

```
Query query = pm.newQuery(Friend.class,
   "lcLastName == 'smith' || lcFirstName == 'bob'"); //wrong
```

# Query filters on fields with multiple values

As introduced in *Chapter 4,* the Datastore allows entities to have properties with multiple values, and this capability is mapped to JDO by allowing fields to contain Collections of core data type values (such as a `List` of a friend's favorite books).

The Datastore query engine regards a multivalued property as equal to a filter value if any of the property's values is equal to the filter value. This behavior can essentially be used to test for membership in a set, a very useful query capability.

Suppose that we added a `tags` multivalued property to our `Friend` class, as suggested in the following code:

```
@PersistenceCapable(identityType = IdentityType.APPLICATION,
    detachable="true")
public class Friend  {

  ...
  @Persistent
  private List<String> tags;
  ...
}
...
tags = new ArrayList<String>();
tags.add("team");
tags.add("coffee");
tags.add("book_club");
```

We could execute a query over this multivalued field to find all `Friend`s who are tagged with a particular tag. For example, we could execute this query:

```
"select from " + Friend.class.getName() + " where tags == 'team'"
```

to find all `Friend`s who are tagged with `team`.

The next query:

```
"select from " + Friend.class.getName() +
    "where tags == 'book_club' && tags == 'coffee' ,
```

would return all `Friend`s who are tagged with both `book_club` and `coffee`—that is, it would match all `Friend`s whose `tags` List contains both values. This would give us the ability to filter `Friend`s on a given group of tags in an efficient manner (the *Connectr* app does not actually include tags but in *Chapter 7* we will introduce a similar use of multivalued properties).

 If a query has multiple inequality filters defined for a multivalued property, an entity will match the query only if it has an individual value for that property that matches *all* of the inequality filters.

## Query sort orders and ranges

Query sort orders can also be specified in several different ways. As illustrated by the previous examples, you can specify sort orders via the string passed to `newQuery`, and/or by calling the `setOrdering` method of `Query`, as in Example 4 of the query examples given earlier. As with `setFilter`, you can invoke the `setOrdering` method multiple times; the sort orders are applied in the order given.

You can specify the range of query results to be returned by calling the `setRange` method of `Query`. It takes the arguments: `setRange(long fromIncl, long toExcl)`

where the first argument is the starting index of the result set you want, and the second argument is the ending index, exclusive, where 0 is the index of the first result. The Datastore query engine implements this by fetching all results up to the last to return, then discarding the results prior to the start offset.

For example, the range, `q.setRange(20, 30)`, will cause the engine to fetch the first 30 results, then return the results from indices 20 to 29. Because all of the results up to the last are fetched, it is typically more efficient to use query cursors instead of a range offset. See the *Query cursors* section of this chapter.

# Executing a query and getting the results

When you execute a query, it will return a `List` of the *kind* of the query. You can iterate over the results as follows, and then **close** the query:

```
try
{
  List<Friend> results = (List<Friend>) query.execute();
      if (results.iterator().hasNext()) {
       for (Friend f : results) {
         // ... do something ...
       }
    } else {
       // ... no results ...
       }
  } finally {
       query.closeAll();
       }
```

You can call the `execute()` method of the same query object multiple times, passing it a different set of parameters each time.

If you expect a query to return only one result, you can call the `setUnique` method of the `Query` object, as in the `UserAccount` class:

```
Query q = pm.newQuery(UserAccount.class, "emailAddress == :email");
q.setUnique(true);
```

In this case, if the query retrieves a single data object, the object will be returned (instead of a `List`). You must cast it to its correct type:

```
oneResult = (UserAccount) q.execute(defaultEmail);
```

If the unique query retrieves more than one object, an exception will be thrown.

# Query cursors

A **query cursor** encodes the location in a query result set of the last result fetched, and can be used to indicate the starting position of a subsequent fetch of additional results for that query. This provides a way to obtain query results in successive batches without needing to pull in the entire set of results at once. The query cursor can be converted to/from a web-safe string, allowing it to be used later. So, query cursors can be used, for example, for pagination, or for batching server-side processing of large amounts of data across multiple web requests.

The cursor's position can be viewed as a marker—it is not an offset calculated from the start of the result set. Thus, if data is added to the Datastore between the time the cursor position was generated and the time it is used for a query, only new results after the cursor's position will be returned. Any new results prior to the cursor position will not be returned (this means that cursors can be used to monitor for new results on a given entity, if they are ordered by timestamp).

When using a cursor, you must always use the same query that was used to generate the cursor; if not, an exception is thrown. For example, you cannot change the kind, the filters, or filter values of the query. You cannot use cursors with != or contains() query filters. A cursor can only be used by the same application in which it was generated.

The following example shows, using JDO, how to obtain the cursor from a query, and to convert it to a web-safe string. The cursor can then be used at some later time, to continue returning results starting from the cursor location.

```java
import javax.jdo.PersistenceManager;
import javax.jdo.Query;
import com.google.appengine.api.datastore.Cursor;
import org.datanucleus.store.appengine.query.JDOCursorHelper;
...

Query q = null;
String cursorString = null;
PersistenceManager pm = PMF.get().getPersistenceManager();
try {
  q = pm.newQuery(Friend.class);
  q.setRange(0, range);
  List<Friend> results = (List<Friend>) q.execute();
  if (results.iterator().hasNext()) {
    for (Friend friend : results) {
      // Do some work...
    }
    Cursor cursor = JDOCursorHelper.getCursor(results);
    cursorString = cursor.toWebSafeString();
  }
}
finally {
  q.closeAll();
  pm.close();
}
```

A common usage is to set a range on the query with offset 0, as shown in the previous code. Perform the query and obtain the cursor from the results:

```
Cursor cursor = JDOCursorHelper.getCursor(results);
String cursorString = cursor.toWebSafeString();
```

In the next iteration, use the cursor as the query starting point:

```
Query q = pm.newQuery(Friend.class);
Cursor cursor = Cursor.fromWebSafeString(cursorString);
Map<String, Object> extensionMap = new HashMap<String, Object>();
extensionMap.put(JDOCursorHelper.CURSOR_EXTENSION, cursor);
q.setExtensions(extensionMap);
q.setRange(0, range);
```

Again set a 0-offset range for the query. This time, the initial element in the results list will be the first result after the cursor position.

The code below puts these pieces together in a method designed to be called multiple times across a series of web requests. It defines and executes a range query, and returns the current query cursor position as a web-safe string. This returned cursor position is passed as an argument in the next web request, and is used to generate the next query, which picks up where the previous one left off, and so on. In *Chapter 7* and later, we will use this pattern a number of times, in order to split up server-side data processing into manageable chunks.

```
import javax.jdo.PersistenceManager;
import javax.jdo.Query;
import com.google.appengine.api.datastore.Cursor;
import org.datanucleus.store.appengine.query.JDOCursorHelper;

...
public String processFriendBatch(String cursorString, int range)
{

Query q = null;
PersistenceManager pm = PMF.get().getPersistenceManager();

try {
  q = pm.newQuery(Friend.class);
  if (cursorString != null) {
    Cursor cursor = Cursor.fromWebSafeString(cursorString);
    Map<String, Object> extensionMap = new HashMap<String,
      Object>();
    extensionMap.put(JDOCursorHelper.CURSOR_EXTENSION, cursor);
    q.setExtensions(extensionMap);
```

```
  }
  q.setRange(0, range);
  List<Friend> results = (List<Friend>) q.execute();
  if (results.iterator().hasNext()) {
    for (Friend friend : results) {
      // Do some work…
    }
    Cursor cursor = JDOCursorHelper.getCursor(results);
    cursorString = cursor.toWebSafeString();
  }
  else {
   // no results
   cursorString = null;
  }
 }
  finally {
    q.closeAll();
    pm.close();
  }
  return cursorString;
}
```

# Unset and unindexed entity fields

Recall that Datastore entities have **soft schemas**, in that entities of a given *kind* are not required to share the same set of properties.

When you query the Datastore for a given entity kind and your query includes a filter or sort order on a given property, then the Datastore will not return any entities that do not include that property. This is because such an entity will not be listed in any index that includes that property. For example, a Friend query with a sort order on the lastName field would not return entities that do not include a lastName property.

If some of your data class fields are unindexed, then these fields cannot be included in query filters or sort orders either for the same reason—indexes are not built for them.

 Note that the Text and Blob core data types are always unindexed.

It is also possible to declare that a field should not be indexed, if you are sure that you will not want to query over it. This can reduce both the index-building time and the amount of storage space your application requires. To do so, add the following annotation to the field:

```
@Extension(vendorName = "datanucleus", key = "gae.unindexed",
    value="true")
```

If you use JDO, the stored entities created from instances of a persistent class will include all fields defined by that class, even if you do not explicitly assign values to them (that is, if some fields are set to `null`). When an object is saved, any null fields will result in the creation of entity properties with null (unset) values, but the properties will exist for those entities (when such an entity is later loaded again into a JDO object, any such unset properties will result in object fields set either to null or to an empty collection/array, depending upon the field type).

So, unless you change your persistence-capable class definitions midstream, you are insulated from the issue of 'missing properties' when using JDO—just remember which fields are not indexed. However, if you use the low-level Datastore API to create some of your entities, or create them via the Admin Console, then be sure that you are explicitly creating all the properties required for your queries.

If you do change the definition of a persistence-capable class, then it is of course possible to introduce Datastore entities of the same *kind* with different sets of properties.

# Deleting by query

Earlier, we saw how to delete objects by passing them to the `deletePersistent()` method of a `PersistenceManager`. For example,

```
pm.deletePersistent(pm.getObjectById(Friend.class, id));
```

It is also possible to delete entities by query. Define a `Query` object just as for a retrieval query. Then, instead of calling the `execute()` method of the `Query`, call the `Query.deletePersistentAll()` method. Query formation is just the same, and the parameter arguments passed to `deletePersistentAll()` are the same as those passed to the `execute()` method. The difference is that the objects (and any dependent children) will be deleted instead of retrieved.

For example, we could do the following:

```
Query q = pm.newQuery(Friend.class, "lcFirstName == :fn");
q.deletePersistentAll("bob");
```

Delete all `Friends` with a `lcFirstName` field of "bob". The dependent `Name` children of those `Friends` will be deleted as well.

# Batch fetches using a list of keys

If you have a list of data object keys, it is possible to do a **batch fetch** of the corresponding objects. This is done via a special query in which the only query filter is on a collection of keys. Define a parameter to hold the key collection and then pass the value of the collection as the argument to `execute()`. The JDO implementation detects that the filter is via a key list and performs a batch get.

We used this technique in the `ConnectrStage1_alt` version of our application to fetch the `Friend` objects corresponding to the list of keys stored by a `UserAccount` object, as follows:

```
List<String> cidList = uinfo.getFriendsList();
Query q = pm.newQuery("select from " + Friend.class.getName() +
    " where id == :keys");
List<Friend> friends = (List<Friend>) q.execute(cidList);
```

# Keys-only queries

It is possible to define and execute a `query` that returns only the matching object's keys, not the full objects. This is done by building a query that selects on only the primary key field of the data class. For example, with our `Friend` class, which has a key field named `id`, such a query would be:

```
Query q = pm.newQuery("select id from Friend where
    lcFirstName == 'bob'");
```

The App Engine JDO implementation interprets that syntax as a *keys-only* query. Then, when you execute the query, a list of IDs (not objects) is returned:

```
List ids = (List) q.execute();
```

Such queries, which return only keys, are faster and less expensive than queries that return data objects. It is important that such a query selects only on the key, otherwise, the full objects will be returned. The returned list will be sorted by key if no other sort order is imposed.

# Extents: fetching all objects of a particular kind

It is possible to fetch all objects of a given *kind*, or data class, from the Datastore. This is done via an `Extent` object.

It is straightforward to use an `Extent`. Create the extent by calling the `getExtent()` method of the `PersistenceManager`. The first argument is the desired data class, and the second indicates whether object subclasses (in the sense of data class inheritance) should be fetched.

Then, iterate over the returned `Extent` to get the results. Every object of the given *kind* in the Datastore will be returned. With an extent, you cannot filter or order the results. When you are done, close the `Extent` by calling its `closeAll()` method.

```
import javax.jdo.Extent;

// ...

    Extent extent = pm.getExtent(Friend.class, false);
    for (Friend f : extent) {
        // ...
    }
    extent.closeAll();
```

# The App Engine Datastore index

For every query performed by an App Engine application, an index table is maintained. More exactly, an index table is maintained for every set of queries that has the same filters and sort orders. In developing App Engine apps, it is useful to have a high-level understanding of the role played by these indexes.

When a query is executed, its corresponding index table is traversed to find the results. The query engine starts scanning the index table at the first row that meets all of the query's filter conditions, and continues until it finds an entry that does not meet the filter conditions (or until it has accumulated the number of results requested by the query). The index table is sorted so that all results for every possible query that will use that table are in consecutive rows in the table.

Whenever Datastore entities are created, modified, or deleted, the relevant indexes must be modified. The Datastore operation does not return until this has occurred. So, the Datastore puts in effort at write time in order to ensure rapid and scalable reads.

The Datastore creates index tables that support certain basic query types automatically, the rest of the index tables must be custom-generated for your application based on the queries used by the application.

In this section, we'll discuss both automatically-generated and custom indexes. Then, we'll revisit some of the constraints on query formation that were introduced in the previous section, and look at their rationale in light of how the indexes are used during query execution.

# Automatically-generated indexes

App Engine builds two indexes for every property of every entity kind, one with values in ascending order and one with values in descending order. It also keeps an index of kinds and keys, sorted by key in ascending order. Be aware that the sort order for multivalued fields can be somewhat unexpected. If an index table sorted is by a multivalued property in ascending order, the value used for ordering is the smallest value, and if a table is sorted by a multivalued property in descending order, the value used for ordering is the greatest value.

As a simple example of an automatically generated table, consider the `Friend` data class. An index table will be automatically built for its `firstName` property, sorted in *ascending* order. Figure 2 suggests this index. Another index table will be built for `firstName` sorted in *descending* order. Analogous indexes will be built for other properties of `Friend`.

| Key | firstName asc |
|-----------|---------------|
| Friend/34 | Alphonse |
| Friend/120 | Bernard |
| Friend/56 | Charlemagne |
| Friend/19 | Edgar |
| . | . |
| . | . |
| . | . |

Figure 2: Example index table for the firstName property of the Friend entity sorted in ascending order

If a new `Friend` were to be created, this index table as well as the other similar indexes on the other fields of `Friend` would be updated before the `makePersistent()` call returns. Similarly, if the `firstName` field of some `Friend` is modified, any index table that includes that field, including the table in Figure 2, will be updated.

With the automatically built indexes, the following types of queries are supported:

- A query on a given kind with no filters or sort orders
- Queries using only equality filters
- Queries using only inequality filters on a single property (recall that it is disallowed to use an inequality filter on more than one property regardless)
- Queries with one sort order on a property and any filters only on the same property

To execute the following query:

```
"select from " + Friend.class.getName() +
   " where firstName == 'Bernard'"
```

The table in Figure 2 would be used (the default sort order is *ascending*). App Engine finds the first row in the index that matches, and then scans to the first row that does not match. Because the table is sorted, this process is very efficient: App Engine can find the first matching row very quickly, and the results are already sorted as required.

Similarly, this query:

```
"select from " + Friend.class.getName() +
   " where firstName > 'Bernard'"
```

would also use the table in Figure 2, and would scan from the first row > "Bernard" to the end of the table.

The class of queries *using only equality filters* is an interesting one in the case where there is more than one filter. Such queries are implemented by scanning the automatically-generated indexes for each of the properties for which an equality filter is specified, in a way that allows the results to be returned as they are encountered. This is called a **merge join**. As long as there are no sort orders specified, this type of query can be performed using just the automatically-generated indexes. It is the only automatically supported query that uses multiple indexes.

# Custom indexes

If a query does not fall into one of the categories listed above and cannot be covered by the automatically-generated indexes, then a **custom index** is required—one built for queries of that given structure with respect to both filters and sort orders.

Queries that require a custom index include:

- Queries with more than one sort order
- Queries with one or more inequality filters on a property and one or more equality filters on other properties
- Queries that have a descending sort order on the key field

Because it would be hugely intractable to build all the indexes that could possibly be needed by an application's queries, App Engine uses application-specific configuration information to specify which custom indexes to build with respect to the queries required by the application.

The development web server makes it easy to generate this information for the most part. When you run your code and execute a query for which the existing indexes aren't sufficient, the configuration information for the needed new custom query is added to a file. This file is called `war/WEB-INF/appengine-generated/datastoreindexes-auto.xml`. As you run your application, entries may be added to this configuration file. If your development testing covers all of the types of queries that your application can generate, then the `datastore-indexes-auto.xml` file will be sufficient for deployment, and you should not have to define additional index configurations.

However, if, based on knowledge of your application, you recognize that further indexes need to be built, you can specify them manually in the `war/WEB-INF/datastore-indexes.xml` file. Both configuration files are used to determine the set of custom indexes generated.

While you are in development mode, a missing index specification never causes an error. Instead, it just triggers a new entry in `war/WEB-INF/appengine-generated/datastore-indexes-auto.xml`. However, once you've deployed your application, if a query is executed for which no index has been built, the query will fail.

The XML index configuration files have the following structure:

```
<datastore-indexes>
    <datastore-index kind="UserAccount" ancestor="false" source="auto">
        <property name="emailAddress" direction="asc"/>
        <property name="name" direction="asc"/>
        <property name="__key__" direction="asc"/>
    </datastore-index>
</datastore-indexes>
```

A `<datastore-indexes>` root node has one or more `<datastore-index>` children. A `<datastore-index>` node indicates the query *kind* and has one or more `<property>` elements. These specify a property name and a sort direction. The order of the `<property>` elements is meaningful—the index is sorted first by the first property, then by the second, and so on. The primary key field of the given kind is referred to in the configuration file by `__key__`.

The previous query configuration file was generated by a query like this:

```
Query query = pm.newQuery(UserAccount.class,
    "name == :nm && emailAddress == :em && id > :id");

List<UserAccount> res =
  (List<UserAccount>)query.execute(name, address, keyid);
```

# Revisiting constraints on queries

With knowledge of the way in which the index tables are constructed and traversed, the reasons for some of the query constraints become clearer. The query engine requires all results for a query to be adjacent in the relevant index table in order to allow the query execution to be implemented by a single scan of the pertinent part of the table (merge join, which does an efficient traversal of multiple tables, is an exception). This requirement is instituted so that the query execution time can scale on the size of the result set, not the data set. Query types that would not meet this requirement are not supported.

Reconsider the two query constraints that we discussed previously. They now make more sense:

- A query may use only inequality filters (<, <=, >=, >, !=) on one property across all of its filters. This is because a single index table cannot represent multiple inequality filters on multiple properties while ensuring that results are consecutive in the table.

- If a query has both a filter with an inequality comparison and one or more sort orders, the query must include a sort order for the property used in the inequality, and the sort order must appear before sort orders on other properties. This is because, for consecutive rows to make up the complete result, the rows must be ordered by the inequality filter before other sort orders.

## Exploding indexes

The Datastore limits the number of index entries that an entity can have across all indexes (both automatic and custom). Normally, this limit will not be of concern to you. However, it is possible that you may run up against it under some circumstances.

If you have a data object with a multivalued field, the Datastore will build an automatically-generated index for it using a row for each value. However, if more than one multivalued field is included in a *custom* query, then the index table must include a row for every permutation of the values of every (multivalued) field. The combinatorics can potentially get out of hand, leading to an "exploding index". If you run up against the index entry limit, you will see indication of an error status when you view the index in the App Engine Admin Console. If this happens, you may need to reformulate your queries.

# Using the Admin Console Datastore index viewer and index vacuuming

From the App Engine Admin Console, you can view the custom indexes that are being used for your application.

Figure 3: A custom index on StreamItem, showing the indexed fields and their sort orders.

Under **Data** in the console's left navigation bar, select **Datastore Indexes**. If you have any custom indexes defined, they will be shown organized by kind, as in Figure 3. For each custom index, the kind (here, `StreamItem`—a class we'll encounter in a later chapter), the fields used in the index table, and their sort orders are shown.

The "status" of an index may be listed as "Building" or "Deleting" if its construction or removal is in process. In Figure 3, the index is ready to be used and **Serving**. If your index status indicates an **error**, it may be an exploding index, as discussed earlier.

If you accidentally generate an exploding index and want to remove it, you currently have to do some work outside Java. After you change your code and redeploy an index configuration that does not include the problematic index, you will still see the index listed in the App Engine console. App Engine does not delete indexes, as they still might be required for an older version of the application. You must explicitly indicate to App Engine that an index should be removed. This is called **vacuuming** the index.

At the time of writing, the Java App Engine SDK does not currently support index vacuuming so you must do this in Python. Future Java support is planned; however, this process is straightforward in Python once it's set up.

To vacuum indexes, you will first need to install Python (if necessary), and then install the App Engine Python SDK. For more information, see the App Engine Python documentation at `http://code.google.com/appengine/docs/python/gettingstarted/`.

On Mac OS X or Windows, when you start the Python Google App Engine Launcher, it should ask your permission to make some Python scripts available in your $PATH, with the result as in Figure 4. You will need to use one of these scripts, `appcfg.py`, to do the vacuuming. If you are not using the Launcher, you will need to locate `appcfg.py` in the Python SDK install.

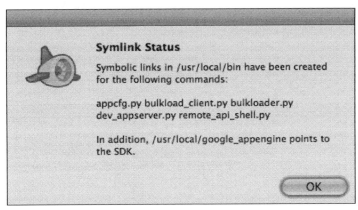

**Symlink Status**

Symbolic links in /usr/local/bin have been created for the following commands:

appcfg.py bulkload_client.py bulkloader.py dev_appserver.py remote_api_shell.py

In addition, /usr/local/google_appengine points to the SDK.

OK

Figure 4: The Python Google App Engine Launcher will make some Python scripts available in your $PATH.

After the Python SDK is installed, build a file called `app.yaml` with the following contents:

```
application: <your_app_id>
version: 1
runtime: python
api_version: 1

handlers:
- url: /.*
  script: anything.py
```

Replace `<your_app_id>` with your actual application ID. You can name the `script` whatever you like (its name is only important if you are developing in Python).

Put this `app.yaml` file in the top-level directory for your Java project. If you are using Eclipse, this directory will be under the Eclipse workspace.

Then, run the following line of code from the command line:

```
appcfg.py vacuum_indexes <app-dir>
```

where `<app-dir>` is replaced with your Java project directory. If you run this command *from* your project directory, you can just type:

```
 appcfg.py vacuum_indexes .
```

If `appcfg.py` is not in your `$PATH`, modify the preceding commands to specify its full path.

You should see something that looks similar to the following (your index details will be different, of course):

```
% appcfg.py vacuum_indexes .
Application: <your_app_id>; version: 1.
Server: appengine.google.com.
Fetching index definitions diff.
Email: [enter your App Engine email address]
Password for <your_email_address>: [enter your password]
This index is no longer defined in your index.yaml file.

kind: UserAccount
properties:
- name: emailAddress
```

```
- name: name
- name: __key__
```

```
Are you sure you want to delete this index? (N/y/a):
```

Follow the prompts to remove problematic indexes.

# Side-stepping query constraints

Earlier, we described some App Engine-related constraints on JDO query formation. For example, you may use an inequality filter on only one property.

A general strategy for getting around these constraints can be to *compute at write time* what might otherwise need to be computed during a query. For example, often you can add extra fields to your data classes whose values are the result of additional domain processing, and then include these fields in your query to circumvent the query restrictions.

Suppose we have User objects with height and age fields. It is not legal to perform a query like this:

```
select user where height > 3  && age < 10
```

because this query uses inequality filters on two different fields.

Instead, we can create age *categories*, guided by our domain semantics, and include them in the query. For example, we may decide that in our domain, we want to place people into 10-year buckets: bucket 1 = = (age < 10), bucket 2 == (10 >= age < 20), and so on. When we create a new User object, we not only record their age but also calculate their age bucket. Then, we can do queries like this, which do not violate the App Engine constraints:

```
select user where height > 3 && age_bucket = 1
```

As another example, you might add another field to categorize the user's name field as falling within "A-F", "G-M", and so on.

Finally, let's look at an example that we have incorporated into our *Connectr* application. As discussed previously, App Engine does not support case-sensitive queries. So, we will store a "canonical", lowercased version of the name of a friend in addition to the version originally provided. We can then search against this normalized version in order to support case-insensitive search. We will implement this via a useful feature of JDO, the *pre-persist callback*.

# Pre-persist callbacks—normalizing Friend name information

It is possible to define a pre-persist callback method for a JDO class which is called prior to saving or modifying a data object of that class. This can be useful for populating generated fields such as the ones in the preceding examples.

We will use such a callback to populate two persistent fields in Friend, lcFirstName, and lcLastName, on save or modify of a Friend object, with the *lowercased* versions of the fields firstName and lastName.

Because Datastore search is case-sensitive, we are generating a "canonical form" of the name string which we can use to search. When the client hands us a name string to search for, we will convert it to lowercase and match it against one of these lowercased fields, not the original string. If we had not done this, then if the client string did not exactly match the capitalization used when the name was originally input, there would not be a match.

To set up the callback, import:

```
import javax.jdo.listener.StoreCallback;
```

Then, define a method in server.domain.Friend called jdoPreStore() (it's required to be so named), which populates the new Friend fields based on the firstName and lastName values. This method will be called by the system prior to the creation or update of a Friend object. The following code shows this addition to the Friend class. We define the new fields— lcFirstName and lcLastName. Then, the jdoPreStore() method sets those fields to the lowercased versions of firstName and lastName.

```
@PersistenceCapable(identityType = IdentityType.APPLICATION,
    detachable="true")
public class Friend implements StoreCallback {

    ...

    @Persistent
    private String lcFirstName;
    @Persistent
    private String lcLastName;
    ...

    public void jdoPreStore() {
        if (getLastName() != null) {
            lcLastName = getLastName().toLowerCase();
        }
        else {
            lcLastName = null;
        }
```

```
      if (getFirstName() != null) {
        lcFirstName = getFirstName().toLowerCase();
      }
      else {
        lcFirstName = null;
      }
    }
    ...
  }
```

Once the callback mechanism is in place, we can perform case-insensitive queries on the name fields by lowercasing the input query arguments, as follows.

```
String inputname = ... // input from client

Query q = pm.newQuery("select from " +   Friend.class.getName() +
    " where lcFirstName == :fn");

List<friend> results =
    (List<Friend>)q.execute(inputname.toLowerCase())
```

Because we're querying against the new lowercased versions of the name strings, the query now works as we want.

[  Inspiration for this example comes from: `http://gae-java-persistence.blogspot.com/2009/11/case-insensitive-queries.html`. ]

# Summary

In this chapter, we continued our development of the *Connectr* application that we'll build throughout the book, by introducing the use of JDO-owned relationships to support one-to-one and one-to-many relationships between data objects.

We covered how to perform Datastore queries using JDOQL the App Engine-imposed restrictions on query formation, and some ways to formulate queries that can help sidestep some of the restrictions.

We also took a closer look at how the Datastore indexes are generated and used, and the constraints that index design imposes upon the types of queries that can be executed.

Based on this foundation, we will continue to develop our application's features in the upcoming chapters.

# 6
# Implementing MVP, an Event Bus, and Other GWT Patterns

In this chapter. we are going to structure the *Connectr* software using the **Model-View-Presenter pattern (MVP)** and add important structural elements:

- **Event Bus:** This is like a phone system between software components. Components send and listen to Events. They can act based on the type of event they receive. An example of an event would be 'somebody logged in' or 'this friend name has changed'.

- **Application Controller**: The *Connectr* Application Controller acts as the conductor of the application. It contains the application-level logic.

- **The Centralized Remote Procedure Call** class brings major improvements to the usability, structure, and robustness of *Connectr*.

  The improvements are three-fold:
  - It retries Remote Procedure Calls on error.
  - It shows users a loading message when the application is busy.
  - It centralizes app-wide exception handling into one place.

Furthermore, in this chapter, we will see how *Connectr* implements **browser history**, allowing users to bookmark the application and to use the back and forward browser buttons.

All code examples can be found in the `ConnectrStage2` code bundle.

Finally, we will implement a standalone example application of MVP with Activities and Places, a new framework that was introduced in GWT 2.1. The code for this example application is available in the ProfileMVP code bundle.

# Introducing MVP – The need for design patterns in software

It is quite easy to create an app that has few widgets. As long as the app is small the code is quite simple to understand. However, as the application grows there is a danger that it enters the spaghetti-code zone—the code has no structure and functionalities are intertwined. It is hard to modify and extend. It becomes buggy and obscure glitches happen sometimes in bizarre circumstances.

To avoid this, good programmers like to structure their application at the very beginning of a project. They like to put things in buckets, files in folders, create coding conventions, naming schemes, and use **design patterns**.

Design patterns are not only used in software, they are used everywhere in our day-to-day lives. Design patterns are here to make our lives easier. In a home, things are placed where you expect them to be as it is built with a particular design pattern in mind. For example, the entrance door is located at floor level on the side of the house that is the closest to the street. It has a reasonable height and width so most people and furniture can easily go through. This is where everyone expects to find it.

If houses were made of software, a home builder, probably called a home programmer in this case, could place the entrance door on the roof with no stair to get to it because the house owner was a parachutist.

Furthermore, if our builder wanted to improve efficiency, knowing most people spend most of their time in the kitchen and in their bed, he could place the bed in the middle of the kitchen thus saving precious room commuting time.

The problem with software that does not use design patterns is that it can have doors on the roof, windows in the basements, stoves in places where you don't expect any. Programmers have different ideas and they implement them with their own inspiration. When new programmers come on board they have to find their way around: where is the entrance door of this software?

Software built without structure and patterns is often buggy, not always fun to work with, and as it grows in size it becomes very costly to bring new programmers onboard because of the time it takes for them to learn its idiosyncrasies.

Enter design patterns.

Design patterns remove programmers' inspiration where it is not needed. They provide a known-to-all way to produce well-architected, easily-maintainable software.

As far as GWT is concerned, the Model-View-Presenter (MVP) pattern seems to be the most commonly used. The MVP pattern preceded GWT. Developers have been using MVP to develop rich applications for decades on many platforms such as Microsoft .NET or Android, and Windows.

There are many advantages to the MVP architecture such as separation of concerns and easy testing.

Separation of concerns allows developers to focus on one part of the application without having to know or worry about what others are doing elsewhere. Making things easy to test means that developers will be more inclined to write and run tests to check their code.

Let's dive into the MVP architecture and explains its different components.

# Introduction to MVP

The following figure shows the MVP class diagram. The key to MVP is to split the view, the presentation, and model into three independent classes.

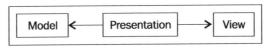

Figure 1: The three components of an MVP triad

This group of three is often called a **triad**. Let's examine the role of each element.

# The view

The view is the user interface. It may contain text fields, images, forms, buttons, links, and many other widgets. The view does not and should not know what it is displaying. This means that it does not know the kind of model it is using because the data sent to the view is in primitive formats such as string, date, and image, via a display interface.

# The model

The model contains the data to be displayed. It is not aware of the component that is going to display it or how it is stored in the Datastore. It is a data container.

The model data can come from a Datastore via a Data Transfer Object (DTO) fetched over a server call or from an **Event Bus**.

In GWT MVP, models are shared between the frontend and the backend. Therefore, models are often Data Transfer Objects (DTOs) that are serialized before transmission.

# The Presenter

The Presenter contains the business logic of the triad. That's the boss. Its role is to send updated data to the view and read back values from it if it changes. It also listens to events sent by other application components. It can also fire its own events on the event bus. The presenter gets its data from the **Model**. Presenters and views are coupled via a **View Interface** as shown in the following image:

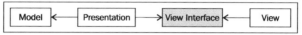

Figure 2: The View Interface connects Presenter with its view

As long as views implement the required **Display Interface**, presenters are able to do their job, that is, send data to the view and read user input.

# *Connectr* MVP application architecture overview

Now that we have reviewed the different components included in the *Connectr* MVP application, we can represent the architecture with the following diagram:

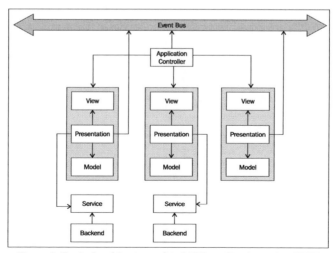

Figure 3: Typical architecture of an MVP application using GWT

In the previous diagram, the event bus serves as the communication backbone between components. The controller orchestrates the behavior of the entire application. Some MVP triads are connected to the backend via a service layer used to access the data store while others are connected to the event bus in order to listen to application events. Whether presenters need a connection to the event bus, or to the backend, or both depends on their specific needs.

## Package and file organization

Implementing the MVP pattern into a project helps organize files and classes in a logical fashion. There can be packages for the views, presenters, and models (labeled shared in the following image because they are shared between the client and the server). Here is how *Connectr's* project layout looks in Eclipse. Since we use Subversion to manage our source code, numbers shown at the end of the package names represent source control version numbers.

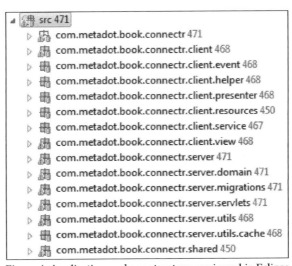

Figure 4: Application package structure as viewed in Eclipse

## Coding MVP into *Connectr*

Now that we have seen the different moving parts of *Connectr* MVP software, let's assemble everything together.

# Starting up the application

1. In GWT, the application entry point is onModuleLoad, located in the ConnectrApp class, which is as follows:

```
package com.metadot.book.connectr.client;

// Imports omitted for better readability

public class ConnectrApp implements EntryPoint {

  ...

  public void onModuleLoad() {

    singleton = this;
    login();
    createUI();
  }
```

2. After creating a singleton reference to itself, onModuleLoad calls login() to get the current user or force a redirection to the login screen. At this stage of the application, since the login method has not been fully implemented, the backend returns a test user. We continue by calling createUI(), which instantiates panels, services, the application controller (that will be explained later in this chapter) and all the necessary **standalone presenters**:

```
...   private void createUI() {

    DockLayoutPanel outer = binder.createAndBindUi(this);
    root = RootLayoutPanel.get();
    root.clear();
    root.add(outer);

    final MessagesServiceAsync messagesService = GWT.
create(MessagesService.class);
    FriendsServiceAsync friendService = GWT.create(FriendsService.
class);

    AppController appViewer = new AppController(friendService,
eventBus);
    appViewer.go();

    friendListPresenter = new FriendListPresenter(friendService,
messagesService, eventBus, new FriendListView());
    friendListPresenter.go(friendListPanel);

  }
```

Standalone presenters can take care of themselves once instantiated. They don't need a controller to do their job. Typically they will listen to the event bus and act upon events they receive. In this case, `FriendListPresenter` is the only standalone presenter. The friend list always stays in the view and does not need to be managed by a controller.

# Inside a presenter

In this section we are going to decompose the `FriendListPresenter` class in order to explain how presenters are connected to their view via a display interface, how they respond to user interface events, and how they listen to the event bus.

The next diagram shows `FriendListView` populated by a list given by the `FriendListPresenter`. The presenter needs to handle clicks from the **+new** link on the property button and on the list itself. It also needs to load the list and know which contacts are in the list.

Figure 5: FriendList user interface

The class `FriendListPresenter` requires its view to implement all methods listed in its **Display Interface**:

```
package com.metadot.book.connectr.client.presenter;

// Imports omitted for increased readabiity

public class FriendListPresenter implements Presenter {

public interface Display {
```

```
        HasClickHandlers getAddButton();
        HasClickHandlers getList();
        void setData(List<String> friendNames);
        int getClickedRow(ClickEvent event);
        ClickPoint getClickedPoint(ClickEvent event);
        List<Integer> getSelectedRows();
        Widget asWidget();
    }
```

It is to be noted that the interface does not use domain specific classes. For example, there is no `Friend` object sent to the view but rather a generic list of strings containing a list of friend names to be displayed. Therefore views are not aware of what they display, which is one of the goals of MVP.

# Populating the Friend list view

In the `FriendListPresenter` class, the presenter gets its list of friends from the backend via a Remote Procedure Call as shown in the following snippet:

```
...
private void fetchFriendSummaryDTO() {
  new RPCCall<ArrayList<FriendSummaryDTO>>() {
    @Override
  protected void callService(AsyncCallback<ArrayList<FriendSummaryD
TO>> cb) {
      rpcService.getFriendSummaries(cb);
    }

    @Override
    public void onSuccess(ArrayList<FriendSummaryDTO> result) {
    friendSummaries = result;
      sortFriendSummaryDTO();
      display.setData(toStringList(friendSummaries));
        eventBus.fireEvent(new FriendListChangedEvent(friendSummari
es));
    }
    ...
  }
```

This way of performing a Remote Procedure Call will be introduced later in this chapter. The important part for now is in the `onSuccess()` method, which is called when the Remote Procedure Call completes successfully. It sorts and sends a list of friends as strings to the view by calling `display.setData()`. Then it proceeds to send the event `FriendListChangedEvent` on the event bus.

Presenters listening to this event type will pick it up and process it accordingly. In *Connectr*, the message list presenter `MessageListPresenter` is listening to these events and will refresh its messages list based on the updated friend list.

## Responding to user interface events

To receive user clicks, the `FriendListPresenter` class needs to bind to the user interface buttons and links. This is done via a `bind` method:

```
...
public void bind() {
    // Bind view
    display.getAddButton().addClickHandler(new ClickHandler() {
      public void onClick(ClickEvent event) {
        eventBus.fireEvent(new FriendAddEvent());
      }
    });

    if (display.getList() != null)
     display.getList().addClickHandler(new ClickHandler() {
        public void onClick(ClickEvent event) {
            int propClicked = display.getClickedRow(event);
            GWT.log("Friend list clicked");
            if (propClicked >= 0) {
              GWT.log("Friend list property button clicked");
              ClickPoint point = display.getClickedPoint(event);
              FriendSummaryDTO friend = friendSummaries
                  .get(propClicked);
              eventBus.fireEvent(new ShowFriendPopupEvent(friend,
    point));
            } else {
              GWT.log("Friend list check box clicked");
              selectedRows = display.getSelectedRows();
              fireFriendListChangeEvent();
            }
          }
        });

    // Listen to events
    eventBus.addHandler(FriendUpdatedEvent.TYPE,
        new FriendUpdatedEventHandler() {
          @Override
          public void onFriendUpdated(FriendUpdatedEvent event) {
            fetchFriendSummaryDTO();
          }
```

```
      });

    eventBus.addHandler(FriendDeletedEvent.TYPE,
        new FriendDeletedEventHandler() {
          @Override
          public void onFriendDeleted(FriendDeletedEvent event) {
            fetchFriendSummaryDTO();
          }
        });
  }
...
```

The previous code shows the presenter adding click handlers to user interface components.

1.  First we add a click handler to the **+new** button:

    ```
    display.getAddButton().addClickHandler(new ClickHandler() {...
    ```

2.  When clicked, it will fire a `FriendAddEvent`.

    ```
    eventBus.fireEvent(new FriendAddEvent());
    ```

Once fired, the presenter listening to this type of event will kick in and open a friend input form.

1.  In order to catch clicks on the friends list we add a click handler using the same mechanism:

    ```
    display.getList().addClickHandler(new ClickHandler() {...
    ```

2.  When a user clicks on the friend list, we first check if the property button was clicked by checking the `propClicked` variable:

    ```
    int propClicked = display.getClickedRow(event);
      if(propClicked >=0)..
    ```

3.  We then assign the x and y coordinates of the click into a `point` variable and fire a `ShowFriendPopupEvent` along with the friend info and the click coordinates.

    ```
    eventBus.fireEvent(new ShowFriendPopupEvent(friend, point));
    ```

4.  `propClicked` triggers a friend information popup window to open up at the location indicated by the `point` object.

5. Finally, if the user click was not located on a property button, it was therefore on a checkbox. We gather the select rows into `selectedRows` and fire a `FriendListChangedEvent` that will trigger a refresh of the message list.

```
if(propClicked >=0)...
// Property button clicked
} else {
    GWT.log("Friend list check box clicked");
    selectedRows = display.getSelectedRows();
    fireFriendListChangeEvent();
}
```

# Listening to the event bus

As the friends list gets updated, `FriendListPresenter` receives the updates by listening to the Event Bus.

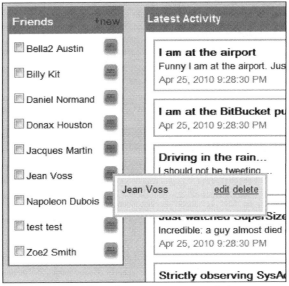

Figure 6: Friend's property popup window

More specifically, since `FriendPopupPresenter` and `FriendEditPresenter` can modify the content of the friend list, `FriendListPresenter` has to listen to friend updates and deletion events to keep its list up-to-date. The two events in charge of conveying this information are `FriendUpdateEvent` and `FriendDeleteEvent` respectively.

Therefore, we add an event bus handler for both these events in the
`FriendEditPresenter` class:

```
...
  public void bind() {
    // Bind view
    ...
    // Listen to events
    eventBus.addHandler(FriendUpdatedEvent.TYPE, new
FriendUpdatedEventHandler() {
      @Override
      public void onFriendUpdated(FriendUpdatedEvent event) {
        fetchFriendSummaryDTO();
      }
    });

      eventBus.addHandler(FriendDeletedEvent.TYPE, new
FriendDeletedEventHandler() {
      @Override
      public void onFriendDeleted(FriendDeletedEvent event) {
        fetchFriendSummaryDTO();
      }
    });
  }
```

When one of these events occurs, `FriendPopupPresenter` triggers a call to
`fetchFriendSummaryDTO()` that returns a fresh list of friends.

# Integrating UiBinder views into MVP

UiBinder is a great way to further compartmentalize view templates from their own
logic. However, if one uses all the power of UiBinder, such as binding events to
views, it can add considerable complexity to the MVP architecture. Therefore, most
views in *Connectr* use only the templating capability of UiBinder. Doing so makes it a
natural fit in our MVP pattern.

Let's examine how `FriendPopupPresenter` builds a popup window for a specified
friend using UiBinder in an MVP triad.

1. The popup window user interface comes from a UIBinder template
   `FriendPopupView.ui.xml` as follows:

   ```
   ...
   <ui:UiBinder xmlns:ui="urn:ui:com.google.gwt.uibinder"
     ...
     <g:HTMLPanel styleName='{style.popup}'>
   ```

```
      <div class='{style.button}'>
         <g:Anchor href='javascript:;' ui:field='edit'>edit</
g:Anchor>
          <g:Anchor href='javascript:;' ui:field='delete'>delete</
g:Anchor>
      </div>
      <div ui:field='nameDiv' />
      <g:Label ui:field='friendNameLabel' >Loading...</g:Label>
   </g:HTMLPanel>
</ui:UiBinder>
```

2.  The previous XML code shows the `FriendPopupView` UiBinder template implementing three widgets: two links (edit and delete) as well as a label that displays the friend's name as shown in the following image:

Figure 7: Friend's popup property window generated from its UiBinder definition

3.  Then in the view Java class, `FriendPopupView`, we associate the three widgets to their respective variables:

```
package com.metadot.book.connectr.client.view;

// Imports omitted for increased readability

public class FriendPopupView extends PopupPanel implements
FriendPopupPresenter.Display {

...
@UiField
Anchor edit, delete;
@UiField
Label friendNameLabel;
...
```

In the FriendPopupPresenter class, the popup window presenter declares the following Display Interface:

```
package com.metadot.book.connectr.client.presenter;
 // Import omitted for increased readability

public class FriendPopupPresenter implements Presenter {
  public interface Display {
    HasClickHandlers getEditButton();
```

```
      HasClickHandlers getDeleteButton();
      HasText getFriendNameLabel();
      void hide();
      void setName(String displayName);
      void setNameAndShow(String displayName, ClickPoint location);
      Widget asWidget();
   }
...
```

4.  In the class, `FriendPopupView`, the view implements this display by returning the UiBinder widget variables. Here is a partial implementation:

```
package com.metadot.book.connectr.client.view;
// Imports omitted for increased readabiity
...
public class FriendPopupView extends PopupPanel implements
FriendPopupPresenter.Display {
...
@Override
  public HasClickHandlers getDeleteButton() {
    return delete;
  }

  @Override
  public HasClickHandlers getEditButton() {
    return edit;
  }
  @Override
  public HasText getFriendNameLabel() {
    return friendNameLabel;
  }
...
```

5.  Finally, the presenter in the `FriendPopupPresenter` class binds the values returned by the display interface:

```
package com.metadot.book.connectr.client.presenter;
 // Import omitted for increased readabiity

public class FriendPopupPresenter implements Presenter {
...
public void bind() {
    this.display.getEditButton().addClickHandler(new
ClickHandler() {
        public void onClick(ClickEvent event) {
          display.hide();
```

```
        eventBus.fireEvent(new FriendEditEvent(friend.getId()));
      }
    });

    this.display.getDeleteButton().addClickHandler(new
ClickHandler() {
public void onClick(ClickEvent event) {
  display.hide();
  if (Window.confirm("Are you sure?")) {
    deleteFriend(friend.getId());
  }
}
}
}
```

# Events and the event bus

The concept of a GWT event bus is rather simple. An event bus is very much like a phone line application that objects can listen to. Objects just tell what kind of conversations they are interested in, by specifying which type of message events they want to receive.

In an application, modules get their information from different channels: RPC calls, files system, event bus, and many others. *Connectr* uses only two. The following diagram shows a *Connectr* MVP triad presentation layer getting its data from an event bus and from a service interface (for RPC calls) connected to the backend.

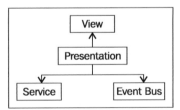

Figure 8:Presentation layer connection getting its data from a service or event bus.

*Connectr's* event bus is built on top of the GWT `SimpleEventBus` which manages event transport and handler management in a transparent fashion. The only thing we need to do to be able to use the GWT event bus is to create our own events. *Connectr* events extend `GwtEvent`. Here are some examples of the events *Connectr* is using:

- `LoginEvent`
- `LogoutEvent`
- `FriendDeleteEvent`
- `FriendEditEvent`

- FriendEditCancelledEvent
- RPCInEvent
- RPCOutEvent
- ShowFriendPopupEvent

# Creating a custom event class

Creating an event class is straightforward. As seen previously, when users click on the friend **edit** button in the friend popup window the application fires a FriendEditEvent. Let's examine how *Connectr's* FriendEditEvent class is built:

```
package com.metadot.book.connectr.client.event;

import com.google.gwt.event.shared.GwtEvent;

public class FriendEditEvent extends GwtEvent<FriendEditEventHandler>{
  public static Type<FriendEditEventHandler> TYPE = new
Type<FriendEditEventHandler>();
  private final String id;

  public FriendEditEvent(String id) {
    this.id = id;
  }

  public String getId() { return id; }

  @Override
  public Type<FriendEditEventHandler> getAssociatedType() {
    return TYPE;
  }

  @Override
  protected void dispatch(FriendEditEventHandler handler) {
    handler.onEditFriend(this);
  }
}
```

Typically, an event will contain a payload. Here the id of the friend being edited is the information the event object transports.

Since events need to override the `dispatch()` method, which takes an `EventHandler` as a parameter, we need to create one event handler for each event class. Therefore, `FriendEditEvent` needs the `FriendEditEventHandler` class:

```
package com.metadot.book.connectr.client.event;

import com.google.gwt.event.shared.EventHandler;

public interface FriendEditEventHandler extends EventHandler {
  void onEditFriend(FriendEditEvent event);
}
```

As we have demonstrated in this section, creating custom events is easy. It simply requires creating the event class and its associated event handler interface.

# Adding an application controller

*Connectr* uses an application controller that contains the application logic. Depending on the complexity of the application, there can be one or more controllers. *Connectr* needs only one. In *Connectr*, the controller is used mostly to handle view transitions via browser history changes.

# Adding support for browser history

Traditional non-AJAX web applications use different URLs to perform different actions. This allows users to use the browser's **back** and **forward** buttons and to **bookmark** pages of their choice.

Unfortunately, most AJAX apps use only one URL or few at best. This presents a number of usability challenges. The browser's back and forward buttons do not result in the expected action and bookmarking does not work.

Luckily, GWT provides a facility to implement browser history management. As a consequence, GWT apps, if programmed appropriately like *Connectr*, can be bookmarked to respond to the browser's back and forward buttons.

In this section, we are going to implement this feature for the *Connectr* controller.

# Introducing the browser history stack and navigation tokens

As users navigate from one URL to another, URLs get added to the browser history stack, allowing the browser back button to behave as expected. If the application button does not provide a specific URL, as is the case for most AJAX-driven buttons, GWT provides the capability to programmatically add tokens to the browser stack.

For example, when users click on a Friend **edit** button we programmatically add the `#edit` token to the browser stack via a call to `History.newItem("edit")`.

The resulting URL will be: `http://connectrapp.appspot.com/#edit`.

The application then gets alerted that the URL has changed and handles the action appropriately.

Let's see how this is implemented in *Connectr*.

# Implementing browser history management

It requires only a few steps to implement browser history using GWT.

1.  First we need to enable it in the application HMTL landing page, namely
    `ConnectrApp.html`:

    ```
    <iframe src="javascript:''" id="__gwt_historyFrame" tabIndex='-1'
    style="position:absolute;width:0;height:0;border:0"></iframe>
    ```

    Since browser history management is supposed to change user interface views, it is coded inside the application controller, named `AppController`.

2.  First the `AppController` class needs to implement the `ValueChangeHandler` interface:

    ```
    package com.metadot.book.connectr.client;

    // Imports omitted for increased readabiity

    public class AppController implements ValueChangeHandler<String> {
    ...
    ```

3. Then we create the `onValueChange` method required by the `ValueChangeHandler` interface, which will be called when the browser history changes.

```
...
public void onValueChange(ValueChangeEvent<String> event) {
  String token = event.getValue();
  if (token != null) {
    Presenter presenter = null;

    if (token.equals("list")) {
      presenter = new MessageListPresenter(messagesService,
      eventBus, new MessageListView());
      presenter.go(ConnectrApp.get().getMainPanel());
      return;
      } else if (token.equals("add")) {
      presenter = new FriendEditPresenter(friendService, evenBus,
new FriendEditView());
      presenter.go(ConnectrApp.get().getMainPanel());
      return;
...
```

4. Finally, the controller needs to subscribe to the history events so that it can receive them:

```
private void bind() {
  History.addValueChangeHandler(this);
...
```

This allows the controller method `onValueChange` to be called in case of changes to the browser's history stack.

Now the application can handle the **back** and **forward** browser buttons. The last thing to be implemented is the application startup behavior.

# Bootstrapping the browser history at application startup

When users first land on the application home page they are likely to be at `http://connectrapp.appspot.com/`, which is the base domain name of the application. However, the application displays the friend and message list only when the URL points to `http://connectrapp.appspot.com/#list`. Therefore, we need to automatically add the `#list` token if there are no tokens in the URL. Otherwise users won't see the expected friend and message list. This is implemented in the `go` method of the `ApplicationController` class:

```
public void go() {

    if (History.getToken().equals("")) {
      History.newItem("list");
    } else {
      History.fireCurrentHistoryState();
    }
}
```

This triggers a call to `onValueChange()`, which results in the display of the appropriate information.

*Connectr* is now equipped with a browser history management facility that greatly enhances the application usability.

# Centralizing RPC calls for better handling and usability and reliability

In this section, we introduce a **centralized Remote Procedure Call class** that brings three major improvements to our application:

- The capability to show **a loading indicator** when the application is busy waiting for the backend
- The ability to **retry failed calls** automatically
- A facility **to centralize the handling of exceptions** sent by the backend

# Introducing an encompassing RPC class

To achieve our goals, we need to centralize all the Remote Procedure Calls into a
higher-level class named RPCCall:

```
package com.metadot.book.connectr.client.helper;

// import omitted for increased readabiity

public abstract class RPCCall<T> implements AsyncCallback<T> {
protected abstract void callService(AsyncCallback<T> cb);
private void call(final int retriesLeft) {
    onRPCOut();

    callService(new AsyncCallback<T>() {
      public void onFailure(Throwable caught) {
        onRPCIn();
        GWT.log(caught.toString(), caught);
        try {
          throw caught;
        } catch (InvocationException invocationException) {
          if (retriesLeft <= 0) {
            RPCCall.this.onFailure(invocationException);
          } else {
            call(retriesLeft - 1); // retry call
          }
        } catch (IncompatibleRemoteServiceException
remoteServiceException) {
          Window.alert("The app maybe out of date. Reload this
page in your browser.");
        } catch (SerializationException serializationException) {
          Window.alert("A serialization error occurred. Try
again.");
        } catch (NotLoggedInException e) {
          // User not logged in. Redirect to login page
        } catch (RequestTimeoutException e) {
          Window.alert("This is taking too long, try again");
        } catch (Throwable e) {// application exception
          RPCCall.this.onFailure(e);
        }
      }

      public void onSuccess(T result) {
        onRPCIn();
        RPCCall.this.onSuccess(result);
```

```
      }
   });
}

private void onRPCIn() {
   ConnectrApp.get().getEventBus().fireEvent(new RPCInEvent());
}

private void onRPCOut() {
   ConnectrApp.get().getEventBus().fireEvent(new RPCOutEvent());
}

public void retry(int retryCount) {
   call(retryCount);
}
}
```

Let's see how this code accomplishes our goals.

# Displaying a loading indicator when the app is busy

Waiting for an application to respond is usually a frustrating experience if it lasts more than a few dozen milliseconds. When calls last longer it is important to give users visual feedback telling them the application is working on their behalf.

When *Connectr* is busy getting information from the backend it displays a loading indicator showing a **Working hard** message as shown in the following screenshot:

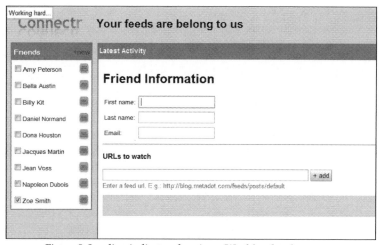

Figure 9: Loading indicator showing a **Working hard** message

Looking at the RPCCall **class,** we see that RPCInEvent and RPCOutEvent events are fired via the onRPCOut() and onRPCComIn() methods for each incoming and outgoing communication.

Since the loading indicator is managed by the BusyIndicator presenter and view, its presenter needs to subscribe to these events as shown in the BusyIndicatorPresenter class:

```
package com.metadot.book.connectr.client.presenter;

// Imports omitted for increased readabiity

public class BusyIndicatorPresenter implements Presenter {
...
  public void bind() {
    eventBus.addHandler(RPCInEvent.TYPE, new RPCInEventHandler() {
      @Override
      public void onRPCIn(RPCInEvent event) {
          outCount = outCount > 0 ? --outCount : 0;
        if (outCount <= 0) {
          display.hide();
        }
      }
    });
    eventBus.addHandler(RPCOutEvent.TYPE, new RPCOutEventHandler() {
        @Override
      public void onRPCOut(RPCOutEvent event) {
          outCount++;
          display.show();
      }
    });
    }
  ...
```

The previous code shows BusyIndicatorPresenter subscribing to RPCInEvent and RPCOutEvent. When a call is made to the backend, RPCCall fires RPCOutEvent and BusyIndicatorPresenter pops up a **Working hard** message. When a response from the backend is received, RPCInEvent is fired by RPCCall. BusyIndicatorPresenter receives the event and hides the message.

In order to keep track of simultaneous communications, we increment the counter outCount when we emit a request and decrement it when the answer is received. This allows us to display the loading messages as long as there is an outstanding communication request waiting for its answer.

From a user interface standpoint, BusyIndicatorView class is a simple extension of the GWT PopupPanel class that provides the facility to show, hide, and animate a popup window. By default, it will show a **Working hard** message but this can be changed during the class instantiation.

```
package com.metadot.book.connectr.client.view;

//Import omitted for increased readability

public class BusyIndicatorView extends PopupPanel implements
BusyIndicatorPresenter.Display{
  private Label message = new Label("Working hard...");

  public BusyIndicatorView() {
    setAnimationEnabled(false);
    add(message);
  }

  public BusyIndicatorView(String msg) {
    this();
    message.setText(msg);
  }

  @Override
  public Widget asWidget() {
    return this;
  }
}
```

In this section, we have seen how the *Connectr*-centralized asynchronous call class RPCCall displays a loading message when the application is making a call to the backend. An improvement left to the reader to implement would be to prevent the loading message from displaying during the first 100ms of an RPCCall in order to avoid unnecessary messages popping up for calls that complete quickly.

# Catching server exceptions

One of the goals of a centralized RPC class is to handle exceptions coming from the backend. Since GWT propagates serialized exceptions from the backend to the client, RPCCall has the opportunity to intercept some types of exceptions. For example, it is a good idea to catch network and system failures as well as exceptions sent by the backend when a user is not logged in. It is implemented in RPCCall as follows:

```
package com.metadot.book.connectr.client.helper;

// Import omitted for increased readability

public abstract class RPCCall<T> implements AsyncCallback<T> {
...
```

```
private void call(final int retriesLeft) {
    onRPCOut();
    callService(new AsyncCallback<T>() {
      public void onFailure(Throwable caught) {
        onRPCIn();
        GWT.log(caught.toString(), caught);
        try {
          throw caught;
        } catch (InvocationException invocationException) {
          if(caught.getMessage().equals(SharedContants.LOGGED_OUT)){
              ConnectrApp.get().getEventBus().fireEvent(new
LogoutEvent());
              return;
          }

          if (retriesLeft <= 0) {
            RPCCall.this.onFailure(invocationException);
          } else {
            call(retriesLeft - 1); // retry call
          }
        } catch (IncompatibleRemoteServiceException
remoteServiceException) {
          Window.alert("The app maybe out of date. Reload this page in
your browser.");
        } catch (SerializationException serializationException) {
          Window.alert("A serialization error occurred. Try again.");
        } catch (NotLoggedInException e) {
          ConnectrApp.get().getEventBus().fireEvent(new
LogoutEvent());
        } catch (RequestTimeoutException e) {
          Window.alert("This is taking too long, try again");
        } catch (Throwable e) {// application exception
          RPCCall.this.onFailure(e);
        }
      }
    }
...
```

To process an exception coming from the backend, RPCCall re-throws it by calling throw caught and tries to catch it back with a catch statement. If the re-thrown exception type is not in the list of catchable exceptions, it is then propagated to the class which initiated the call by calling RPCCall.this.onFailure(e).

# Retrying a call after failure

As we have seen in the previous section, since RPCCall allows centralizing **error handling,** there is an opportunity to choose to **retry calls when an error occurs.** RPCCall **achieves this** by calling itself recursively several times till the call succeeds. Here, we show how the RPCCall class retries calls only when it catches an InvocationException, which is a network error:

```
private void call(final int retriesLeft) {
  onRPCOut();
  callService(new AsyncCallback<T>() {
    public void onFailure(Throwable caught) {
    onRPCIn();
    GWT.log(caught.toString(), caught);
      try {
      throw caught;
    } catch (InvocationException invocationException) {
      if (retriesLeft <= 0) {
        RPCCall.this.onFailure(invocationException);
    } else {
        call(retriesLeft - 1); // retry call
      }
  ...
```

We avoid retrying an infinite number of times by allowing caller methods to specify a maximum number of retries via the variable, retriesLeft. RPCCall will retry on failure until retriesLeft is less than one, at which point RPCCall gives up and sends the exception to the calling class by invoking:

```
RPCCall.this.onFailure(invocationException);
```

# Putting it all together

Now that we have seen how our centralized RPC management class RPCCall works, we can look at a concrete implementation example. Here is how the FriendPopupPresenter class implements RPCCall in order to delete a friend object:

```
package com.metadot.book.connectr.client.presenter;

// Imports omitted for increased readabilty

public class FriendPopupPresenter implements Presenter {

...
private void deleteFriend(final String id) {
```

```
new RPCCall<String>() {
  @Override
  protected void callService(AsyncCallback<String> cb) {
      friendsService.deleteFriend(id, cb);
    }
  @Override
  public void onSuccess(String idDeleted) {
    eventBus.fireEvent(new FriendDeletedEvent());
  }
  @Override
  public void onFailure(Throwable caught) {
    Window.alert("An error occurred: " + caught.toString());
  }   }.retry(3);   }
```

As for GWT RPC calls, `RPCCall` must implement `onSuccess` and `onFailure`. Additionally, `RPCCall` requires one more method to be implemented: `callService`. It specifies which service to use. Finally, we specify that the call should be retried up to three times by invoking `retry(3)`.

In case of error, the `onFailure` method catches the exception and displays the error message, **An error occurred**.

# MVP Development with Activities and Places

As we have seen in the previous MVP section, the MVP pattern that we described provides a great way to structure code, but requires view navigation and history management (which allows users to bookmark an app at a certain state) as well as event management, which allows different elements of the application to signal state changes to other listening elements.

Google Web Toolkit 2.1 introduces a new MVP framework called **MVP with Activities and Places**, which simplifies management of certain aspects of this model. This framework encapsulates some of the low-level code plumbing with higher-level classes that can be easier to use. However, Activities and Places should not be viewed as a replacement for the traditional MVP pattern presented above; the former deals with views attached to URLs, whereas the latter allows more flexibility, and can be used as a general-purpose UI design pattern, encompassing complex UI design scenarios such as nested views.

In this section we cover the following topics:

- A comparison of traditional MVP versus MVP with **Activities and Places**
- An explanation of Activities and Places
- Introduction of the **browser factory**, which allows a deferred binding mechanism to support alternate views, for example for iPhone and Android devices.

The example application we build in this section is called *ProfileMVP*. It is based on Google's "HelloMVP" example. We modified it to provide a more realistic example, and cover the use of browser factories that use deferred binding to load views for multiple devices— such as Android devices, iPhones, and iPads— in a transparent fashion.

You can download the `ProfileMVP` source code from the Packt website.

# Building a basic application

*ProfileMVP* is a minimal application that displays a user name on the main page and provides a link to allow users to modify it in an edit page. Here is how it looks on a mobile device:

Figure 10: ProfileMVP application as seen on mobile phones

# Traditional MVP versus MVP with Activities and Places

Both the 'traditional' MVP pattern described previously in this chapter, and the GWT2.1 Activities and Places framework, follow a **triad** model. As shown in the figure below, the concept of **Model** remains unchanged with Activities and Places, the **Presenter** is roughly equivalent to an **Activity**, and a **View** becomes a **Place**. A Place is a view with state. For example, a Place might be an email client inbox view showing a given email. Places are bookmarkable.

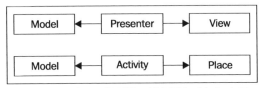

Figure 11 : comparing traditional MVP with MVP with Activities and Places

Let's see how we can create an example application using MVP with Activities and Places.

# Moving parts of ProfileMVP

In this section, we introduce new concepts that we loosely refer to as the app's "moving parts". While they are simple to understand, there are many parts to deal with, and putting them together requires quite a bit of boilerplate coding.

## Activities

Activities are controllers. They work very much like we have seen previously. Here is the profile view activity:

```
package com.profilemvp.client.activity;

import com.profilemvp.client.place.ProfilePlace;
import com.profilemvp.client.ui.ProfileView;
import com.google.gwt.activity.shared.AbstractActivity;
import com.google.gwt.event.shared.EventBus;
import com.google.gwt.place.shared.Place;
import com.google.gwt.user.client.ui.AcceptsOneWidget;
import com.profilemvp.client.BrowserFactory

public class ProfileActivity extends AbstractActivity implements
    ProfileView.Presenter {
  private BrowserFactory browserFactory;
  private String name;
```

```
    public ProfileActivity(ProfilePlace place, BrowserFactory
browserFactory) {
        this.name = place.getProfileName();
        this.browserFactory = browserFactory;
    }

    @Override
    public void start(AcceptsOneWidget containerWidget, EventBus
eventBus) {
        ProfileView profileView = browserFactory.getProfileView();
        profileView.setName(name);
        profileView.setPresenter(this);
        containerWidget.setWidget(profileView.asWidget());
    }

    public void goTo(Place place) {
        browserFactory.getPlaceController().goTo(place);
    }

    @Override
    public String mayStop() {
        return "Are you sure you want to leave this view?";
    }

}
```

This activity, ProfileActivity, makes use of the com.profilemvp.client.
BrowserFactory.BrowserFactory interface, which provides access to the interface
to the view. Using an interface instead of a class allows us to swap classes based on
which kind of browser (e.g. an Android phone) is requesting the view. Later in this
section, we will show how to implement a view for mobile devices.

The constructor parameters are optional and can be modified as needed. The start
method is invoked by the activity manager. The method prepares the view and
presenter, then inserts the view inside its container.

Finally, a useful feature of the AbstractActivity class is the ability to warn users
when leaving a view. This is done with the mayStop method. If the string returned is
null, then no warning will be displayed.

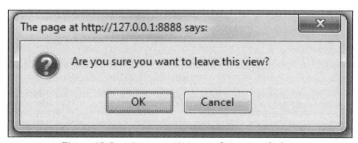

Figure 12: Leaving an activity confirmation dialog.

# Places and the Place History Mapper

**Places** correspond to a URL associated with a view. GWT provides a default naming scheme, which is the class name of the activity followed by a semicolon and optional parameters. For example,

`http://<yourdomain>/#ProfileEditPlace:supercobra` corresponds to the view editing activity of the `ProfileEditPlace` class, with `supercobra` as a parameter, which corresponds to the value of the name being edited.

Here is how a place is created:

```
package com.profilemvp.client.place;

import com.google.gwt.place.shared.Place;
import com.google.gwt.place.shared.PlaceTokenizer;

public class ProfilePlace extends Place {
  private String profileName;

  public ProfilePlace(String token) {
    this.profileName = token;
  }

  public String getProfileName() {
    return profileName;
  }

  public static class Tokenizer implements
PlaceTokenizer<ProfilePlace> {
    @Override public String getToken(ProfilePlace place) {
      return place.getProfileName();
    }

    @Override public ProfilePlace getPlace(String token) {
      return new ProfilePlace(token);
    }
  }
}
```

Furthermore, a `Place` class must implement a `Tokenizer` inner class, which provides a way to serialize the place state into a URL token.

Once the application places are defined, they need to be specified in the com.google.gwt.place.shared.PlaceHistoryMapper interface via the @WithTokenizers annotation:

```
package com.profilemvp.client.mvp;

import com.google.gwt.place.shared.PlaceHistoryMapper;
import com.google.gwt.place.shared.WithTokenizers;
import com.profilemvp.client.place.ProfileEditPlace;
import com.profilemvp.client.place.ProfilePlace;

@WithTokenizers( { ProfilePlace.Tokenizer.class, ProfileEditPlace.
Tokenizer.class })
public interface AppPlaceHistoryMapper extends PlaceHistoryMapper {
}
```

# Views

*ProfileMVP* implements a profile and an edit view, named ProfileViewImpl and ProfileEditViewImpl respectively. They are constructed with a UI Binder template file in XML and an associated Java class that contains the view logic.

Figure 13: The profile view

The profile view is coded against an interface, so we can interchange it based on browser abilities. The interface defines a name and a presenter.

```java
public interface ProfileView extends IsWidget {
  void setName(String name);
  void setPresenter(Presenter listener);

  public interface Presenter {
    void goTo(Place place);
  }
}
```

The default view is as follows:

```java
package com.profilemvp.client.ui;

// Imports omitted

public class ProfileViewImpl extends Composite implements ProfileView
{
  private static ProfileViewImplUiBinder uiBinder =
    GWT.create(ProfileViewImplUiBinder.class);
  interface ProfileViewImplUiBinder extends UiBinder<Widget,
ProfileViewImpl> {
  }

  @UiField SpanElement nameSpan;
  @UiField Anchor editLink;
  private Presenter listener;
  private String name;

  public ProfileViewImpl() {
    initWidget(uiBinder.createAndBindUi(this));
  }

  @Override
  public void setName(String name) {
    this.name = name;
    nameSpan.setInnerText(name);
  }

  @UiHandler("editLink")
  void onClickGoodbye(ClickEvent e) {
    listener.goTo(new ProfileEditPlace(name));
  }

  @Override
  public void setPresenter(Presenter listener) {
    this.listener = listener;
  }
}
```

and the associated UI Binder template:

```
<!DOCTYPE ui:UiBinder SYSTEM "http://dl.google.com/gwt/DTD/xhtml.ent">
<ui:UiBinder xmlns:ui="urn:ui:com.google.gwt.uibinder"
       xmlns:g="urn:import:com.google.gwt.user.client.ui">
  <ui:style>
    .important {font-weight: bold;}
  </ui:style>
  <g:HTMLPanel>
  <h1>User Profile</h1>
  <hr/>
    Your name is:
    <span class="{style.important}" ui:field="nameSpan" />
    <g:Anchor ui:field="editLink" text=" - Edit your profile"></
g:Anchor>
    <hr/>
  </g:HTMLPanel>
</ui:UiBinder>
```

The edit profile view is structured exactly the same way, with a UIBinder UI declaration `ProfileEditViewImpl.ui.xml` and `ProfileEditViewImpl.java` that implements its logic.

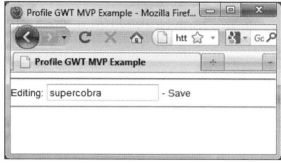

Figure 14: Edit profile view

Finally, we also created a different profile view for mobile devices. This view's files are named `ProfileViewMobileImpl.ui.xml` and `ProfileViewMobileImpl.java`. This view implementation is automatically used when *ProfileMVP* detects an iPhone, Android device, or iPad. To achieve this, we set up GWT **deferred binding** in the application configuration file `ProfileMVP.gwt.xml`. We will describe this configuration shortly, after we introduce `BrowserFactory`.

Figure 15: ProfileMVP supports different browser implementations via the deferred binding technique

# The Browser Factory

A Browser Factory is not part of MVP per se, but it is a useful complement to any GWT application that needs to support multiple browser versions, including mobile devices. Each Browser Factory implements `com.profilemvp.client.BrowserFactory`, and defines specific components for a given browser version, including the event bus, controller, and browser-specific views.

Typically there will be a default browser implementation like this one:

```
package com.profilemvp.client;

// Imports omitted

public class BrowserFactoryImpl implements BrowserFactory {
  private static final EventBus eventBus = new SimpleEventBus();
  private static final PlaceController placeController = new
PlaceController(eventBus);
  private static final ProfileView profileView = new
ProfileViewImpl();
  private static final ProfileEditView profileEditView = new
ProfileEditViewImpl();
```

```
  @Override
  public EventBus getEventBus(){
    return eventBus;
  }

  @Override
  public ProfileView getProfileView(){
    return profileView;
  }

  @Override
  public PlaceController getPlaceController(){
    return placeController;
  }

  @Override
  public ProfileEditView getGoodbyeView(){
    return profileEditView;
  }

}
```

And there will be one or more browser specific implementations such as this one for mobile devices:

```
package com.profilemvp.client;

// Imports omitted

public class BrowserFactoryMobileImpl implements BrowserFactory {
  private static final EventBus eventBus = new SimpleEventBus();
  private static final PlaceController placeController = new
PlaceController(eventBus);
  private static final ProfileView profileView = new
ProfileViewMobileImpl();
  private static final ProfileEditView profileEditView = new
ProfileEditViewImpl();

  // Getters and setters omitted

}
```

Note that in our example, the only difference between the default browser implementation and the one for mobile users is that the latter implementation specifies a different profile view:

```
private static final ProfileView profileView =
  new ProfileViewMobileImpl();
```

Now the only thing required for **deferred binding** to work, is to configure the application so it uses the right browser implementation based on **automatic client detection**. This is discussed next.

# Adding deferred binding for iPhone and Android views

Deferred binding allows GWT clients to receive only the kind of code it is compatible with. In our example, an Android phone will receive only the view specific to mobile devices. The advantage is that the code downloaded a given client is much smaller, because it does not contain other browser-specific implementation.

To configure deferred binding, we need first to add the default implementation in `ProfileMVP.gwt.xml`:

```
<!-- Use BrowserFactoryImpl by default -->
<replace-with class="com.profilemvp.client.BrowserFactoryImpl">
  <when-type-is class="com.profilemvp.client.BrowserFactory" />
</replace-with>
```

Then we need to add a snippet of code that detects what browser is being used:

```
<!-- Smart phone detection -->
<define-property name="ismobile" values="yes,no" />
<property-provider name="ismobile"><![CDATA[
    return (navigator.userAgent.indexOf('iPhone') > -1 \
    || navigator.userAgent.indexOf('Android') > -1 \
    || navigator.userAgent.indexOf('iPad') > -1) ? 'yes' : 'no';
  ]]>
</property-provider>
```

In the above snippet, the property `ismobile` is set to `yes` when the browser user agent string contains the word `iPhone`, `Android` or `iPad`.

Finally we add a `replace-with` clause that instructs the application to use `BrowserFactoryMobileImpl` when `ismobile` is set to `yes`:

```
<replace-with class="com.profilemvp.client.
BrowserFactoryMobileImpl">
    <when-type-is class="com.profilemvp.client.BrowserFactory" />
     <when-property-is name="ismobile" value="yes" />
    </replace-with>
```

This completes the setup of deferred binding. Mobile users will now enjoy a specific view for their device.

# Activity mapper

We also need to create an activity mapper, which implements `com.google.gwt.activity.shared.ActivityMapper`. Its role is to instantiate Activities based on their Place. For our app, we define a class called `AppActivityMapper`:

```
package com.profilemvp.client.mvp;
// Imports omitted

public class AppActivityMapper implements ActivityMapper {

  private BrowserFactory browserFactory;

  public AppActivityMapper(BrowserFactory browserFactory) {
    super();
    this.browserFactory = browserFactory;
  }

  @Override public Activity getActivity(Place place) {
    if (place instanceof ProfilePlace)
      return new ProfileActivity((ProfilePlace) place,
browserFactory);
    else if (place instanceof ProfileEditPlace)
      return new ProfileEditActivity((ProfileEditPlace) place,
browserFactory);

    return null;
  }

}
```

The `AppActivityMapper` constructor takes a `BrowserFactory` instance as a parameter, so that the specifics of each browser implementation can be accessed.

# Putting the pieces together: the onModuleLoad method

Finally, the method onModuleLoad, located in our main application class ProfileMVP, assembles all the moving parts together and launches the default Place.

```
package com.profilemvp.client;

// Imports omitted

public class ProfileMVP implements EntryPoint {
  private Place defaultPlace = new ProfilePlace("supercobra");
  private SimplePanel appWidget = new SimplePanel();

  public void onModuleLoad() {
    // Browser factory for deferred binding
    BrowserFactory browserFactory = GWT.create(BrowserFactory.class);
    EventBus eventBus = browserFactory.getEventBus();
    PlaceController placeController = browserFactory.
getPlaceController();

    // Start ActivityManager
    ActivityMapper activityMapper =
      new AppActivityMapper(browserFactory);
    ActivityManager activityManager = new
ActivityManager(activityMapper, eventBus);
    activityManager.setDisplay(appWidget);

    // Start PlaceHistoryHandler
    AppPlaceHistoryMapper historyMapper =
      GWT.create(AppPlaceHistoryMapper.class);
    PlaceHistoryHandler historyHandler = new PlaceHistoryHandler(hist
oryMapper);
    historyHandler.register(placeController, eventBus, defaultPlace);

    RootPanel.get().add(appWidget);

    // Go to current URL or default place
    historyHandler.handleCurrentHistory();

    // Log user agent to see deferred binding at work
    GWT.log("User agent: " + Window.Navigator.getUserAgent());
  }
}
```

Since the GWT team did such a great job of explaining how the pieces fit together, we include an excerpt from the GWT documentation:

The `ActivityManager` keeps track of all Activities running within the context of one container widget. It listens for `PlaceChangeRequestEvents` and notifies the current activity when a new Place has been requested. If the current Activity allows the Place change (`Activity.onMayStop()` returns `null`) or the user allows it (by clicking on **OK** in the confirmation dialog), the `ActivityManager` discards the current Activity and starts the new one. In order to find the new one, it uses your app's `ActivityMapper` to obtain the Activity associated with the requested Place.

Along with the `ActivityManager`, two other GWT classes work to keep track of Places in your app. `PlaceController` initiates navigation to a new Place and is responsible for warning the user before doing so. `PlaceHistoryHandler` provides bi-directional mapping between Places and the URL. Whenever your app navigates to a new Place, the URL will be updated with the new token representing the Place so it can be bookmarked and saved in the browser history. Likewise, when the user clicks the back button or pulls up a bookmark, `PlaceHistoryHandler` ensures that your application loads the corresponding Place.

# Summary

In this chapter, we structured *Connectr* software architecture by implementing an MVP software pattern. We also added some key facilities that were needed for our application. We first added an Event Bus allowing software components to communicate among themselves. We explained how GWT helps programmers handle browser history management, by allowing users to use the back and forward browser buttons and allowing the app to be bookmark-able. We added an application controller that orchestrates application-wide view transitions. The application controller is also the home of the browser history management. We also introduced a centralized way to do asynchronous calls that provides centralized exception handling, automatic retries on errors, and also improves the application usability by displaying a loading message when the application is waiting for the backend to answer.

Finally, we covered an example of using the 'MVP with Activities and Places' framework, which was released with GWT 2.1.

The next chapter will focus exclusively on the backend. We'll add the capability to fetch friends' feeds using App Engine's built-in services.

# 7
# Background Processing and Feed Management

In this chapter, we will extend the functionality of *Connectr* by adding the ability to specify various feeds (say, a Twitter or blog stream) associated with a given friend's data, and to pull in the content for those feeds. As described in *Chapter 1, Introduction, Connectr* will display a stream of status information related to (some set of) a user's `Friends`. In this chapter, we will build the foundation of the server-side functionality that supports that feature. In the process, we'll use Servlets and some of the App Engine **services**—in particular, **URL Fetch** and the **Task Queue**—and look at how to support background processing asynchronously with client requests.

The chapter will focus on the server-side aspects of Friend feed management—specifying, creating, fetching, and updating feed information. Later chapters will build on these capabilities.

We have several objectives in the design of this new application functionality. We want the application to be responsive in displaying requested feeds, and to be robust to feed-related errors. Furthermore, we want it to support asynchronous and decoupled feed fetch while avoiding duplication of effort.

The approach that we'll take has several facets:

- We will use the App Engine URL Fetch service to grab the feed content. To do this, we will use the open source ROME RSS/Atom libraries. We'll use a conditional HTTP GET (where supported) so that feeds are re-fetched only if they have changed.

- We'll construct shared feed objects so that we don't duplicate effort if multiple `Friends` have the same feed specified for them, and we will design the feed objects so that it is efficient to retrieve the feeds associated with a given `Friend`.

- We will enable asynchronous background feed processing using the App Engine Task Queue, and define Servlets to update the feeds independent of any particular client request. This will allow focused, proactive feed updating to occur when the application is not busy at other tasks. In that way, less updating effort is likely to be required when a set of feeds are requested by the client.

- Our design will allow a small amount of latency in order to reduce workload: if a feed has just been checked within a given period of time, it will be served up without checking if it needs updating again. The application won't spend time retrying feeds with transient fetch errors, instead; it will just retain existing feed content, and try again the next time the feed is fetched.

# Overview of the chapter

This chapter uses the `ConnectrStage2` version of the *Connectr* app.

The first section, *Using Servlets in App Engine*, will provide an overview of App Engine Servlet support. Then, *Using migrations to evolve the Datastore* will discuss the need for data migrations and present an approach for managing data changes in a structured manner. We'll use this approach to migrate the Friend data in the Datastore to include a new field for feed URLs.

*Pulling in Feeds: The URL Fetch Service* will examine using the URL Fetch service via App Engine's `java.net.URLConnection` implementation, and describe what's required to add the third-party ROME libraries to the deployed application as well as the development environment.

Then, in *Using RSS/Atom feeds in the Connectr App*, we'll build the new data classes to support Friend feeds in *Connectr*. Finally, in *Enabling background feed updating and processing*, we will implement some feed management tasks using Servlets and the App Engine Task Queue.

# Using Servlets in App Engine

So far in *Connectr*, we've used `RemoteServiceServlet` to support client requests.

We can also build regular Servlets, and use them to directly support server-side admin or backend tasks, invoked asynchronously from any GWT RPC requests. For example, in this chapter we will build a Servlet to support the Datastore entity *migration*. We will also build Servlets that trigger an asynchronous background update of all the current RSS/Atom feeds associated with our application's `Friend` objects so that client requests require less work to be done.

These Servlets do not need to support GWT RPC. App Engine uses the Java Servlet API and our non-RPC Servlets will simply extend `javax.servlet.http.HttpServlet`; thus the Servlet API may be familiar to you already.

However, the App Engine imposes some limitations on Servlet behavior, which we will describe below. Note that `RemoteServiceServlet` extends `javax.servlet.http.HttpServlet` and is subject to the same limitations.

# Making your Servlets accessible—the deployment descriptor

If you've not used Java Servlets before, one of the first things to understand is the way in which a web request is connected to a Servlet. An application's **deployment descriptor** (DD) is used to map incoming web requests to the code that should handle the request. The deployment descriptor in your App Engine project is the `war/WEB-INF/web.xml` file.

The `web.xml` file can include pairs of `<servlet>` and `<servlet-mapping>` nodes, as shown in the following example. The `<servlet>` nodes associate a name with a given application class. The `<servlet-class>` is specified as the fully qualified name of the data class. In the example, the Servlet class is `packagepath.server.servlets.MigrationServlet`; where you would replace `packagepath` with your actual package path. The `<servlet>` node may also include the specification of Servlet initialization parameters.

```
<servlet>
  <servlet-name>Migration</servlet-name>
  <servlet-class>
    packagepath.server.servlets.MigrationServlet
  </servlet-class>
</servlet>
<servlet-mapping>
  <servlet-name>Migration</servlet-name>
  <url-pattern>/migration</url-pattern>
</servlet-mapping>
```

 See `http://www.oracle.com/technetwork/java/index-jsp-135475.html` for more information about the Java Servlet API.

**[ 219 ]**

Then, the `<servlet-mapping>` nodes associate a given Servlet *name* with a URL pattern. A wildcard * is allowed at the beginning or end of the pattern. The order in which the mappings are defined is significant: the first matching mapping is used. In the previous example, we are mapping the `/migration` URL request to the `Migration` Servlet name, which indicates the `MigrationServlet` class. So now, when we access the URL `http://<your-domain>/migration`, the `MigrationServlet` code will be run.

In this chapter, we will be creating several Servlets, and so we will make several such additions to `web.xml`.

You will also notice a `<welcome-file-list>` node in `web.xml`. This specifies which page to load when the user accesses a path that represents a `war` directory (that is not already explicitly mapped to a Servlet). For *Connectr*, we specify to load `ConnectrApp.html`, which in turn loads the GWT module for our application. The `<welcome-file-list>` node may contain multiple `<welcome-file>` children. If there are more than one, they are checked in the order listed.

The `web.xml` file supports other configuration options, including support for security and authentication, and we will return to it again later.

> The Tomcat `web.xml` reference guide is a good general source for further information about the `web.xml` standard: `http://wiki.metawerx.net/wiki/Web.xml`.
>
> There are a few `web.xml` features not supported in App Engine; see `http://code.google.com/appengine/docs/java/config/webxml.html` for details.

# Defining a Servlet

A Servlet class is defined by extending `javax.servlet.http.HttpServlet`.

```java
import java.io.IOException;
import javax.servlet.http.*;
@SuppressWarnings("serial")
public class YourServlet extends HttpServlet {

public void doPost(HttpServletRequest req, HttpServletResponse resp)
    throws IOException {
        //… Process the request…
    }
  …
}
```

HttpServlet supports all of the HTTP methods (GET, POST, PUT, DELETE, and HEAD). The doGet and doPost methods (which will be our focus here) are called upon receipt of a GET or POST HTTP request respectively. All are passed the HttpServletRequest req and HttpServletResponse resp objects, as shown in the previous example. The req parameter provides access to the request information and the resp parameter is used to generate the Servlet's response.

If the method corresponding to the HTTP request type is not implemented by the HttpServlet subclass, that request type is not handled by the app (more exactly, the default implementation generates a 405 error). This means that it is a bit more secure not to define a doGet method if the Servlet should be accessed only via POST requests—this prevents casual access to such Servlets.

In addition, it is possible to restrict a Servlet's access only to users logged in with a Google Account or only to application admins, by adding <security-constraint> specifications to the web.xml file. We will show some such examples in the following sections.

## Servlet requests and responses

The typical flow of control for a Servlet is to access information about the incoming HTTP request (for example, the parameters and headers that were sent), do some processing, and then generate a response.

```java
import java.io.IOException;
import javax.servlet.http.*;

@SuppressWarnings("serial")
public class YourServlet extends HttpServlet {


public void doPost(HttpServletRequest req, HttpServletResponse resp)
  throwsIOException {

String p1 = req.getParameter("param1");
String name = req.getParameter("name");
String rangestring = req.getParameter("num");
String resultstring;
    ...
resp.setContentType("text/plain");
resp.getWriter().println(resultstring);
    }
    ...
}
```

You can obtain the request parameters using the `getParameter` method of the `HttpServletRequest` object, as shown in the previous example. For example, when a request is sent to the URL:

```
http://<yourdomain>/yourservlet?num=123&param1=abc&name=bob
```

the following line of code:

```
String p1 = req.getParameter("param1");
```

would set `p1` to the string `abc`.

If `getParameter()` accesses a parameter that was not provided in the request, its value will be `null`. Otherwise, `getParameter()` always returns a `String`. So, if you wanted to use the `num` parameter as an integer, you would need to first parse it, for example:

```
int range = Integer.parseInt(rangestring);.
```

You can access HTTP header information by calling the `getHeader` method. For example,

```
String host = req.getHeader("Host");
```

would obtain the name of the host that made the request.

## Generating a response

Generate a Servlet response by writing to the `HttpServletResponse` object. If an uncaught exception is thrown by the Servlet processing, this generates a server error of status 500. (The `RemoteServiceServlet` subclass instead overrides `doPost` to swallow all exceptions, logs them in the `ServletContext`, and returns a `GENERIC_FAILURE_MSG` response with status code 500).

To send character data, use the `PrintWriter` object returned by `getWriter()`, as shown in the code above. To send binary data in the response, use the `ServletOutputStream` returned by `getOutputStream()`.

With App Engine, it is not possible to "stream" the response; the response will be sent in one single chunk when the Servlet method returns. The Servlets will send compressed content, if so requested by the client. Clients can receive zipped content by specifying both `Accept-Encoding` and `User-Agent` headers with a value of `gzip`.

# App Engine Servlet limitations

App Engine imposes some limitations on Servlet use.

- Servlets time out after 30 seconds. If a Servlet has not generated a response after 30 seconds, it will throw a `com.google.apphosting.api.DeadlineExceededException`. This exception can be caught in order to do some brief cleanup before exiting. If the exception is not caught, a server error of status 500 is returned. If it is caught, but cleanup does not occur within a short interval, an uncatchable exception is thrown (and an error is returned).

- App Engine imposes a 10 MB limit on the size of both the request and response data. Recall that entities have a size limit of 1MB, so it is possible to receive request data that cannot be stored wholesale in a single entity.

- App Engine puts a limit on the maximum number of simultaneous dynamic requests allowed—it is approximately 30.

 If you have a paid account, you can request that this limit on the maximum number of requests be raised. *Chapter 11* will discuss the App Engine billing model.

# Restricting access to a Servlet

At times, you may want to restrict Servlet access to only *site* administrators, or to only users who have logged in using a Google Account. This can be specified via `<security-constraint>` declarations in the `war/WEB-INF/web.xml` file.

```
<security-constraint>
 <web-resource-collection>
  <url-pattern>/migration</url-pattern>
 </web-resource-collection>
 <auth-constraint>
  <role-name>admin</role-name>
 </auth-constraint>
</security-constraint>

<security-constraint>
  <web-resource-collection>
    <url-pattern>/prefs/*</url-pattern>
  </web-resource-collection>
  <auth-constraint>
    <role-name>*</role-name>
  </auth-constraint>
</security-constraint>
```

These declarations have the structure shown in the previous code snippet, where a URL pattern and a role are specified.

With the `admin<role-name>` specification, the URL `/migration` will be accessible only to admin users.

You, as the creator of the App Engine application, are an admin. Via the App Engine Admin Console, you can designate other people as developers of a given application, and they too will have admin access when logged in. See the **Permissions** link in the left navigation bar of the Admin Console.

If a user has not yet authenticated as an admin, they will be met with an App Engine-generated login window when they try to access a Servlet with admin-level protection. In the development environment, you will see a "mock" login page (as in Figure 1). It doesn't matter what e-mail address you use, just be sure to check the admin box.

Figure 1: The "mock" login page in the development environment

When accessing an admin URL in a deployed application, you will see an actual Google login page generated by App Engine, and here you will need to authenticate as an actual admin for the application.

A `*` `role-name` in the `<security-constraint>` declaration indicates any user authenticated with a Google account. Thus, in the `web.xml` example above, URLs that match the `/prefs/*` pattern will only be available to users who have authenticated with a Google Account login. When you access a "login-required" URL in your development environment, you will again see the window of Figure 1, though this time you will not need to check the "admin" box to obtain access. When accessing such a URL in a deployed application, you will need to log in with a Google Account to access the URL.

The App Engine Task Queue can access admin-only URLs directly. Thus, if you have developed a Servlet that should be invoked only as a task action, you should declare an admin-role <security-constraint> for it. We will show several examples of employing the admin security constraint in upcoming sections.

We will revisit authentication in *Chapter 8, Authentication using Facebook and Twitter OAuth, and Google Accounts,* when we add a user login and account framework to *Connectr.* However, a nice thing about this model is that these protections work regardless—essentially, much of a user account framework is already in place and supported by App Engine, if you want to use Google Accounts for authentication.

# Sessions

App Engine includes an implementation of **sessions** (`javax.servlet.http. HttpSession`), but you must explicitly enable this feature. To do so, add:

`<sessions-enabled>true</sessions-enabled>`

to `war/WEB-INF/appengine-web.xml`.

You can then access the `HttpSession` object via the `getSession()` method of the `HttpServletRequest` object as usual for Servlets.

>  See `http://download.oracle.com/docs/cd/ E17802_01/products/products/servlet/2.5/ docs/servlet-2_5-mr2/javax/servlet/http/ HttpSession.html` for more information about sessions.

To access the session from a `RemoteServiceServlet` (such as `FriendsServiceImpl`), do the following to get the `request` object:

`HttpServletRequest request = this.getThreadLocalRequest();`

You can then access the session as shown previously:

```
HttpSession session = request.getSession();
```

The App Engine implementation of sessions uses both the Datastore and Memcache service (which we will introduce in *Chapter 9*). This is so that the session data will be properly shared across the multiple JVMs that may be serving the app requests. Thus, anything that you store in the session must implement `java. io.Serializable`. Note that because session information is being serialized/ deserialized and loaded to/from the Datastore, heavy use of the session in App Engine can potentially impact performance if you are storing lots of data.

In the Datastore, session information will have the *kind* _ah_SESSION. In Memcache, the session information keys will be prefixed with _ahs.

# The JRE whitelist and system restrictions

App Engine apps run in a "sandbox", which imposes a number of restrictions in order to increase application security and robustness.

App Engine supports only a subset of the Java JRE classes, called the **whitelist**. You can find the list here: http://code.google.com/appengine/docs/java/jrewhitelist.html.

Threading is not supported by App Engine, nor are system calls. The only allowed network requests are via HTTPS using the **URL Fetch** service (which is discussed in the *Pulling in feeds: The URL Fetch service* section). This means that you cannot use FTP, directly open a socket, and so on.

No dynamic file creation is possible—your code can only write to the Datastore, or use the App Engine's **Blobstore** service.

However, App Engine does provide support for a large subset of the JRE classes and many existing third-party packages port to App Engine with little or no modification. We will see this later in this chapter, in our use of the ROME RSS/Atom libraries.

# Accessing static application files

Since the App Engine app sandbox has no general filesystem, there is no access to classes that write to the filesystem, such as java.io.FileWriter, so such classes are not on the JRE class whitelist.

However, your application does have read access to the files under the war directory, using java.io classes such as FileReader or FileInputStream. Only files designated as app "resource files" can be accessed in this manner. By default, all files under the war directory are considered resource files (except for JSP files). You can exclude files from this set via war/WEB-INF/appengine-web.xml.

See the App Engine documentation for more information on resource and static file management: http://code.google.com/appengine/docs/java/config/appconfig.html#Static_Files_and_Resource_Files.

Resource files are accessed using pathnames *relative* to the war root. For example, you might create a `boilerplate` subdirectory under the war directory, which holds canned text used by your Servlets. You would access a file in this directory as in the following code:

```
new FileInputStream("boilerplate/error.txt");
```

App Engine imposes restrictions on the total number of application files allowed — 3000, at the time of writing — as well as a limit on total application file size — currently, 150MB.

If it is necessary to reduce the application file count, then in addition to explicit exclusion of files via `appengine-web.xml`, you can reduce the file count by creating a jar of the files under `WEB-INF/classes` and moving that `.jar` file to `WEB-INF/lib`. The `ClientBundle` described in *Chapter 3* can also aid in reducing the number of application files.

# Using migrations to evolve the Datastore entities

During the process of application development, it is nearly inevitable that you will want to change the "schema" of the entities in the Datastore. While it can make application development easier when you don't need to explicitly define your database schemas — as is the case with the Datastore — if you don't exercise care in making your changes, problems can arise. Frameworks such as Rails have the concept of data *migration*, which impose structure on the process of schema modification (and other related tasks, such as generating sample data), in order to avoid these problems. We will make use of that concept for our application.

If you want to use a `local_db.bin` Datastore file from one App Engine project in another (for example, as part of a migration), both projects must be using the same App Engine app ID, as set in Eclipse under the project's **Properties**. Otherwise, the entities in the `local_db.bin` file won't be visible to the other app.

The persistence-capable JDO data classes introduced in *Chapter 4* provide wrappers for the Datastore entities. If we add or remove a field of an existing JDO data class — that is, one for which entities already exist in the Datastore — this impacts the structure of the entities of that kind created from then on, and affects how the existing entities of that kind are mapped into JDO instances.

We must pay attention to this now as we will need to add a field to the `Friend` class in this next stage of the *Connectr* application. The new field will hold a set of feed URLs associated with that Friend. The use of migrations lets us manage such changes.

We'll first take a look at what happens in the Datastore in the case of both JDO field removals and additions, and then discuss how to build and use migrations that manage this process.

# Removing a field from a JDO data class definition

JDO field removal is straightforward in its effects. If a field is removed from the data class after some entities of that *kind* have been created, the corresponding property in the existing entities is simply ignored from then on—that property is not included when the entities are mapped to JDO data class instances. Any new instances built using the new class definition will not include that property (though it will still exist in the Datastore). So, there is no particular action that you need to take as long as JDO is your only programmatic access to the entities. JDO does not allow you to directly delete unused entity properties but if you want to do so, the low-level Datastore API (`http://code.google.com/appengine/docs/java/javadoc/com/google/appengine/api/datastore/package-summary.html`) supports this operation.

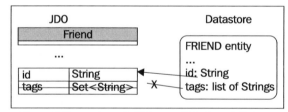

Figure 2: Removing a field from a JDO class definition

Figure 2 suggests this situation. Suppose that for the sake of example, we decided to remove a `tags` persistent field from the JDO `Friend` class. All the existing `Friend` Datastore entities would retain the `tags` property, but the JDO instances would no longer include that field.

# Adding a field to a JDO data class definition

Adding a field to an existing JDO class, for which there are already entities in the Datastore, requires more care. The issue relates to how existing Datastore entities are mapped to JDO instances. If a retrieved Datastore entity does not contain a property corresponding to the new field, then JDO will attempt to set the instance field corresponding to the property to `null`, or to the appropriate empty Collection in the case of a multi-valued property.

If the new instance field is of a **primitive** type (such as `boolean` or `int`), then this mapping will fail (a primitive can't be set to `null`) and an exception will be thrown. Thus, with JDO, if you add a new field to a data class for which there are existing entities without that field, the new field must be an object type (for example, `java.lang.Boolean` or `java.lang.Integer`), *not* a primitive.

If an existing Datastore entity is updated and re-persisted, the property corresponding to the new field, if modified, will be created upon persistence. Of course, any new entities created after the change to the class definition will include the new property.

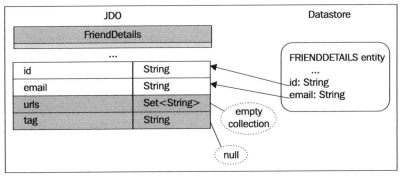

Figure 3: Adding a field to a JDO class definition

Figure 3 suggests the scenario when two new JDO fields, `urls` and `tag`, are added to a data class. The existing Datastore entities do not include those properties. So, the JDO instances to which the entities are mapped set the value of the new fields to an empty set and `null`, respectively. When those fields are updated and the JDO instance persisted, new properties will be created for the underlying entity.

 Don't change the type of an existing field in a JDO data class definition.

It's not possible to change the type of a JDO class field. This will cause an error if entities of that kind already exist. Instead, declare a new field with a different name to hold the new type. If you want to convert the data stored in the old field to the new, then you can first run a migration (as in the next section) to populate the new field based on the old. Once that process is complete, you can remove the old field from the class definition.

# Facilitating "schema" transitions via migrations

We will use the concept of data migrations to manage changes to our application's JDO data classes. We will first define a `Migration` interface. Then, for each change to an existing JDO class definition, we can define a migration class that implements that interface and specifies any processing necessary to make that change.

For *Connectr*, we will be adding a new `urls` field to the `server.domain.FriendDetails` data class. Recall that each `server.domain.Friend` has a `FriendDetails` child object, which holds details about the `Friend`. The new field will be of the type `Set<String>`.

We will create and run a "**Friend migration**" that accesses each existing `FriendDetails` entity in turn. These existing entities won't have a `urls` property, thus, JDO will set the corresponding field value to an empty set when it maps the retrieved entity to the JDO instance. The migration will explicitly create the new `urls` property for the existing entities.

This is a rather artificial example—in this case, it is not really necessary to pre-emptively create the new `urls` property before it is needed. However, we show the migration for the purpose of example. Often the conversion will be more complex and using a structured migration makes the transition much more robust.

Often, less migration work is required for new JDO classes that we add to the application. Because the Datastore entity's "soft" schemas do not need to be explicitly defined, we do not need to define migrations for the new classes unless we wish to generate sample data or otherwise populate existing entities. Later in this chapter, we will be creating new "feed" entities to hold RSS/Atom feed information. We can simply create these entities on demand without issue.

# Approach—defining a migration

To implement the migrations, we will first define a `server.migrations.Migration` interface, which requires each migration to have a `migrate_up` and a `migrate_down` method. The `up` method is run when the schema modifications are *added*, and the `down` method is run to back out of the changes.

The migration will be triggered via the `server.servlets.MigrationServlet` Servlet, which takes as input the name of a `Migration` class to run.

We won't be able to migrate a large data set in a single request, as the Servlet will receive a timeout error after 30 seconds. So, we will design the Servlet to run the migration in batches. Thus, the arguments to `migrate_up` and `migrate_down` are a Datastore query cursor string (as was described in *Chapter 5*), a query batch size, and a `Map` holding any additional necessary parameters. Each invocation of a migration method will run a query to retrieve a batch of instances of the given size, starting from the point indicated by the cursor string. The migration method returns a result `Map` that includes the updated query cursor for the next batch. If the returned query cursor is `null`, the migration terminates.

The batches will be run as separate Tasks using the App Engine Task Queue, which we'll introduce shortly. The migrations should be effectively **idempotent**. This means that their actions can be performed multiple times without changing the result. Thus, you should be able to run a given migration more than once without causing problems or inconsistencies. This is necessary as a Task may be retried if there is an error or system issue.

We will build a `server.migrations.FriendMigration` class that implements the `Migration` interface and sets up the new `urls` field. For the example in this chapter, we will not actually use a "down" migration, and so the `migrate_down` method will be just a stub (or, an "exercise for the reader").

## The Migration interface

We will define the `server.migrations.Migration` interface as follows. The interface requires any implementers to provide both a `migrate_up` and a `migrate_down` method. Both methods take a `String` cursor argument, which will be interpreted as a query cursor, a range used to indicate the query result size, and a `Map` containing any other parameters used by the migration. For our example here, we will not require any other parameters.

```
public interface Migration  {
    public Map<String,String> migrate_up(String cursor,
        int range, Map<String,String> params);
```

```
public Map<String,String> migrate_down(String cursor,
    int range, Map<String,String> params);
}
```

This model will allow the implementing methods to run one batch of the migration task at a time. Thus, a more time-consuming migration operation can be run in smaller batches to avoid timeouts.

# Implementing a Migration: The FriendMigration class

Before migrating the `server.domain.FriendDetails` class, our first step is to add the new `urls` field to the `FriendDetails` class definition (we'll add the usual accessor methods as well).

```
@PersistenceCapable(identityType = IdentityType.APPLICATION,
    detachable="true")
public class FriendDetails {
    ...
    @Persistent
private Set<String> urls;
    ...
}
```

Once we've made the change, then JDO's instantiation of Datastore `FriendDetails` entities will include that new field— set to an empty set if the property does not exist in the entity. So, we're now set up to build the migration itself.

To do this, we'll build an implementation of the `Migration` interface called `FriendMigration` and define a `migrate_up` method.

Our migration should operate over all `FriendDetails` entities, so we create a query that simply selects on `FriendDetails`. The `migrate_up` method is passed a cursor string. As shown in the following example from `server.migrations.FriendMigration`, the next step is to determine if the cursor string is non-null, and if so, whether we can reconstruct the query cursor from it. If so, the query is set with that cursor. We'll then set the query range. Because we're using a cursor, the `start` offset is with respect to the cursor starting point.

```
import javax.jdo.PersistenceManager;
import javax.jdo.Query;
import com.google.appengine.api.datastore.Cursor;
```

```
import org.datanucleus.store.appengine.query.JDOCursorHelper;

… Other imports…

public class FriendMigration implements Migration
{
  public Map<String, String> migrate_up(String cursorString,
    int range, Map<String,String> params)
  {

    Query q = null;
    PersistenceManager pm = PMF.get().getPersistenceManager();

    try {
      q = pm.newQuery(FriendDetails.class);
      if (cursorString != null) {
        Cursor cursor = Cursor.fromWebSafeString(cursorString);
        Map<String, Object> extensionMap = new HashMap<String,
          Object>();
        extensionMap.put(JDOCursorHelper.CURSOR_EXTENSION, cursor);
        q.setExtensions(extensionMap);
      }
      q.setRange(0, range);
      …migration actions here…

    }
    finally {
      q.closeAll();
      pm.close();
    }
    Map<String,String> res = new HashMap<String,String>();
    res.put("cursor", cursorString);
    return res;
  }
  …
}
```

After the query is set up, we execute it and iterate over the results, as shown below in server.migrations.FriendMigration. For each instantiated FriendDetails object, the new urls field will be set by JDO to an empty set. We will mark this field as modified so that when we persist the object, the urls entity property will be created as necessary.

As mentioned earlier, this is a rather artificial example, as in this case it is not strictly necessary to pre-emptively create the `urls` property. Typically, however, migrations require more complex changes and a structured migration process makes them much easier to manage.

```java
public class FriendMigration implements Migration  {

  public Map<String, String> migrate_up(String cursorString,
      int range, Map<String,String> params) {

    ...
   try {
    ... query setup ...
    List<FriendDetails> results = (List<FriendDetails>) q.execute();
    if (results.size() > 0) {
        for (FriendDetails friendd : results) {
           // initialize the new field if necessary
           Set<String> urls = friendd.getUrls();
           if (urls == null || urls.isEmpty()) {
             if (urls == null) {
               friendd.setUrls(new HashSet<String>());
             }
              JDOHelper.makeDirty(friendd, "urls");
           }
        }
        Cursor cursor = JDOCursorHelper.getCursor(results);
        cursorString = cursor.toWebSafeString();
    }
    else {
       // no results
       cursorString = null;
    }

   }
   finally {
      q.closeAll();
      pm.close();
   }
   Map<String,String> res = new HashMap<String,String>();
   res.put("cursor", cursorString);
   return res;
  }
```

If there are no results, a `null` cursor is returned; otherwise we return the ending cursor position. This will be used to invoke processing of the next batch for the migration.

We do not include a "down" migration in this example. A reasonable implementation might be to set the `urls` fields to null (then revert the `Friend` class definition so that it does not include that field). The `urls` property in the `Friend` entities would still exist, though it would not be used. As mentioned previously, you can use the "low-level" Datastore API if you wish to remove a property altogether.

# Running the Migration: A Migration Servlet and the Task Queue

To run the `server.migrations.FriendMigration` migration, we'll build a general-purpose `server.servlets.MigrationServlet`, which expects to be handed the name of a `Migration` class. An instance of the given `Migration` class will be created and its appropriate migration method invoked with the proper parameters. We will run the migration as a server-side *admin* task, independent of the user-facing GWT interface that we've dealt with up to this point.

As discussed earlier, we will run the migration in batches in order to avoid timeouts. So, in `MigrationServlet`, we will introduce use of the App Engine **Task Queue**, which we will use to initiate each "batch" of processing. We will use the Task Queue in its simplest default form here and will return to it in more detail in the upcoming chapters.

The following code shows a portion of the `doPost` method of `server.servlets.MigrationServlet` (its `doGet` method, not shown, essentially wraps the `doPost`). `doPost` first processes the request parameters. It then attempts to create an instance of the given migration class. If no migration parameter is provided, if the given string does not resolve to a known class, or if the class is not of type `Migration`, it generates a response with that information and exits.

```
public void doPost(HttpServletRequest req, HttpServletResponse resp)
  throws IOException
{

  String migration = req.getParameter("migration");
  String direction = req.getParameter("dir");
  String cursor = req.getParameter("cursor");
  String rangestring = req.getParameter("num");

  int range;
```

```
Long prior = null;
Map<String,String> params = new HashMap<String,String>();
Map<String,String> res = null;

  if (migration == null || migration.equals("")) {
    resp.setContentType("text/plain");
    resp.getWriter().println("error: no migration class provided");
    return;
  }
  if (direction == null || !direction.equalsIgnoreCase("down")) {
    direction = "up";
  }
  range = setBatch(rangestring);
  Enumeration en = req.getParameterNames();
  while (en.hasMoreElements())
  {
    String paramName = (String) en.nextElement();
      if (!paramName.equals("cursor") && !paramName.equals("num")
        && !paramName.equals("dir") &&
        !paramName.equals("migration"))
      {
      params.put(paramName, req.getParameter(paramName));
    }
  }
  try
  {
    // make an instance of the passed-in class...
    Class<?> [] classParm = null;
    Object [] objectParm = null;
    Class<?> cl = Class.forName(migration);
    java.lang.reflect.Constructor<?> co =
        cl.getConstructor(classParm);
    // there will be a cast exception here if the object does not
    //implement Migration
    Migration mg = (Migration) co.newInstance(objectParm);
     migration run here…

  }
  catch (ClassNotFoundException e) {
    logger.warning(e.getMessage());
    resp.setContentType("text/plain");
    resp.getWriter().println("error: got a 'class not found'
      exception for " + migration);
    }
  …
}
```

Once an instance of the `Migration` class has been created, its appropriate
`up` or `down` method is invoked as shown in the following code from
`server.servlet.MigrationServlet`:

```
public void doPost(HttpServletRequest req, HttpServletResponse resp)
  throws IOException {
    ...
    try {
      ... create an instance of the migration class...
      // then call the migrate up or down method as
      // appropriate, which every class of type Migration
      // must support.
      if (direction.equals("down")) {
        logger.info("migrating down: " + mg);
            res = mg.migrate_down(cursor, range, params);
        cursor = res.get("cursor");
      }
      else {
        logger.info("migrating up: " + mg);
        res = mg.migrate_up(cursor, range, params);
        cursor = res.get("cursor");
      }
      if (cursor != null) {
        Queue queue = QueueFactory.getDefaultQueue();
        TaskOptions topt = TaskOptions.Builder.url("/migration");
        for (String rkey : res.keySet()) {
          if (!rkey.equals("cursor")) {
            topt = topt.param(rkey, ""+ res.get(rkey));
          }
        }
        queue.add(topt.param("cursor", cursor).param("num", ""+range).
        param("dir", direction).param("migration", migration));
      }
    }
    ...
    catch (DatastoreTimeoutException e) {
      throw e;
    }
    catch (Exception e) {
        logger.warning(e.getMessage());
      resp.setContentType("text/plain");
      resp.getWriter().println(e.getMessage());
    }
}
```

When we call the up or down method for the initial migration batch, the cursor string is null (so the first query will be run from offset 0). The method returns the updated cursor value. If the returned cursor is not null, we create an App Engine Task to do the next batch of migrations. The migration Servlet URL is indicated as the task action, and we specify the new cursor and other information as task parameters:

```
Queue queue = QueueFactory.getDefaultQueue();
TaskOptions topt = TaskOptions.Builder.url("/migration");
for (String rkey : res.keySet()) {
  if (!rkey.equals("cursor")) {
    topt = topt.param(rkey, ""+ res.get(rkey));
  }
}
queue.add(topt.param("cursor", cursor).param("num", ""+range).
  param("dir", direction).param("migration", migration));}
```

This code adds the migration Servlet as a Task on the *default* App Engine Task Queue, which always exists. We will describe the com.google.appengine.api. labs.taskqueue package's TaskOptions and Queue classes in more detail in *Chapter 12, Asynchronous Processing with Cron, Task Queue, and XMPP*. Once enqueued, the task will be run asynchronously.

In this manner, the migration batches are chained—when each is finished running, it adds the next batch as a task to the default Task Queue using the returned cursor. Tasks are automatically retried if they terminate in an exception.

For this task specification to work, we must define the /migration URL to map to MigrationServlet in web.xml. We'll do that next.

## Invoking the Servlet as a web request

To be able to access the Servlet via a web request, we need to add its specification to the deployment descriptor. We'll do that by adding the following code to the war/WEB-INF/web.xml file, where you would replace packagepath with your actual package for the Servlet.

```
<servlet>
  <servlet-name>Migration</servlet-name>
  <servlet-class>
    packagepath.server.servlets.migrations.MigrationServlet
  </servlet-class>
</servlet>
<servlet-mapping>
  <servlet-name>Migration</servlet-name>
```

```
  <url-pattern>/migration</url-pattern>
</servlet-mapping>
```

Once the Servlet mapping is specified, we can invoke the Servlet as a GET request like this:

```
http://localhost:8888/migration?migration=packagepath.server.
servlets.migrations.FriendMigration&num=4 ,
```

where the `migration` parameter is the `Migration` to invoke and the `num` parameter is the batch size (up is the default migration direction). This will initiate the migration.

# Servlet admin authentication

We don't want just anyone to be able to run this migration task. So, we will specify that the Servlet URL requires *admin* authentication. The following code shows the `security-constraint` specification in `web.xml`.

```
<security-constraint>
  <web-resource-collection>
    <url-pattern>/migration</url-pattern>
  </web-resource-collection>
  <auth-constraint>
    <role-name>admin</role-name>
  </auth-constraint>
</security-constraint>
```

Once this specification is in place, then to run the migration, we will need to log in as an admin for the app. The App Engine Task Queue can access admin-only URLs automatically but we need to authenticate to initiate the migration.

Recall that in the development environment, you log in as an admin as shown in Figure 1. For the deployed application you will need to use a real admin account. For now, if you want to log out, as we have not yet added proper login/logout functionality to *Connectr*—we will do that in *Chapter 8*—you will need to delete the app's cookies.

It is helpful to use *logging* to track what is going on during the series of task invocations, and you may have noticed the use of the `java.util.logging.Logger` in the preceding code. Logger output will appear in the App Engine Admin Console logs as well as in the development console. We will describe the Logger in more detail in *Chapter 11, Managing and Backing Up your App Engine Application*.

# Pulling in Feeds: The URL Fetch service

We've converted the *Connectr* `Friend` entities to hold a set of URLs. So, each `Friend` can have a set of feed URLs associated with it, pointing to the feeds for the friend's blog, Twitter and Flickr accounts, and so on.

Now, we'll add the classes and methods that allow us to fetch, store, and manage the feeds. To help implement the feed fetch, we will use the App Engine's **URL Fetch service**, which allows HTTP(S) access to web services and the ROME open source RSS/Atom libraries.

In this chapter, we focus on building the foundations of the server-side feed management. *Chapter 10* will address the frontend implementation required to display and refresh the feed items, and *Chapter 12* will further extend the server-side architecture.

# App Engine services

The App Engine **URL Fetch** service, which we will be using to grab RSS/Atom feeds, is—along with our introduction of the Task Queue—the first use in *Connectr* of the set of **services** provided by App Engine.

As the App Engine documentation states:

> *App Engine provides a variety of services that enable you to perform common operations when managing your application.*

These services are accessed via APIs and amongst other functionality they allow your application to have contact with the "outside world"— other types of connectivity not listed here, such as using FTP or opening an arbitrary socket, are not permitted. This restricted access model allows App Engine to have more control over the security, responsiveness, and robustness of its applications.

The services include:

- **URL Fetch**: Internet access via HTTP and HTTPS.
- **Mail**: Uses the App Engine infrastructure to send and receive e-mails.
- **Memcache**: An efficient in-memory key-value cache.
- **Task Queues and scheduled "Cron" tasks**: Perform background processing.
- **Blobstore**: Upload and serve large objects of up to 50MB in size.
- **Google Accounts authentication**: Allows your users to log in using their Google Accounts (an experimental OpenID option exists as well).

- **Image Manipulation**: Gives you the ability to perform a number of image manipulation tasks such as resizing, cropping, and rotating.
- **XMPP**: Communicates with users or other apps via XMPP (Jabber).

The Datastore, of course, can be considered a service as well. At the time of writing, the Task Queue and Blobstore services are still considered experimental, which means that their APIs may change.

We will focus on URL Fetch in this chapter and return to other services in later chapters.

# URL Fetch

The URL Fetch service allows an application to send HTTP and HTTPS requests and receive responses. It uses HTTP/1.1. Both synchronous and asynchronous requests are supported. URL Fetch has two Java implementations, described below.

The URL Fetch service has a number of limitations:

- URL Fetch does not maintain a persistent connection with the remote host.
- URL Fetch supports only `GET`, `POST`, `PUT`, `HEAD`, and `DELETE` requests.
- It can connect only to standard TCP ports — port 80 for HTTP and port 443 for HTTPS.
- The request and the response size are both limited to 1MB.
- The proxy used by the service accepts all certificates. This means that while communication is encrypted, "man-in-the-middle" attacks are not prevented.
- For security reasons, the following headers cannot be modified by the application: `Content-Length`, `Host`, `Vary`, `Via`, and `X-Forwarded-For`. Instead, the App Engine sets these headers itself.
- As a protection against looping, URL Fetch cannot fetch the URL that maps to the Servlet doing the fetching.

 Other related protocols, such as FTP, are not supported — only HTTP(S).

If your application needs to connect to sites inside your company or organization's firewall (for example, an LDAP server), then URL Fetch alone is not sufficient; you will need to enable the connection using a Secure Data Connector. A **Secure Data Connector** agent must be installed on the relevant machine inside the firewall, and App Engine apps can authenticate with it. See the Google documentation for more information: `http://code.google.com/securedataconnector/`.

# Java support for URL Fetch

There are two Java wrappers for App Engine's URL Fetch service. The first is App Engine's re-implementation of `java.net.URLConnection` and related classes from the Java standard library. We will use this implementation for *Connectr*. App Engine's re-implementation of this standard and familiar API means that many existing third-party packages can be used by App Engine apps. We will see this in *Connectr*, when we use the open source ROME RSS/Atom library.

>  See the Java documentation for more information on `URLConnection`:
> `http://download.oracle.com/javase/6/docs/api/java/net/`
> `URLConnection.html`.

The second Java implementation of URL Fetch is App Engine's "low-level" API, `com.google.appengine.api.urlfetch`. We will not use this API in the *Connectr* app. However, it does expose a bit more of URL Fetch's capabilities, as described in *The "low-level" Java URL Fetch API* section.

# Using java.net.URLConnection

The implementation of URL fetch via `java.net.URLConnection` allows `java.net`-based code to be moved in and out of App Engine fairly transparently. If you are already familiar with the `java.net` API then you will not have much more to learn. However, there are a few limitations and differences to be aware of.

- Because of the underlying functionality of URL Fetch, *persistent HTTP connections are not supported* by App Engine's implementation.

- When using the `java.net API`, data larger than the *1MB* limit is truncated without notification (the low-level API allows an exception to be reported instead of truncation).

- The URL Fetch service buffers the full response into the application's memory—that is, the app reads the response data from memory, not from a network stream.

- When you are using `URLConnection`, URL Fetch will automatically support up to five redirects (the low-level API allows you to disallow redirects).

- A request waits up to five seconds for a response by default. The maximum wait can be ten seconds. You can set the amount of time to wait (between one and ten seconds) via the `setConnectTimeout` method of `URLConnection`.

In this section, we will give some examples of common usage of the `java.net` implementation.

# Making an HTTP request

If you are making a GET request and you do not need to set any connection headers or otherwise configure your request, then the following example illustrates the most straightforward usage. Use the URL openStream convenience method to read the response line-by-line.

```java
import java.net.MalformedURLException;
import java.net.URL;
import java.io.BufferedReader;
import java.io.InputStreamReader;
import java.io.IOException;

// ...
 try{
   URL url = new URL("http://www.somedomain.com/atom.xml");
   BufferedReader reader = new BufferedReader(
    new InputStreamReader(url.openStream()));
   String line;

   while((line = reader.readLine())!=null){
   // ...
   }
   reader.close();

 }
 catch(MalformedURLException e){
  // ...
 }catch(IOException e){
  // ...
 }
```

# Using HTTP(S) URLConnection objects

If you want to configure your HTTP requests, including setting the headers and/or the request method, then call the URL object's openConnection method. This will return a URLConnection object—more specifically, either an HttpURLConnection or an HttpsURLConnection, depending upon the connection type.

## Setting request headers

The following code shows an example of setting and adding request header properties.

Establish the connection after setting the request information. The response can be read from the connection's input stream via the `getInputStream` method. After the response data has been accessed, the request data cannot be modified.

```
HttpURLConnection connection = (HttpURLConnection)
  url.openConnection();
connection.setRequestProperty("Accept-Encoding", "gzip");
connection.addRequestProperty("User-Agent", getUserAgent());
// …
connection.connect();
InputStream inputStream = connection.getInputStream();
```

## Making a POST request

In order to make a POST request, it is necessary to both set the connection request method to POST, and to write to the connection output stream.

```
import java.net.HttpURLConnection;
import java.net.MalformedURLException;
import java.net.URL;
import java.net.URLEncoder;
import java.io.BufferedReader;
import java.io.InputStreamReader;
import java.io.IOException;
import java.io.OutputStreamWriter;

// ...
 String param1 = URLEncoder.encode("param1 data","UTF-8");
 String param2 = URLEncoder.encode("param2 data","UTF-8");

 Try
 {
   URL url =newURL("http://www.someblog.com/comment");
   HttpURLConnection connection =
     (HttpURLConnection)url.openConnection();
   connection.setDoOutput(true);
   connection.setRequestMethod("POST");
   connection.setRequestProperty("Content-Type",
       "application/x-www-form-urlencoded");

   OutputStreamWriter writer =
     new OutputStreamWriter(connection.getOutputStream());
```

```
    writer.write("param1="+ param1 + "&param2=" + param2);
    writer.close();

    if(connection.getResponseCode()== HttpURLConnection.HTTP_OK){
    // OK
    }else{
      // Server returned HTTP error code.
    }
}catch(MalformedURLException e){
  // ...
 }catch(IOException e){
  // ...
  }
```

The preceding code shows an example of a POST request. A connection is opened on the URL and the setDoOutput method is called with true, which indicates that the application intends to write data to the URL connection (the default value is false). The request method is set as POST. Then, the post parameter content (which must be URL-encoded) is written to the connection's output stream. When the output stream is closed, the request is sent. The response code can then be inspected.

## Using a Blob to store a binary response

As indicated in *The JRE whitelist and system restrictions*, App Engine provides no mechanism for creating new static files. You must store any generated data in the Datastore instead. Be sure to save data from large responses in Blob or Text fields. However, recall that Datastore entities cannot be over 1MB in size. The App Engine's **Blobstore** can also be an option for larger-sized data in some circumstances.

With binary response data, you should store the data in a Blob.

1. Define your data class to have a persistent field of type Blob. For example:

    ```
    @Persistent
    Blob imageData;
    ```

2. Process the connection input stream as a byte stream and create a new Blob with the resultant byte array by passing the array to the Blob constructor. For example:

    ```
    public void storeImage(byte[] bytes) {
          this.imageData = new Blob(bytes);
     }
    ```

3. To later generate a byte array from the `Blob`, call its `getBytes()` method. For instance:

```
public byte[] getBytes() {
return imageData.getBytes();
    }
```

# The "low-level" Java URL Fetch API

We will not cover the low-level Java URL Fetch API in this book. You can find more information about it in the App Engine documentation: `http://code.google.com/appengine/docs/java/javadoc/com/google/appengine/api/urlfetch/package-summary.html`.

The low-level API does expose more configuration options and functionality than the `java.net` implementation. There are several circumstances under which you might want to use this API instead:

- You wish to have an exception thrown when the response size limit is exceeded (rather than having the response silently truncated).

- You wish to indicate that redirects should not be followed.

- You want to use an **asynchronous fetch** — this means that the fetch request does not block waiting for the response but instead immediately returns an object that can be used later to access the results. The application code can continue with its work immediately and then later call a method on the `response` object to get the results. This method will wait until the results are complete (as necessary), and then return the results. An application can have up to ten simultaneous asynchronous URL Fetch calls. At the time of writing, asynchronous fetch is not supported by the `java.net` implementation.

# The ROME and ROME Fetcher RSS/Atom libraries

Earlier, we added the ability to store a list of feed URLs associated with each `Friend` in its `FriendDetails` child. We will use the ROME and ROME Fetcher RSS/Atom libraries to fetch the feeds corresponding to those URLs.

These libraries provide a set of open source Java tools for parsing, generating, and publishing RSS and Atom feeds, which have grown out of a project started by engineers at Sun. It turns out that these libraries run on App Engine. They use `java.net.URLConnection` to access the feeds and do not use any `URLConnection` features unsupported by App Engine's implementation over the URL Fetch service.

In *Connectr*, we will use these libraries to fetch the feeds, to parse them, and to build Java objects representing the feed information.

In this section, we'll describe how to install the **JAR** files for these libraries and their dependencies, so that our deployed App Engine application can use them successfully.

Then, in the *Using RSS/Atom feeds in the Connectr* section, we'll show how to use the libraries.

# Downloading the ROME and ROME Fetcher jars and their dependencies

ROME requires the JDOM library that provides utilities for XML parsing. You can download the JDOM JAR here: `http://www.jdom.org/`. At the time of writing, the most current version is 1.1.1.

Then, you can download the ROME JAR from: `https://rome.dev.java.net/`. At the time of writing, the most current version is 1.0. Obtain the ROME Fetcher JAR from: `http://wiki.java.net/bin/view/Javawsxml/RomeFetcherRelease1_0`.

We need to obtain one additional JAR file. The ROME library has a dependency that may not cause you trouble when you are running locally in *development* mode, but would cause an error when you deploy to App Engine. The GAE runtime environment is missing the `xercesImpl` package from the Xerces Apache project. Xerces provides a processor for parsing, validating, serializing, and manipulating XML. Download the binary files for Xerces2 Java (version 2.9.1 as of this writing) from `http://xerces.apache.org/` and locate the `xercesImpl.jar` file.

 You can also find all of these jars in our download available at the Packt website.

# Installing the library JAR files

Copy all of the JAR files mentioned previously (`rome`, `rome-fetcher`, `jdom`, and `xercesImpl`) to the `war/WEB-INF/lib` directory of your Eclipse project. All of the files in this directory will be uploaded when you deploy to App Engine, thus your deployed application will have access to these libraries.

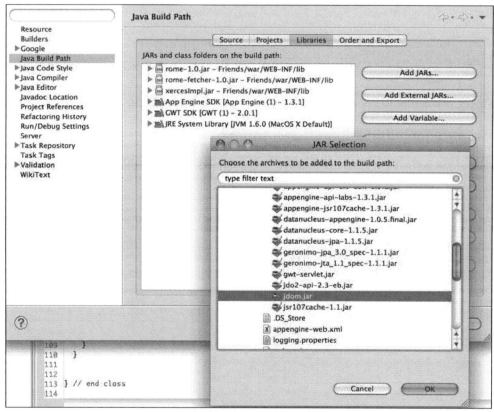

Figure 4: Adding JAR files to a project's Build Path.

Then, add these jars to the build path (classpath) for your Eclipse project. To do this, right-click on the project name and select **Build Path | Configure Build Path** from the context menu. Select the **Libraries** tab, and click on **Add JARs**. This will bring up a dialog window in which you can locate the JAR to add to the path, as shown in Figure 4. Navigate to the `war/WEB-INF/lib` directory of your project and add each jar in turn.

# Using RSS/Atom feeds in the *Connectr* app

Now that we're set up with the necessary third-party libraries, we'll use them as a basis for the feed management of *Connectr*.

As discussed earlier, we have a number of design objectives in building this new functionality. We want our application to be responsive in displaying requested feeds and to be robust to feed-related errors. We would also like it to support asynchronous and decoupled feed fetch while avoiding duplication of effort.

In this section, we will define two new data classes—`server.domain.FeedInfo` and `server.domain.FeedIndex`—which we will use to store feed information. Their design will support the objectives mentioned earlier. We will also subclass a ROME Fetcher class to allow us to integrate with the Datastore; it will use the URL Fetch service.

Then, in the *Enabling background feed updating and processing* section, we will write some "admin" Servlets that operate asynchronously over the feed information in order to perform various tasks (such as updating all of the feeds for a given user's Friends).

## Adding feed support

We'll take the following approach in adding the new feed functionality:

- We will create new classes to hold the feed information. The feed objects will be shared between `Friend`s wherever possible, so that we don't unnecessarily redo feed fetches. For example, if two different users are friends with Bob and enter his blog URL, only one corresponding feed object for Bob's blog will be created. We will design the new feed classes so that it is efficient to query for the feed objects associated with a given `Friend`. We will do this via queries on multi-valued properties.

- We will use the App Engine URL Fetch service to pull in the feeds, using `URLConnection` via the ROME libraries. We will subclass a `Fetcher` class to integrate it with our use of the Datastore to persist feeds. The fetch code supports a *conditional GET*, so that we don't pull in a feed if its server indicates that it does not need to be updated.

- We will allow a small amount of information latency in order to reduce workload: if a feed has just been checked within $X$ period of time, serve it up without checking whether it needs updating again.

- We will essentially ignore transient feed fetch errors (after a feed has been validated initially). So, we won't waste time retrying fetches. We will just retain the existing feed content and try again to fetch the feed at some point after the latency window has passed.

- *Connectr* will support decoupled background feed processing: we will use Servlets and the App Engine Task Queue to update the feeds of any particular client request asynchronously. This will allow the app to keep relevant feeds updated—both proactively and in response to client events—so that it can responsively display current feed content. We'll lay the foundations in this chapter and develop the approach further in *Chapter 12*.

In this chapter, we're not yet discussing the use of App Engine's Memcache service to store objects in-memory between requests. When we introduce Memcache in *Chapter 9*, we will see how to use the cache to make this model even more efficient.

# The feed classes

We've now extended the FriendDetails data class with a urls field to store the feed URLs associated with that friend. Multiple users may have the same friend, and/or related Friends may be associated with the same blog, and so on, and so multiple FriendDetails objects may list the same feed URL.

To support the feed management, we will define two new classes. The first is the server.domain.FeedInfo class. Each FeedInfo object will store the contents of a given RSS/Atom feed parsed by the ROME libraries. The primary key for a FeedInfo object, named urlstring, is its feed URL string.

In addition, we will build a related class—server.domain.FeedIndex. Each FeedInfo class will have a FeedIndex child. A FeedIndex object contains a set of the *keys* of those Friends that store the URL of the parent FeedInfo. This set is maintained in a friendKeys field of FeedIndex. The rationale for building a pair of objects—FeedInfo and FeedIndex—rather than a single object, relates to the efficiency of Datastore access and is described in *Chapter 9*. For now, we will simply focus on the information stored by the objects.

So, Friend and FeedInfo (with its FeedIndex child) have a many-to-many relationship, as shown in Figure 5: one "feed information" pair may list multiple Friend keys and a Friend may list multiple URLs (that is, multiple FeedInfo IDs).

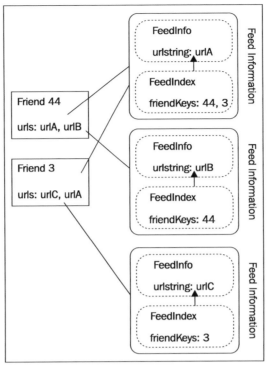

Figure 5: The many-to-many relationship between Friend objects and feed information.

A key to this design is that it is simple and efficient to find all of the feed objects for a given `Friend` by performing a query on the multi-valued `friendKeys` property:

```
q = pm.newQuery(FeedIndex.class, "friendKeys == :id");
```

If the Friend ID is in its `friendKeys` set, a `FeedIndex` object will be matched by this query.

The fields and constructor of the `FeedInfo` class are shown below. The primary key of `FeedInfo`, `urlstring`, is the URL string for the feed. The `feedInfo` field stores a serialized `SyndFeedInfo` object that holds the actual feed contents already parsed into its component object and subobjects. `SyndFeedInfo` and its associated classes are defined in the open source ROME and ROME Fetcher libraries that we'll use.

The `server.domain.FeedInfo` instance and class variables are defined as follows:

```
import com.sun.syndication.fetcher.impl.SyndFeedInfo;
import packagepath.server.FriendFeedFetcher;
… Other imports…
```

```
@PersistenceCapable(identityType = IdentityType.APPLICATION,
  detachable="true")
public class FeedInfo implements Serializable, Cacheable
{

  protected static FriendFeedFetcher feedFetcher =
    new FriendFeedFetcher();

  @Persistent
  @PrimaryKey
  private String urlstring;


  @Persistent
  private Date dateChecked;
  @Persistent
  private Date dateUpdated;
  @Persistent
  private Date dateRequested;

  @Persistent(serialized = "true")
  private SyndFeedInfo feedInfo;

  @Persistent
  private Long lastModified;
  @Persistent
  private String eTag;

  @Persistent
  private String feedTitle;

  @Persistent
  Set<Long> ukeys;

  private static Logger logger =
    Logger.getLogger(FeedInfo.class.getName());
  private int update_mins;
  private static Properties props = System.getProperties();

  private static final int DEFAULT_UPDATE_MINS = 2;


  ...
}
```

A new `FeedInfo` instance will be created only for a valid feed. One of the arguments to the `server.domain.FeedInfo` constructor, shown below, is the `SyndFeedInfo` object `feedInfo`, encoding information about that feed and its HTTP response.

```java
public FeedInfo(SyndFeedInfo feedInfo, String url, String fkey) {
  this.feedInfo = feedInfo;
  this.feedTitle = feedInfo.getSyndFeed().getTitle();
  this.dateChecked = new Date();
  this.dateUpdated = new Date();
  this.dateRequested = new Date();
  this.urlstring = url;
  this.ukeys = new HashSet<Long>();

  try
  {
     update_mins =  Integer.parseInt(props.getProperty(
        "com.metadot.connectr.mins-feed-check"));
  }
  catch (Exception e) {
     update_mins = DEFAULT_UPDATE_MINS;
  }

  if (feedInfo.getLastModified() instanceof Long) {
    this.lastModified = (Long)feedInfo.getLastModified();
  }
  else {
    this.lastModified = new Long(0);
  }
   this.eTag = feedInfo.getETag();
}

  ...
}
```

Included in the information maintained by the `FeedInfo` object is the `lastModified` and `eTag` information returned by the HTTP fetch response for the feed. This information allows a conditional HTTP GET to be used when the feed is fetched, essentially allowing a GET request to specify, "Send me the feed only if it has changed since time *T*". Not all feed servers support this request; those that do not will always just indicate that the feed has new content.

Each `FeedInfo` object keeps track of three dates—when its feed was last checked, when it was last updated (because with the conditional GET, feeds do not always need to be updated when checked), and when the feed was last requested by a client. As we'll see next, the last-requested date is used to focus proactive background updates on feeds likely to be accessed again soon. These values are stored in the `dateChecked`, `dateUpdated`, and `dateRequested` fields.

We will return to the `ukeys` instance variable in *Chapter 12*; it will hold some bookkeeping done to make certain queries more efficient.

The constructor uses a system property, `packagepath.mins-feed-check`, to define how long (in minutes) *Connectr* should wait after checking a feed before checking again whether it needs refreshing (where you would replace `packagepath` with your package path). You can see that if no system property is set, the default is two minutes.

 System properties are defined in the `appengine-web.xml` file; we will discuss setting system properties in *Chapter 11*.

The `server.domain.FeedIndex` instance variables are shown next. The `friendKeys` set holds the IDs of those `Friend` objects that have listed that feed's URL.

```
@PersistenceCapable(identityType = IdentityType.APPLICATION,
    detachable="true")
public class FeedIndex implements Serializable {

  @PrimaryKey
  @Persistent(valueStrategy = IdGeneratorStrategy.IDENTITY)
  private Key key;

  @Persistent
  private Set<String> friendKeys;
```

A `key` of `FeedIndex` will be constructed in a particular way so that we can derive the parent `FeedInfo` `urlstring` key directly from it, and conversely construct the child `FeedIndex` key given the URL. This will be described in *Chapter 9*; the details are not important for this chapter.

# Adding and removing friend feeds

The static `server.domain.FeedIndex` methods shown below are called when URLs are removed or added from a Friend's data.

When a Friend removes a URL, we must check whether that Friend was the only one listing the URL and thus the only object pointing to the corresponding `FeedInfo` object. If no other Friend points to that `FeedInfo` object, it is deleted.

The following code shows the removal methods as well as a "helper" method, `findFeedIndex`, which retrieves the `FeedIndex` associated with a given URL if it exists, and returns `null` if it does not.

```
@PersistenceCapable(identityType = IdentityType.APPLICATION,
    detachable="true")
public class FeedInfo{
    ...

  public static FeedIndex findFeedIndex(String url,
    PersistenceManager pm)
{
    FeedIndex fi = null;
    // query for a feed index with the given url
    try {
      KeyFactory.Builder keyBuilder =
        new KeyFactory.Builder(FeedInfo.class.getSimpleName(), url);
      keyBuilder.addChild(FeedIndex.class.getSimpleName(), url);
      Key ckey = keyBuilder.getKey();
      fi = pm.getObjectById(FeedIndex.class, ckey);
    }
    catch (javax.jdo.JDOObjectNotFoundException e) {
      logger.info(e.getMessage());
    }
    return fi;
}

  public static void removeFeedsFriend(Set<String> urls, String fkey)
  {
    for (String url : urls) {
      removeFeedFriend(url, fkey);
    }
  }

  public static void removeFeedFriend(String urlstring, String fkey)
```

```
    {

        PersistenceManager pm =
        PMF.get().getPersistenceManager();

        try {
            FeedIndex findex = findFeedIndex(urlstring, pm);
            if (findex != null) {
              Set<String> fkeys = findex.getFriendKeys();
              fkeys.remove(fkey);
              if (fkeys.isEmpty()) {
                logger.info("orphaned feed - deleting " + urlstring);
                // then delete parent
                pm.deletePersistent(pm.getObjectById(FeedInfo.class,
                  findex.getKey().getParent()));
                // then delete index obj
                 pm.deletePersistent(findex);
            }
            else {
              // update the set of users associated
              // with this feed
              FeedInfo feedInfo =
              pm.getObjectById(FeedInfo.class, urlstring);
              Set<Long> ukeys = findex.findUkeys();
              feedInfo.setUkeys(ukeys);
              }
                pm.makePersistent(findex);
            }
        }
        finally {
            pm.close();
        }
      }
    ...
    }
```

Similarly, the following code shows the `server.domain.FeedIndex` methods called when URLs are added to `Friend` data. When URLs are added, new `FeedInfo` and `FeedIndex` objects are created for each (valid) URL, if one does not exist already. If feed objects for a given URL already exist, the `Friend` key is added to the `friendKey` list of `FeedIndex`.

```
@PersistenceCapable(identityType = IdentityType.APPLICATION,
    detachable="true")
```

```
public class FeedIndex{

  ...

public static Set<String> addFeedsFriend(Set<String> urls,
   String fkey)
{

  boolean status;
  Set<String> badUrls = new HashSet<String>();
  for (String url: urls) {
    try {
      status = FeedIndex.addFeedFriend(url, fkey);
      if (status == false)
      { // then malformed url or some issue with the feed
         badUrls.add(url);
      }
    }
    catch (Exception e)
    { // also treat url as bad if anything else goes wrong
       badUrls.add(url);
    }
  } // end for
   return badUrls;
 }


    // build a new feed object if necessary, otherwise add
    // friend key to existing feedinfo object
public static boolean addFeedFriend(String urlstring, String fkey)
{

  FeedInfo feedInfo = null;
  FeedIndex findex = null;
  boolean status = false;
  SyndFeedInfo fi = null;

  PersistenceManager pm = PMF.get().getPersistenceManager();
  PersistenceManager pm2 =  PMF.get().getPersistenceManager();

  try {
    // first just check if the url is valid --
      if it's not, nothing else to do.
    URL url = new URL(urlstring);
```

```
        logger.fine("looking for feedindex for " + urlstring);
        findex = findFeedIndex(urlstring, pm);
        if (findex == null) {
          // then build new
          logger.fine("building new feed for " + urlstring);
          fi = FeedInfo.feedFetcher.retrieveFeedInfo(url, null);
          // create parent
          feedInfo = new FeedInfo(fi, urlstring, fkey);
          pm.makePersistent(feedInfo);
          // create child
          findex = new FeedIndex(fkey, urlstring);
          pm.makePersistent(findex);
        }
        else
        { // existing feed info for that url
          findex.addFriendKey(fkey);
          logger.info("added friendKey " + fkey + " for "   + urlstring);
          pm.makePersistent(findex);
        }
        feedInfo = pm2.getObjectById(FeedInfo.class, urlstring);
        // update the set of users associated with this feed
        Set<Long> ukeys = findex.findUkeys();
        feedInfo.setUkeys(ukeys);
        feedInfo.updateRequestedFeed(pm2);
        status = true; // success
      }
      catch (Exception e) {
          logger.warning(e.getMessage());
      }
      finally {
        pm2.close();
        pm.close();
      }
        return status;
      }

      ...

    }
```

New feed objects are created for a URL only if its feed is valid. A check is first made to ensure that it parses as a URL; if it does, then the retrieveFeedInfo method of feedFetcher is called to actually fetch the feed (we'll see more of the feedFetcher shortly). If this method returns null or throws an exception, new feed objects are not created for that URL. If all is well, the new FeedInfo object is created with the fetched feed content.

# Fetching and updating feeds

The `server.domain.FeedInfo` methods of the following listing contain the logic for checking whether a feed needs updating and initiating its update if so. As introduced earlier, a configurable latency period is defined and a feed is not updated again until it has passed that window of time. Any update errors are ignored (with the current feed content retained); the fetcher will try again next time. We can identify persistently bad feeds by their last-updated date if we want to prune them.

```
@PersistenceCapable(identityType = IdentityType.APPLICATION,
    detachable="true")
public class FeedInfo
{

  private static FriendFeedFetcher feedFetcher =
    new FriendFeedFetcher();
  ...

  public SyndFeedInfo updateRequestedFeed(PersistenceManager pm)
  {
    this.dateRequested = new Date();
    updateIfNeeded(pm);
    return this.feedInfo;
  }

  public void updateIfNeeded(PersistenceManager pm) {
    try
    {
      if (feedNeedsChecking()) {
        logger.info("feed needs checking: "+ urlstring);
        updateFeed(pm);
        pm.makePersistent(this);
      }
    }
    catch (Exception e) {
      logger.warning(e.getMessage());
    }
  }


  // update the feed contents
  private void updateFeed(PersistenceManager pm)
  {
```

```
        logger.info("in UpdateFeed: " + urlstring);
        try {

          this.dateChecked = new Date();
          SyndFeedInfo fi = feedFetcher.retrieveFeedInfo(
              new URL(this.urlstring), this);
          // if non-null was returned, update the feed contents.
          // null indicates either that the feed did not need
         // updating, or that there was an error fetching it.
          if (fi != null) {
           this.feedInfo = fi;
           this.eTag = fi.getETag();
           setLastModified(fi.getLastModified());
           this.dateUpdated = new Date();
           JDOHelper.makeDirty(this, "feedInfo");
           logger.info("updating feed " + urlstring + " at " +
              dateUpdated);
          }
        } //end try
        catch (Exception e)
        {
          logger.warning(e.getMessage());
        }
      }


      private Boolean feedNeedsChecking()
      {

        long delay = 1000 * 60 * this.update_mins; // default 2-min delay
        Date now = new Date();
        long diff = now.getTime() - dateChecked.getTime();
        return (diff > delay);
      }

    }// end class
```

The `updateIfNeeded` method will update the feed if the time since the last check has been greater than the latency window.

The `updateFeed` method manages the actual feed update. It calls the `retrieveFeedInfo` method of the `feedFetcher` object (described next). If this call returns `null`, it means that either the feed's content had not changed, or there was some error in fetching it. Otherwise, there was a content update: the `feedInfo` field is set to the returned feed (`JDOHelper.makeDirty(this, "feedInfo")` is called to indicate to JDO that the serialized field should be re-persisted).

Additionally, the `FeedInfo` object is updated with the `eTag` and `lastModified` information from the returned feed. This information lets us perform a conditional GET next time the feed is updated.

The `updateRequestedFeed` method returns the feed contents freshened as needed. It updates the `dateRequested` field.

# Subclassing the ROME Fetcher HttpURLFeedFetcher class

The ROME and ROME Fetcher libraries are used to grab and parse the feed content. It is here that we use the `java.net` implementation of URL Fetch.

To use the ROME Fetcher libraries, we need to make a few small changes. We are storing feed structures in the Datastore and accessing them on update. So, we will subclass the Fetcher's `com.sun.syndication.fetcher.impl.HttpURLFeedFetcher` class to support these changes—the subclass is called `server.FriendFeedFetcher`. We won't go through the code of `FriendFeedFetcher` in detail (the ROME Fetcher documentation contains more information), but as shown in the following code, it contains examples of setting request headers, making a connection, and reading the response code.

```
// subclass of HttpURLFeedFetcher, which works with the
// FeedInfo persistent object
public class FriendFeedFetcher extends
  com.sun.syndication.fetcher.impl.HttpURLFeedFetcher
{

  ...
  public SyndFeedInfo retrieveFeedInfo(URL feedUrl,
    FeedInfo dtsFeedInfo) throws IllegalArgumentException,
    IOException, FeedException, FetcherException
{
  if(feedUrl == null){
    throw new IllegalArgumentException("null is not a valid URL");
  }

  URLConnection connection = feedUrl.openConnection();
  if(!(connection instanceof HttpURLConnection))
  {
    throw new llegalArgumentException(feedUrl.toExternalForm()+
    " is not a valid HTTP Url");
  }
```

```
     HttpURLConnection httpConnection = (HttpURLConnection)connection;

     SyndFeedInfo syndFeedInfo =null;
     if(dtsFeedInfo !=null){
       setRequestHeaders(connection, dtsFeedInfo.getLastModified(),
         dtsFeedInfo.getETag());
     }
     else{
       setRequestHeaders(connection,null,null);
     }
     httpConnection.connect();
     try
     {
       fireEvent(FetcherEvent.EVENT_TYPE_FEED_POLLED, connection);

       if(dtsFeedInfo == null){
         // this is a feed that hasn't been retrieved
         syndFeedInfo = new SyndFeedInfo();
         resetFeedInfo(feedUrl, syndFeedInfo, httpConnection);
       }
       else{
         // check the response code
         int responseCode = httpConnection.getResponseCode();
         if(responseCode != HttpURLConnection.HTTP_NOT_MODIFIED){
           // the feed needs retrieving
           syndFeedInfo = new SyndFeedInfo();
           resetFeedInfo(feedUrl, syndFeedInfo, httpConnection);
         }
         else{
           // the feed does not need retrieving
           fireEvent(FetcherEvent.EVENT_TYPE_FEED_UNCHANGED,
             connection);
         }
       }
       // if null is returned, feed did not need updating, or
       // there was an error fetching it.
        return syndFeedInfo;
     }
     finally{
       httpConnection.disconnect();
     }
  }
```

```
protected void setRequestHeaders(URLConnection connection,
  Long lm, String eTag)
{
  // support the use of both last modified and eTag headers
  if(lm != null){
    connection.setIfModifiedSince(lm.longValue());
  }
  if(eTag != null){
    connection.setRequestProperty("If-None-Match", eTag);
  }
// header to retrieve feed gzipped
  connection.setRequestProperty("Accept-Encoding","gzip");

  // set the user agent
  connection.addRequestProperty("User-Agent", getUserAgent());
  if(isUsingDeltaEncoding()){
    connection.addRequestProperty("A-IM","feed");
  }
}

  ...
}
```

The setRequestHeaders method uses information persisted in the FeedInfo object since the last fetch (if available). More specifically, it uses the last-modified and eTag (If-None-Match) information obtained from the response of the last fetch and saved in the FeedInfo object passed in as a parameter. If the feed server supports one of these protocols, it can determine whether the feed has changed since last request, and if so, it will not send the full feed content, responding with a HttpURLConnection.HTTP_NOT_MODIFIED response code instead. This is the *conditional* GET. The header information must be set before the connection is established.

If the feed needs to be updated, the fetcher's resetFeedInfo method is called (this method is defined in the com.sun.syndication.fetcher.impl. HttpURLFeedFetcher class). It populates the syndFeedInfo object with the updated and parsed feed contents, as well as the last-modified and eTag information, as available from the response. Then, the updated syndFeedInfo object is returned. As shown in the previous code listings, the SyndFeedInfo object is used to construct and update the persisted FeedInfo object. The (updated) last-Modified and eTag fields will be used next time the feed is fetched.

# Processing changes to Friend URLs

In the *Using migrations to evolve the Datastore entities* section, we added a `urls` field to the `Friend` class, which stores the set of feed URLs associated with that `Friend`.

We've not yet looked at the process by which changes to this URL list, via the client UI, are reflected in changes to the set of feed information objects.

We support this by first adding two methods to `server.domain.FeedIndex` — `addFeedURLs` and `updateFeedURLs`, shown in the following code.

`server.domain.FeedIndex`

```
  // used for existing URLs lists.
  public static Set<String> updateFeedURLs (Set<String> newurls,
    Set<String> origUrls, String id, boolean replace)
  {
    if (id == null || newurls == null || origUrls == null )
    {
      return null;
    }
    Set<String> added = new HashSet<String>(newurls);
    added.removeAll(origUrls);
    Set<String> badUrls = FeedIndex.addFeedsFriend(added, id);
    if (replace) {
      Set<String> removed = new HashSet<String>(origUrls);
      removed.removeAll(newurls);
      FeedIndex.removeFeedsFriend(removed, id);
    }
    return badUrls;
  }


  // used for Friends with no existing urls
  public static Set<String> addFeedURLs (Set<String> urls,
    String id)
  {
    if (id == null || urls == null) {
      return null;
    }
    Set<String> badUrls = FeedIndex.addFeedsFriend(urls, id);
    return badUrls;
  }
```

The `addFeedURls` method is called if the `Friend` data object does not have an existing list of URLs. In this case, feed objects are created for the URLs or existing feed objects are updated with the new `Friend` key. The `updateFeedURLs` method is called if there is an existing list of URLs that has been modified, in which case, some feed objects may also need to be removed.

These methods are called (as necessary) when changes to the `Friend` data are made via the client. Our approach is designed for App Engine's transactional model, and so we will not describe it in detail here but will revisit this stage of the process in *Chapter 9*, when we introduce **transactions**. As a preview, in the `server.FriendsServiceImpl` method, tasks are placed on a Task Queue (via the `/updatefeedurls` URL) to perform any necessary feed bookkeeping whenever a `Friend` is modified. We do this because (as we'll see in *Chapter 9*) that lets us perform the feed operations in the same transactional context as the `Friend` modifications.

# Enabling background feed updating and processing

With the `FeedInfo`, `FeedIndex`, and `FriendFeedFetcher` classes, we have the foundation in place to set up background feed-related processing. We want to be able to update the feeds (that is, refresh their content) asynchronously of any particular client request. If we do this, then for a particular client request, we can immediately display nearly up-to-date content to give the client something to look at right away, and it is much less likely that we will need to do a lot of on-request feed fetching to bring the content fully up-to-date.

We will enable the background processing via some new Servlets. We'll build two feed update request handlers (for now):

- Update feeds for the more recently requested FeedInfo objects: This is appropriate to do regularly as a lower-priority task. This will help to keep relevant feed content (close to) current.
- Update all FeedInfo objects belonging to the Friends of a given user: This is useful to do periodically for all logged-in active users, in order to pre-emptively fetch the feeds that they will likely want to display.

For both of these update models we cannot assume that we will be able to perform the update as a single processing episode. Because App Engine imposes a 30-second response timeout, we will split up the processing into batches to ensure that each batch has time to finish. We will again do this via the App Engine Task Queue. As before, we'll just use the existing default queue.

# Add some test feeds to your app

To best explore the Servlets described in this section, you may want to first add some feed URLs—any Atom or RSS feeds should work—for your *Connectr* Friends.

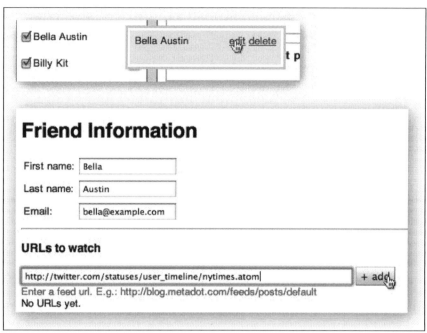

Figure 6: Adding some feed URLs to a Friend's details

In the *Connectr* browser interface, edit a Friend's information by clicking on the icon beside their name and selecting **edit**.

Paste in one or more Atom or RSS URL(s), such as the NY Times Twitter feed shown in Figure 6, clicking on **Add** after each one, and then **Save**.

As you edit the Friends' URLs lists, you can track the consequent modifications to the feed objects in the development console. You will not yet see the feed content reflected in the app's main panel (that functionality will be added in *Chapter 10*), but see the next section for another way to view the feed content.

# Updating the most recently requested FeedInfo objects

To update the `FeedInfo` feed content, we'll use an approach similar to the one taken with the `Migration` code in *Using migrations to evolve the Datastore entities*: we will perform the feed update in batches, passing along a string encoding of the query cursor from each batch to the next.

In order to keep the feed update process scalable, we will retrieve the `FeedInfo` objects ordered by the last date the feed was requested by a client. We'll specify a maximum number of batches to process. Essentially, we are using a heuristic: it is useful to perform proactive background updates for those feeds that have been most recently viewed.

This functionality is specified in `server.servlets.FeedUpdateServlet` , as follows. We use the query cursor to identify the starting point for each query. For each feed in the current batch, we call its `updateIfNeeded` method. Recall that a feed will not actually be updated if it was checked recently, or if its contents have not changed.

```
import javax.jdo.Query;
import com.google.appengine.api.datastore.Cursor;
import org.datanucleus.store.appengine.query.JDOCursorHelper;

import com.google.appengine.api.labs.taskqueue.Queue;
import com.google.appengine.api.labs.taskqueue.QueueFactory;
import com.google.appengine.api.labs.taskqueue.TaskOptions.Method;
import static com.google.appengine.api.labs.taskqueue.TaskOptions.
Builder.*;
// .. Other imports…

// update the most recently-requested feeds up to the
// given max number of batches
public void doPost(HttpServletRequest req, HttpServletResponse resp)
  throws IOException {

    int batch, max, batchcount= 0;
    String cursorString = req.getParameter("cursor");
    String numstring = req.getParameter("num");
    String maxstring = req.getParameter("max");
    String bc = req.getParameter("bc");
    batch = setNum(numstring);
    max = setMax(maxstring);
    logger.fine("bc is: "+ bc + " and num is: " + batch);
```

```
if (bc != null) {
  try {
     batchcount = Integer.parseInt(bc);
  }
  catch (Exception e) {
    logger.warning(e.getMessage());
    return;
  }
  if (batchcount >= max) {
    logger.info("Reached max number of feed update batches: "
        + max);
    return;
  }
}

PersistenceManager pm = PMF.get().getPersistenceManager();

Query q = null;
try {
  q = pm.newQuery(FeedInfo.class);
  q.setOrdering("dateRequested desc");
  if (cursorString != null)
  {
    Cursor cursor =  Cursor.fromWebSafeString(cursorString);
    Map<String, Object> extensionMap =
      new HashMap<String, Object>();
    extensionMap.put(JDOCursorHelper.CURSOR_EXTENSION, cursor);
    q.setExtensions(extensionMap);
  }
  q.setRange(0, batch);
  List<FeedInfo> results = (List<FeedInfo>) q.execute();
  if (results.size() > 0) {
    batchcount++;
    Cursor cursor = JDOCursorHelper.getCursor(results);
    cursorString = cursor.toWebSafeString();
    Queue queue = QueueFactory.getDefaultQueue();
    queue.add(url("/feedupdate").param(
      "cursor",cursorString).param("num", ""+batch).
      param("max", ""+max).param("bc", ""+batchcount));

    for (FeedInfo f : results) {
      // update the feed if needed
      // [if it has not just been updated]
      logger.info("working on feed: "+ f.getFeedTitle());
      f.updateIfNeeded(pm);
```

```
        }
      }
      else {
        cursorString = null;
      }
    }
    catch (Exception e) {
      logger.warning(e.getMessage());
    }
    finally {
      q.closeAll();
      pm.close();
    }
  }


  ...
}
```

# The FeedUpdateServlet mapping

To run FeedUpdateServlet and its resultant series of tasks, we will map the Servlet to a URL, /feedupdate:

```
<servlet>
 <servlet-name>FeedUpdate</servlet-name>
 <servlet-class>
   packagepath.server.servlets.FeedUpdateServlet
 </servlet-class>
</servlet>
<servlet-mapping>
 <servlet-name>FeedUpdate</servlet-name>
 <url-pattern>/feedupdate</url-pattern>
</servlet-mapping>
```

Once mapped, the feed update can be initiated locally as so:

```
http://localhost:8888/feedupdate?num=2&max=3
```

where, by using num=2, we are specifying a batch size of two feed updates per task, instead of the default 5, and where max=3 indicates that a maximum of three batches of feeds should be processed. In actuality, we would probably want this number to be larger. For the initial request, we of course have no query cursor parameter.

When each query returns, if there are more results, the Servlet adds the next /feedupdate Task to the default Task Queue to perform the next batch of updates. Each invocation passes on the updated cursor information to the next, as well as the running count for the number of batches processed thus far.

 Note that the next task in the series is enqueued as soon as the cursor is obtained, before the Servlet processes the results from the current query. This increases throughput.

In this way, we iterate over the FeedInfo objects in the Datastore, terminating when we have processed max batches of feeds, or run out of feeds.

The FeedInfo updates are (essentially) *idempotent*—it does not matter if we fetch a feed multiple times. This characteristic is important for actions running as tasks because if the task terminates in an exception for any reason, it will be rerun.

The FeedUpdateServlet can be used to proactively fetch feeds in the background so that the initial client feed display is fresh, and it is likely to take less work to handle a client feed update request. In *Chapter 12*, we will see how to set up this activity as a **Cron** Job and how to run the feed update tasks at a lower priority than other tasks.

If you run and rerun this Servlet you will see some diagnostics printed in the development console that indicate what is happening with respect to feed checking. You will be able to see that if a feed has just been checked, it won't be checked again during its latency period. You can also observe that not all feed servers support a conditional GET—those that do not will always be updated once the latency window has passed.

## Using an admin-only Servlet URL for the feed update job

We will configure our feed update Servlet URL to allow only admin access. As before, this is done via a security-constraint specification in the war/WEB-INF/web.xml file. Recall that the App Engine Task Queue can access admin-only URLs.

```
<security-constraint>
    <web-resource-collection>
      <url-pattern>/feedupdate</url-pattern>
    </web-resource-collection>
    <auth-constraint>
       <role-name>admin</role-name>
    </auth-constraint>
  </security-constraint>
```

Once this declaration is in place, you will need to log in as an admin to initiate the feed update task.

# Updating all feeds for the Friends of a UserAccount

The second Servlet that we will define is the one that updates the feeds associated with all Friends for a given `UserAccount`. For now, we will just run this Servlet manually. However, once the *Connectr* login mechanism is in place, we will configure this task to be run asynchronously when a user logs in, and re-invoked periodically while the user is active.

With this Servlet, we will use a slightly different model than that of the `FeedUpdateServlet` mentioned previously. In a "parent" Servlet called `server.servlets.FeedUpdateUserServlet`, we will find all instances of `Friend` associated with the given user. Then, we will define a feed update Task for each `Friend`, implemented by `server.servlets.FeedUpdateFriendServlet`, and will add all such tasks to the queue at once. Then, the parent Servlet will terminate and its child update tasks will be run when they reach their turn in the queue.

It is possible that some of the child tasks will be run in parallel. For our feed model, this does not cause problems—in fact, we view it as a benefit—but in general, this issue must be considered. *Chapter 9* will introduce the use of transactional control.

So, here we have two Servlets to define: the parent `server.servlets.FeedUpdateUserServlet`, and the child `server.servlets.FeedUpdateFriendServlet`. `FeedUpdateFriendServlet` is used only as a task action, and we will define it to support only HTTP POST requests.

 Any Servlets that are used only for tasks should, as a matter of course, require admin authentication.

```
import com.google.appengine.api.labs.taskqueue.Queue;
import com.google.appengine.api.labs.taskqueue.QueueFactory;
import com.google.appengine.api.labs.taskqueue.TaskOptions.Method;
import static com.google.appengine.api.labs.taskqueue.TaskOptions.Builder.*;


@SuppressWarnings("serial")
public class FeedUpdateUserServlet extends HttpServlet
```

```
  {

  private static Logger logger =
    Logger.getLogger(FeedUpdateUserServlet.class.getName());

  private UserAccount getUserAccount(String userEmail,
    PersistenceManager pm)
  {
    UserAccount userAccount = null;
    Query q = null;
    try
    {
      q = pm.newQuery(UserAccount.class,
      "emailAddress == :emailAddress");
      q.setRange(0,1);
      List<UserAccount> results =
        (List<UserAccount>) q.execute(userEmail);
      if (results.iterator().hasNext())
      {
        for (UserAccount u : results)
        {
          userAccount = u;
        }
      }
    }
    catch (Exception e) {
      logger.warning(e.getMessage());
    }
    finally {
      q.closeAll();
    }
    return userAccount;
  }

...
// update all feeds for friends of the given UserAccount
public void doPost(HttpServletRequest req, HttpServletResponse resp)
  throws IOException
{

  PersistenceManager pm = PMF.get().getPersistenceManager();
  String userEmail = req.getParameter("useremail");
  UserAccount userAccount = null;
  try {
    userAccount = getUserAccount(userEmail, pm);
```

```
      if (userAccount != null)
      {
        Set<Friend> friends = userAccount.getFriends();
        // get the default queue
        Queue queue = QueueFactory.getDefaultQueue();
        for (Friend fr : friends )
        {
          // spawn off tasks to fetch the Friend-associated urls
          queue.add(url("/feedupdatefr").param("fkey", fr.getId()));
        }
      }
    }
    finally {
      pm.close();
    }
    resp.setContentType("text/plain");
    if (userAccount != null) {
      resp.getWriter().println("queued up friend feed fetches");
    }
    else {
      resp.getWriter().println("no matching user found");
    }
  }
```

```
}//end class
```

As shown in the previous code, in `FeedUpdateUserServlet`, a `UserAccount` object is first retrieved from the Datastore. At the moment, our application includes only the "default user", which for convenience we will retrieve via its e-mail, `default@default.com`. This model will change and the choice of users will become more exciting, after we add login and account capabilities in *Chapter 8*.

The user's Friends are obtained from the retrieved `UserAccount` object, and a `/feedupdatefr` task is added to the default queue for each. The task parameter is the Friend's ID. This will allow the task to retrieve the `FeedInfo` objects associated with the Friend.

The /feedupdateuser URL is mapped to FeedUpdateUserServlet and the /feedupdatefr URL is mapped to FeedUpdateFriendServlet. We require admin access for both. The additions to web.xml are as follows:

```
<servlet>
 <servlet-name>FeedUpdateUser</servlet-name>
 <servlet-class>
   packagepath.server.servlets.FeedUpdateUserServlet
 </servlet-class>
</servlet>
<servlet-mapping>
 <servlet-name>FeedUpdateUser</servlet-name>
   <url-pattern>/feedupdateuser</url-pattern>
</servlet-mapping>

<servlet>
  <servlet-name>FeedUpdateFriend</servlet-name>
  <servlet-class>
   packagepath.server.servlets.FeedUpdateFriendServlet
  </servlet-class>
</servlet>
<servlet-mapping>
  <servlet-name>FeedUpdateFriend</servlet-name>
  <url-pattern>/feedupdatefr</url-pattern>
</servlet-mapping>

<security-constraint>
  <web-resource-collection>
      <url-pattern>/feedupdateuser</url-pattern>
  </web-resource-collection>
  <auth-constraint>
      <role-name>admin</role-name>
  </auth-constraint>
</security-constraint>

<security-constraint>
   <web-resource-collection>
      <url-pattern>/feedupdatefr</url-pattern>
   </web-resource-collection>
   <auth-constraint>
     <role-name>admin</role-name>
   </auth-constraint>
</security-constraint>
```

# Updating the feeds for a specific Friend

The `server.servlets.FeedUpdateFriendServlet` performs feed updates for the feeds associated with a given `Friend`. This Servlet demonstrates some useful and efficient Datastore query tricks.

```java
@SuppressWarnings("serial")
public class FeedUpdateFriendServlet extends HttpServlet
{

  private static Logger logger =
    Logger.getLogger(FeedUpdateFriendServlet.class.getName());

  public void doPost(HttpServletRequest req,
    HttpServletResponse resp) throws IOException
  {

    PersistenceManager pm = PMF.get().getPersistenceManager();

  Query q = null;
  try {
    String fkey = req.getParameter("fkey");
    if (fkey != null) {
      // query for matching FeedIndex keys
      q = pm.newQuery("select key from " +
        FeedIndex.class.getName() +
        " where friendKeys == :id");
      List ids = (List) q.execute(fkey);
      if (ids.size() == 0) {
          return;
      }
      // get the parent keys of the ids
      Key k = null;
      List<Key> parentlist = new ArrayList<Key>();
      for (Object id : ids) {
        // cast to key
        k = (Key)id;
        parentlist.add(k.getParent());
      }
      // fetch the parents using the keys
      Query q2 = pm.newQuery("select from " +
      FeedInfo.class.getName() +
      " where urlstring == :keys");
```

```
// setting query deadline, allowing eventual consistency
 on read
q2.addExtension(
  "datanucleus.appengine.datastoreReadConsistency",
  "EVENTUAL");
List<FeedInfo> results =
  (List<FeedInfo>) q2.execute(parentlist);

if (results.iterator().hasNext()) {
  for (FeedInfo fi : results) {
    fi.updateRequestedFeed(pm);
  }
}
    }
  }
  catch (Exception e) {
     logger.warning(e.getMessage());
  }
  finally {
     if (q != null) {
        q.closeAll();
     }
     pm.close();
  }
 }
}
```

The Friend key (fkey) is passed in as a parameter to FeedUpdateFriendServlet.
That key is used to find the FeedIndex objects associated with the URLs of a Friend.
As described in *Chapter 5*, *multi-valued properties* can be very useful in supporting "set
membership" types of queries. Because friendKeys is a multi-valued property, a
filter like the following on FeedIndex:

```
friendKeys == :id
```

will return all FeedIndex objects with the given Friend ID in their friendKeys list.
Note that it is not necessary to actually instantiate the Friend itself. Furthermore,
the query is a *keys-only* query (as described in *Chapter 5*), which means that only
the FeedIndex keys are returned—a much more efficient process than obtaining
the instances.

From the FeedIndex keys we can obtain the parent FeedInfo keys. This derivation
is possible because of how the object keys are constructed, and will be described
in *Chapter 9*.

We can then do a *batch* fetch of all the indicated `FeedInfo` objects at once, as introduced in *Chapter 5*, by passing the *list* of `FeedInfo` keys as a query argument. This again is much more efficient than retrieving each of them individually. The batch query returns the list of `FeedInfo` objects to update as necessary.

The `updateIfNeeded` method is then called for each associated `FeedInfo` object in turn.

The design of the `FeedUpdateFriendServlet` assumes that a single `Friend` will not have "too many" associated feeds, such that the Servlet times out at the 30-second deadline before finishing all its updates. If this turns out not to be the case, then the feed updates could themselves be divided into subtasks.

To manually initiate an update of all the feeds for the Friends of the "default" user, invoke the `FeedUpdateUserServlet` like this in the development environment:

```
http://localhost:8888/feedupdateuser?useremail=default@default.com
```

As before, use of the default user's e-mail address is only temporary; we will change this model in *Chapter 8*. Make sure that you use the e-mail address corresponding to your one test user—you can see it listed in the development Datastore browser if you want to check. Later, once our login framework is set up, this task will be invoked automatically for a given user.

# A simple Servlet to display feed contents

Now that we've added and are fetching `Friend` feeds, it's a bit unsatisfying that the frontend UI is not hooked up yet in this version of the app, and so we can't see the contents of the feeds that we're fetching. So, we have generated a rather low-rent Servlet to let us display the data anyway. It is called `server.servlets.ShowUserFriendFeedsServlet`. You can run it locally as so:

```
http://localhost:8888/showfeedsuser?useremail=default@default.com
```

where the `useremail` parameter is the e-mail address of the default `UserAccount` object. This Servlet simply displays (without any finesse) the titles of the feed items for all of the feeds associated with all of the Friends of the default user. It will first update the feeds as necessary.

If you reload this Servlet multiple times, you will notice from the console diagnostics that, as intended, feeds aren't re-fetched again within the update latency window. Similarly, try running one of the feed update Servlets first, before running the ShowUserFriendFeedsServlet. As expected, after they've been executed, the ShowUserFriendFeedsServlet will do less work, both with respect to not needing to re-fetch within the latency window, and with respect to the higher likelihood that a given feed source will indicate that it does not need to be updated yet.

# Summary

In this chapter, we've used Servlets, URL Fetch, and Task Queues (and string-encoded query cursors) to support data migration and to add RSS/Atom feed support to *Connectr*, with the help of the open source ROME and ROME Fetcher libraries.

We built a simple Migration framework and built a model and framework for storing, updating, and accessing feed information associated with Friends. We used Servlets and the Task Queue to support various background update tasks, independent of a specific client-side request.

The application supports asynchronous and decoupled feed updates, so the Servlets can work both proactively and on-demand in the background to keep feed content updated—as application resources permit, and focusing on those users currently logged in. In that way, the application can be more responsive in displaying relevant feed information for a given user, and in updating that user's feeds quickly. We will put this functionality to use in the following chapters and further develop and refine this asynchronous model in *Chapter 12*.

# 8

# Authentication using Twitter, Facebook OAuth, and Google Accounts

In this chapter, we integrate *Connectr* with Google Accounts, Facebook, and Twitter for user authentication and information retrieval.

By using third party services, users can login to their favorite service in order to use *Connectr*. This allows *Connectr* to log its users in without asking them to remember and use yet another username and password.

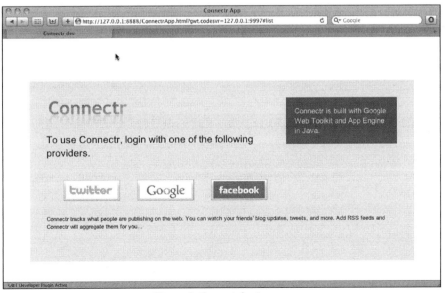

Figure 1: *Connectr* login page

Figure 2: *Connectr* login page

Since *Connectr* retrieves a user's information such as name and, when available, e-mail address or unique identifier from the authentication provider, it has enough information to identify them uniquely and can register them in *Connectr* automatically. This not only simplifies the user experience but also programming because credential management does not need to be implemented.

Implementing integrations to different authentication providers boils down to a few steps as explained in the following section.

# *Connectr* login implementation

Typically a login implementation using multiple third party authentication providers happens in a sequence of chronological events:

1.  Display of the *Connectr* login page: the user has to choose from preferred authentication services

2.  The user is redirected to the chosen service which authenticates and grants access to *Connectr*.

3.  The service redirects the user back to *Connectr*. The user session is created.

4.  *Connectr* presents the application to the user.

Let's explore how to implement Google Accounts, Facebook, and Twitter authentication in *Connectr*. To do so, we will explain each step as presented in the following image:

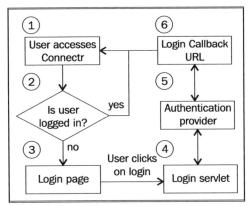

Figure 3: Login sequence

# Step-by-step implementation of the login sequence

1. In step 1, shown in the previous image, when users access *Connectr* , it checks whether they are logged in or not (step 2).

2. This check is done in the main class `ConnectrApp` as soon as the application loads:

```
package com.metadot.book.connectr.client;
// Imports omitted

public class ConnectrApp implements EntryPoint {

...
  public void onModuleLoad() {
...
    getLoggedInUser();
  }
...
```

3. The `getLoggedInUser` method is as follows:

```
private void getLoggedInUser() {
  new RPCCall<UserAccountDTO>() {
    @Override protected void callService(AsyncCallback<UserAccount
DTO> cb) {
```

```
        loginService.getLoggedInUserDTO(cb);
    }
    @Override public void onSuccess(UserAccountDTO
loggedInUserDTO) {
        if (loggedInUserDTO == null) {
            // nobody is logged in
            showLoginView();

} else {
            // user is logged in
            setCurrentUser(loggedInUserDTO);
             goAfterLogin();
    eventBus.fireEvent(new LoginEvent(currentUser));
}
    ...
```

4. The previous code snippet shows that if a user is logged in then `loggedInUserDTO` is not `null` and sets the current user, constructs the user interface, and finally fires a login event. The user can then use the application.

5. However, when nobody is logged in the RPC calls return a `null` `loggedInUserDTO` object. This triggers a call to the `showLoginView()` method, which presents users with a login page (step 3).

```
if (loggedInUserDTO == null) {                     nobody is
logged in
    showLoginView();
```

6. At the login page, users can choose Facebook, Google, or Twitter as their authentication provider. Once they click on their choice, the LoginPresenter instance redirects them to a backend Servlet (step 4) as shown in the following code:

```
package com.metadot.book.connectr.client.presenter;

// Imports omitted

...
  private void doLoginFacebook() {
    Window.Location.assign("/loginfacebook");
  }

  private void doLoginGoogle() {
     Window.Location.assign("/logingoogle");
  }

  private void doLoginTwitter() {
    Window.Location.assign("/logintwitter");
  }
...
```

It must be noted that `Location.assign(URL)` instructs the browser to completely unload the GWT app and to replace its content with what is found at URL. The advantage of this is that it allows the current browser window to conduct the entire authentication and authorization transaction without having to pop up an additional window. The drawback is that the application has to be reloaded at the end of the login process. However, this drawback is mitigated by the fact that, first, *Connectr* uses code splitting so only the necessary parts of the application are downloaded, and second, because the client application is cached by the browser so reloading it has minimum performance impact. We feel confident that the advantages gained by redirecting the browser to the backend outweigh this drawback.

In step 4 and step 5, once the *Connectr* backend Servlet is in action mode, a back and forth discussion takes place where tokens, application ID, and secret keys depending on provider requirements, are exchanged.

At the end of step 5, once the provider has everything it needs, it calls a callback URL provided by *Connectr*.

In step 6, the Servlet at the callback URL wraps up the authentication process, creates a login session, and updates or creates the user's record. The specific implementation of each authentication provider is slightly different and will be covered in subsequent sections. The code used for Google Accounts is as follows:

```
package com.metadot.book.connectr.server.servlets;

public class LoginGoogleCallbackServlet extends HttpServlet {
  ...


  public void doGet(HttpServletRequest request,
    HttpServletResponse response)
      throws IOException {
    Principal googleUser = request.getUserPrincipal();
    if (googleUser != null) {
        // start login process
...
    }
    response.sendRedirect(LoginHelper.getApplitionURL(request));
  }
}
```

At this point, the login process is completed. The Servlet redirects the user back to the *Connectr* front page using a call to `response.sendRedirect(URL)`. The *Connectr* GWT client is then reloaded in the user's browser.

Now that we have seen how the login sequence works, let's look at the specific implementations for Facebook, Google, and Twitter.

# OAuth: a new way to login and authorize

OAuth is short for Open Authorization. OAuth is an open standard. It allows users to grant applications access to their personal information stored in other applications. For example, a user could grant application X access to his or her list of Facebook friends. The type of information exchanged among applications is not limited in any way. It can be as simple as a user's name and e-mail address or can be complex data structures such as pictures, videos, contact lists, blog entries, or Twitter tweets.

Once a user grants access to an application, a set of tokens is used to identify the requesting application. These tokens replace traditional username and password authentication.

OAuth 2.0, which we use in this book, focuses on simplicity while providing a lot of capabilities programmers can tap into. Both Facebook and Twitter use the OAuth standard for authentication.

# Integrating with Facebook

The official Facebook recommendation is to use the Graph API that allows read and write access to Facebook for third party application integration. *Connectr* uses it for authentication and user information retrieval. The Graph API uses OAuth 2.0 as its authentication protocol.

On top of using Facebook as an authentication gateway we will also make *Connectr* available from within Facebook as a Facebook app located at

```
http://apps.facebook.com/connectrapp
```

Before we can start coding the integration, first we need to register *Connectr* to Facebook.

# Registering *Connectr* with Facebook

Registering an app is easy and takes only a few steps. This can be done at the following URL:

```
http://www.facebook.com/developers/createapp.php
```

Once we enter the name of the application and upload our logo along with a favicon (16 by 16 pixels icon), Facebook presents us with the application settings:

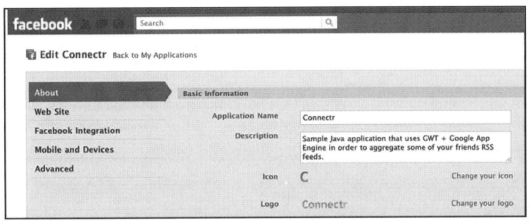

Figure 4: Registering *Connectr* with Facebook

The **Web Site** tab provides us with our **Application ID** and our **Application Secret**. We can also enter the **Site URL** where the application lives.

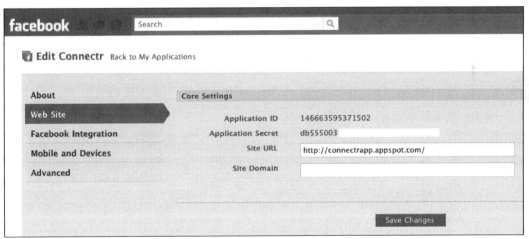

Figure 5: Adding *Connectr* website information

Once the changes are saved, we click on **Back to My Applications** to view the application summary including the *Connectr* **Application ID, API key**, and **Application Secret**, as shown in the following image:

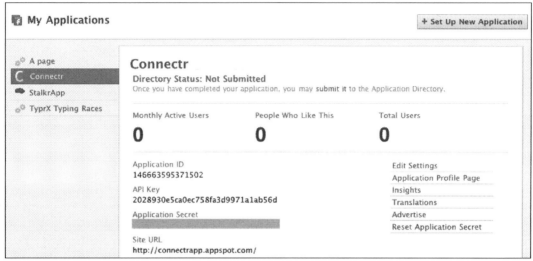

Figure 6: *Connectr* application Facebook status page

The application is now set up on Facebook and we can start implementing Facebook authentication.

# Authenticating with Facebook OAuth

Before we start coding the Facebook authentication, first we need to configure our app with the **Application ID, API Key**, and **Application Secret** that we were granted during the Facebook application registration process. In addition, Facebook will be using the callback URL when the users authenticate.

All this information should reside in `appengine-web.xml` as shown in the following code:

```
<system-properties>
..
    <property name="fb_app_id" value="your_app_id" />
    <property name="fb_api_key" value="your_app_key" />
    <property name="fb_secret" value="your_app_secret " />
    <property name="fb_callback_url" value="http://connectrapp.
appspot.com/loginfacebook" />
...
```

Obviously, readers will have to replace the values shown in the previous code with their own.

In order to expose the details of a typical OAuth authentication process *Connectr* implements Facebook authentication and graph query straight into Java, without using any third party library, so that each step of the process can be atomized to its simplest expression.

The authentication process consists of the following steps:

- From the login page, a user clicks on the Facebook link and is redirected to Facebook for authentication. After authenticating, the user is required to authorize *Connectr* to access his or her data.

- After authorization, Facebook redirects the user back to *Connectr* , with a Facebook verification code.

- *Connectr* then exchanges this code for the access token needed to query the Graph API in order to get the user information.

Let's examine how the authentication is implemented.

First, when a user clicks on the **Login with Facebook** button, the user is redirected to the `LoginFacebookServlet` Servlet that constructs the Facebook login URL. The URL includes the *Connectr* Facebook application ID `appid` and a callback URL, which Facebook will use to call *Connectr* back after the user authenticates and grants us permission. We then redirect to Facebook where the authentication and authorization takes place. The login and authorization is done by the `LoginFacebookServlet` using the following code:

```
package com.metadot.book.connectr.server.servlets;
// Imports omitted

public class LoginFacebookServlet extends LoginSuperServlet {

public void doGet(HttpServletRequest request, HttpServletResponse
response) throws IOException {
...
```

```
String fbLoginPage = "https://graph.facebook.com/oauth/authorize"
    + "?client_id=" + appId
    + "&redirect_uri=" + callbackURL;

response.sendRedirect(fbLoginPage);
```

Figure 7: First time login permission request

After users login to Facebook and authorize *Connectr* to access their information, Facebook redirects them to the callback URL.

The callback URL points to the same Servlet that initiated the process, namely LoginFacebookServlet. We identify that this call is a callback because Facebook sends a verification code as a parameter. We exchange it for an access token with a call to UrLFetcher:

```
if (code != null && !code.isEmpty()) {
    request.getSession().setAttribute("facebook_code", code);
    String tokenURL = "https://graph.facebook.com/oauth/access_token"
    + "?client_id=" + appId
    + "&redirect_uri="
    + callbackURL
    + "&client_secret=" + clientSecret + "&code=" + code;

    String resp = UrLFetcher.get(tokenURL);
```

Once the response is received for UrLFetcher, we extract the access token from the response string resp:

```
int beginIndex = "access_token=".length();
String token = resp.substring(beginIndex);
```

Finally, we fetch the user information by making another UrLFetcher call to the Graph API using the access token we were just granted. We then extract the user information using the custom method extractUserInfo—which we created:

```
String URL = "https://graph.facebook.com/me?access_token=" + token;
resp = UrLFetcher.get(URL);
log.info("Response: " + resp);
UserAccount connectr = extractUserInfo(resp);
```

Once the previous code is executed, we can start our login process and redirect users to the front page.

```
connectr = new LoginHelper().loginStarts(request.getSession(),
connectr );
log.info("connectr id is logged in:" + connectr.getId().toString());
response.sendRedirect(LoginHelper.getApplitionURL(request));
```

The entire LoginFacebookServlet Servlet code is as follows:

```
package com.metadot.book.connectr.server.servlets;

// Imports omitted

public class LoginFacebookServlet extends LoginSuperServlet {
   private static final long serialVersionUID = -1187933703374946249L;
   private static Logger log = Logger.getLogger(LoginFacebookServlet.
class.getName());

   public void doGet(HttpServletRequest request, HttpServletResponse
response) throws IOException {
     String callbackURL = null, clientSecret = null, appId = null;

     clientSecret = getFbParam("fb_secret");
     appId = getFbParam("fb_app_id");
     callbackURL = getFbParam("fb_callback_url");
     String code = request.getParameter("code");

     if (code != null && !code.isEmpty()) {
       // Facebook authentication has been done and Facebook is calling
us back here:
       String keyNValues = getParams(request);

      /*
       * Save code in session
       */
       request.getSession().setAttribute("facebook_code", code);

      /*
```

```
     * Get access token
     */
    String tokenURL = "https://graph.facebook.com/oauth/access_
token" + "?client_id=" + appId + "&redirect_uri="
          + callbackURL + "&client_secret=" + clientSecret + "&code="
+ code;

    log.info("requesting access token url=" + tokenURL);
    String resp = UrlFetcher.get(tokenURL);
    log.info("Response = " + resp);
    int beginIndex = "access_token=".length();
    String token = resp.substring(beginIndex);
    log.info("Extracted token = " + token);

    /*
     * Get user info
     */
    String url = "https://graph.facebook.com/me?access_token=" +
token;
    log.info("requesting user info: " + url);
    resp = UrlFetcher.get(url);
    log.info("Response: " + resp);
    UserAccount connectr = extractUserInfo(resp);
    connectr = new LoginHelper().loginStarts(request.getSession(),
connectr);
    log.info("User id is logged in:" + connectr.getId().toString());

    /*
     * All done. Let's go home.
     */
    response.sendRedirect(LoginHelper.getApplitionURL(request));

  } else {
    // Redirect to Facebook login page
    log.info("Starting FB authentication appid: " + appId + " -
callback: " + callbackURL);
    String fbLoginPage = "https://graph.facebook.com/oauth/
authorize"
        + "?client_id=" + appId
        + "&redirect_uri=" + callbackURL;

    response.sendRedirect(fbLoginPage);
  }

}

...
```

# Integrating *Connectr* inside Facebook

Facebook provides an **iFrame** mechanism by which an app can be seen as if it was coming directly from Facebook itself. The page in which the iFrame can be found is called a **Canvas** page.

To set up this feature we have to edit the *Connectr* Facebook application settings and enter additional information in the **Canvas** tab:

- The canvas Page is where *Connectr* lives on Facebook. We choose `http://apps.facebook.com/connectrapp`

- The canvas URL is where Facebook pulls the content from. Since we want the login page with automatic Facebook authentication we choose: `http://connectrapp.appspot.com/loginfacebook?`

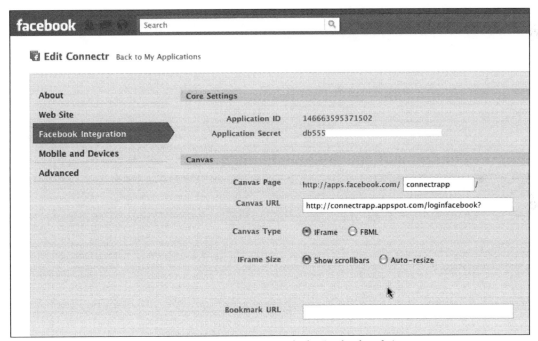

Figure 8: Installing *Connectr* inside the Facebook website

After saving all the settings, we can visit `http://apps.facebook.com/connectrapp` to use the application inside Facebook.

Figure 9:The *Connectr* application as seen inside the Facebook website

# Authenticating against Google

Since *Connectr* lives on Google App Engine, it makes authenticating against the Google Accounts service a breeze. To authenticate against Google Accounts, we will use the AppEngine Java Google Account API.

The login process is handled by two Servlets attached to two distinct URLs: a Servlet named `LoginGoogleServlet` whose job is mainly to redirect users to the Google Account login page, and a callback Servlet named `LoginGoogleCallbackServlet` that Google Account Service calls after users authenticate. Having two Servlets instead of one can make the application source code more readable. However, this is a software design consideration and does not affect the application behavior.

1. In the following snippet, the `LoginGoogleServlet` first creates the callback URL named `callbackURL` by calling `buildCallBackURL(...)`. This method is smart enough to distinguish between production and development environments.

```
package com.metadot.book.connectr.server.servlets;
// Imports and variable declarations omitted

  public void doGet(HttpServletRequest request,
HttpServletResponse response) throws IOException {
    String callbackURL = buildCallBackURL(request,
AuthenticationProvider.GOOGLE);
    UserService userService = UserServiceFactory.getUserService();
    String googleLoginUrl = userService.
createLoginURL(callbackURL);
    log.info("Going to Google login URL: " + googleLoginUrl);
    response.sendRedirect(googleLoginUrl);
    }
  }
```

2. Then we get the Google Account login URL by calling

```
userService.createLoginURL(callbackURL) that redirects the user
to the Google login page:
    response.sendRedirect(googleLoginUrl);
```

At this point, the user authenticates on the Google login page and is redirected to the *Connectr* callback URL that points to the `LoginGoogleCallbackServlet`. This Servlet finishes the login process:

```
package com.metadot.book.connectr.server.servlets;



// Imports omitted

public class LoginGoogleCallbackServlet extends HttpServlet {

    private static Logger log = Logger.getLogger(LoginGoogleCallback
```

```
Servlet.class

    .getName());



  public void doGet(HttpServletRequest request,
HttpServletResponse response)

    throws IOException {

  Principal googleUser = request.getUserPrincipal();

  if (googleUser != null) {
    // update or create user
    UserAccount u = new UserAccount(googleUser.getName(),
AuthenticationProvider.GOOGLE);

    u.setName(googleUser.getName());
    UserAccount connectr = new LoginHelper().
    loginStarts(request.getSession(), u);

  }

  response.sendRedirect(LoginHelper.getApplitionURL(request));

 }

}
```

First, the Servlet checks if the authentication was successful by requesting the user object via a call to `request.getUserPrincipal()`.

If the object is `null` it means that nobody is logged in so it redirects to the front page where users will have the choice to login again, otherwise we instantiate a `UserAccount` object with the Google user information and start the login process by calling `new LoginHelper().loginStarts(...)`.

`loginStarts(...)` creates a *Connectr* session and then either updates or creates the user account record if it did not previously exist.

The login process is now completed and we can redirect the user back to the *Connectr* front page.

```
response.sendRedirect(LoginHelper.getApplitionURL(request));
```

# Authenticating against Twitter with OAuth

Twitter authentication implementation is structured the same way as Facebook's and Google's. We first initiate a redirect to Twitter where users authenticate and grant access to *Connectr*. Then Twitter redirects them back to a callback URL where the login sequence is completed.

Instead of coding the OAuth authentication fully in Java without using a third party library, like we did for Facebook authentication, we use a library called twitter4j. This library provides easy access to the Twitter OAuth API, which we use to authenticate and get the current user's information. More information about this library can be found at `http://twitter4j.org`.

## Registering *Connectr* with Twitter

The first step is to register *Connectr* with Twitter at `http://twitter.com/apps/new`:

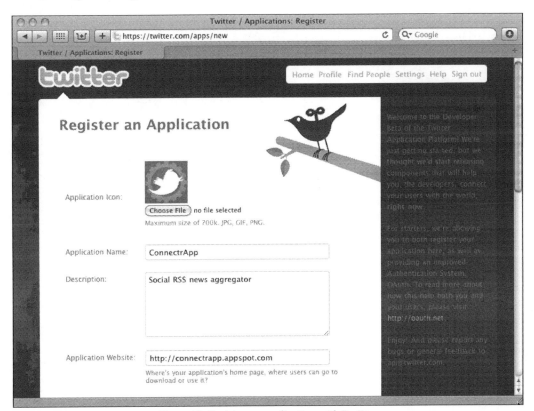

Figure10: Register an application with Twitter

Once created, Twitter provides us with both OAuth consumer and secret keys as shown in the following image:

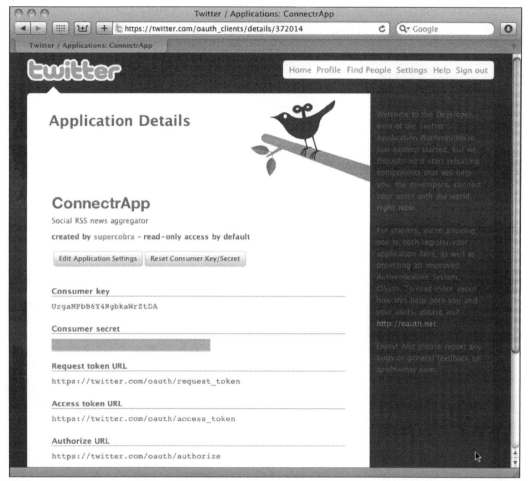

Figure11: *Connectr* application details

We save the following information into our application configuration file `appengine-web.xml`:

```
<system-properties>
    <property name="twitter-consumer-key" value="your-key" />
    <property name="twitter-consumer-secret" value="your-secret" />
    ...
<system-properties>
```

Readers should make sure that they replace the values in the previous code sample with their own.

# Introducing the Twitter login servlet

As for Google authentication, we use two Servlets, one that initiates the authentication and redirects the user to Twitter and another one, a callback Servlet, which completes the login process.

1. First, the login Servlet instantiates an instance of the Twitter class:

   ```
   Twitter twitter = new TwitterFactory().getInstance();
   ```

2. Then it asks for a request token. To do so, we need to provide our application credentials, which we got when we registered *Connectr* to Twitter:

   ```
   // Get info from system properties
   String key = AuthenticationProvidergetProp("twitter-consumerkey");
   String secret =
     AuthenticationProvider.getProp ("twitter-consumersecret");
   ...
   twitter.setOAuthConsumer(key, secret);
   RequestToken token = twitter.getOAuthRequestToken(callbackURL);
   ```

3. We then redirect users to Twitter for authentication using the following code:

   ```
   request.getSession().setAttribute("requestToken", token);
   String loginURL = token.getAuthenticationURL() + "&force_
   login=true";
   response.sendRedirect(loginURL);
   ```

4. Special attention should be paid to the parameter force_login that is set to true. This tells Twitter not to keep users logged in Twitter after this OAuth authentication session. The login Servlet code in its entirety is as follows:

   ```
   public class LoginTwitterServlet extends LoginSuperServlet {
     private static Logger log = Logger.
   getLogger(LoginTwitterServlet.class
       .getName());

     public void doGet(HttpServletRequest request,
   HttpServletResponse response)
       throws IOException {

     Twitter twitter = new TwitterFactory().getInstance();
     // get auth info from system properties
     String key = AuthenticationProvider.getProp("twitter-consumer-
   key");
     String secret = AuthenticationProvider.getProp("twitter-
   consumer-secret");
     try {
       twitter.setOAuthConsumer(key, secret);
       String callbackURL = buildCallBackURL(request,
   AuthenticationProvider.TWITTER);
   ```

```
        RequestToken token = twitter.getOAuthRequestToken(callbackUR
L);
        request.getSession().setAttribute("requestToken", token);
        String loginURL = token.getAuthenticationURL() + "&force_
login=true";
        log.info("Redirecting to: " + loginURL);
        response.sendRedirect(loginURL);

    } catch (TwitterException e) {
        e.printStackTrace();
    }

  }
}
```

# Analyzing the Twitter callback servlet

After users authenticate against Twitter and grant access to *Connectr* , they are redirected to the *Connectr* Twitter callback Servlet.

1.  First, the Servlet retrieves its Twitter instance , the Twitter key and secrets, as well as token and verifier code:

    ```
    Twitter twitter = new TwitterFactory().getInstance();
    String key = AuthenticationProvider.getProp("twitter-consumer-
    key");
    String secret = AuthenticationProvider.getProp("twitter-consumer-
    secret");

    RequestToken token = (RequestToken) request.getSession().
    getAttribute("requestToken");
    String verifier = request.getParameter("oauth_verifier");
    twitter.setOAuthConsumer(key, secret);
    ```

2.  Then it proceeds to get the OAuth access token:

    ```
    twitter.getOAuthAccessToken(token, verifier);
    ```

3.  Finally we fetch the user information from Twitter via a call to the verifyCredential method:

    ```
    User user = twitter.verifyCredentials();
    ```

After this we have everything we need to login our *Connectr* user:

```
UserAccount u =
  new UserAccount(sid, AuthenticationProvider.TWITTER);
u.setName(user.getName());
UserAccount Connectr =
  new LoginHelper().loginStarts(request.getSession(), u);
```

4. Here is the callback Servlet in its entirety:

```
package com.metadot.book.connectr.server.servlets;

// Imports omitted

@SuppressWarnings("serial")
public class LoginTwitterServlet extends LoginSuperServlet {
  private static Logger log = Logger.
getLogger(LoginTwitterServlet.class.getName());

  public void doGet(HttpServletRequest request,
HttpServletResponse response) throws IOException {

    Twitter twitter = new TwitterFactory().getInstance();
    // get auth info from system properties
    String key = AuthenticationProvider.getProp("twitter-consumer-
key");
    String secret = AuthenticationProvider.getProp("twitter-
consumer-secret");

    try {
      twitter.setOAuthConsumer(key, secret);
      String callbackURL = buildCallBackURL(request,
AuthenticationProvider.TWITTER);
      RequestToken token = twitter.getOAuthRequestToken(callbackUR
L);
      request.getSession().setAttribute("requestToken", token);
      String loginURL = token.getAuthenticationURL() + "&force_
login=true";
      log.info("Redirecting to: " + loginURL);
      response.sendRedirect(loginURL);
    } catch (TwitterException e) {
      e.printStackTrace();
    }
  }
}
```

# Logging out

In a nutshell, a logout action consists of telling the backend to invalidate the current user's session and to redirect users to the login screen.

Unfortunately, since Facebook logs users in when they authorize third party applications like *Connectr* to use their Facebook credentials, the logout process we have to implement will not only consist of login users of *Connectr* but also of Facebook.

Since *Connectr* uses the MVP pattern the logout action is part of the presenter of the `UserBadge` triad.

In this presenter, the logout action for Google and Twitter users consists of a call to the logout backend login service method, and for Facebook users we simply redirect them to a JSP document.

```
package com.metadot.book.connectr.client.presenter;
// Imports omitted

public class UserBadgePresenter implements Presenter {
...
private void doLogout() {
  new RPCCall<Void>() {
    @Override
    protected void callService(AsyncCallback<Void> cb) {
      if(facebookUser()){
        Window.Location.assign("/facebooklogout.jsp");
      } else { // Twitter, Google.
         rpcService.logout(cb);
            }
    }
    @Override
    public void onSuccess(Void result) {
      // logout event already fired by RPCCall
    }
    ...
  }.retry(3);
}
```

# Logging out when authenticating against Google or Twitter

When users log out of *Connectr*, while they previously logged in Google or Twitter, the `LoginService` logout method implemented in the `LoginServiceImpl` class, first invalidates the user session, then throws a special type of exception named `NotLoggedInException`, which is sent back to the client.

```
package com.metadot.book.connectr.server;
// Imports omitted

public class LoginServiceImpl extends RemoteServiceServlet implements
...
public void logout() throws NotLoggedInException {
  getThreadLocalRequest().getSession().invalidate();
    throw new NotLoggedInException("Logged out");
  }
```

This exception named `NotLoggedInException` is a custom Java exception as shown in the following piece of code:

```
package com.metadot.book.connectr.shared.exception;
import java.io.Serializable;

public class NotLoggedInException extends Exception implements
Serializable{
  public NotLoggedInException() {
  }
  public NotLoggedInException(String message) {
    super(message);
  }
  public NotLoggedInException(String message, Throwable cause) {
    super(message, cause);
  }
  public NotLoggedInException(Throwable cause) {
    super(cause);
  }
}
```

On the client side, the role of the *Connectr* `RPCCall` class is to centralize asynchronous calls, and it also intercepts preconfigured exceptions including `NotLoggedInException`. Once intercepted, a logout event is fired.

```
package com.metadot.book.connectr.client.helper;
// Imports omitted

public abstract class RPCCall<T> implements AsyncCallback<T> {

...
  } catch (NotLoggedInException e) {
    ConnectrApp.get().getEventBus().fireEvent(new LogoutEvent());
  }
...
```

As the application controller `AppController` has been configured to listen to logout events in the `bind` method, it is able to intercept it in order to call `doLogout()`.

```
package com.metadot.book.connectr.client;
// Imports omitted
...
  public AppController(FriendsServiceAsync rpcService, HandlerManager
eventBus) {
...
  private void bind() {
```

```
...
eventBus.addHandler(LogoutEvent.TYPE, new LogoutEventHandler() {
    @Override
    public void onLogout(LogoutEvent event) {
      doLogout();
        }
    });
...
```

The method doLogout() adds a "login" entry to the browser history.

```
private void doLogout() {
    History.newItem("login");
  }
```

Finally, the browser history change triggers a call to onValueChange, which requests the application to display the login page.

```
public void onValueChange(ValueChangeEvent<String> event) {
...
} else if (token.equals("login"))
  {
  ConnectrApp.get().loginView();
  return;
...
```

At this point, the user is logged out from *Connectr* and is presented with the application login page.

# Logging out of Facebook

When users login to *Connectr* via Facebook they end up logged in both applications because Facebook logs them in without their knowledge. This represents a serious security issue when users use a shared computer because if they log out of *Connectr*, the next user using the same computer, whose login provider is Facebook, will end up being logged in automatically to *Connectr* because Facebook will tell the new users the old user is still logged in.

Therefore logging users out cannot be accomplished only by invalidating their current *Connectr* session we also need to log them out of Facebook.

Unfortunately, Facebook fails to provide an API or a Java library, that *Connectr* could use to log users out. Therefore, it is up to the application to clean up the Facebook login session.

To do so, we are constrained to use the Facebook Javascript library, which provides a logout facility. We therefore create a JSP document that both invalidates the current *Connectr* user session and also calls the Facebook logout method via Facebook's own Javascript library.

When users click on logout, they are redirected to facebooklogout.jsp, which is as follows:

```
<%@ page import="java.util.List,com.metadot.book.connectr.shared.*,
com.metadot.book.connectr.server.utils.*"%>

<html>
<title>Logging out of Facebook</title>
<body>
<p>Please wait...</p>
<% session.invalidate(); %>
<div id="fb-root"></div>
<script src="http://connect.facebook.net/en_US/all.js"></script>
<script>
FB.init({ apiKey: '<%=AuthenticationProvider.fb_api_key()%>' });
FB.getLoginStatus(onResponse);
function onResponse(response) {
    if (!response.session) {
        window.location = "http://connectrapp.appspot.com/";
        return;
    }
    FB.logout(onResponse);
}
</script>
</body>
</html>
```

In this JSP document, we first display a 'please wait' message, then we proceed to invalidate the *Connectr* session by calling session.invalidate(). Since the session variable is available as an implicit object in JSP pages, we can access it right away.

Then we declare the mandatory Facebook HTML div with the mandatory fb-root ID and load the Javascript library directly from Facebook.

```
<div id="fb-root"></div>
<script src="http://connect.facebook.net/en_US/all.js"></script>
```

Then we initialize the library with *Connectr's* Facebook API key and request the user's login status:

```
FB.init({ apiKey: '<%=AuthenticationProvider.fb_api_key()%>' });
FB.getLoginStatus(onResponse);
```

The response is received via a callback function `onResponse()`.

In the `onResponse()` function we check whether we received a session. Since the user is still logged in in Facebook, the `response.session` object is present. Therefore, we call `FB.logout()` to log the user out with the same callback function.

```
function onResponse(response) {
    if (!response.session) {
        window.location = "http://connectrapp.appspot.com/";
        return;
    }
    FB.logout(onResponse);
}
```

Once `FB.logout()` returns, the user is logged out so we have no session available and can redirect the user back to the application:

```
window.location = "http://connectrapp.appspot.com/";
```

An upgrade of this functionality left to the reader to implement, would be to ask users if they wish to logout of Facebook instead of the application logging them out automatically.

This completes the Facebook logout implementation. We have seen that we can accomplish it with a little extra work because we have to log users out of Facebook on top of *Connectr*.

# Uniquely identifying *Connectr* users

When users log in for the first time, *Connectr* creates an account record for each of them. The goal of the record is to uniquely identify users and to store their information such as unique ID, name, and e-mail address.

To uniquely identify users, *Connectr* assigns them a `uniqueId`, which is a field of the `UserAccount` class:

```
package com.metadot.book.connectr.server.domain;
public class UserAccount implements Serializable, Cacheable{
...
  @Persistent
  private String uniqueId;
...
```

This unique ID is in the form of `<authentication provider user unique id>-<authentication provider id>`.

The unique user IDs assigned by Twitter and Facebook are numerical identifiers. In contrast, Google assigns the user's e-mail address, which is unique in the Google e-mail address namespace. Therefore, a *Connectr* `uniqueId` for a user authenticating via Google will appear as `bob@test.com-1`, as 14644763-2 for Twitter users and finally as 578742859-3 for Facebook junkies. The authentication provider ID is a simple constant declared in the `AuthenticationProvider` class:

```
package com.metadot.book.connectr.server.utils;
// Imports omitted
public class AuthenticationProvider {
  public static Integer GOOGLE=1, TWITTER=2, FACEBOOK=3;
}
```

# Automatically registering users when they login

Since users are not required to register by themselves before they use our application, *Connectr* needs to do this automatically on their behalf, so it can store their application settings for later retrieval. This automatic creation of user records happens when users use *Connectr* for the first time. It is implemented at login time via a call to `loginStart(session, user)`.

As an example, here is a fragment of the Google callback Servlet `LoginGoogleCallbackServlet`:

```
package com.metadot.book.connectr.server.servlets;
// Imports omitted

public class LoginGoogleCallbackServlet extends HttpServlet {

public void doGet(HttpServletRequest request, HttpServletResponse response)
    ...
// Logs user in
   UserAccount connectr = new LoginHelper().loginStarts(request.getSession(), u);
    . . .
```

In `loginStarts()`, which is part of the `LoginHelper` class, a call to `findOrCreate(user)` either finds an existing user record or creates it:

```
package com.metadot.book.connectr.server;
// Imports omitted
public class LoginHelper extends RemoteServiceServlet {
...
   public UserAccount loginStarts(HttpSession session, UserAccount
user){
      UserAccount connectr = AppLib.findOrCreateUser(user);
      // updated last logon date, etc...
      return connectr ;
   }
...
```

Finally, the method `findOrCreate(user)`, which is part of the `UserAccount` class, contains trivial Datastore entity manipulations that retrieve or create a new user entity:

```
package com.metadot.book.connectr.server.domain;
// Imports omitted

public class UserAccount implements Serializable, Cacheable {...
   public static UserAccount findOrCreateUser(UserAccount user) {
      PersistenceManager pm = PMF.get().getPersistenceManager();
      UserAccount oneResult = null, detached = null;

      String uniqueId = user.getUniqueId();

      Query q = pm.newQuery(UserAccount.class, "uniqueId == :uniqueId");
      q.setUnique(true);

      try {
        oneResult = (UserAccount) q.execute(uniqueId);
        if (oneResult != null) {
          log.info("User uniqueId already exists: " + uniqueId);
          detached = pm.detachCopy(oneResult);
        } else {
          log.info("UserAccount " + uniqueId + " does not exist,
creating...");
          AppLib.addFriends(user);
          pm.makePersistent(user);
          detached = pm.detachCopy(user);
        }
```

```
    } catch (Exception e) {
      e.printStackTrace();
    } finally {
      pm.close();
      q.closeAll();
    }

    return detached;
}
```

Et voila. The `detached` variable contains the current logged in user that is sent back to the GWT client. This concludes the automatic user registration feature of *Connectr*.

# Summary

In this chapter, we integrated *Connectr* with Google Accounts, Twitter, and Facebook in order to provide *Connectr* with authentication and user information retrieval services. This allows users to logon to *Connectr* by using their existing account from any of the three providers.

We then decomposed the login sequence in a series of steps that are common to all providers whether they implement OAuth or not. We highlighted the fact that users are sent from *Connectr* to their chosen authentication provider and then sent back to *Connectr* via the callback that URL *Connectr* provides.

We coded all the steps in straight Java for Facebook, and by using third party libraries for Google and Twitter.

We discovered that logging out from *Connectr* is done by invalidating the session. Depending on the authentication provider, especially in the case of Facebook, additional steps are required in order to log users out from their provider.

In the next chapter we will switch to the backend where we introduce techniques to increase the speed, robustness, and scalability of the Datastore.

# 9

# Robustness and Scalability: Transactions, Memcache, and Datastore Design

*Chapter 4* and *Chapter 5* explored the basics of using the App Engine Datastore. In this chapter, we'll delve deeper to investigate Datastore-related ways to help increase the robustness, speed, and scalability of an App Engine app, and apply these techniques to our *Connectr* app.

First, in the *Data modeling and scalability* section we look at ways to structure and access your data objects to make your application faster and more scalable.

Then, the *Using transactions* section describes the Datastore **transactions**, what they do, and when and how to use them. Finally, *Using Memcache* will introduce App Engine's **Memcache** service, which provides a volatile-memory key-value store, and discuss the use of Memcache to speed up your app.

In this chapter, we will use for our examples the full version of the *Connectr* app, `ConnectrFinal`.

## Data modeling and scalability

In deciding how to design your application's data models, there are a number of ways in which your approach can increase the app's scalability and responsiveness. In this section, we discuss several such approaches and how they are applied in the *Connectr* app. In particular, we describe how the Datastore access latency can sometimes be reduced; ways to split data models across entities to increase the efficiency of data object access and use; and how property lists can be used to support "join-like" behavior with Datastore entities.

# Reducing latency—read consistency and Datastore access deadlines

By default, when an entity is updated in the Datastore, all subsequent reads of that entity will see the update at the same time; this is called **strong consistency**. To achieve it, each entity has a primary storage location, and with a strongly consistent read, the read waits for a machine at that location to become available. Strong consistency is the default in App Engine.

However, App Engine allows you to change this default and use **eventual consistency** for a given Datastore read. With eventual consistency, the query may access a copy of the data from a secondary location if the primary location is temporarily unavailable. Changes to data will propagate to the secondary locations fairly quickly, but it is possible that an "eventually consistent" read may access a secondary location before the changes have been incorporated. However, eventually consistent reads are faster on average, so they trade consistency for availability. In many contexts, for example, with web apps such as *Connectr* that display "activity stream" information, this is an acceptable tradeoff—completely up-to-date freshness of information is not required.

This touches on a complex and interesting field beyond the scope of this book. See `http://googleappengine.blogspot.com/2010/03/read-consistency-deadlines-more-control.html`, `http://googleappengine.blogspot.com/2009/09/migration-to-better-datastore.html`, and `http://code.google.com/events/io/2009/sessions/TransactionsAcrossDatacenters.html` for more background on this and related topics.

In *Connectr*, we will add the use of eventual consistency to some of our feed object reads; specifically, those for feed content updates. We are willing to take the small chance that a feed object is slightly out-of-date in order to have the advantage of quicker reads on these objects.

The following code shows how to set eventual read consistency for a query, using `server.servlets.FeedUpdateFriendServlet` as an example.

```
Query q = pm.newQuery("select from " + FeedInfo.class.getName() +
    "where urlstring == :keys");
//Use eventual read consistency for this query
q.addExtension("datanucleus.appengine.datastoreReadConsistency",
    "EVENTUAL");
```

App Engine also allows you to change the default Datastore *access deadline*. By default, the Datastore will retry access automatically for up to about 30 seconds. You can set this deadline to a smaller amount of time. It can often be appropriate to set a shorter deadline if you are concerned with response latency, and are willing to use a cached version of the data for which you got the timeout, or are willing to do without it.

The following code shows how to set an access timeout interval (in milliseconds) for a given JDO query.

```
Query q = pm.newQuery("...");
// Set a Datastore access timeout
q.setTimeoutMillis(10000);
```

# Splitting big data models into multiple entities to make access more efficient

Often, the fields in a data model can be divided into two groups: main and/or summary information that you need often/first, and *details*—the data that you might not need or tend not to need immediately. If this is the case, then it can be productive to split the data model into multiple entities and set the *details* entity to be a child of the summary entity, for instance, by using JDO owned relationships. The child field will be fetched lazily, and so the child entity won't be pulled in from the Datastore unless needed.

In our app, the `Friend` model can be viewed like this: initially, only a certain amount of summary information about each `Friend` is sent over RPC to the app's frontend (the Friend's name). Only if there is a request to view details of or edit a particular `Friend`, is more information needed.

So, we can make retrieval more efficient by defining a parent *summary* entity, and a child *details* entity. We do this by keeping the "summary" information in `Friend`, and placing "details" in a `FriendDetails` object, which is set as a child of `Friend` via a JDO bidirectional, one-to-one owned relationship, as shown in Figure 1. We store the `Friend`'s e-mail address and its list of associated URLs in `FriendDetails`. We'll keep the name information in `Friend`. That way, when we construct the initial 'FriendSummaries' list displayed on application load, and send it over RPC, we only need to access the summary object.

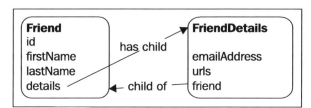

Figure 1: Splitting `Friend` data between a "main" `Friend` persistent class and a `FriendDetails` child class.

A `details` field of `Friend` points to the `FriendDetails` child, which we create when we create a `Friend`. In this way, the details will always be transparently available when we need them, but they will be lazily fetched—the `details` child object won't be initially retrieved from the database when we query `Friend`, and won't be fetched unless we need that information.

As you may have noticed, the `Friend` model is already set up in this manner—this is the rationale for that design.

## Discussion

When splitting a data model like this, consider the queries your app will perform and how the design of the data objects will support those queries. For example, if your app often needs to query for `property1 == x` and `property2 == y`, and especially if both individual filters can produce large result sets, you are probably better off keeping both those properties on the same entity (for example, retaining both fields on the "main" entity, rather than moving one to a "details" entity).

For persistent classes (that is, "data classes") that you often access and update, it is also worth considering whether any of its fields do not require indexes. This would be the case if you never perform a query which includes that field. The fewer the indexed fields of a persistent class, the quicker are the writes of objects of that class.

# Splitting a model by creating an "index" and a "data" entity

You can also consider splitting a model if you identify fields that you access only when performing queries, but don't require once you've actually retrieved the object. Often, this is the case with multi-valued properties. For example, in the *Connectr* app, this is the case with the friendKeys list of the server.domain.FeedIndex class (first encountered in *Chapter 7*). This multi-valued property is used to find relevant feed objects but is not used when displaying feed content information.

With App Engine, there is no way for a query to retrieve only the fields that you need (with the exception of *keys-only* queries, as introduced in *Chapter 5*), so the full object must always be pulled in. If the multi-valued property lists are long, this is inefficient.

To avoid this inefficiency, we can split up such a model into two parts, and put each one in a different entity—an index entity and a data entity. The **index entity** holds only the multi-valued properties (or other data) used only for querying, and the **data entity** holds the information that we actually want to use once we've identified the relevant objects. The trick to this new design is that the data entity key is defined to be the parent of the index entity key.

More specifically, when an entity is created, its key can be defined as a "child" of another entity's key, which becomes its parent. The child is then in the same **entity group** as the parent (we discuss entity groups further in the *Using transactions* section). Because such a child key is based on the path of its parent key, it is possible to derive the parent key given only the child key, using the getParent() method of Key, without requiring the child to be instantiated.

So with this design, we can first do a *keys-only* query on the index kind (which is faster than full object retrieval) to get a list of the keys of the relevant index entities. With that list, even though we've not actually retrieved the index objects themselves, we can derive the parent data entity keys from the index entity keys. We can then do a *batch fetch* with the list of relevant parent keys to grab all the data entities at once. This lets us retrieve the information we're interested in, without having to retrieve the properties that we do not need.

See Brett Slatkin's presentation, *Building scalable, complex apps on App Engine* (`http://code.google.com/events/io/2009/sessions/BuildingScalableComplexApps.html`) for more on this index/data design.

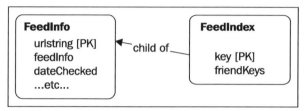

Figure 2: Splitting the feed model into an "index" part (`server.domain.FeedIndex`) and a "data" part (`server.domain.FeedInfo`)

Our feed model (which was introduced in *Chapter 7*) maps well to this design—we filter on the `FeedIndex.friendKeys` multi-valued property (which contains the list of keys of Friends that point to this feed) when we query for the feeds associated with a given `Friend`.

But, once we have retrieved those feeds, we don't need the `friendKeys` list further. So, we would like to avoid retrieving them along with the feed content. With our app's sample data, these property lists will not comprise a lot of data, but they would be likely to do so if the app was scaled up. For example, many users might have the same friends, or many different contacts might include the same company blog in their associated feeds.

So, we split up the feed model into an index part and a parent data part, as shown in Figure 2. The index class is `server.domain.FeedIndex`; it contains the `friendKeys` list for a feed. The data part, containing the actual feed content, is `server.domain.FeedInfo`. When a new `FeedIndex` object is created, its key will be constructed so that its corresponding `FeedInfo` object's key is its parent key. This construction must of course take place at object creation, as Datastore entity keys cannot be changed.

 For a small-scale app, the payoff from this split model would perhaps not be worth it. But for the sake of example, let's assume that we expect our app to grow significantly.

The FeedInfo persistent class—the parent class—simply uses an app-assigned String primary key, urlstring (the feed URL string). The server.domain. FeedIndex constructor, shown in the code below, uses the key of its FeedInfo parent—the URL string—to construct its key. (The *Using transactions* section will describe the key-construction code of the figure in more detail). This places the two entities into the same **entity group** and allows the parent FeedInfo key to be derived from the FeedIndex entity's key.

```
@PersistenceCapable(identityType = IdentityType.APPLICATION,
    detachable="true")
public class FeedIndex implements Serializable {

  @PrimaryKey
  @Persistent(valueStrategy = IdGeneratorStrategy.IDENTITY)
  private Key key;
  ...

  public FeedIndex(String fkey, String url) {
    this.friendKeys = new HashSet<String>();
    this.friendKeys.add(fkey);
    KeyFactory.Builder keyBuilder =
        new KeyFactory.Builder(FeedInfo.class.getSimpleName(), url);
    keyBuilder.addChild(FeedIndex.class.getSimpleName(), url);
    Key ckey = keyBuilder.getKey();
    this.key= ckey;
  }
```

The following code, from server.servlets.FeedUpdateFriendServlet, shows how this model is used to efficiently retrieve the FeedInfo objects associated with a given Friend. Given a Friend key, a query is performed for the *keys* of the FeedIndex entities that contain this Friend key in their friendKeys list. Because this is a *keys-only* query, it is much more efficient than returning the actual objects. Then, each FeedIndex key is used to derive the parent (FeedInfo) key. Using that list of parent keys, a *batch fetch* is performed to fetch the FeedInfo objects associated with the given Friend. We did this without needing to actually fetch the FeedIndex objects.

```
... imports...
@SuppressWarnings("serial")
public class FeedUpdateFriendServlet extends HttpServlet{

  private static Logger logger =
      Logger.getLogger(FeedUpdateFriendServlet.class.getName());
```

```
public void doPost(HttpServletRequest req, HttpServletResponse resp)
   throws IOException {

PersistenceManager pm = PMF.get().getPersistenceManager();

Query q = null;
try {
  String fkey = req.getParameter("fkey");
  if (fkey != null) {
    logger.info("in FeedUpdateFriendServlet, updating feeds for:"
       +fkey);
    // query for matching FeedIndex keys
    q = pm.newQuery("select key from "+FeedIndex.class.getName()+"
       where friendKeys == :id");
    List ids=(List)q.execute(fkey);
    if (ids.size()==0) {
      return;
    }
    // else, get the parent keys of the ids
    Key k = null;
    List<Key>parent list = new ArrayList<Key>();
    for (Object id : ids) {
      // cast to key
      k = (Key)id;
      parentlist.add(k.getParent());
    }
    // fetch the parents using the keys
    Query q2 = pm.newQuery("select from +FeedInfo.class.getName()+
       "where urlstring == :keys");
    // allow eventual consistency on read
    q2.addExtension(
      "datanucleus.appengine.datastoreReadConsistency",
      "EVENTUAL");
    List<FeedInfo>results =
      (List<FeedInfo>)q2.execute(parentlist);
    if(results.iterator().hasNext()){
       for(FeedInfo fi : results){
         fi.updateRequestedFeed(pm);
       }
    }
  }
}
catch (Exception e) {
   logger.warning(e.getMessage());
}
```

```
    finally {
      if q!=null) {
        q.closeAll();
      }
      pm.close();
    }
  }
}//end class
```

# Use of property lists to support "join" behavior

Google App Engine does not support joins with the same generality as a relational database. However, property lists along with accompanying denormalization can often be used in GAE to support join-like functionality in a very efficient manner.

 At the time of writing, there is GAE work in progress to support simple joins. However, this functionality is not yet officially part of the SDK.

Consider the many-to-many relationship between `Friend` and feed information in our application. With a relational database, we might support this relationship by using three tables: one for Friend data, one for Feed data, and a "join table" (sometimes called a "cross-reference table"), named, say, `FeedFriend`, with two columns — one for the friend ID and one for the feed ID. The rows in the join table would indicate which feeds were associated with which friends.

In our hypothetical relational database, a query to find the feeds associated with a given `Friend fid` would look something like this:

```
select feed.feedname from Feed feed, FeedFriend ff
  where ff.friendid = 'fid' and ff.feedid = feed.id
```

If we wanted to find those feeds that *both* Friend 1 (`fid1`) and Friend 2 (`fid2`) had listed, the query would look something like this:

```
select feed.feedname from Feed feed, FeedFriend f1, FeedFriend f2
  where f1.friendid = 'fid1' and f1.feedid = feed.id
  and f2.friendid = 'fid2' and f2.feedid = feed.id
```

With Google App Engine, to support this type of query, we can denormalize the "join table" information and use Datastore multi-valued properties to hold the denormalized information. (Denormalization should not be considered a second-class citizen in GAE).

In *Connectr*, feed objects hold a list of the keys of the `Friend`s that list that feed (`friendKeys`), and each `Friend` holds a list of the feed `URL`s associated with it. *Chapter 7* included a figure illustrating this many-to-many relationship.

So, with the first query above, the analogous JDQL query is:

```
select from FeedIndex where friendKeys == 'fid'
```

If we want to find those feeds that are listed by *both* Friend 1 and Friend 2, the JDQL query is:

```
select from FeedIndex where friendKeys == 'fid1' and
    friendKeys == 'fid2'
```

Our data model, and its use of multi-valued properties, has allowed these queries to be very straightforward and efficient in GAE.

# Supporting the semantics of more complex joins

The semantics of more complex join queries can sometimes be supported in GAE with multiple synchronously-ordered multi-valued properties.

For example, suppose we decided to categorize the associated feeds of Friends by whether they were "Technical", "PR", "Personal", "Photography-related", and so on (and that we had some way of determining this categorization on a feed-by-feed basis). Then, suppose we wanted to find all the Friends whose feeds include "PR" feed(s), and to list those feed URLs for each `Friend`.

In a relational database, we might support this by adding a "Category" table to hold category names and IDs, and adding a category ID column to the Feed table. Then, the query might look like this:

```
select f.lastName, feed.feedname from Friend f, Category c,
    Feed feed, FeedFriend ff
    where c.id = 'PR' and feed.cat_id = c.id and ff.feedid = feed.id
    and ff.friend.id = f.id
```

We might attempt to support this type of query in GAE by adding a `feedCategories` multi-valued property list to `Friend`, which contained all the categories in which their feeds fell. Every time a feed was added to the `Friend`, this list would be updated with the new category as necessary. We could then perform a JDQL query to find all such Friends:

```
select from Friend where feedCategories == 'PR'
```

However, for each returned `Friend` we would then need to check each of their feeds in turn to determine which feed(s) were the PR ones—requiring further Datastore access.

To address this, we could build a `Friend feedCategories` multi-valued property list whose ordering was synchronized with the `urls` list ordering, with the *nth* position in the categories list indicating the category of the *nth* feed. For example, suppose that `url1` and `url3` are of category 'PR', and `url2` is of category 'Technical'. The two lists would then be sorted as follows:

```
urls =  [url1, url2, url3, … ]

feedCategories = [PR, TECHNICAL, PR, …]
```

(For efficiency, we would probably map the categories to integers). Then, for each `Friend` returned from the previous query, we could determine which feed URLs were the 'PR' ones by their position in the feed list, without requiring further Datastore queries. In the previous example, it would be the URLs at positions 0 and 2—`url1` and `url3`.

This technique requires more expense at write time, in exchange for more efficient queries at read time. The approach is not always applicable—for example, it requires a one-to-one mapping between the items in the synchronized property lists, but can be very effective when it does apply.

# Using transactions

As the App Engine documentation states,

> *A transaction is a Datastore operation or a set of Datastore operations that either succeed completely, or fail completely. If the transaction succeeds, then all of its intended effects are applied to the Datastore. If the transaction fails, then none of the effects are applied.*

The use of transactions can be the key to the stability of a multiprocess application (such as a web app) whose different processes share the same persistent Datastore. Without transactional control, the processes can overwrite each other's data updates midstream, essentially stomping all over each other's toes. Many database implementations support some form of transactions, and you may be familiar with RDBMS transactions. App Engine Datastore transactions have a different set of requirements and usage model than you may be used to.

First, it is important to understand that a "regular" Datastore write on a given entity is *atomic*—in the sense that if you are updating multiple fields in that entity, they will either all be updated, or the write will fail and none of the fields will be updated. Thus, a single update can essentially be considered a (small, implicit) transaction—one that you as the developer do not explicitly declare. If one single update is initiated while another update on that entity is in progress, this can generate a "concurrency failure" exception. In the more recent versions of App Engine, such failures on single writes are now retried transparently by App Engine, so that you rarely need to deal with them in application-level code.

However, often your application needs stronger control over the atomicity and isolation of its operations, as multiple processes may be trying to read and write to the same objects at the same time. Transactions provide this control.

For example, suppose we are keeping a count of some value in a "counter" field of an object, which various methods can increment. It is important to ensure that if one Servlet reads the "counter" field and then updates it based on its current value, no other request has updated the same field between the time that its value is read and when it is updated. Transactions let you ensure that this is the case: if a transaction succeeds, it is as if it were done in isolation, with no other concurrent processes 'dirtying' its data.

Another common scenario: you may be making multiple changes to the Datastore, and you may want to ensure that the changes either all go through atomically, or none do. For example, when adding a new `Friend` to a `UserAccount`, we want to make sure that if the `Friend` is created, any related `UserAcount` object changes are also performed.

While a Datastore transaction is ongoing, no other transactions or operations can see the work being done in that transaction; it becomes visible only if the transaction succeeds.

Additionally, queries inside a transaction see a consistent "snapshot" of the Datastore as it was when the transaction was initiated. This consistent snapshot is preserved even after the in-transaction writes are performed. Unlike some other transaction models, with App Engine, a within-transaction read after a write will still show the Datastore as it was at the beginning of the transaction.

Datastore transactions can operate only on entities that are in the same **entity group**. We discuss entity groups later in this chapter.

# Transaction commits and rollbacks

To specify a transaction, we need the concepts of a transaction **commit** and **rollback**.

A transaction must make an explicit "commit" call when all of its actions have been completed. On successful transaction commit, all of the create, update, and delete operations performed during the transaction are effected atomically.

If a transaction is rolled back, none of its Datastore modifications will be performed. If you do not commit a transaction, it will be rolled back automatically when its Servlet exits. However, it is good practice to wrap a transaction in a try/finally block, and explicitly perform a rollback if the commit was not performed for some reason. This could occur, for example, if an exception was thrown.

If a transaction commit fails, as would be the case if the objects under its control had been modified by some other process since the transaction was started the transaction is automatically rolled back.

## Example—a JDO transaction

With JDO, a transaction is initiated and terminated as follows:

```
import javax.jdo.PersistenceManager;
import javax.jdo.Transaction;
...
  PersistenceManager pm = PMF.get().getPersistenceManager();
  Transaction tx;

    ...
  try {
     tx = pm.currentTransaction();
     tx.begin();
     // Do the transaction work
     tx.commit();
  }
  finally {
    if (tx.isActive()) {
       tx.rollback();
    }
  }
```

A transaction is obtained by calling the currentTransaction() method of the PersistenceManager. Then, initiate the transaction by calling its begin() method. To commit the transaction, call its commit() method. The finally clause in the example above checks to see if the transaction is still active, and does a rollback if that is the case.

While the preceding code is correct as far as it goes, it does not check to see if the commit was successful, and retry if it was not. We will add that next.

# App Engine transactions use optimistic concurrency

In contrast to some other transactional models, the *initiation* of an App Engine transaction is never blocked. However, when the transaction attempts to commit, if there has been a modification in the meantime (by some other process) of any objects in the same entity group as the objects involved in the transaction, the transaction commit will fail. That is, the commit not only fails if the objects in the transaction have been modified by some other process, but also if any objects in its entity group have been modified. For example, if one request were to modify a FeedInfo object while its FeedIndex child was involved in a transaction as part of another request, that transaction would not successfully commit, as those two objects share an entity group.

App Engine uses an *optimistic concurrency* model. This means that there is no check when the transaction initiates, as to whether the transaction's resources are currently involved in some other transaction, and no blocking on transaction start. The commit simply fails if it turns out that these resources have been modified elsewhere after initiating the transaction. Optimistic concurrency tends to work well in scenarios where quick response is valuable (as is the case with web apps) but contention is rare, and thus, transaction failures are relatively rare.

# Transaction retries

With optimistic concurrency, a commit can fail simply due to concurrent activity on the shared resource. In that case, if the transaction is retried, it is likely to succeed.

So, one thing missing from the previous example is that it does not take any action if the transaction commit did not succeed. Typically, if a commit fails, it is worth simply retrying the transaction. If there is some contention for the objects in the transaction, it will probably be resolved when it is retried.

```
PersistenceManager pm = PMF.get().getPersistenceManager();
  // ...
  try {
    for (int i =0; i < NUM_RETRIES; i++) {
      pm.currentTransaction().begin();
      // ...do the transaction work ...
      try {
        pm.currentTransaction().commit();
        break;
      }
```

```
      catch (JDOCanRetryException e1) {
        if (i == (NUM_RETRIES - 1)) {
          throw e1;
        }
      }
    }
  }
  finally {
    if (pm.currentTransaction().isActive()) {
      pm.currentTransaction().rollback();
    }
    pm.close();
  }
```

As shown in the example above, you can wrap a transaction in a retry loop, where NUM_RETRIES is set to the number of times you want to re-attempt the transaction. If a commit fails, a JDOCanRetryException will be thrown. If the commit succeeds, the for loop will be terminated.

If a transaction commit fails, this likely means that the Datastore has changed in the interim. So, next time through the retry loop, be sure to start over in gathering any information required to perform the transaction.

# Transactions and entity groups

An entity's **entity group** is determined by its key. When an entity is created, its key can be defined as a child of another entity's key, which becomes its *parent*. The child is then in the same entity group as the parent. That child's key could in turn be used to define another entity's key, which becomes *its* child, and so on. An entity's key can be viewed as a path of ancestor relationships, traced back to a *root* entity with no parent. Every entity with the same root is in the same entity group. If an entity has no parent, it is its own root.

Because entity group membership is determined by an entity's key, and the key cannot be changed after the object is created, this means that **entity group membership cannot be changed** either.

As introduced earlier, a transaction can only operate on entities from the same entity group. If you try to access entities from different groups within the same transaction, an error will occur and the transaction will fail.

You may recall from *Chapter 5* that in App Engine, JDO owned relationships place the parent and child entities in the same entity group. That is why, when constructing an owned relationship, you cannot explicitly persist the children ahead of time, but must let the JDO implementation create them for you when the parent is made persistent. JDO will define the keys of the children in an owned relationship such that they are the child keys of the parent object key. This means that the parent and children in a JDO owned relationship can always be safely used in the same transaction. (The same holds with JPA owned relationships).

So in the *Connectr* app, for example, you could create a transaction that encompasses work on a `UserAccount` object and its list of `Friends`—they will all be in the same entity group. But, you could not include a `Friend` from a different `UserAccount` in that same transaction—it will not be in the same entity group.

This App Engine constraint on transactions—that they can only encompass members of the same entity group—is enforced in order to allow transactions to be handled in a scalable way across App Engine's distributed Datastores. Entity group members are always stored together, not distributed.

# Creating entities in the same entity group

As discussed earlier, one way to place entities in the same entity group is to create a JDO owned relationship between them; JDO will manage the child key creation so that the parent and children are in the same entity group.

To explicitly create an entity with an entity group parent, you can use the App Engine `KeyFactory.Builder` class. This is the approach used in the `FeedIndex` constructor example shown previously. Recall that you cannot change an object's key after it is created, so you have to make this decision when you are creating the object.

Your "child" entity must use a primary key of type `Key` or String-encoded Key (as described in *Chapter 5*); these key types allow parent path information to be encoded in them. As you may recall, it is required to use one of these two types of keys for JDO owned relationship children, for the same reason.

If the data class of the object for which you want to create an entity group parent uses an app-assigned string ID, you can build its key as follows:

```
// you can construct a Builder as follows:
KeyFactory.Builder keyBuilder =
  new KeyFactory.Builder(Class1.class.getSimpleName(),
parentIDString);

// alternatively, pass the parent Key object:
Key pkey = KeyFactory.Builder keyBuilder =
```

```
    new KeyFactory.Builder(pkey);

  // Then construct the child key
   keyBuilder.addChild(Class2.class.getSimpleName(), childIDString);
   Key ckey = keyBuilder.getKey();
```

Create a new `KeyFactory.Builder` using the key of the desired parent. You may specify the parent key as either a `Key` object or via its entity name (the simple name of its class) and its app-assigned (String) or system-assigned (numeric) ID, as appropriate. Then, call the `addChild` method of the `Builder` with its arguments—the entity name and the app-assigned ID string that you want to use. Then, call the `getKey()` method of `Builder`. The generated child key encodes parent path information. Assign the result to the child entity's key field. When the entity is persisted, its entity group parent will be that entity whose key was used as the parent.

This is the approach we showed previously in the constructor of `FeedIndex`, creating its key using its parent `FeedInfo` key.

> See `http://code.google.com/appengine/docs/java/javadoc/com/google/appengine/api/datastore/KeyFactory.Builder.html` for more information on key construction.

If the data class of the object for which you want to create an entity group parent uses a system-assigned ID, then (because you don't know this ID ahead of time), you must go about creating the key in a different way. Create an additional field in your data class for the parent key, of the appropriate type for the parent key, as shown in the following code:

```
@PrimaryKey
@Persistent(valueStrategy = IdGeneratorStrategy.IDENTITY)
private Key key;

...

@Persistent
  @Extension(vendorName="datanucleus", key="gae.parent-pk",
    value="true")
  private String parentKey;
```

Assign the parent key to this field prior to creating the object. When the object is persisted, the data object's primary key field will be populated using the parent key as the entity group parent. You can use this technique with any child key type.

# Getting the entity parent key from the child key

Once a "child" key has been created, you can call the `getParent()` method of `Key` on that key to get the key of its entity group parent. You need only the key to make this determination; it is not necessary to access the actual entity. `getParent()` returns a `Key` object. We used this technique earlier in the *Splitting a model by creating an "index" and a "data" entity* section.

If the primary key field of the parent data class is an app-assigned string ID or system-assigned numeric ID, you can extract that value by calling the `getName()` or `getID()` method of the `Key`, respectively.

You can convert to/from the `Key` and String-encoded `Key` formats using the `stringToKey()` and `keyToString()` methods of the `KeyFactory`.

# Entity group design considerations

Entity group design considerations can be very important for the efficient execution of your application.

Entity groups that get too large can be problematic, as an update to any entity in a group while a transaction on that group is ongoing will cause the transaction's commit to fail. If this happens a lot, it affects the throughput. But, you do want your entity groups to support transactions useful to your application. In particular, it is often useful to place objects with parent/child semantics into the same entity group. Of course, JDO does this for you, for its owned relationships. The same is true for JPA's version of owned relationships.

It is often possible to design relatively small entity groups, and then use **transactional tasks** to achieve required coordination between groups. Transactional tasks are initiated from within a transaction, and are enqueued only if the transaction commits. However, they operate outside the transaction, and thus it is not required that the objects accessed by the transactional task be in the transaction's entity group. We discuss and use transactional tasks in the *Transactional tasks* section of this chapter.

Also, it can be problematic if too many requests (processes) are trying to access the same entity at once. This situation is easy to generate if, for example, you have a counter that is updated each time a web page is accessed. Contention for the shared object will produce lots of transaction retries and cause significant slowdown. One solution is to **shard** the counter (or similar shared object), creating multiple counter instances that are updated at random and whose values are aggregated to provide the total when necessary. Of course, this approach can be useful for objects other than counters.

We will not discuss entity sharding further here, but the App Engine documentation provides more detail: `http://code.google.com/appengine/articles/sharding_counters.html`.

# What you can do inside a transaction

As discussed earlier, a transaction can operate only over data objects from the same entity group. Each entity group has a root entity. If you try to include multiple objects with different root entities within the same transaction, it is an error.

Within a transaction, you can operate only on (include in the transaction) those entities obtained via retrieval by key, or via a query that includes an ancestor filter. That is, only objects obtained in those ways will be under transactional control. Queries that do not include an ancestor filter may be performed within the transactional block of code without throwing an error, but the retrieved objects will not be under transactional control.

 Queries with an "ancestor filter" restrict the set of possible hits to objects only with the given ancestor, thus restricting the hits to the same entity group. JDO allows querying on "entity group parent key fields", specified as such via the `@Extension(vendorName="datanucleus", key="gae.parent-pk", value="true")` annotation, as a form of ancestor filter. See the JDO documentation for more information.

So, you may often want to do some preparatory work to find the keys of the object(s) that you wish to place under transactional control, then initiate the transaction and actually fetch the objects by their IDs within the transactional context. Again, if there are multiple such objects, they must all be in the same entity group.

As discussed earlier, after you have initiated a transaction, you will be working with a consistent "snapshot" of the Datastore at the time of transaction initiation. If you perform any writes during the transaction, the snapshot will not be updated to reflect them. Any subsequent reads you make within the transaction will still reflect the initial snapshot and will not show your modifications.

# When to use a transaction

There are several scenarios where you should be sure to use a transaction. They should be employed if:

- You are changing a data object field relative to its current value. For example, this would be the case if you are modifying (say, adding to) a list. It is necessary to prevent other processes from updating that same list between the time you read it and the time you store it again. In our app, for example, this will be necessary when updating a `Friend` and modifying its list of `urls`.

  In contrast, if a field update is not based on the field's current value, then by definition, it suggests that you don't care if/when other updates to the field occur. In such a case, you probably don't need to employ a transaction, as the entity update itself is guaranteed to be atomic.

- You want operations on multiple entities to be treated atomically. That is, there are a set of modifications for which you want them all to happen, or none to happen. In our app, for example, we will see this when creating a `Friend` in conjunction with updating a `UserAccount`. Similarly, we want to ensure that a `FeedInfo` object and its corresponding `FeedIndex` are created together.

- You are using app-assigned IDs and you want to either create a new object with that ID, or update the existing object that has that ID. This requires a test and then a create/update, and these should be done atomically. In our app, for example, we will see this when creating feed objects, whose IDs are URLs.

  If you are using system-assigned IDs, then this situation will not arise.

- You want a consistent "snapshot" of state in order to do some work. This might arise, for example, if you need to generate a report with mutually consistent values.

# Adding transactional control to the *Connectr* application

We are now equipped to add transactional control to the *Connectr* application.

First, we will wrap transactions around the activities of creating, deleting, and modifying `Friend` objects. We will also use transactions when creating feed objects: because `FeedInfo` objects use an app-assigned ID (the feed URL string), we must atomically test whether that ID already exists, and if not, create a new object and its associated `FeedIndex` object. We will also use transactions when modifying the list of `Friend` keys associated with a feed, as this is a case where we are updating a field (the `friendKeys` list) relative to its current value.

We will not place the feed content updates under transactional control. The content updates are effectively idempotent—we don't really care if one content update overwrites another—and we want these updates to be as quick as possible.

However, there is a complication with this approach. When we update a Friend's data, their list of urls may change. We want to make any accompanying changes to the relevant feed objects at the same time—this may involve creating or deleting feed objects or editing the friendKey lists of the existing ones.

We'd like this series of operations to be under control of the same transaction, so that we don't update the Friend, but then fail to make the required feed object changes. But they can't be—a Friend object is not in the same entity group as the feed objects. The Friend and feed objects have a many-to-many relationship and we do not want to place them all in one very large entity group.

App Engine's **transactional tasks** will come to our rescue.

# Transactional tasks

App Engine supports a feature called **transactional tasks**. We have already introduced some use of tasks and Task Queues in *Chapter 7* (and will return to the details of task configuration in *Chapter 12*). Tasks have specific semantics in the context of a transaction.

 If you add a task to a Task Queue within the scope of a transaction, that task will be enqueued *if and only if* the transaction is successful.

A transactional task will not be placed in the queue and executed unless the transaction successfully commits. If the transaction rolls back, the task will not be run. The specified task is run outside of the transaction and is not restricted to objects in the same entity group as the original transaction. At the time of writing, you can enqueue up to five transactional tasks per transaction.

You may recall from *Chapter 7* that once a task is enqueued and executed, if it returns with error status, it is re-enqueued to be retried until it succeeds. So, you can use transactional tasks to ensure that either all of the actions across multiple entity groups are eventually performed or none are performed. There will be a (usually small) period of time when the enqueued task has not yet been performed and thus not all of the actions are completed, but eventually, they will all (or none) be done. That is, transactional tasks can be used to provide **eventual consistency** across more than one entity group.

We will use transactional tasks to manage the updates, deletes, and adds of feed URLs when a `Friend` is updated. We place the changes to the `Friend` object under transactional control. As shown in the following code from `server.FriendsServiceImpl`, within that transaction we enqueue a transactional task that performs the related feed object modifications. This task will be executed if and only if the transaction on the `Friend` object commits.

```java
@SuppressWarnings("serial")
public class FriendsServiceImpl extends RemoteServiceServlet
  implements FriendsService {

  private static final int NUM_RETRIES =5;
  ...
  public FriendDTO updateFriend(FriendDTO friendDTO){

    PersistenceManager pm = PMF.getTxnPm();
    if (friendDTO.getId() == null) { // create new
      Friend newFriend = addFriend(friendDTO);
      return newFriend.toDTO();
    }

    Friend friend = null;
    try {
     for (int i=0;i<NUM_RETRIES;i++) {
       pm.currentTransaction().begin();
       friend = pm.getObjectById(Friend.class,friendDTO.getId());

       Set<String> origurls = new HashSet<String>(friend.getUrls());

       // delete feed information from feedids cache
       // we only need to do this if the URLs set has changed...
       if (!origurls.equals(friendDTO.getUrls())) {
         CacheSupport.cacheDelete(feedids_nmspce,friendDTO.getId());
       }

       friend.updateFromDTO(friendDTO);

       if (!(origurls.isEmpty() && friendDTO.getUrls().isEmpty())) {
         // build task payload:
         Map<String,Object> hm = new HashMap<String,Object>();
         hm.put("newurls", friendDTO.getUrls());
         hm.put("origurls", origurls);
         hm.put("replace", true);
         hm.put("fid",friendDTO.getId());
```

```
        byte[]data = Utils.serialize(hm);

        // add transactional task to update the
        // url information
        // the task will not be run if the
        // transaction does not commit.
        Queue queue = QueueFactory.getDefaultQueue();
        queue.add(url("/updatefeedurls").payload(data,
          "application/x-java-serialized-object"));
      }
      try {
        pm.currentTransaction().commit();
        logger.info("in updateFriend, did successful commit");
        break;
      }
      catch (JDOCanRetryException e1) {
        logger.warning(e1.getMessage());
        if (i==(NUM_RETRIES-1)) {
          throw e1;
        }
      }
    }// end for
  } catch (Exception e) {
    logger.warning(e.getMessage());
    friendDTO = null;
  } finally {
    if (pm.currentTransaction().isActive()) {
      pm.currentTransaction().rollback();
      logger.warning("did transaction rollback");
      friendDTO = null;
    }
    pm.close();
  }
  return friendDTO;
}
```

The previous code shows the updateFriend method of server.
FriendsServiceImpl. Prior to calling the transaction commit, a task (to update
the feed URLs) is added to the default Task Queue. The task won't be actually
enqueued unless the transaction commits. A similar model, including the use of a
transactional task, is employed for the deleteFriend and addFriend methods of
FriendsServiceImpl.

We configure the task with information about the "new" and "original" Friend urls lists, which it will use to update the feed objects accordingly. Because this task requires a more complex set of task parameters than we have used previously, we convert the task parameters to a Map, and pass the Map in serialized form as a byte[] task payload. See the *Task Parameters: Sending a Payload of byte[] Data as the Request* section of this chapter for more information about payload generation and use.

This task is implemented by a Servlet, servlet.server.servlets. UpdateFeedUrlsServlet, which is accessed via /updatefeedurls. This Servlet covers the three cases of URL list modification—adds, deletes, and updates.

The following code is from the server.servlets.UpdateFeedUrlsServlet class.

```
@SuppressWarnings("serial")
public class UpdateFeedUrlsServlet extends HttpServlet {
   ...
   public void doPost(HttpServletRequest req, HttpServletResponse
      resp) throws IOException {

    Set<String> badurls = null;
    // deserialize the request
    Object o = Utils.deserialize(req);
    Map<String,Object> hm = (Map<String, Object>) o;
    Set<String> origurls = (Set<String>)hm.get("origurls");
    Set<String> newurls = (Set<String>)hm.get("newurls");
    Boolean replace = (Boolean)hm.get("replace");
    Boolean delete = (Boolean)hm.get("delete");
    String fid = (String)hm.get("fid");
   ...

    if (delete != null && delete) {
      if (origurls != null) {
        FeedIndex.removeFeedsFriend(origurls, fid);
      }
       else {
        return;
       }
    }
     ...
  }
}
```

The previous code shows the initial portion of the doPost method of UpdateFeedUrlsServlet. It shows the Servlet deserialization of the request, which holds the task payload. The resulting Map is used to define the task parameters. If the delete flag is set, the origurls Set is used to indicate the FeedIndex objects from which the Friend key (fid) should be removed.

Similarly, the following code shows the latter portion of the doPost method of server.servlets.UpdateFeedUrlsServlet. If the task is not a deletion request, then depending upon how the different task parameters are set, either the FeedIndex.addFeedURLs method or the FeedIndex.updateFeedURLs method is called.

```
@SuppressWarnings("serial")
public class UpdateFeedUrlsServlet extends HttpServlet {

  private static final int NUM_RETRIES = 5;
  public void doPost(HttpServletRequest req, HttpServletResponse
    resp) throws IOException {

      ...
    if (origurls == null) {
      // then add only -- no old URLs to deal with
      badurls = FeedIndex.addFeedURLs(newurls, fid);
    }
    else { //update
      badurls = FeedIndex.updateFeedURLs(newurls, origurls, fid,
        replace);
    }
    if (!badurls.isEmpty()) {
     // then update the Friend to remove those bad urls from its set.
     // Perform this operation in a transaction
     PersistenceManager pm = PMF.getTxnPm();
     try {
       for (int i =0; i < NUM_RETRIES; i++) {
         pm.currentTransaction().begin();
         Friend.removeBadURLs(badurls, fid, pm);
         try {
           pm.currentTransaction().commit();
           break;
         }
         catch (JDOCanRetryException e1) {
           if (i == (NUM_RETRIES -1)) {
           throw e1;
         } } } }
       finally {
         if (pm.currentTransaction().isActive()) {
```

```
        pm.currentTransaction().rollback();
        logger.warning("did transaction rollback");
    }
    pm.close();
} } }
    }
  }
```

In the case where URLs were added to the `urls` list of a `Friend`, some of the new URLs may have been malformed, or their endpoints unresponsive. In this case, they are returned as `badurls`. It is necessary to update the `Friend` object with this information—specifically, to remove any bad URLs from its `urls` list. This operation is performed in a transaction within the task Servlet. As with previous examples, the transaction may be retried several times if there are commit problems.

## What if something goes wrong during the feed update task?

In `UpdateFeedUrlsServlet`, in addition to the `Friend` transaction, the operations on the feed objects are using transactions under the hood (in the `FeedIndex` methods).

Because all the transactions initiated by the task may be retried multiple times, it is quite unlikely that any of them will not go through eventually. However, it is not impossible that one might fail to eventually commit. So, we want to consider what happens if a failure were to take place.

The `FeedIndex` operations can be repeated multiple times without changing their effect, as we are just adding and removing specified friend keys from the sets of keys. So, if the task's `Friend` update transaction in the example above fails after its multiple retries, the Servlet will throw an exception and the entire task will be retried until it succeeds (recall that if a task returns an error, it is automatically retried). It is okay to redo the task's feed operations, so this scenario will cause no problems.

If a `FeedIndex` URL add/update transaction fails after multiple retries, this will result in that URL being marked as "bad". So, no information in the system ends up as inconsistent, though the client user will have to re-enter the "bad" URL.

If a `FeedIndex` URL delete transaction fails after multiple retries, it will throw an exception, which will result in the task being retried until it succeeds. Again, this causes no problems.

So, even if the transactions performed in the task themselves fail to go through on the first invocation of the task, the system will nevertheless reach an eventually consistent state.

## Task parameters—sending a payload of byte[ ] data as the request

The previous code, from `FriendsServiceImpl`, showed a task using a `byte[]` "payload" as specification, rather than the individual string params that we had employed in *Chapter 7*. The following syntax is used to specify a payload, where `data` refers to a `byte[]`:

```
Queue queue = QueueFactory.getDefaultQueue();
queue.add(url("/updatefeedurls").payload(data,
  "application/x-java-serialized-object"));
```

When the task is invoked, the task Servlet's request parameter, `req`, will hold the payload data and may be deserialized from the request byte stream back into its original object, for example, as shown in the previous code, `UpdateFeedUrlsServlet`. This can be a useful technique when the task parameters are too complex to easily deal with as Strings. In our case, we want to pass `Sets` as parameters. So for the `UpdateFeedUrlsServlet` task, a `Map` containing the various task parameters is constructed and used for the payload, then deserialized in the task Servlet. Methods of `server.utils.Utils.java` support the serialization and deserialization. As an alternative approach, you could also pass as task params the identifier(s) of Datastore objects containing the parameter information. The task would then load the information from the Datastore when it is executed.

 Due to a GAE issue at the time of writing, base64 encoding and decoding is necessary for successful (de)serialization; this is done in `server.utils.Utils` (thanks to a post by Vince Bonfanti for this insight).

# Using Memcache

**Memcache** is one of the App Engine *services*. It is a volatile-memory key-value store. It operates over all your JVM instances; as long as an item remains in Memcache, it can be accessed by any of your application's processes.

Memcache contents remain indefinitely if you don't set them to expire, but can be removed ("evicted") by App Engine at any time. So, never count on a Memcache entry to exist in order for your application to work correctly. The service is meant only as a cache that allows you quicker access to information that you would otherwise obtain from the Datastore or have to generate. Memcache is often used both for storing copies of data objects and for storing relatively static display information, allowing web pages to be built more quickly.

Transactions over Memcache operations are not supported—any Memcache changes you make within a transaction are not undone if the transaction is rolled back.

The basic Memcache operations are `put`, `get`, and `delete`: `put` stores an object in the cache indexed by a key; `get` accesses an object based on its cache key; and `delete` removes the object stored at a given cache key. A Memcache `put` is *atomic*—the entire object will be stored properly or not at all. Memcache also has the ability to perform increments and decrements of cache values as atomic operations.

Objects must be serializable in order to be stored in Memcache. At the time of writing, Memcache has a 1MB size limit on a given cached value, and data transfer to/from Memcache counts towards an app quota (we further discuss quotas in *Chapter 11*).

Memcache has two features that can be particularly useful in organizing your cached data—the ability to define cache namespaces and the ability to define when a cache entry expires. We'll use these features in *Connectr*.

App Engine supports two different ways to access Memcache—via an implementation of the JCache API or via an App Engine Java API. JCache is a (not-yet-official) proposed interface standard, JSR 107.

The *Connectr* app will use the App Engine's Memcache API, which exposes a bit more of its functionality.

This page and its related links have more information on uses for Memcache: `http://code.google.com/appengine/articles/scaling/memcache.html`.

For more information on JCache, see `http://jcp.org/en/jsr/detail?id=107` and `http://code.google.com/appengine/docs/java/memcache/usingjcache.html`.

# Using the App Engine Memcache Java API in *Connectr*

To access the Memcache service in *Connectr*, we will use the `com.google.appengine.api.memcache` package (`http://code.google.com/appengine/docs/java/javadoc/com/google/appengine/api/memcache/package-summary.html`). To facilitate this, we'll build a "wrapper" class, `server.utils.cache.CacheSupport`, which does some management of Memcache namespaces, expiration times, and exception handling. The code for the `server.utils.cache.CacheSupport` class is as follows:

```
import com.google.appengine.api.memcache.Expiration;
import com.google.appengine.api.memcache.MemcacheService;
import com.google.appengine.api.memcache.MemcacheServiceException;
import com.google.appengine.api.memcache.MemcacheServiceFactory;

public class CacheSupport {
  private static MemcacheService cacheInit(String nameSpace){
   MemcacheService memcache =
    MemcacheServiceFactory.getMemcacheService(nameSpace);
   return memcache;
  }
  public static Object cacheGet(String nameSpace, Object id){
    Object r = null;
    MemcacheService memcache = cacheInit(nameSpace);
    try {
      r = memcache.get(id);
    }
    catch (MemcacheServiceException e) {
     // nothing can be done.
    }
   return r;
  }
  public static void cacheDelete(String namespace, Object id){
    MemcacheService memcache = cacheInit(nameSpace);
    memcache.delete(id);
  }
  public static void cachePutExp(String nameSpace, Object id,
   Serializable o, int exp)  {
    MemcacheService memcache = cacheInit(nameSpace);
    try {
      if (exp>0) {
        memcache.put(id, o, Expiration.byDeltaSeconds(exp));
      }
     else {
       memcache.put(id, o);
     }
    }
    catch (MemcacheServiceException e) {
      // nothing can be done.
    }
  }
  public static void cachePut(String nameSpace, Object id,
    Serializable o){
    cachePutExp(nameSpace, id, o, 0);
  }
}
```

As seen in the `cacheInit` method, to use the cache, first obtain a handle to the Memcache service via the `MemcacheServiceFactory`, optionally setting the **namespace** to be used:

```
MemcacheService memcache =
    MemcacheServiceFactory.getMemcacheService(nameSpace);
```

Memcache **namespaces** allow you to partition the cache. If the namespace is not specified, or if it is reset to null, a default namespace is used.

Namespaces can be useful for organizing your cached objects. For example (to peek ahead to the next section), when storing copies of JDO data objects, we'll use the classname as the namespace. In this way, we can always use an object's app-assigned String ID or system-assigned Long ID as the key without concern for key clashes.

You can reset the namespace accessed by the Memcache handle at any time by calling:

```
memcache.setNamespace(nameSpace);
```

Once set for a Memcache handle, the given namespace is used for the Memcache API calls. Therefore, any subsequent gets, puts, or deletes via that handle will access that namespace.

As this book goes to press, a new Namespace API is now part of App Engine. The **Namespace API** supports *multitenancy*, allowing one app to serve multiple "tenants" or client organizations via the use of multiple namespaces to separate tenant data.

A number of App Engine service APIs, including the Datastore and Memcache, are now namespace-aware, and a namespace may be set using a new **Namespace Manager**. The `getMemcacheService()` method used in this chapter, if set with a namespace, will override the more general settings of the Namespace Manager. So, for the most part, you do not want to use these two techniques together—that is, if you use the new Namespace API to implement multitenancy, do not additionally explicitly set Memcache namespaces as described in this chapter. Instead, leave it to the Namespace Manager to determine the broader namespace that you are using, and ensure that your cache keys are unique in a given "tenant" context. `http://code.google.com/appengine/docs/java/multitenancy/overview.html` provides more information about multitenancy.

To store an object in Memcache, call:

```
memcache.put(key, value);
```

where `memcache` is the handle to the Memcache service, and both the `key` and the `value` may be objects of any type. The `value` object must be serializable. The `put` method may take a third argument, which specifies when the cache entry expires. See the documentation for more information on the different ways in which expiration values can be specified.

To retrieve an object with a given key from Memcache, call:

```
Object r = memcache.get(key);
```

where again `memcache` is the handle to the Memcache service. If the object is not found, `get` will return `null`.

To delete an object with a given key from Memcache, call:

```
memcache.delete(key);
```

If these operations encounter a Memcache service error, they may throw a `MemcacheServiceException`. It is usually a good idea to just catch any Memcache-generated errors.

Thus, the `cacheGet`, `cacheDelete`, and `cachePut`/`cachePutExp` methods of `CacheSupport` create a namespace-specific handler based on their namespace argument, perform the specified operation in the context of that namespace, and catch any `MemcacheServiceExceptions` thrown. The `cachePutExp` method takes an expiration time, in seconds, and sets the cached object to expire accordingly.

`CacheSupport` requires the cache value argument to implement `Serializable` (if the wrapper class had not imposed that requirement, a `put` error would be thrown if the value were not `Serializable`).

# Memcache error handlers

The default error handler for the Memcache service is the `LogAndContinueErrorHandler`, which just logs service errors instead of throwing them. The result is that service errors act like cache misses. So if you use the default error handler, `MemcacheServiceException` will in fact not be thrown. However, it is possible to set your own error handler, or to use the `StrictErrorHandler`, which will throw a `MemcacheServiceException` for any service error. See the `com.google.appengine.api.memcache` documentation (http://code.google.com/appengine/docs/java/javadoc/com/google/appengine/api/memcache/package-summary.html) for more information.

# Memcache statistics

It is possible to access statistics on Memcache use. Using the `com.google.appengine.api.memcache` API, you can get information about things such as the number of cache hits and misses, the number and size of the items currently in the cache, the age of the least-recently accessed cache item, and the total size of data returned from the cache.

The statistics are gathered over the service's current uptime (and you can not explicitly reset them), but they can be useful for local analysis and relative comparisons.

# Atomic increment/decrement of Memcache values

Using the `com.google.appengine.api.memcache` API, it is possible to perform atomic increments and decrements on cache values. That is, the read of the value, its modification, and the storage of the new value can be performed atomically, so that no other process may update the value between the time it is read and the time it is updated. Because Memcache operations cannot be a part of regular transactions, this can be a useful feature. For example, it can allow the implementation of short-term volatile-memory locks. Just remember that the items in the cache can be evicted by the system at any time, so you should not depend upon any Memcache content for the correct operation of your app.

The atomic increments and decrements are performed using the variants of the `increment()` and `incrementAll()` methods of `MemcacheService`. You specify the delta by which to increment and can perform a decrement by passing a negative delta. See the `com.google.appengine.api.memcache` documentation for more information.

# Using Memcache with JDO data objects

One common use of the Memcache service is to cache copies of persistent data objects in volatile memory so that you don't always have to make a more time-consuming Datastore fetch to access them: you can check the cache for the object first, and only if you have a cache miss do you need to access the Datastore. Objects must be serializable in order to be stored in Memcache, so any such cached data classes must implement Serializable. When storing a JDO object in Memcache, you are essentially storing a detached copy, so be sure to prefetch any lazily loaded fields that you want to include in the cached object before storing it.

When using Memcache to cache data objects, be aware that there is no way to guarantee that related Memcache and Datastore operations always happen together—you can't perform the Memcache operations under transactional control, and a Memcache access might transiently fail (this is not common, but is possible), leaving you with stale cached data.

Thus, it is not impossible for a Memcache object to get out of sync with its Datastore counterpart. Typically, the speedup benefits of using Memcache far outweigh such disadvantages. However, you may want to give all of your cached objects an expiration date. This helps the cache "re-sync" after a period of time if there are any inconsistencies.

The pattern of cache usage for data objects is typically as follows, depending upon whether or not an object is being accessed in a transaction.

- **Within a transaction**

  When accessing an object from within a transaction, you should not use the cached version of that object, nor update the cache inside the transaction. This is because Memcache is not under transactional control. If you were to update the cache within a transactional block, and then the transaction failed to commit, the Memcache data would be inconsistent with the Datastore. So when you access objects inside a transaction, purge the cache of these objects.

  Post-transaction, you can cache a detached copy of such an object, once you have determined that the commit was successful.

- **Outside a transaction**

  If a Datastore access is not under transactional control, this means that it is not problematic to have multiple processes accessing that object at the same time. In that case, you can use Memcache as follows:

  When reading an object: first check to see if the object is in the cache; if not, then fetch it from the Datastore and add it to the cache.

  When creating or modifying an object: save it to the Datastore first, then update the cache if the Datastore operation was successful.

  When deleting an object: delete from the cache first, then delete from the Datastore.

In all cases, be sure to catch any errors thrown by the Memcache service so that they do not prevent you from doing your other work.

When using Memcache to store data objects, it can be useful to employ some form of caching framework, so that you do not have to add object cache management code for every individual method and access. In the next section, we will look at one way to do this—using capabilities provided by JDO.

# JDO lifecycle listeners

JDO 2.0 defines an interface for the `PersistenceManager` (and `PersistenceManagerFactory`) that allows a listener to be registered for persistence events in the "lifecycle" of a data object—creating, deleting, loading, or storing the object. Once a listener is set up for a `PersistenceManager`, the JDO implementation will call methods on the listener when specified persistence events occur. This allows the application to define methods that monitor the persistence process (for specified persistent classes). We will use this feature to support object cache management in *Connectr*.

To set up a JDO lifecycle listener, create a class that implements any number of the following `javax.jdo.listener` interfaces—`DeleteLifecycleListener`, `CreateLifecycleListener`, `LoadLifecycleListener`, and `StoreLifecycleListener`. Each interface requires that the implementing class implements a "pre" and/or "post" method for the associated event type. These methods, often referred to as *callbacks*, are called before and after the persistence event. For example, `preDelete()` and `postDelete()` methods are defined for the `DeleteLifecycleListenerinterface`, which are called before and after a *delete* event.

Each method takes as its argument the `InstanceLifecycleEvent` event that triggered it. If triggered within a transaction, the listener actions are performed within the context of that same transaction.

 See `http://www.datanucleus.org/products/accessplatform_1_1/jdo/lifecycle_listeners.html` for further details on Lifecycle listeners.

The following code shows one of the listener classes used in *Connectr*, `server.utils.cache.CacheMgmtTxnLifecycleListener`. It implements the `DeleteLifecycleListener` and `LoadLifecycleListener` interfaces, and thus is required to define methods called on *delete* and *load* events.

```
import javax.jdo.listener.DeleteLifecycleListener;
import javax.jdo.listener.InstanceLifecycleEvent;
import javax.jdo.listener.LoadLifecycleListener;


public class CacheMgmtTxnLifecycleListener implements
  DeleteLifecycleListener, LoadLifecycleListener {

  public void preDelete(InstanceLifecycleEvent event) {
    removeFromCache(event);
  }
```

```
public void postDelete(InstanceLifecycleEvent event) {
  // must be defined even though not used
}

public void postLoad(InstanceLifecycleEvent event) {
  removeFromCache(event);
}

private void removeFromCache(InstanceLifecycleEvent event) {
  Object o = event.getSource();
  if(o instanceof Cacheable) {
    Cacheable f = (Cacheable) o;
    f.removeFromCache();
  }
}
}
```

Once a listener class has been defined, you can associate it with a given `PersistenceManager` instance as follows:

```
pm.addInstanceLifecycleListener(
    new CacheMgmtTxnLifecycleListener(), classes);
```

where `classes` is an array of `java.lang.Class` objects for which changes should be listened for. That is, the `PersistenceManager` will listen for *delete* and *load* events on the given classes and call the defined listener methods when they occur.

# Defining a cacheable interface

To use the JDO listeners to support Memcache management in *Connectr*, we'll first define a `server.utils.cache.Cacheable` interface:

```
public interface Cacheable
{
  public void addToCache();
  public void removeFromCache();
}
```

Any data class that implements this interface must define two instance methodsâ€"an `addToCache()` method, which adds that object to Memcache, and a `removeFromCache()` method, which deletes that object from Memcache. The lifecycle listener methods (as in the previous example, `server.utils.cache.CacheMgmtTxnLifecycleListener`) can thus safely call `addToCache()` and `removeFromCache()` on any `Cacheable` object.

The implementations of these methods will in turn use the `server.utils.cache.` `CacheSupport` class (described previously) to actually access the cache, using the class name to set the Memcache *namespace*.

In *Connectr*, both the `Friend` and `FeedInfo` classes implement `Cacheable`. The following code shows the `server.domain.FeedInfo` implementation of `addToCache()` and `removeFromCache()` in support of that interface. For `FeedInfo`, the call to `getFeedInfo()` prior to adding the object to Memcache forces the feed content field to be fetched. Otherwise (because it is lazily loaded), that field would not be included when the object was serialized for Memcache.

```
@PersistenceCapable(identityType = IdentityType.APPLICATION,
    detachable="true")
public class FeedInfo implements Serializable, Cacheable {

  ...
  @Persistent
  @PrimaryKey
  private String urlstring;
  ...
  private int update_mins;


  public void removeFromCache() {
    CacheSupport.cacheDelete(this.getClass().getName(), urlstring);
  }

  public void addToCache() {
    getFeedInfo();
    CacheSupport.cachePut(this.getClass().getName(),urlstring,this);
  }
  ...
}
```

# The *Connectr* application's lifecycle listeners

Any number of lifecycle listener classes can be defined, which implement handlers for some or all of the persistence events. For *Connectr*, we have defined two—one for the case where the `PersistenceManager` is being used to manage a transaction, and one for the case where there is non-transactional Datastore access. This simple distinction works for our application; more complex applications might use others.

As discussed earlier, with transactions, it is safest to conservatively remove cached information for any object that the transaction accesses. In that way, if the transaction does not commit, the cache will not be out of sync. The `server.utils.cache.` `CacheMgmtTxnLifecycleListener` class listed previously will be used for accesses inside transactions, and deletes the object from the cache after the object is loaded or before it is deleted from the Datastore. It does not add to the cache at any point.

If not operating within a transaction—for example, for a read—then the `server.` `utils.cache.CacheMgmtLifecycleListener` class, which follows, is used. It too deletes an object from the cache before it is deleted in the Datastore. However, this Listener caches an object after it is loaded or stored.

```
public class CacheMgmtLifecycleListener implements
   DeleteLifecycleListener, LoadLifecycleListener,
   StoreLifecycleListener {

   public void preDelete(InstanceLifecycleEvent event) {
      Object o = event.getSource();
      If (o instanceof Cacheable) {
        Cacheable f = (Cacheable) o;
        f.removeFromCache();
      }
   }

   public void postDelete(InstanceLifecycleEvent event) {
      // must be defined even though not used
   }

   public void postLoad(InstanceLifecycleEvent event) {
      addToCache(event);
   }

   public void preStore(InstanceLifecycleEvent event) {
   }

   public void postStore(InstanceLifecycleEventevent) {
    addToCache(event);
   }

   private void addToCache(InstanceLifecycleEvent event) {
      Object o = event.getSource();
      if (o instanceof Cacheable) {
        Cacheable f = (Cacheable) o;
        f.addToCache();
      }
   }
}
```

## Using the lifecycle listeners consistently

In *Connectr*, we will use Memcache to cache objects of the FeedInfo and Friend (and child) data classes. In later chapters, as we further develop the app, we will make additional use of the cache as well. We can use our two JDO lifecycle listeners to impose consistency on our object caching: we can enforce the use of one of the two listeners with each PersistenceManager and set the listeners to apply only to the FeedInfo and Friend classes, so that the listeners are not being employed unnecessarily.

To facilitate this, we will modify the app's server.PMF singleton class (shown as follows) to define the list of data classes for which the app uses Listener-based caching. Then, we'll add two methods (getTxnPm() and getNonTxnPm()) that return a PersistenceManager with the appropriate lifecycle listener set. Now, instead of simply grabbing a generic PersistenceManager, we will obtain a configured one via getTxnPm() or getNonTxnPm(), depending upon whether or not the PersistenceManager will be used inside a transaction.

The following code shows the modified server.PMF class (in the classes array, replace 'packagepath' with your path).

```java
import javax.jdo.JDOHelper;
import javax.jdo.PersistenceManagerFactory;
import javax.jdo.PersistenceManager;

public final class PMF {

  private static final java.lang.Class[] classes =
    new java.lang.Class[]{
    packagepath.server.domain.FeedInfo.class,
    packagepath.server.domain.Friend.class};
  private static final PersistenceManagerFactory pmfInstance =
    JDOHelper.getPersistenceManagerFactory("transactions-optional");

    privatePMF(){
    }

  public static PersistenceManagerFactory get(){
     return pmfInstance;
  }

  public static PersistenceManager getNonTxnPm(){
    PersistenceManager pm = pmfInstance.getPersistenceManager();
    pm.addInstanceLifecycleListener(new CacheMgmtLifecycleListener(),
        classes);
    return pm;
```

```
    }

    public static PersistenceManager getTxnPm(){
        PersistenceManager pm = pmfInstance.getPersistenceManager();
        pm.addInstanceLifecycleListener(
            new CacheMgmtTxnLifecycleListener(), classes);
        return pm;
    }
}
```

## Checking for a cache hit

Once the Listener-based mechanism is in place to add objects to the cache appropriately, we can check the cache on reads, given the ID of an object. If we get a cache *hit*, we use the cached copy of the object. If we have a cache *miss*, we simply load the object from the Datastore. Using the CacheMgmtLifecycleListener, a Datastore load invokes the postLoad() Listener method. This will cache the object, making it available for subsequent reads.

The following code illustrates this approach in the getFriendViaCache() method of server.FriendsServiceImpl.

```
@SuppressWarnings("serial")
public class FriendsServiceImpl extends RemoteServiceServlet
    implements FriendsService
{
    ...
    private Friend getFriendViaCache(String id, PersistenceManager pm){
        Friend dsFriend = null, detached = null;

        // check cache first
        Object o = null;
         o = CacheSupport.cacheGet(Friend.class.getName(), id);
         if (o != null && o instanceof Friend) {
             detached = (Friend) o;
         }
         else {
          // the fetch will automatically add to cache via the lifecycle
          // listener
          dsFriend = pm.getObjectById(Friend.class, id);
          dsFriend.getDetails();
          detached = pm.detachCopy(dsFriend);
         }
         return detached;
    }
    ...
}
```

Memcache is not useful solely for data object caching. It is often used to cache display-related information as well. We will see this usage of Memcache in a later chapter.

# Summary

In this chapter, we've explored ways in which you can make a GAE application more robust, responsive, and scalable in its interactions with the Datastore, and applied these techniques to our *Connectr* app.

We first took a look at how Datastore access configuration and data modeling can impact application efficiency and discussed some approaches to entity design towards scalability.

Then, we introduced transactions—what they are, the constraints on a transaction in App Engine, and when to use them.

Finally, we discussed the App Engine's Memcache service, how caching can speed up your app's server-side operations, and looked at an approach to integrating caching with access to "lifecycle events" on JDO data objects.

# 10
# Pushing Fresh Content to Clients with the Channel API

## Why use push technology

When it comes to displaying rapidly changing information coming from the backend to web clients, there are two strategies available to software programmers: either they implement a polling system that will ask the server if there is new information on a regular basis, or they can choose to program a push system that will send information from the server to the clients as information becomes available.

Most client applications **poll** their backend servers every few minutes for updates. A typical example of software using a polling strategy is an e-mail client application that will check mail every five minutes.

Polling is widely used because it is simple to implement. One way that developers can use is to create a timer that goes off at regular intervals. However even though polling fulfills its roles it nevertheless has severe limitations.

First, new information is only fetched at polling time even though it could have been available long before. Secondly, the backend may do unnecessary work when asked to check for new items when there are none available. This is the reason why **polling does not scale** well for apps used by thousands or millions of users.

The opposite of polling technology is **push** technology. Instead of clients requesting updates on a periodic basis, the backend pushes updates as they become available to its clients. Chat applications are a good example of apps using push technology. Push technology does not have any of the inherent issues poll technology has. However, push is harder to implement than poll because it requires in-depth knowledge of low level networking such as socket programming.

Luckily, Google provides a library that encapsulates the low-level programming into an easy-to-understand API, making push technology accessible to more programmers.

In the next section, we show how to implement push technology in *Connectr*.

# Implementation overview

At the time of this writing the ChannelAPI currently only works in local development mode-- its classes are included in the App Engine libs, so it can be used locally, but it is not yet officially supported for deployed appspot apps. It is anticipated that one of the next release of App Engine will include official Channel API support. *Connectr's* push implementation is based on Google's Dance Dance Robot showcase example. This example is located on Google code at `http://code.google.com/p/dance-dance-robot/`. It has been modified to meet *Connectr's* requirements. Before we jump right into Java code, let's see how a typical message push sequence works in *Connectr*:

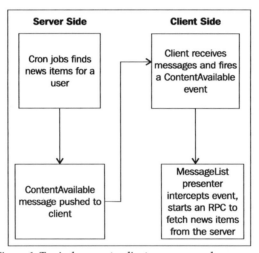

Figure 1: Typical server-to-client message push sequence

As continuously running Cron Jobs scour the Internet to find news items for its users, *Connectr* pushes a special type of message named `ContentAvailable` to clients as news items become available. Once clients receive this message, they generate an ad hoc event named `ContentAvailableEvent` that `MessageList` presenters listen to. When received, presenters fetch the news items by triggering a Remote Procedure Call to the server.

# Setting up the application to handle pushed messages

In order to implement a push system, the server needs to create **one channel for each client**. Clients need to **listen** to their own channel by creating a **network socket listener**.

## Server side channel creation

Channels are created on the server side during the login sequence via a call to the LoginStart method, which is located in the LoginHelper class:

```
package com.metadot.book.connectr.server;
// Imports omitted

public class LoginHelper extends RemoteServiceServlet {
...
  public UserAccount loginStarts(HttpSession session, UserAccount
user) {
...
u = (UserAccount) pm.getObjectById(UserAccount.class, aUser.getId());
        String channelId = ChannelServer.createChannel(u.
getUniqueId());
      u.setChannelId(channelId);

...

      tx.commit();
...
```

Once we have the user information, u, a call to ChannelServer.createChannel(u.getUniqueId()) with the user's unique ID as input parameter creates a channel. It is important for this parameter to represent users uniquely since channels have to be unique for each user. The result of this call is a string channelId containing the channel identifier for this particular user. An example of a channel identifier is channel--eurysa-Connectr-email@example.com-1, where the e-mail part (including the last digit) is the user unique identifier.

We then save the identifier channelId in a user field and make it persistent by committing the changes in the Datastore:

```
u.setChannelId(channelId);
...
tx.commit();
```

# Under the hood of ChannelServer

We abstract some of the Channel API inner workings by using a class called ChannelServer that encapsulates the lower level App Engine Channel API.

Details of a channel creation are as follows:

```
package com.metadot.book.connectr.server.utils;
import com.google.appengine.api.channel.ChannelMessage;
import com.google.appengine.api.channel.ChannelService;
import com.google.appengine.api.channel.ChannelServiceFactory;
//Other imports omitted'

public class ChannelServer {
...

public static String createChannel(String uniqueId) {
  String channelId = getChannelService().createChannel(
      APP_KEY + uniqueId);
  return channelId;
}
```

To create a channel on the backend side, we use a Channel API call getChannelService().createChannel(...). It requires one parameter, APP_KEY, combined with the user's unique identifier uniqueId. APP_KEY represents a string identifying the application, whose value is Connectr- in this case. The method getChannelService() is a private ChannelServer class method that uses the Channel API factory to return a channel service as shown in the following code:

```
private static ChannelService getChannelService() {
  return ChannelServiceFactory.getChannelService();
}
...
```

This concludes the server side channel creation. In the next section, we set up the GWT client to listen to and receive pushed messages.

# Preparing the GWT client for pushed messages

Once a server-side channel is created, the web client needs to listen to it in order to receive pushed messages. This initialization is performed in the main client class `Connectr`.

```
package com.metadot.book.connectr.client;
// Imports omitted


public class ConnectrApp implements EntryPoint {
...
  private void listenToChannel() {
    Channel channel =
      ChannelFactory.createChannel(currentUser.getChannelId());
    channel.open(new SocketListener() {
      public void onOpen() {

        ...
      }

      public void onMessage(String encodedData) {
        try {
          SerializationStreamReader reader =
            pushServiceStreamFactory.createStreamReader(encodedData);
          Message message = (Message) reader.readObject();
          handleMessage(message);
        } catch (SerializationException e) {
          throw new RuntimeException("Unable to deserialize " +
encodedData, e);
        }
      }
    });
  }
...
```

First, we create a client channel by calling our own `ChannelFactory` method, `createChannel`, that uses the channel identifier of the current logged in user via a call to `currentUser.getChannelId()`. This channel identifier was created when the channel was created on the server side.

We then open the channel with `channel.open(new SocketListener...)`. When creating a new socket listener, we need to create two interface methods, `onOpen()` and `onMessage()`. The first one is called when the socket opens up. Here we could just log a message for debugging purposes. The second interface method, `onMessage()`, is called when a pushed message is received. At this point the method `onMessage()`, after some deserialization magic, calls our custom made message handler `handleMessage()`.

# Adding a handler to process pushed messages

Once a pushed message is received, *Connectr's* message handler, `handleMessage`, located in the `Connectr` class, takes over. It is set up to process two types of messages, text messages and new content available messages, as shown in the following code:

```
package com.metadot.book.connectr.client;
// Imports omitted

public class ConnectrApp implements EntryPoint {
...
public void handleMessage(Message msg) {
    switch (msg.getType()) {

    case TEXT_MESSAGE:
      GWT.log("Pushed msg received: TEXT_MESSAGE: " +
((ChannelTextMessage) msg).get());
        break;


    case NEW_CONTENT_AVAILABLE:
      GWT.log("Pushed msg received: NEW_CONTENT_AVAILABLE");
      eventBus.fireEvent(new ContentAvailableEvent());
      break;


    default:
        Window.alert("Unknown message type: " + msg.getType());
    }
  }
...
```

The first type, identified by the constant TEXT_MESSAGE, handles simple strings pushed by the server. This type of message is used mostly for debugging purposes. It will be a developer's best friend during the development of a push system and should get copious usage.

The second type, identified by the constant NEW_CONTENT_AVAILABLE, handles messages indicating that new content is available. This new content needs to be fetched from the server by the GWT client. In this case, *Connectr* fires a custom event named ContentAvailableEvent on the event bus.

Then a presenter named MessageListPresenter, in charge of managing the MVP triad displaying the latest friends' messages to users, receives the event and handles it accordingly, as described by the following snippet.

```
...
public void bind() {
...
    eventBus.addHandler(ContentAvailableEvent.TYPE, new
ContentAvailableEventHandler() {
        @Override
        public void onContentAvailable(ContentAvailableEvent event) {
          getMessageList();
        }
    });
...
}
```

Once a ContentAvailableEvent event is received, the method getMessageList() initiates a Remote Procedure Call to the backend in order to get the most recent items.

This concludes the channel setup for the *Connectr* GWT client. *Connectr* is now ready to receive pushed messages from the server and can handle them appropriately.

# Pushing messages to clients

Now that both the backend and GWT client wiring is completed, we are ready to push messages from the server to the client. This can be done in a very simple way by making a call to the method ChannelServer.pushMessage(...):

```
ChannelServer.pushMessage(user, message)
```

These calls are only made on the server side. As an example, *Connectr* backend notifies clients of new content in `UserNotifServlet` as follows:

```
package com.metadot.book.connectr.server.servlets;
// Imports omitted

public class UserNotifServlet extends HttpServlet {
...
public void doPost(HttpServletRequest req, HttpServletResponse resp)
  ...
  // new content available
  ChannelServer.pushMessage(user,
    new ContentAvailableMessage());
  ...
```

This couldn't be simpler.

# Creating custom classes of pushed messages

*Connectr* is set up to handle only a few types of pushed messages. Real world applications create their own message types based on their needs. Any complex object can be sent via our push message facility. This is achievable because messages are serialized before they are transmitted to clients.

For example, here is the code *Connectr's* text message class name `ChannelTextMessage` that encapsulates a message `ttext` of type String:

```
package com.metadot.book.connectr.shared.messages;

@SuppressWarnings("serial") public class ChannelTextMessage extends
Message {
  private String ttext;

  private ChannelTextMessage() {
    super(Type.TEXT_MESSAGE);
  }

  public ChannelTextMessage(String ttext) {
    this();
    this.ttext = ttext;
  }

  public String get() {
    return ttext;
  }
}
```

On the client side, the message `ttext` can be extracted from the message class by doing a cast to its original class as shown in the following code:

```
package com.metadot.book.connectr.client;
// Imports omitted

public class ConnectrApp implements EntryPoint {
...
public void handleMessage(Message msg) {
    switch (msg.getType()) {

...

    case TEXT_MESSAGE:
        String ttext = ((ChannelTextMessage) msg).get();

...

    }
```

In order to create a new message class we first need to modify the abstract class `Message` and add a constant representing this new class. For example, say we are going to add a complex blob message type, we would therefore add COMPLEX_BLOB_ MESSAGE constant to the types of messages already available. Here is how we would modify the `Message` class.

```
package com.metadot.book.connectr.shared.messages;
...
@SuppressWarnings("serial") public abstract class Message implements
Serializable {

  public enum Type {
      NEW_CONTENT_AVAILABLE,
      TEXT_MESSAGE,
      COMPLEX_BLOB_MESSAGE,
    }

  private Type type;

  private Message() {
  }

  protected Message(Type type) {
    this.type = type;
  }

  public Type getType() {
    return type;
  }
}
```

Then, we would create the `ComplexBlobMessage` class as follows:

```java
package com.metadot.book.connectr.shared.messages;

@SuppressWarnings("serial") public class ComplexBlobMessage extends
Message {

  private Blob blob;

  @SuppressWarnings({ "UnusedDeclaration" })
  private ComplexBlobMessage() {
      super(Type.COMPLEX_BLOB_MESSAGE);
  }

  public ComplexBlobMessage (Blob blob) {
    this();
    this.blob = blob;
  }

    public Blob get() {
       return blob;
    }
  }
}
```

Finally, on the client side, in the `Connectr` class' `handleMessage` method we can receive blob objects after performing a cast of the received message to its initial class:

```java
package com.metadot.book.connectr.client;
// Imports omitted

public class ConnectrApp implements EntryPoint {
...
  public void handleMessage(Message msg) {
    switch (msg.getType()) {
    ...
    case TEXT_MESSAGE:
    ...
    case COMPLEX_BLOB_MESSAGE:
      Blob blob = ((ComplexBlobMessage) msg).get();

    ...
    }
  ...
```

This is all the knowledge needed in order to create custom message classes. Since we rely on the robust GWT serialization mechanism, any type of complex class can be transmitted via a push service.

# Telling the server a client is inactive

One of the challenges that we face when using a push system is that servers may do unnecessary work if client applications are left unattended. For example, a backend could keep sending messages to clients even though their users may not be in front of their monitor staring at their web app. Therefore, in order to avoid doing unnecessary work when a web client is unused, *Connectr* implements a mechanism that indicates to the backend when users are active. In the context of *Connectr*, active means that users are performing a *certain kind of action* that triggers Remote Procedure Calls to the backend. Different types of applications will implement different strategies in order to detect inactive users.

In *Connectr*, each time this kind of action occurs, a user record field storing the last activity date is updated. The backend checks this before doing any kind of work or before pushing any messages. This avoids unnecessary work if users are inactive.

Here is how it is implemented. Each time users' actions generate calls to the server, the server identifies them by calling getLoggedInUser. In this method, we update the user u attribute lastActiveOn with the current date as shown in the following code:

```
package com.metadot.book.connectr.server;
// Imports omitted

public class LoginHelper extends RemoteServiceServlet {
...
  static public UserAccount getLoggedInUser(HttpSession session,
    PersistenceManager pm) {
  ...
    u.setLastActive(new Date());
...
```

It is now up to the backend to check the value of this field before deciding whether to perform work or not.

# Adding a refresh button to allow on-demand news updates

It is useful to provide users with the ability to refresh friends' news on demand. *Connectr* provides a **Refresh now** button located on the right-hand side of the message list as shown in the next screenshot:

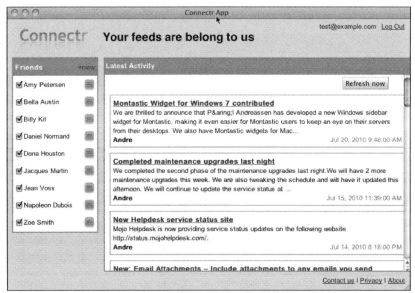

Figure 2: *Connectr* Refresh-now button provides users a way to get the latest items.

The presenter in charge of the message list wires this button to a method that gets the latest messages. This method is named getMessageList() as shown in the following code.

```
this.display.getRefreshButton().addClickHandler(new ClickHandler() {
    public void onClick(ClickEvent event) {
      getMessageList();
    }
});
```

# Summary

In this chapter, we covered the implementation of a message push system using the App Engine Channel API.

We have seen how to create a channel for each GWT client on the server side and a socket listener on the client side. In case users log in with several browser sessions, all sessions will receive the push notifications. To avoid this behavior, which can consume quite a bit of resources for large user bases, a multi-session push system will need to be developed. We have also explained how to create a client-side handler to process pushed messages. We have presented the *Connectr* server that pushes messages to clients with a call to the `ChannelServer.pushMessage()` method. We also covered the basic implementation of custom Message classes that can encapsulate complex objects. This will be useful to adapt *Connectr* to fit specific developers' needs. Finally, we reviewed how a server can avoid sending messages to unattended GWT clients and how users can use the on-demand refresh button to force a friend message list refresh. This could be extended to implement an automatic refresh when an inactive session becomes active again.

In the next chapter, we are going to discuss the more mundane tasks of managing an application on App Engine such as deploying, monitoring, as well as importing and backing up its data.

# 11
# Managing and Backing Up your App Engine Application

In this chapter, we'll take a break from developing the *Connectr* application code and look in more detail at what's involved in configuring, deploying, monitoring, and maintaining an App Engine app.

*Configuration and deployment* will detail application configuration options, deployment of application versions, and dealing with deployment file limits.

Then, *The Admin Console* section will take a closer look—than we have done thus far—at the App Engine's Admin Console features, including quotas and billing.

*Command-line administration* will look at some useful command-line utilities (one Python-based), which let you do application maintenance, download your logs, and back up your application data by downloading and uploading Datastore contents.

*Using Appstats* will describe how to configure and use a package called `Appstats` that lets you monitor request performance and browse performance statistics.

Finally, *Using your own domain for an app* will describe how to set up a custom domain for your App Engine app via a Google Apps account.

## Configuration and deployment

In previous chapters, we've introduced various aspects of App Engine app configuration and deployment as they came up in the process of developing the *Connectr* application's functionality.

This section covers some of the configuration and deployment features that we haven't described yet. We'll first survey many of the application configuration options available. Then, we will discuss some deployment issues and tactics. We will cover management of multiple app versions, how and when to switch between them, the limits that App Engine places on the number and size of files that you can deploy, and some ways to repackage your app if you bump up against the limits.

# Configuration

In this section, we'll explore in more detail the different ways in which you can configure an App Engine app. This includes `web.xml` (deployment descriptor) configuration, `appengine-web.xml` configuration, and configuring a Denial of Service (`dos.xml`) file for specifying IP addresses or subnets that you want your app to block.

We will postpone two aspects of app configuration to a later chapter. We will describe Task Queue configuration (this uses the `queue.xml` file, which lets you define multiple queues of different priorities) and Cron job configuration (which uses the `cron.xml` file) in *Chapter 12*.

## The deployment descriptor—web.xml

The `war/WEB-INF/web.xml` file is the **deployment descriptor** file used by Java Servlet-based web applications; it is a part of the Servlet specification. For more general information, see the Java Servlet specification or the Tomcat reference guide (`http://wiki.metawerx.net/wiki/Web.xml`). Previous chapters introduced some `web.xml` features. This section provides a bit more detail.

App Engine does not support all features of the `web.xml` standard. See the App Engine documentation at: `http://code.google.com/appengine/docs/java/config/webxml.html`, for more information on the unsupported features as well as more detail on the features described in the next section.

## Servlet declarations and mappings, security, and authentication

*Chapter 7* showed examples of declaring Servlets (using the `<servlet>` element) and defining Servlet mappings (using the `<servlet-mapping>` element) in the `web.xml` file. The Servlet declarations define a name for a Servlet invocation and can include initialization parameters. The Servlet mappings tell App Engine what Servlet to call, given an incoming URL path request, and can include the use of a wildcard `*` at the beginning or end of the URL pattern.

*Chapter 7* also described the use of the `<security-constraint>` element to place restrictions on which users can access a given URL pattern. If you indicate a `<role-name>` of `*`, this allows all Google-authenticated users to access the URL—either via their general Google Account or via their Google Apps account for a custom domain, depending upon how the app is set up at creation time (see *Using your own domain for an app*). If you indicate a `<role-name>` of admin, then only the application admins (developers) can access the URL. These two options are shown in the following code snippet:

```
<security-constraint>
   <web-resource-collection>
      <url-pattern>/login/*</url-pattern>
   </web-resource-collection>
   <auth-constraint>
      <role-name>*</role-name>
   </auth-constraint>
</security-constraint>

<security-constraint>
   <web-resource-collection>
      <url-pattern>/admin/*</url-pattern>
   </web-resource-collection>
   <auth-constraint>
      <role-name>admin</role-name>
   </auth-constraint>
</security-constraint>
```

You can require that a given URL be only accessible via HTTPS—this is done by indicating the `<transport-guarantee>` element with a value of CONFIDENTIAL, as shown in the example below. This works only for URLs using the `appspot.com` domain. As will be further discussed in *Using your own domain for an app*, custom domains administered via Google Apps do not currently support HTTPS.

```
<security-constraint>
  <web-resource-collection>
     <url-pattern>/login/*</url-pattern>
  </web-resource-collection>
  <user-data-constraint>
     <transport-guarantee>CONFIDENTIAL</transport-guarantee>
  </user-data-constraint>
</security-constraint>
```

# Servlet filters

If you have built other Servlet-based web-apps before, you may be familiar with Servlet filters. **Filters** can be used to perform auxiliary tasks associated with a Servlet (or with a URL pattern) before invoking the Servlet to which the URL is mapped, and may be *chained*. App Engine supports filters, and *Connectr* uses a filter to check whether a requester of an app URL is logged in.

A `Filter` class must implement the `javax.servlet.Filter` interface. It requires implementation of the `doFilter()`, `init()`, and `destroy()` methods. `doFilter()` has access to the Servlet request and response. The *Connectr* app includes an example filter, `server.servlets.LogFilter` (disabled by default), which logs information about the associated Servlet's request URL and parameters. This filter is shown below.

```
// … imports …
public final class LogFilter implements Filter {

  private static Logger logger =
   Logger.getLogger(LogFilter.class.getName());


  @Override
  public void doFilter(ServletRequest request,
    ServletResponse response, FilterChain chain)
    throws IOException, ServletException {

    Enumeration<String> pnames = request.getParameterNames();
    String p;
    String pval = null;
    String reqUrl =
      ((HttpServletRequest)(request)).getRequestURL().toString();

    logger.info("request URL: " + reqUrl);
    while(pnames.hasMoreElements()) {
      p = (String)pnames.nextElement();
      pval = request.getParameter(p);
      logger.info("request parameter " + p + "has value" + pval);
    }
    chain.doFilter(request, response);

  }
  …
}
```

*Connectr* also includes the `server.servlets.LoginFilter` class. This filter blocks access to the application if the requester is not logged in.

Analogous to the `<servlet>` and `<servlet-mapping>` declarations, filters are set up in `web.xml` by declaring a named `<filter>` and then by defining the `<filter-mapping>` elements that use it. As shown in the next code snippet, you can define `web.xml` filter mappings for both URL patterns and Servlet names (where you would replace `packagepath` with your package path). In this example, the log filter defined previously is mapped to all request handlers via the `/*` pattern, so each time a request is made, information about that request will be logged (this will slow things down; we probably wouldn't want to enable this filter for a production app). The `myFilter` filter declaration that includes the initialization parameters will be called for `testServlet` only.

We will see filters again later in this chapter; a filter is used to support the `Appstats` functionality described in the *Using Appstats* section.

```xml
<filter>
  <filter-name>logfilter</filter-name>
  <filter-class>packagepath.server.servlets.LogFilter
  </filter-class>
</filter>
<filter-mapping>
  <filter-name>logfilter</filter-name>
  <url-pattern>/*</url-pattern>
</filter-mapping>

<filter>
  <filter-name>myFilter</filter-name>
  <filter-class>packagepath.server.MyFilterImpl
  </filter-class>
  <init-param>
    <param-name>param1</param-name>
    <param-value>defaultval</param-value>
  </init-param>
</filter>

<filter-mapping>
  <filter-name>myFilter</filter-name>
  <servlet-name>testServlet</servlet-name>
</filter-mapping>
```

Other features are also configurable via web.xml. It is possible to define custom error handler pages that are accessed when a particular error code or exception type is generated. You can also define a <welcome-file-list> (as was introduced in *Chapter 7*), which specifies the list of filenames that the server should try when it accesses a war (sub-) directory for which a specific Servlet mapping is not defined.

## Configuring DoS protection blacklists—dos.xml

If you want to deny access to your app from a particular set of IP addresses, for example, for **Denial of Service (DoS)** protection, you can do this by creating a war/WEB-INF/dos.xml file. You can specify the addresses to block via IP address (either IPv4 or IPv6) or via a subnet. The dos.xml file should have the format as shown in the next code snippet, where the <blacklistentries> element contains some number of <blacklist> entries. Each <blacklist> entry contains a <subnet> element and an optional <description> element. The <subnet> can contain any valid IPv4 or IPv6 address or subnet in CIDR notation (for examples, see http://en.wikipedia.org/wiki/CIDR_notation).

```
<blacklistentries>
  <blacklist>
    <subnet>0.1.2.3</subnet>
    <description>an IPv4 address</description>
  </blacklist>
  <blacklist>
    ...
  </blacklist>
  ...
</blacklistentries>
```

You can list as many blacklisted IPs or subnets as you want.

Clicking on the **Blacklist** link in the App Engine Admin Console sidebar will show you the top 25 recent visitors for an app, as well as any blacklisted IPs or subnets that you have set up. Figure 1 shows a (fabricated) example of what the start of a DoS attack might look like.

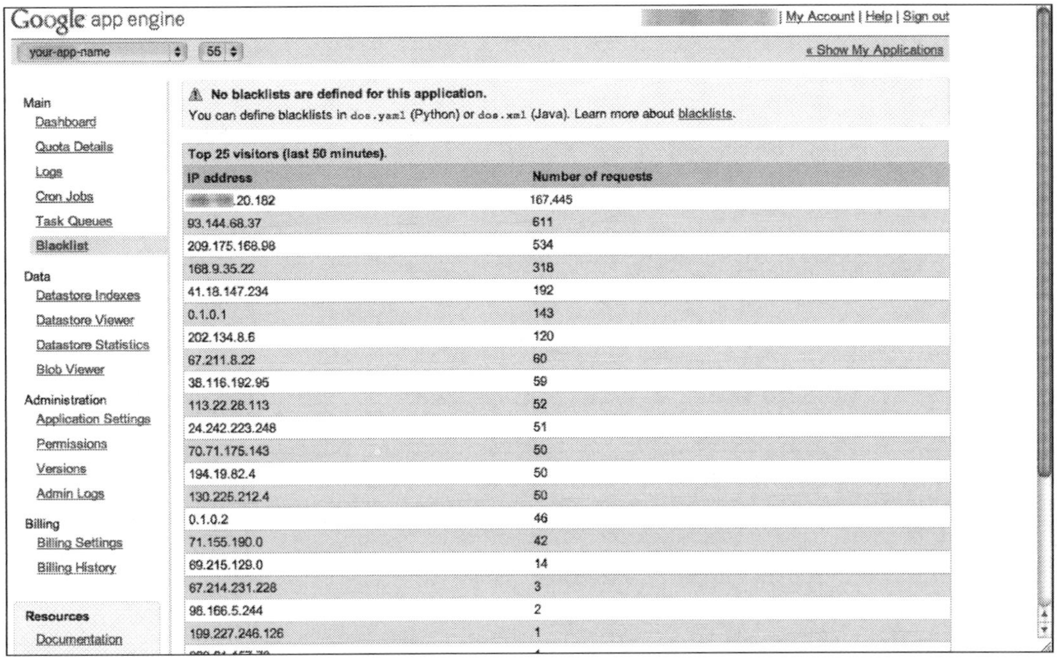

Figure 1: What the start of a DoS attack might look like

If you were to set up a `dos.xml` file that listed the offending IP address, the **"Blacklist"** page would then list this IP at the top of the page, as in Figure 2, and requests from that IP address would be blocked.

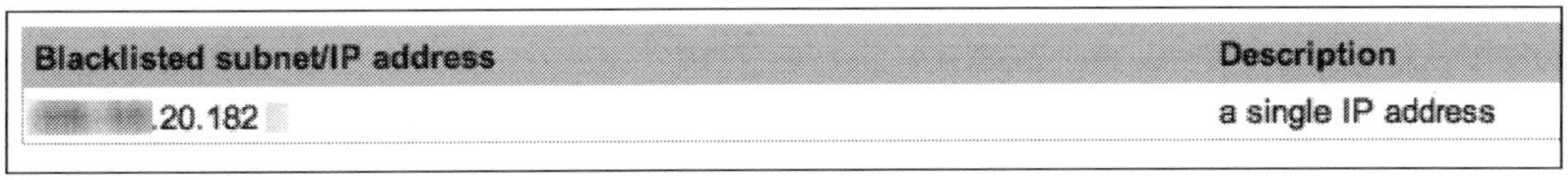

| Blacklisted subnet/IP address | Description |
| --- | --- |
| .20.182 | a single IP address |

Figure 2: Blacklisted IPs or subnets will be listed at the top of the "Blacklist" page in the Admin Console.

As will be described in the *Command-line administration* section, it is possible to edit and re-upload just the `dos.xml` file without re-deploying the entire application (this holds also for some other files such as index definition files). This allows you to be quite agile in responding to suspected DoS incidents. Once deployed, the blacklist will be applied to all versions of that app.

# App configuration—appengine-web.xml

The `war/WEB-INF/appengine-web.xml` file holds application configuration information. This is where system properties and environment variables are defined. `appengine-web.xml` also holds the specification of which uploaded files are to be treated as *static* and/or *resource* files.

 In this section, we describe some of the most useful application configuration options. For more detail, see the App Engine documentation, `http://code.google.com/appengine/docs/java/config/appconfig.html`.

## Enabling Servlet sessions

Servlet *sessions* are not automatically enabled. To enable sessions for your application, add the following line to `appengine-web.xml`:

```
<sessions-enabled>true</sessions-enabled>
```

*Chapter 7* introduced how to access the session. You can see session examples throughout the *Connectr* code, particularly with the login and authentication classes described in *Chapter 8*.

## Adding Admin Console pages

If you have built pages that require admin authentication to access, you can add a declaration for the page so that a link to it is shown in the Admin Console, which when clicked displays the page in the console (via an `iframe`). For example, you may build admin pages for activities such as initiating bookkeeping tasks, managing a set of data migrations, or sending an e-mail to a user. The Admin Console provides a convenient place to list the URLs for those pages.

To do this, add an `<admin-console>` element to `appengine-web.xml`, in which the admin pages are listed via `<page>` elements. For each page, indicate its name (to be displayed in the sidebar) and its relative URL, as shown in the following code. Note that if your admin URLs include ampersands (`&`), you will need to replace the ampersands with `&amp;` in the definition in order to be XML-compliant; if you do not do this, deployment of the `appengine-web.xml` file will fail. This is illustrated in the following code with a parameterized request based on one of the *Connectr* admin Servlets.

```
<admin-console>
  <page name="Generate analytics" url="/admin/analytics" />
  <page name="feed data migration"
     url="/migration?migration=packagpath.server.
     migrations.FeedInfoDataMigration&amp;num=3" />
</admin-console>
```

The links to your custom admin pages will show up under a new category in the left-hand sidebar—**Custom**.

## System properties and logging

You can set system properties for your app in the `appengine-web.xml` file. To do this, enclose the properties in a `<system-properties>` tag. Use the `<property>` tag to specify the property name and values. For example, as shown in the following code, *Connectr* uses a system property, `packagepath.mins-feed-check`, to indicate the default interval in minutes before checking for new content on a feed URL (where you would replace `packagepath` with your *Connectr* app path. A property name can be anything unique, but it is best to base properties on package names to avoid clashes.

```
<appengine-web-app xmlns="http://appengine.google.com/ns/1.0">
  ...
<system-properties>
  <property name="java.util.logging.config.file"
      value="WEB-INF/logging.properties"/>
  <property name="packagepath.mins-feed-check" value="3" />
</system-properties>
  ...
</appengine-web-app>
```

To access a property value in your code, import
```
import java.util.Properties;
```

then access the value as follows (properties are of type String, so if you want to handle them as a different type, you will have to convert them):

```
Properties p = System.getProperties();
update_mins =
  Integer.parseInt(p.getProperty("packagepath.mins-feed-check"));
```

## Logging properties

App Engine supports logging at varying log levels, and allows configuration of the log level for a given app package. When you set a log level for a package, any log messages in that package's code that write to a less-severe level will not be output. This allows you to keep debugging and informational log messages in your code, but to suppress the generation of these messages in your deployed app, which will be more efficient.

App Engine's log levels, in increasing order of severity, are DEBUG, INFO, WARNING, ERROR, and CRITICAL, where only CRITICAL is system-generated, and cannot be logged by the user. In GAE/Java, the JRE java.util.logging package is supported and is implemented to map its log levels to App Engine log levels.

One of the properties in the previous system properties configuration example, java.util.logging.config.file, specifies the logging configuration file. The property's default value is WEB-INF/logging.properties (you can change this value to point to a different file if you like). The logging.properties file allows you to set the log levels for the different packages used by your application. Eclipse will generate this logging property setting and logging.properties file for you when you create a new project.

In the default logging.properties file, you will see this line:

```
.level = WARNING
```

which sets the default app log level (if not otherwise specified) to WARNING. To set a different log level for a specific package, for instance, the INFO level, indicate it as so:

```
packagepath.level = INFO
```

(where packagepath is replaced by a given package). In general, you probably want to set log levels for third-party and App Engine packages at WARNING or higher to reduce noise. For the development stage of your own code, you will often want to set a more verbose log level.

You can see the log output in your local development console and in App Engine's Admin Console logs. Even if your application-level code is not doing any logging, you will see log messages from the App Engine code — the extent of these messages depends upon the log level set.

## Generating log messages

The java.util.logging log levels are mapped to the App Engine log levels as follows — finest, finer, fine, and config all correspond to the App Engine DEBUG level; info maps to the App Engine INFO level; warning to WARNING; and severe to ERROR. CRITICAL log entries are generated by App Engine when there is an exception that is not caught by the Servlet (the app itself cannot log errors at this level).

To generate log messages in your code, import:

```
import java.util.logging.Logger;
```

Then, create a logger (for efficiency, as a class variable):

```
private static final Logger logger =
  Logger.getLogger(YourClass.class.getName());
```

where the argument to getLogger (here, the class name) will be used in the log entry. Use the logger to output a log message at the desired log level, for example:

```
logger.warning("this is a warning message...");
```

or

```
logger.info("this is an informational message...");
```

You will see many examples of Logger used throughout the *Connectr* server-side code. For example, the following code fragment, from server.servlets. FeedUpdateServlet, shows the creation of the Logger as a class variable and the generation of an INFO-level log message.

```
public class FeedUpdateServlet extends HttpServlet {

  ...
  private static Logger logger =
    Logger.getLogger(FeedUpdateServlet.class.getName());
  ...

  public void doPost(HttpServletRequest req, HttpServletResponse resp)
   throws IOException {

    ...
  if (batchcount >= max) {
    logger.info("Reached max number of feed update batches: " + max);
     return;
  }
    ...
}
```

The App Engine Admin Console allows you to browse the log messages you generate for each deployed version of your app, and filter them by level. In addition, you can download the logs for an application version. See the *Browsing an app version's logs* and *Downloading application logs* sections for more information on these activities.

# Static and resource files

*Chapter 7* mentioned **static** and **resource** files. **Static files** hold static content such as images, CSS stylesheets, JavaScript, and so on. These files do not need to be stored on the app server instances. Instead, they are served from dedicated servers.

**Resource files** are any files that may be accessed by the application code. These are pushed to the app server instances. Resource files are accessed using pathnames relative to the war root. For example, if a class were to use a WEB-INF/appdata/ feedlist.txt file as a resource file, it would be accessed in the code as so:

```
FileInputStream fstream =
  new FileInputStream("WEB-INF/appdata/feedlist.txt");
```

All files under the war directory are by default treated as both static files and resource files, with the exception of **JSP** files and WEB-INF files. WEB-INF files are never treated as static files and are always available as resource files.

## Specifying static and resource files

In appengine-web.xml, you can specify more exactly which files are treated as static and which are treated as resource files. One reason that you may want to do so is that there are limits on the number of files that can be associated with an app (see *Application file limits*).

To indicate which files should be treated or excluded as static files, define <include> and <exclude> elements within a <static-files> element, as in the next example. The * indicates zero or more of any character in a file or directory name, and the ** matches any number of characters including subdirectories.

 Remember that you cannot define files under WEB-INF to be static files. Any <exclude> element is applied after the <include> patterns.

For example, the following appengine-web.xml entry includes all .js files, except those in the extras directory and its subdirectories (and, of course, not the WEB-INF directory).

```
<static-files>
  <include path="/**.js" />
    <exclude path="/extras/**.js" />
</static-files>
```

The same `include` and `exclude` elements are used within a `<resource-files>` element to indicate which files should be included or excluded as resource files. The next example excludes as resource files all files under the `image` directory and subdirectories, except the `sample.jpg` file.

```
<resource-files>
  <include path="/images/sample.jpg" />
  <exclude path="/images/**" />
</resource-files>
```

You can specify a browser cache expiration period for static files by adding an expiration element, as so:

```
<include path="/**.js" expiration="2d 12h" />
```

The `expiration` attribute's value should be a string of numbers and time units, separated by spaces, where units can be `d` for days, `h` for hours, `m` for minutes, and `s` for seconds.

# App engine application versions

*Chapter 2* showed how to create an App Engine app ID, how to set the app ID and app **version** in an Eclipse project, and how to deploy that version of the app via Eclipse. Here we delve a bit more deeply into app version management.

Each app ID can have multiple deployed versions associated with it, up to a maximum of ten. Examples will often show numbers used for the version identifiers, for convenience, but in fact the identifier can be any ASCII string valid as a subdomain. Each time you deploy your Eclipse project as a new version of an App Engine application, you specify the version string to use—it can be one that you've used before, or a new one.

Then, in the App Engine Admin Console, you can see all your deployed versions listed, for each app that you have created. One version is designated as the default version of the application—this is the app that is loaded when `http://<app-id>.appspot.com` is accessed. You may use your own domain as well, via Google Apps—see *Using your own domain for an app*.

The other non-default versions of an app may be accessed via this syntax: `http://<version>.latest.<app-id>.appspot.com/`, indicating the app's version string as a subdomain.

You can see a list of the URLs for all versions as well as information on when the version was deployed and by which admin, by clicking on the **Versions** link in the Admin Console's left sidebar.

In this page, you can also indicate which version should be the default, and can delete versions. Typically, you will want to deploy a new version of an app as a non-default version, then designate it the default after testing. You can delete older versions to make room for new ones if you are approaching your maximum of ten.

Anyone who knows your app ID and knows or can guess your version IDs can access your app versions via the previously shown URL syntax. To prevent this, you can restrict access to all app URLs to app *admins* only during development. This is done via a `<security-constraint>` element in `web.xml`, as described in the *Configuration* section. Define the `<url-pattern>` for the security constraint to match any URL, as shown in the following code. Just remember to remove this restriction before switching that version to be the default.

```
<security-constraint>
  <web-resource-collection>
    <url-pattern>/*</url-pattern>
  </web-resource-collection>
  <auth-constraint>
    <role-name>admin</role-name>
  </auth-constraint>
</security-constraint>
```

If there has previously been a deployment against a given version of an app, then when you deploy to that version again, App Engine will replace the existing installation with your current files. No uploaded files from the previous incarnation of that version will remain. However, service-related data that exists across app versions, including the DataStore and Memcache contents, is not removed. Recall in particular that all versions of an app share the same Datastore entities, so ensure that existing Datastore contents will not "break" a new version of your app.

## Application deployment and Datastore indexes

If a new deployment of an app includes any changes to custom index files, then these new indexes must be built. This can take a while (the more data in the Datastore, the longer to build the indexes). If you run a query that depends upon an index still under construction, this will cause an error.

You can track the progress of new-index building by clicking on the **Datastore Indexes** link in the Admin Console sidebar. As discussed in *Chapter 5*, if you have inadvertently generated an "exploding index", then you will need to "vacuum" the offending index and restructure your query and/or entities. So, be sure that you check the status of the indexes before switching a new deployment over to the default. Even though all apps share the same Datastore indexes as well as the same Datastore contents, different apps may require different indexes.

# App versions and the Admin Console

Some Admin Console information panels, such as the Logs or the Dashboard, are specific to an app *version*. Others, such as Datastore information, are not. For version-specific information, be sure to select the version you want to browse from the pulldown in the upper-left of the window.

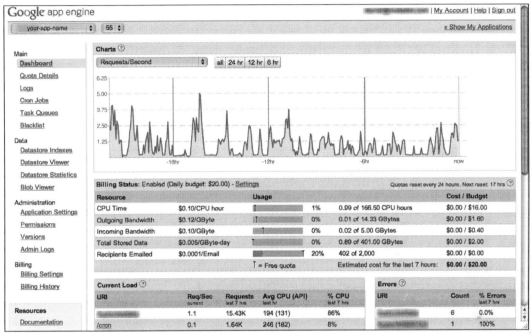

Figure 3: The Dashboard of the Admin Console with usage information for a given application version (version "55") selected. The *your-app-name* pulldown would in actuality show one of your apps.

The previous screenshot shows the **Dashboard** with a specific version of a billing-enabled app (version "55") selected (where the **your-app-name** pulldown would show your app name). For each resource graphed, a marker shows where the free quota lies, as discussed in the *Quotas and billing* section. Switching to a different version of the app displays different chart information.

# Application file limits

There are several file-related limits to be aware of when deploying an App Engine app. As of this writing:

- The maximum total number of files cannot exceed 3000
- There may be 1000 files max per directory (not counting files in subdirectories)

- An individual file cannot be larger than 10MB in size
- The maximum total size of all files cannot exceed 150MB

If you run up against the maximum total file limit, there are several ways that you might reduce it.

First, if your app has too many .class files, you can put them into a .jar file. For example, you can jar all files from WEB-INF/classes.

Second, you can use the <static-files> and <resource-files> directives in appengine-web.xml, as described in *Specifying static and resource files* , to reduce the file count. By default, all files (outside of WEB-INF) belong to both groups—*static files* and *resource files*. The files are counted twice, once for each group—that is, the file count includes the total count for both groups. So, restricting your static and resource files to only those you specifically need, will reduce this count.

Finally, you can consider building a GWT ClientBundle to reduce the number of image and CSS files, as described in *Chapter 3*.

# The Admin Console

The App Engine's app Admin Console allows you to perform a wide range of application management and monitoring tasks. This section explores some of its capabilities in more detail. Recall that you can log in to the Admin Console at http://appengine.google.com.

# Browsing an app version's logs

In addition to the **Dashboard** statistics, the Admin Console logs provide a lot of information about what your application is doing, and what resources it is consuming. Select the **Logs** link in the Admin Console sidebar to view them. Make sure that in the top-left pulldowns, you have selected the application and the app version that you want to browse.

For a given application version, you can either browse all requests or view those with log messages at or above the selected minimum severity level. By expanding the **Options** link—as shown in Figure 4—you can also filter the entries with a regular expression, or limit the entries displayed to be since a given date.

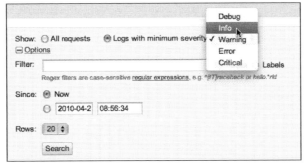

Figure 4: Various options exist to filter an app version's logs.

A request has information such as the referrer URL and the "user agent" of the request. The log also indicates the resources used for each request.

Figure 5: Viewing an app's logs

Figure 5 shows a typical log listing. Each entry shows time and resources used and the referrer for the given request. Each entry can be expanded to see details and logger output for the request. Requests initiated via Cron Jobs or the Task Queue will appear here as well, with the referrer as AppEngine-Google.

The *Command-line administration* section describes how to download an app's logs to your local machine.

# App server startup latency

When you make a request to a deployed App Engine app, a new app server instance may need to be allocated to it. This can be the case either if your app has not received any other requests recently (and so its servers were de-allocated), or if the number of allocated server instances needs to be scaled up.

> **W** 04-26 08:55AM 03.802
>
> This request caused a new process to be started for your application, and thus caused your application code to be loaded for the first time. This request may thus take longer and use more CPU than a typical request for your application.

Figure 6: The logs will show you where app server instance "spin-up" occurred

The "spin-up" time required to do this is noticeable both in terms of CPU usage and response time. If this was the case, you will see an indication in your logs, as shown in Figure 6. Once the process has started up, subsequent requests to it will take less time.

This startup latency, while not excessively long for an individual instance, can add up. For lightly used apps, App Engine may have to spin up a JVM, including all the Servlet context and any framework initialization, on a large percentage of requests. This can be one of the main issues that people mention with respect to developing on App Engine. The App Engine roadmap indicates that in future there may be paid support for retaining "warm", or reserved JVM instances for an app, which would not require the same *spin-up* time.

# Quotas and billing

As you have probably noticed from your exploration of the App Engine Admin Console, there are some billing-related tabs on the left-hand side. You can deploy and run an app for free, but its usage quotas, while reasonable, are limited. For instance, at the time of writing, you get 1GB of storage in the Datastore and 1,300,000 requests per day for a free account.

To deploy an app that will get "real" usage, you will likely need to set up billing, which will enable you to increase your quota levels. You can set up billing via Google Checkout by clicking on the **Enable Billing** button in the **Billing Settings** panel.

When you set up billing, some quotas are *billable* and some increase by a *fixed* amount.

The billable quotas let you set up a budget, indicating how much you want to pay per day total for these resources and split this budget between the billable resources. The billable resources are:

- CPU time
- Bandwidth in
- Bandwidth out
- Stored data
- E-mails sent

For example, the amount of data stored in the Datastore by your apps is billable. You start with your free quota of 1GB, and with billing set up there is no storage maximum—you pay for what you use. Other billable resources such as CPU usage do have a maximum, but it is much higher than for the free accounts. You can accept defaults for how your daily budget is split amongst these resource categories, or customize your budget. As your app grows, you can increase your daily budget at any time.

In contrast, other resources such as Datastore API calls have a fixed quota, both with respect to their daily limit and the number of calls allowed per minute. These limits are higher for billing-enabled apps than free apps. Billing must be enabled to use the **Blobstore** (which allows storage of large chunks of data); however, you won't get charged if you don't go over the free quota.

The resource maximums for both fixed and billable resources set resource constraints that help preserve App Engine integrity, so that one app cannot impact the performance of another. In some cases, if you are running up against a resource maximum, you can submit a form to request an increase.

See `http://code.google.com/appengine/docs/quotas.html` for detailed information about the current quotas—for both free and billed accounts—on application resources. Currently, quotas are reset every 24 hours, and the Admin Console will indicate when the next reset will occur for your app.

`http://code.google.com/appengine/docs/billing.html` has current information on the charges for these resources, and walks you through the process of setting up a daily budget. As the App Engine documentation states:

*Any developer who has access to an application's Administration Console can take over billing responsibilities. This will relieve the currently-billed administrator of responsibility for charges. The new developer will be responsible for any outstanding balance on the application's account.*

# Monitoring your quota levels and resource usage

Once you have an app deployed—and especially once you've set up a budget for your billable resources—you will want to keep an eye on your app's quotas. See the **Quota Details** link on the left sidebar of your Admin Console. Use the pulldown menu in the upper-left to select an application. The quota information shown will be for all deployed versions of that app.

| Main | The quota details for this application are grouped by API and are listed below. If your application exceeds 50% of any particular quota halfway through the day, it may exceed the quota before the day is over. To learn more about how quotas work, read Understanding Quotas and Why is My App Over Quota? | | | | |
|---|---|---|---|---|---|
| Dashboard | | | | | |
| **Quota Details** | **Requests** | | | Quotas are reset every 24 hours. Next reset: 12 hours | |
| Logs | Resource | Daily Quota | | | Rate |
| Cron Jobs | CPU Time | | 2% | 4.07 of 166.50 CPU hours | Okay |
| Task Queues | Requests | | 0% | 75,753 of 43,200,000 | Okay |
| Blacklist | Outgoing Bandwidth | | 0% | 0.05 of 14.33 GBytes | Okay |
| Data | Incoming Bandwidth | | 2% | 0.09 of 5.00 GBytes | Okay |
| Datastore Indexes | Secure Requests | | 0% | 0 of 43,200,000 | Okay |
| Datastore Viewer | Secure Outgoing Bandwidth | | 0% | 0.00 of 14.33 GBytes | Okay |
| Datastore Statistics | Secure Incoming Bandwidth | | 0% | 0.00 of 5.00 GBytes | Okay |
| Blob Viewer | **Storage** | | | | |
| Administration | Datastore API Calls | | 0% | 90,202 of 141,241,791 | Okay |
| Application Settings | Datastore Queries | | 0% | 38,765 of 208,655,584 | Okay |
| Permissions | Blobstore API Calls | | 0% | 0 of 141,241,791 | Okay |
| Versions | Total Stored Data | | 0% | 0.90 of 401.00 GBytes | Okay |
| Admin Logs | Blobstore Stored Data | | 0% | 0.00 of 401.00 GBytes | Okay |
| Billing | Data Sent to Datastore API | | 0% | 0.02 of 72.00 GBytes | Okay |
| Billing Settings | Data Received from Datastore API | | 0% | 0.10 of 696.00 GBytes | Okay |
| Billing History | Datastore CPU Time | | 0% | 2.81 of 1,243.85 CPU hours | Okay |
| | Number of Indexes | | 12% | 24 of 200 | Okay |

Figure 7: Quota details for an app

The **Billing History** page in the Admin Console will show a summary of your billable usage over time, even for free accounts.

It can be useful to track how these resources are being consumed by individual requests, and to see which requests are the most expensive. The Admin Console **Dashboard**, as seen in Figure 3, shows a summary of recent activity and resource usage per app version, and indicates where your free quotas lie.

For more detail, the Admin Console logs provide information about the resource usage of a specific request, as was described in *Browsing an app version's logs*. In addition, if you are signed in as an app developer when you request a URL from an app, the HTTP headers will include information about the resources that were used for that request.

It is also possible to monitor your quota usage from your application code via the `com.google.appengine.api.quota` package and the `QuotaService` interface. See `http://code.google.com/appengine/docs/java/javadoc/com/google/appengine/api/quota/package-summary.html` for more information.

Finally, the `Appstats` package can provide more information about your app's resource consumption (see *Using Appstats*).

## Application behavior when a quota is depleted

When an app consumes its quota of a given resource, the resource is unavailable until the quota is reset. For resources that must be available in order to initiate a request, such as CPU time or incoming/outgoing bandwidth, App Engine will return an HTTP 403 Forbidden status code for the request after the resource is exhausted. For all other resources, your application will get a `com.google.apphosting.api.ApiProxy.OverQuotaException`. If a resource is consumed to its limits, it will be indicated as **Limited** in the **Quota Details** panel of the Admin Console.

## Adding developers for an application

Once you have created an App Engine application, you can add additional developers or admins for that app via the **Permissions** link in the sidebar. It is best to invite a new admin using the same e-mail account with which they will administer the app. Be aware that all developers for an app have the same rights and access permissions. For example, all developers can initiate a suspension or deletion of an app and as we saw earlier, can take over billing responsibilities.

# Command-line administration

Some App Engine-related administrative activities are not supported by Eclipse. In this section, we describe how to perform some useful tasks from the command line.

## Using appcfg.sh

In general, it is most convenient to deploy your Java App Engine application using Eclipse. However, it is possible to deploy it from the command line as well, using a script included with the App Engine SDK called `appcfg.sh` (or `appcfg.cmd` on Windows). This script is a wrapper around the Java class `com.google.appengine.tools.admin.AppCfg` in `appengine-java-sdk/lib/appengine-tools-api.jar`.

The `appcfg.sh` script can also be used to update specific app files without re-deploying the entire application, and this can be very useful when you need to make a quick change to a file or do not want to re-deploy the full project in its current state. Specifically, `appcfg.sh` supports individual updates of:

- Datastore index definitions (as were described in *Chapter 5*)
- The Task Queue configuration file, `queue.xml` (we will discuss Task Queue configuration in *Chapter 12*)
- The Cron configuration file, `cron.xml` (we will use Cron jobs in *Chapter 12*)
- The Denial of Service (DoS) protection configuration file, `dos.xml` (which was described in the *Configuration* section of this chapter)

You can also use `appcfg.sh` to download application log files and check your Cron settings.

# Locating appcfg.sh

The first step in using `appcfg.sh` is locating it in your App Engine SDK installation. Assuming you installed the SDK via Eclipse, it will be in: `<eclipse_install_dir>/plugins/<appengine-java-sdk>/bin`, where `<eclipse_install_dir>` is the directory where you installed Eclipse, and `<appengine-java-sdk>` is dependent upon the version and will look something like: `com.google.appengine.eclipse.sdkbundle.1.3.x_1.3.x.v201008311405` `/appengine-java-sdk-1.3.x`.

On Windows, the script will be named `appcfg.cmd`. On Mac OSX or Linux, it will be called `appcfg.sh`. For convenience, you may want to give this script executable permissions. For brevity, we will refer to the script throughout the rest of this section as `appcfg.sh`.

# Using appcfg.sh

`appcfg.sh` is used as follows:

```
appcfg.sh [options] <action> <war-directory>
```

where `<war-directory>` is the path to your app's `war` directory. You will need to provide an app admin e-mail address and password at the command line and ensure that your app ID and version number are configured for that app. If you have already deployed that project's app via Eclipse, it will have ensured that this configuration is correct.

You can use the update action to deploy a full application (though again, you will probably find it easier to do this via Eclipse). See the GWT and App Engine documentation for more details on doing this. You will need to ensure that your GWT files are compiled beforehand.

However, Eclipse does not let you upload individual configuration files. This is where appcfg.sh is particularly handy.

To upload an individual configuration file, use the appropriate update action as follows.

To update the dos.xml file, use:

```
appcfg.sh [options] update_dos <war-directory>
```

To update the cron.xml file, use:

```
appcfg.sh [options] update_cron <war-directory>
```

To update the queue.xml file, use:

```
appcfg.sh [options] update_queues <war-directory>
```

To update the Datastore index files, use:

```
appcfg.sh [options] update_indexes <war-directory>
```

To list your Cron configuration, use:

```
appcfg.sh [options] cron_info <war-directory>
```

# Downloading application logs

AppCfg also gives you the ability to download your app logs so you can examine and store them locally. Do so via:

```
appcfg.sh [options] request_logs <war-directory> <output-file>
```

where <output-file> is the name of the file to write the logs to. If you use - (a hyphen) as the filename, the log information is written to STDOUT instead.

You can use the following options specific to the request_logs action, as described in the App Engine documentation:

```
--num_days=...
```

The number of days of log data to retrieve, ending on the current date at midnight UTC. A value of 0 retrieves all available logs. If `--append` is given, then the default is 0, otherwise the default is 1.

> `--severity=...`

This flag indicates the minimum log level for the log messages to retrieve. The value is a number corresponding to the log level: 4 for CRITICAL, 3 for ERROR, 2 for WARNING, 1 for INFO, and 0 for DEBUG. All messages at the given log level and above will be retrieved. The default is 1 (INFO).

> `--append`

This flag tells AppCfg to append logs to the log output file instead of overwriting the file. This simply appends the requested data but does not guarantee that the file won't contain duplicate error messages. If this argument is not specified, AppCfg will overwrite the log output file.

 See the App Engine documentation, `http://code.google.com/appengine/docs/java/tools/uploadinganapp.html`, for further details.

# Bulk download and upload of an app's Datastore

With a little extra setup, you can do command-line bulk downloads and uploads/restores of the contents of an app's Datastore. This can be useful for making backups, restoring a previous data "snapshot", and generating data for a new App Engine app. Just remember that all versions of an app share the same Datastore content.

This functionality currently requires use of the App Engine Python SDK's bulk loader script, although you can do the necessary app configuration in the context of your Java project.

First, if you have not already done so, install the Python App Engine SDK, as was described in *Chapter 5* (you may recall that the Python SDK is also required to perform index "vacuuming". As described in that chapter, running the Launcher software (for Mac OS X and Windows) should result in some App Engine Python scripts—or symbolic links to them—added to your environment's $PATH. Here, we will be using the `bulkloader.py` script. If it is not in your $PATH, then you can just locate it directly in the Python App Engine SDK installation and use its full path.

Then, add the following code to your `war/WEB-INF/web.xml` file. It defines access to the `RemoteApiServlet` and a `remote_api` endpoint.

```xml
<servlet>
  <servlet-name>remoteapi</servlet-name>
  <servlet-class>
      com.google.apphosting.utils.remoteapi.RemoteApiServlet
  </servlet-class>
</servlet>
<servlet-mapping>
  <servlet-name>remoteapi</servlet-name>
  <url-pattern>/remote_api</url-pattern>
</servlet-mapping>

<security-constraint>
  <web-resource-collection>
      <web-resource-name>remoteapi</web-resource-name>
      <url-pattern>/remote_api</url-pattern>
  </web-resource-collection>
  <auth-constraint>
      <role-name>admin</role-name>
  </auth-constraint>
</security-constraint>
```

After the app has been re-deployed with these new definitions, you can use the Python bulk uploader from the command line as in the following sections.

# Downloading data

To download a dump of the Datastore contents, call this script on the command line:

```
bulkloader.py --dump --app_id=<app-id>
  --url=<your-app-url>/remote_api
  --filename=dump.csv
```

(all on one line) where `<app-id>` is replaced with your app ID, and `<your-app-url>` is replaced with the URL for the app version of the project in which you defined the `remote_api` endpoint. For example, if your project *version* was named `upload`, the `url` argument would be: `http://upload.latest.<app-id>.appspot.com/remote_api`.

As specified by the `web.xml` file, you will need to authenticate your access to the `remote_api` URL with an admin e-mail and password. If you are accessing an app configured to authenticate only to a Google Apps custom domain (as described in the *Using your own domain for an app* section), you will need to use an admin e-mail from that domain to authenticate, and you must add this option to the `bulkloader.py` call:

```
--auth_domain=<domain>
```

where `<domain>` is your Google Apps custom domain.

If you want to download just the data for a specific *kind*, add the following option:

```
--kind=<kind>
```

where `<kind>` is one of your entity kinds. For example, with *Connectr*, you could use:

```
--kind=Friend
```

to download a dump of all `Friend` entities.

# Uploading or restoring data

To upload a previously downloaded data file to the app's Datastore, use the following command, with the `--restore` instead of the `--dump` option:

```
bulkloader.py --restore --app_id=<app-id>
  --url=http://<appname>.appspot.com/remote_api
  --filename=dump.csv
```

(again, all on one line) where the `--kind` specification is optional. As in the previous code, you must also use the `--auth_domain` option as necessary.

When data is downloaded, the entities are stored along with their original keys. When the data is restored, these same keys are used. If an entity exists in the Datastore with the same key as an entity being restored, the entity in the Datastore is *replaced*.

You can use the `--restore` option to upload to the same app from which the Datastore dump was created, or you can use it to upload data to a different application.

As an alternative to using the `bulkloader.py` script, you can also call the `appcfg.py` script (introduced in *Chapter 5*) with the `upload_data` or `download_data` actions; this does the same thing.

While beyond the scope of this book, use of the `BulkLoader` with `.yml` load configuration files allows further control in uploading and downloading data so that you are not restricted to dealing only with files generated with the `-dump` and `-restore` options. You can define connectors and transformers that specify how to map existing data to Datastore entities.

See `http://code.google.com/appengine/docs/python/tools/uploadingdata.html` and `http://goo.gl/Z0PU` for more information.

# Using Appstats

**Appstats** is a group of tools for collecting information about your app's performance and browsing that information via a web interface. It is included as part of the App Engine SDK.

Appstats is not automatically enabled. You must set it up by adding configuration information to your `war/WEB-INF/web.xml` file. Because its information collection incurs an overhead, you will probably not want to enable it on a deployed production site.

# Enabling and configuring Appstats

Appstats is a Servlet *filter*, as described earlier in this chapter. You must define it as such, and then define a `<filter-mapping>` to indicate the requests you want Appstats to monitor. The Appstats filter records statistics for API calls made during the request, and stores its statistics in Memcache (using its own *namespace*).

To define the Appstats filter and then monitor all requests, add the following code to your `web.xml` file.

```
<filter>
  <filter-name>appstats</filter-name>
  <filter-class>
    com.google.appengine.tools.appstats.AppstatsFilter
  </filter-class>
  <init-param>
    <param-name>logMessage</param-name>
    <param-value>Appstats available: /appstats/details?time={ID}
    </param-value>
```

```
      </init-param>
  </filter>
  <filter-mapping>
    <filter-name>appstats</filter-name>
    <url-pattern>/*</url-pattern>
  </filter-mapping>
```

Once the filter has been set up, the next step is to define a Servlet that gives you access to the Appstats web interface, and requires admin access to do so (as you don't want just anyone looking at your application stats). To set this up, add the next code snippet to your web.xml file as well.

```
  <servlet>
    <servlet-name>appstats</servlet-name>
    <servlet-class>
        com.google.appengine.tools.appstats.AppstatsServlet
    </servlet-class>
  </servlet>
  <servlet-mapping>
    <servlet-name>appstats</servlet-name>
    <url-pattern>/appstats/*</url-pattern>
  </servlet-mapping>

  <security-constraint>
    <web-resource-collection>
        <url-pattern>/appstats/*</url-pattern>
    </web-resource-collection>
    <auth-constraint>
      <role-name>admin</role-name>
    </auth-constraint>
  </security-constraint>
```

# Browsing the Appstats statistics page

Once you've enabled Appstats in web.xml, then visit the Appstats interface in your development environment via: http://127.0.0.1:8888/appstats/ (if your app is running locally under http://127.0.0.1:8888/). If you added a security constraint to web.xml as in the example above, you will need to authenticate as an admin to view the Appstats pages. Recall that in your development environment, this simply requires checking the "admin" box on the authentication page—any e-mail address is fine. In a deployed app version, the Appstats URL will similarly be http://<your-app-version-url>/appstats/, and you will need to properly authenticate as an admin.

Remember that you probably do not want to leave Appstats enabled for a production version of an app, as it will slow down your page loads.

| RPC Stats | | Path Stats | | | |
|---|---|---|---|---|---|
| RPC | Count | Path | #RPCs | #Requests | Most Recent requests |
| ⊞ memcache.Get | 253 | ⊞ POST /connectr/messagesService | 375 | 6 | (2) (3) (14) (15) (18) (21) |
| ⊞ memcache.Set | 116 | ⊞ POST /updatefeedurls | 72 | 2 | (4) (16) |
| ⊞ datastore_v3.RunQuery | 79 | ⊞ POST /connectr/friendsService | 30 | 2 | (5) (17) |
| ⊞ datastore_v3.Put | 49 | ⊞ POST /feedupdatefr | 24 | 1 | (19) |
| ⊞ taskqueue.BulkAdd | 9 | ⊞ POST /feedupdateuser | 11 | 1 | (20) |
| ⊞ datastore_v3.Get | 8 | ⊞ /_ah/admin/datastore | 8 | 4 | (7) (9) (11) (13) |
| ⊞ datastore_v3.Count | 4 | ⊞ /logingooglecallback | 5 | 1 | (23) |
| ⊞ datastore_v3.BeginTransaction | 2 | ⊞ /logingoogle | 1 | 1 | (25) |
| ⊞ datastore_v3.Commit | 2 | ⊞ POST /connectr/loginService | 1 | 2 | (22) (26) |
| ⊞ memcache.Delete | 2 | ⊞ /_ah/login | 0 | 1 | (24) |
| ⊞ urlfetch.Fetch | 2 | ⊞ /_ah/resources | 0 | 4 | (6) (8) (10) (12) |
| ⊞ user.CreateLoginURL | 1 | ⊞ /appstats | 0 | 1 | (1) |

**Requests History** ⊞ Expand All

Request

⊞ (1) 2010-09-13 18:13:21.516 "GET /appstats" 307 real=82ms cpu=0ms api=0ms overhead=0ms (0 RPCs)
⊞ (2) 2010-09-13 18:12:51.106 "POST /connectr/messagesService" 200 real=131ms cpu=0ms api=0ms overhead=0ms (49 RPCs)
⊞ (3) 2010-09-13 18:12:50.359 "POST /connectr/messagesService" 200 real=194ms cpu=0ms api=0ms overhead=0ms (49 RPCs)
⊞ (4) 2010-09-13 18:12:49.543 "POST /updatefeedurls" 200 real=541ms cpu=0ms api=0ms overhead=0ms (71 RPCs)
⊞ (5) 2010-09-13 18:12:39.532 "POST /connectr/friendsService" 200 real=41ms cpu=0ms api=0ms overhead=0ms (15 RPCs)
⊞ (6) 2010-09-13 18:12:29.005 "GET /_ah/resources?resource=google" 200 real=9ms cpu=0ms api=0ms overhead=0ms (0 RPCs)
⊞ (7) 2010-09-13 18:12:28.964 "GET /_ah/admin/datastore?kind=FriendDetails" 200 real=40ms cpu=0ms api=0ms overhead=0ms (2 RPCs)
⊞ (8) 2010-09-13 18:12:25.348 "GET /_ah/resources?resource=google" 200 real=9ms cpu=0ms api=0ms overhead=0ms (0 RPCs)
⊞ (9) 2010-09-13 18:12:25.285 "GET /_ah/admin/datastore?kind=FeedIndex" 200 real=6ms cpu=0ms api=0ms overhead=0ms (2 RPCs)
⊞ (10) 2010-09-13 18:12:21.036 "GET /_ah/resources?resource=google" 200 real=11ms cpu=0ms api=0ms overhead=0ms (0 RPCs)
⊞ (11) 2010-09-13 18:12:20.956 "GET /_ah/admin/datastore?kind=FeedIndex" 200 real=25ms cpu=0ms api=0ms overhead=0ms (2 RPCs)

Figure 8: The GAE/Java Appstats interface

As shown in Figure 8, the Appstats interface lets you browse statistics on your page requests, the API calls they make, and the resources used.

# Using your own domain for an app

You can use your own domain name for an App Engine app. This is done by setting up a **Google Apps** account for that domain. Then, you must set up the App Engine app as a service with the Google Apps account, which then enables you to associate a subdomain of your domain with the App Engine app.

You can set up a Google Apps account for your domain ahead of time, for example, by starting here: `http://www.google.com/apps/intl/en/group/index.html` (you can start with a domain name that you already own, or buy it in the process). Alternatively, you can do the Google Apps setup after you've created your App Engine app.

When you create a new App Engine app, you have two options with respect to user authentication via App Engine's Google Accounts. You are not required to use the Google Accounts API for authentication—you can build your own authentication framework if you like, for example, by using **OAuth**, as in *Chapter 8*. However, if you plan to use Google Accounts, then when you create your application, you must decide which authentication variant you want, as shown in Figure 9. Click on the **Edit** link in the **Create An Application** page to choose an option. You can open authentication to all Google Accounts users (the default), or restrict authentication only to users of a given Google Apps domain. An experimental OpenID option also exists. You cannot change this configuration once the app is created.

Figure 9: You must select an authentication option when you create an app, and it cannot be changed later.

So, if you are building an app that you want to open only to users of a given Google Apps domain, choose the second option in Figure 9. If you do so, only users with accounts under that Google Apps domain will be able to authenticate with your app via the App Engine authentication API. This authentication model could be useful if, for example, you are building an application for use within a small company.

If you select the latter option, and restrict authentication to only users of a given Google Apps domain, then you must set up the new App Engine app as a *service* of your Google Apps for that domain in order for the authentication to work. You can do this via the Google Apps **Dashboard** page, once you are logged in to Google Apps. The dashboard can be accessed via `https://www.google.com/a/cpanel/<your_domain>/Dashboard`, where `<your_domain>` is replaced with the domain associated with your Google Apps account. Click on the **Add More Services** link, then find **App Engine** under **Other Services**, as in Figure 10, and enter your App Engine app ID.

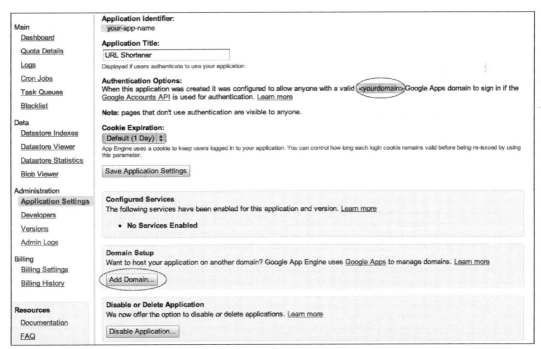

Figure 10: Add your App Engine app as a Google Apps service

Alternatively, you can initiate this setup via the App Engine Admin Console, by clicking on **Add Domain...** in the **Application Settings** panel in the Administration section, as shown in Figure 11. If the app was set up to require authentication with a Google Apps domain (indicated by **<yourdomain>** in Figure 11), add that domain.

Figure 11: You can add a custom domain from the App Engine Application Settings.

Enter your Google Apps domain when prompted. You can associate only the default version of an App Engine app with Google Apps—that is, the app's `appspot` URL without any version subdomain modifiers.

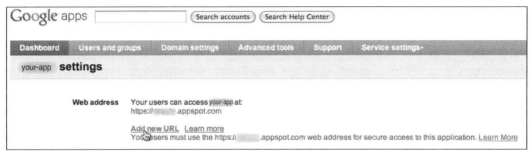

Figure 12: In the Google Apps settings, add a URL to set up a custom domain for an App Engine app. (Instead of `your-app`, your actual app name is displayed).

Once your App Engine app is entered as a *service* with your Google Apps account, you can select that service, then click on the **Add new URL** link, as in Figure 12, to specify a subdomain of your own domain, which points to the App Engine app. The URL that you define must include a subdomain (it cannot be a so-called "naked" top-level domain). However, you can use www as the subdomain, and define requests to the "naked" URL to redirect to www if you like. The subdomain does not have to be the same as the App Engine app ID.

You will need to correctly set up the CNAME record for a subdomain at your registrar before Google Apps will accept the new URL, as per the instructions that Google Apps will display.

You can map multiple subdomains to the same App Engine app if you like—just go through the **Add New URL** process for each such subdomain. You will need to set up a CNAME record for each subdomain as well.

You can add your App Engine app as a Google Apps service, then map it to a subdomain of your domain, regardless of which type of authentication the app is set up to use—that is, if an app is configured to authenticate for all Google Accounts (the default), it too can be set up to use a custom domain. But, if the app is set up to authenticate *only* for the users of a Google Apps domain, then as of this writing you *must* add it as a Google Apps service for the authentication to work.

App Engine currently supports HTTPS requests only for an app's `appspot.com` URL. You can use the `appspot` URL and your custom domain URL at the same time, so if you need to use HTTPS for certain requests, you can redirect to the `appspot` URL.

The `appspot.com` URL has another capability not supported by the custom domain URL—it will accept an additional domain part, for example:

`<anything>.app-id.appspot.com`

where `<anything>` is any valid single domain name part. All such requests will be routed to the app with the given app ID. This can be useful, for example, in setting up an application where each user gets his/her "own" URL. Google Apps domains do not currently support this feature.

# Summary

This chapter looked at various aspects of App Engine application configuration, management, and monitoring. We first looked in more detail at application configuration, deployment and version management, and logging. Then, we discussed using the App Engine's extensive Admin Console for various monitoring and app management tasks, and setting up billing and quotas in order to give your app more resources.

Next, we described some useful command-line app management programs (one currently Python-based), which amongst other capabilities, allow you to download your application's logs and to download and restore Datastore contents.

We also took a look at setting up and using Appstats—a statistics-gathering package and web interface included with App Engine. Finally, we discussed the process required to set up an app using a custom domain name, via Google Apps, and the constraints on using such domains.

In the next chapter, we'll return to the *Connectr* application, and look at the server-side framework and services that generate and provide the activity stream of *Connectr*.

# 12

# Asynchronous Processing with Cron, Task Queue, and XMPP

## Introduction

*Chapter 10, Pushing Fresh Content to Clients with the Channel API,* described the client-side support for the 'activity stream' that a *Connectr* user sees in the main panel of the app's display. In this chapter, we describe the server-side framework used to generate that activity stream data.

We introduce the use of App Engine Cron Jobs and application-defined (non-default) Task Queues. In addition, we introduce the App Engine **XMPP** service and use it to let *Connectr* receive push content—in the form of 'breaking news items'—which are also incorporated into the activity display.

We also incorporate and refine a number of concepts introduced in earlier chapters. In particular, support for the activity stream requires performing background tasks asynchronously from the client side requests; the use of Task Queues to asynchronously pre-fetch content and perform bookkeeping tasks; the use of caching using the Memcache service; the use of query cursors to split tasks into manageable chunks; and leverage of a number of techniques for performing efficient Datastore queries.

The code in this chapter builds upon on the `FeedInfo` and `FeedIndex` persistent classes described in *Chapter 7* and *Chapter 9* and adds further layers of functionality in order to serve up the activity StreamItems to the client side.

This chapter uses the `ConnectrFinal` version of the *Connectr* app.

 As mentioned previously, our use of the term "activity stream" is not to be confused with its more technical reference to an extension of the Atom feed format (`http://activitystrea.ms/`)—though the use of Activity Stream-formatted feeds would be consistent with the semantics of *Connectr's* functionality.

# What the client sees

In *Connectr*, when the user adds or edits a `Friend`, they can add one or more URLs for RSS or Atom feeds that they associate with that `Friend`. Then, as shown in Figure 1, in a **Latest Activity** panel in the main view, a stream of items from these feeds is displayed for selected friends, with the panel contents updating as new items are available.

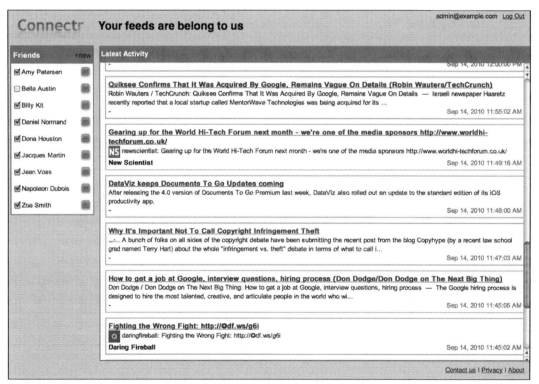

Figure 1: *Connectr's* main view, showing a list of friends for a user and a stream of items for selected friends.

# What goes on behind the scenes

In *Connectr*, a primary job of the server is to provide requested activity stream data quickly to the client. To help accomplish this, we will design the server-side code so that we can run tasks asynchronously from each other, reduce required client synchronization, and support safe task repetition. Such a framework is robust and responsive and its actions largely parallelizable, which supports efficient processing on a platform like App Engine where many tasks can be run at the same time.

This design has two primary components.

**Connectr decouples the backend activities related to fetching or updating feed content from the client-side requests so that no synchronization is required for these activities.**

We always want to design our apps so that the client does not have to wait long for a response to his/her requests to the server.

We can help to accomplish this by moving as much server-side work as possible to background jobs that run asynchronously—decoupled from any specific client request. But then, to reap the benefits of doing this, we need to ensure that when the client does make a request, the server does not need to wait for some background activity to finish before returning a response.

With our requirements for *Connectr*, this is straightforward for activity stream management. We do not require a stream of items to be completely up-to-date when we display it as we will refresh it with new content within a short period of time. This tactic makes sense from a UI perspective as well since it gives the client something to look at initially. Similarly, we do not require instant updates to our app when a feed changes online.

So, we need to ensure that client queries can tap into the activity stream at any time without issue, and that we are running the right background jobs to usefully generate the stream data.

Feed content updates, as described in *Chapter 7* and *Chapter 9*, already support an asynchronous update model. These updates are essentially *idempotent*. It does not matter if multiple content updates are triggered at the same time, and transactional control is not required when updating feed content, which allows high throughput. Feeds have a short latency period within which they are not refreshed after a recent update, and if two tasks should happen to be updating the same feed (if, say they were started at essentially the same time), this does no harm.

From the feed content, we will build new objects of the class StreamItem (so-called to suggest Friends' activity streams), holding feed item information. StreamItem objects will encode the feed item information used for display and will also serve to archive more of the feed histories than provided by the transient feed object content. The StreamItem objects are constructed and added to Memcache when the feeds are updated. As with the feed objects themselves, transactional control will not be required in creating StreamItem objects, and they can be overwritten or updated without harm; thus they too support effective idempotency.

The StreamItem objects can potentially come from multiple source categories, not just feed updates. We will use App Engine's XMPP service to demonstrate this. XMPP push notifications will result in 'news' StreamItem objects injected into the stream along with the feed items.

The client-facing methods can then tap into this sequence of StreamItem objects (or more often, their corresponding cached versions) regardless of whether or not updates on the feeds are currently occurring, since Datastore object saves and Memcache writes are performed atomically. That is, the client requests can remain fully independent and decoupled from whatever backend updates might currently be in progress.

We must update the feeds regularly, guided in part by client activity (what users are logged in, what feeds are actively in use) so that they are current. Note that while we want to stay current, we must also guard against doing a lot of refresh work, which will not be required by the clients, both with respect to the degree of freshness (how often updated) and what gets refreshed when. Guided by some heuristics, we will use tasks, application-defined (non-default) Task Queues, and Cron Jobs to accomplish this.

**Connectr's client-facing methods guide the generation of fresh information and use efficient queries and caching to obtain 'activity stream' content quickly.**

The client-facing methods that deliver the activity stream content are implemented in the server.MessagesServiceImpl class, which extends RemoteServiceServlet.

These methods support content delivery via a combination of Datastore queries to identify StreamItem objects relevant to a given client request, and use of the cache to support fast delivery.

To support this, we will design the StreamItem objects so that they support the types of queries we need to perform, and let us use keys-only queries (in which only keys, not the full objects, are returned) in conjunction with caching.

In addition, the MessagesServiceImpl class will support communication of information from the client to the server about what background feed updates to initiate. For example, when a user logs in, this will trigger the initiation of updates for the feeds associated with that user's Friend objects.

## Overview of the chapter

The organization of this chapter is as follows. In *Activity stream classes*, we'll briefly describe the new server-side data class, StreamItem, and its DTOs (Data Transfer Objects).

Then, *Server-Side asynchronous processing* will discuss the asynchronous activities that support StreamItem generation. In the process, we will introduce the use of **Cron Jobs** and non-default **Task Queue** configuration and use.

*Supporting synchronous content delivery: Datastore queries and caching* will describe how the products of these server-side tasks are consumed and managed by the server. MessagesServiceImpl RPC methods, which deliver content to the client. The implementation of the client-facing methods brings up some interesting Datastore-related issues.

Finally, *XMPP: Information push to the app* will introduce the App Engine's **XMPP** service and its API, and show how we can use this service to incorporate the push of 'breaking news' items into *Connectr's* feed streams.

# Activity stream classes

In this section, we'll lay the groundwork for the rest of the chapter by first briefly describing the new persistent class, server.domain.StreamItem, and its DTOs. Instances of these classes will be used to generate the contents of *Connectr's* activity stream panel.

## The StreamItem persistent class

We add a new server.domain.StreamItem class to *Connectr's* set of persistent classes. The server.domain.FeedInfo objects, described in previous chapters, hold in serialized form the content fetched and parsed by the ROME libraries. The new StreamItem instances store information about the individual feed items, and their keys are the feed item URLs.

The `StreamItem` objects serve several purposes: we can consume the `StreamItem` without worrying about whether or not a feed update is in progress; we are pulling the feed items out of the serialized field so that we can query on them directly; and by extracting only the data we need and adding some additional query-related fields, Datastore access is efficient. In addition, a feed object stores only the most recent feed items (usually about 20), so `StreamItem` persistence allows us to maintain an archive of older feed contents.

The following code lists the `StreamItem@Persistent` instance variables and constructor. The instance variables show what information we are extracting from the feed data. The ROME parse results include other information that we are not extracting.

In the code, you will notice that not all the StreamItem persistent fields are indexed, as indicated by exclusion annotations:

```
@Extension(vendorName = "datanucleus", key = "gae.unindexed",
    value="true")
```

This is because *Connectr* does not need to query over all the `StreamItem` fields. The fewer the indexes that need to be updated when an object is stored in the Datastore, the faster its storage time will be. Reducing storage time can be particularly helpful in cases where many objects are created rapidly, as will be the case for the `StreamItem` objects.

```
@SuppressWarnings("serial")
@PersistenceCapable(identityType = IdentityType.APPLICATION,
detachable="true")
public class StreamItem implements Serializable, Cacheable {

  private static final int CACHE_EXPIR = 500 * 60;
  private static final int SUMMARY_LENGTH = 100;

  @PrimaryKey
  @Persistent(valueStrategy = IdGeneratorStrategy.IDENTITY)
  @Extension(vendorName="datanucleus", key="gae.encoded-pk",
   value="true")
  private String id;

  @Persistent
  @Extension(vendorName="datanucleus", key="gae.pk-name",
   value="true")
  private String url;
```

```
@Persistent
private String title;
@Persistent
@Extension(vendorName = "datanucleus",
 key = "gae.unindexed", value="true")
private Text description;

@Persistent
@Extension(vendorName = "datanucleus",
 key = "gae.unindexed", value="true")
private String descrSummary;

@Persistent
@Extension(vendorName = "datanucleus",
 key = "gae.unindexed", value="true")
private String feedDescription;

@Persistent
private String feedUrl;

@Persistent
@Extension(vendorName = "datanucleus",
 key = "gae.unindexed", value="true")
private String imageUrl;

@Persistent
@Extension(vendorName = "datanucleus",
 key = "gae.unindexed", value="true")
private String feedTitle;
@Persistent
@Extension(vendorName = "datanucleus",
 key = "gae.unindexed", value="true")
private String author;

@Persistent
private Date date;

@Persistent
Set<Long> ukeys;

public StreamItem(String title, String description,
 String feedDescription, Date date,
 String feedTitle, String author, String url,
 String feedUrl, String imageUrl, Set<Long> ukeys) {
```

```
        this.title = title;
        this.description = new Text(description);
        this.feedDescription = feedDescription;
        this.date = date;
        this.author = author;
        this.feedTitle = feedTitle;
        this.url = url;
        this.feedUrl = feedUrl;
         this.imageUrl = imageUrl;
        this.descrSummary = null;
        this.ukeys = ukeys;


    }
```

In the previous code, note that the `description` field is of type `com.google.appengine.api.datastore.Text`. This is important— recall that `String` fields stored in the Datastore must be less than 500 characters long. Our description fields may often be longer than this. The `StreamItem` constructor performs the conversion to `Text` from `String`:

```
        this.description = new Text(description);
```

One implication of using a `Text` field is that it rules out the possibility of directly sending detached `StreamItem` objects to the client—the `Text` type will be incompatible. Instead, we will use DTOs in which the `Text` is converted back to a `String`.

When a feed is updated, we will now generate its corresponding series of `server.domain.StreamItem` methods at the same time. The static `StreamItem` methods `buildItems()` and `builditem()` map the `SyndFeed` structures generated by the ROME parser to `StreamItem`. The `StreamItem.builditems()` method is called from the `FeedInfo.updateFeed()` method whenever a feed is updated.

> Recall that, if the app saves a Datastore object with an app-assigned key, and there is already an object of that *kind* in the Datastore with that key, the object will be overwritten. This is applicable to our `StreamItems`, whose keys are the item URLs, since feed items may sometimes have updated content.

The `StreamItem` constructor populates the new `StreamItem` with the extracted feed item data. It stores one additional piece of information, in the `ukeys` multi-valued property. This is a list of `UserAccount` IDs, for all those users for which one or more of their `Friends` has this feed listed. As will be described in *Making StreamItem queries fast*, this information will be used to perform efficient `StreamItem` queries in the context of a given user's account.

Note that the `StreamItem` class implements `Cacheable`. Additionally, the `StreamItem` class is added to the class list in `PMF.java`, as described in *Chapter 9*. This adds `StreamItem` to the list of classes for which `LifecycleListener`-enabled `PersistenceManagers` are constructed. As a result, whenever a `StreamItem` is saved to the Datastore (either created or updated), its `addToCache()` method is called as shown in the following code, adding the object to Memcache:

```
public void addToCache() {
    CacheSupport.cachePutExp(this.getClass().getName(),
        id, this, CACHE_EXPIR);
    addSummaryToCache();
}
```

In addition to caching the `StreamItem` itself, `addToCache()` calls an additional method: `addSummaryToCache()`. This method creates a DTO that summarizes the information stored in the `StreamItem` and then caches the summary item as well. This 'loads up' Memcache in preparation for client requests. It is these summary DTOs that will be sent initially to the client when the activity stream panel is built.

As we will discuss in more detail below, feed updates, and accompanying `StreamItem` construction, are done as background tasks. Thus we are doing more work asynchronously at 'write time' (loosely speaking) so that the synchronous client-facing access can be more efficient.

# HTML 'sanitization'

In the process of creating the `StreamItem` objects from the feed data, we are 'sanitizing' the information that will be displayed as HTML: the `title` and `description`, and additionally, a truncated version of the description (the `descrSummary` field) that will be used in the summary DTOs described later. We do this to ensure that no malicious HTML or script code will be included in the activity stream data that our app displays.

To accomplish this, we use the JSOUP open-source library (`http://jsoup.org/`), which is a Java library for working with HTML. It includes the ability to *clean* HTML against a specified *whitelist* (and includes a number of pre-specified whitelists). Using JSOUP's pre-defined whitelists, we will remove all HTML from the `descrSummary`, remove all but b, em, i, strong, and u tags from the `title` field, and allow only 'basic' HTML (with images) in the `description`.

For example, the title is cleaned using the following code:

```
import org.jsoup.Jsoup;
import org.jsoup.safety.Whitelist;
...
title = Jsoup.clean(entry.getTitle(),
  Whitelist.simpleText());
```

# The StreamItem DTOs

Two classes of DTOs (Data Transfer Objects) are built from the `StreamItem` data. The structure and use of these DTOs follows the same pattern that was used with the `Friend`-based DTOs. The DTOs are defined in the `shared` subpackage since they need to be available to both the client-side and server-side code.

The `StreamItemSummaryDTO` class holds the feed item `title`, `url`, `date`, `author`, and the short (and sanitized) `descrSummary`, and is set with the same `id` as its `StreamItem`. The DTO is used—unsurprisingly—to send summary data upon the initial request from the client. That is, the `StreamItemSummaryDTO` classes are used to build the scrolling 'activity stream' list in *Connectr's* main panel.

If the client requests more detail about a particular item, its `StreamItemDTO` is sent. The `StreamItemDTO` encodes all the `StreamItem` fields except for the description summary.

Both DTOs use as their ID the associated `StreamItem` ID (the URL of the corresponding feed item). The DTOs are always cached to Memcache when created, and as with the `Friend` DTOs, consistent use of the same ID as their originating persistent object makes it straightforward to determine if a DTO is in the cache.

The `StreamItem` class is in charge of generating its associated DTOs. To use the `description` field in a DTO, it must convert the `Text` field to a `String` by calling the `Text` object's `getValue()` method.

The feed objects—the `StreamItems`, and their DTOs—provide the building blocks for the framework of asynchronous tasks described in the next section.

# Server-Side asynchronous processing

In this section, we drill down into *Connectr's* use of feed-related server-side processing. First, we will discuss some configuration options and design considerations for the Task Queue, and describe how to set up Cron Jobs.

Then, we will discuss *Connectr's* use of both of these features to implement and support its feed-update-related background activities.

# Tasks and Task Queues

In the previous chapters, we introduced the App Engine Task Queue service (`com.google.appengine.api.labs.taskqueue.Queue`) and showed the basics of defining and enqueuing tasks. We have used the Task Queue both to formulate long-running server-side activities as a series of tasks (for example, the migrations of *Chapter 7*), as well as to spawn *transactional tasks* from RPC methods as in *Chapter 9*. We have already seen that the Task Queue allows us to **initiate work that is executed asynchronously in the background**—which is key for the *Connectr* app's successful operation. Here, we look at Tasks and the Task Queue in more detail.

 The Task Queue API can be found at the following URL: `http://code.google.com/appengine/docs/java/javadoc/com/google/appengine/api/labs/taskqueue/package-summary.html`. At the time of writing, the Task Queue is still considered 'experimental' (as indicated by the 'labs' in its package path), which means that its API could change in the future.

Roughly speaking, a task can be viewed as code to run, identified via a request URL, along with accompanying task parameters, or data.

In App Engine, as we have seen, **web hooks** (essentially, "HTTP callbacks") are used to trigger tasks. To run a task, a request is made to a defined URL using the parameters that you have specified for the task. You define the mapping between the URL and its handler in `web.xml`, as with any other handler. You can specify that the Task Queue requests be made via either POST or GET. POST is the default.

As with any other App Engine web request, tasks must finish in 30 seconds. If a task fails, App Engine will retry it until it succeeds, gradually ratcheting down the rate of retry. From the Admin Console, you can delete tasks from a queue.

You can enqueue Tasks on either the **default Task Queue**—always available without configuration—or a queue that you have specified, and the tasks are then run as soon as possible, subject to the queue's scheduling criteria and the system's available resources. The tasks will be run asynchronously and potentially in parallel. A Task Queue always runs with admin privileges. This means that you can (and probably should) impose admin constraints on your task URLs so that they cannot be invoked by a non-admin from the browser.

As described in *Chapter 9*, if you enqueue a task in the context of a transaction, it will be enqueued if and only if the transaction is committed successfully. Such tasks are termed **transactional tasks**.

Thus far, we have just used the default Task Queue. However, it is possible to specify additional Task Queues with non-default characteristics. In particular, it is possible to define additional Task Queues with different **throughput rates** and **bucket sizes**.

## Task Queue specification

Task queues are specified in the war/WEB-INF/queue.xml file. As shown in the following code, this file contains a <queue-entries> element, containing one or more <queue> elements. Each <queue> includes a <name> element, which will be used to refer to the queue from within your application code, a <rate>, and a <bucket-size>.

A queue's <rate> defines how often tasks are processed from the queue. For example, a queue might be set to have a rate of 100 tasks per minute. Rates are specified by giving a numeric value followed by a '/' and then a time unit. The unit s indicates seconds, m indicates minutes, h indicates hours, and d indicates days. For example, 100/m would indicate a rate of 100 tasks per minute on the given queue. If not specified, the default rate is 5/s. The <bucket-size> (so named because a 'token bucket' dequeueing algorithm is used) regulates how many tasks can be running at once. The maximum bucket size is 100. Reducing this number will reduce resource usage. If not specified, the default bucket size is 5.

```
<queue-entries>
  <queue>
    <name>frfeedupdates</name>
     <rate>3/s</rate>
    <bucket-size>4</bucket-size>
  </queue>
  <queue>
    <name>userfeedupdates</name>
    <rate>7/s</rate>
    <bucket-size>7</bucket-size>
  </queue>
</queue-entries>
```

The development server does not model the 'rate' and 'bucket-size' configurations (nor retain queues across a restart). All versions of an application share the same Task Queues.

The specification in the previous example shows two queues defined for *Connectr*. The first is called `frfeedupdates` (you can of course name your own queues whatever you like). This queue is used to process the regular feed updates run by the Cron Job, as described in *Asynchronous server-side tasks in Connectr* It has a rate of `3/s` — slower than the default— and a bucket size of `4` —smaller than the default. Thus, the `frfeedupdates` queue limits resource usage as compared to the default and does not process tasks as quickly. This makes sense for a task that will run regularly in the background, and is not required to generate results particularly quickly.

The second queue is called `userfeedupdates`. It is used to run the tasks, triggered by a user's login, that update the feeds associated with that user's Friends. We want this queue to run a bit faster than normal, with more parallelization, and so we set it with a higher bucket size and rate than the default.

The `queue.xml` file can include an entry named `default`—if this is the case, that definition redefines the default queue. Otherwise, as seen in previous chapters, it is not necessary to explicitly define the default queue or even to have a `queue.xml` file to use the default queue.

You can also specify a `<total-storage-limit>` element of `<queue-entries>`. This indicates the total allowed storage over all queues. The default is 100M.

## Task Queue quotas and limits

As with a regular request, task invocations are counted against request, CPU, and bandwidth quotas. App Engine also maintains quotas for Task Queue API calls, Task Queue stored task count, and Task Queue stored task bytes. The specifics depend upon whether or not billing has been enabled, and you can see the details by following the **Task Queues** and **Quota** links in your Admin Console sidebar. In addition, the limits in the table below, from the App Engine documentation, applied to Task Queues when this book was written.

| Limit | Amount |
| --- | --- |
| task object size | 10 kilobytes |
| number of active queues (not including the default queue) | 10 |
| queue execution rate | 50 task invocations per second per queue |
| maximum countdown/ETA for a task | 30 days from the current date and time |
| maximum number of tasks that can be added in a batch | 100 tasks |

These limits may be subject to change, particularly while the Task Queue has 'experimental' status.

# Monitoring tasks in the App Engine Admin Console

In the Admin Console for a deployed app, click on **Task Queues** in the sidebar to see quota information for your tasks as well as current information about the Task Queues. You can see how many tasks are currently in each queue, as in Figure 2.

| Queue Name | Maximum Rate | Bucket Size | Oldest Task | Tasks in Queue | Run in Last Minute |
|---|---|---|---|---|---|
| default | 5.00/s | 5.0 | | | 0 |
| frfeedupdates | 3.0/s | 4.0 | | | 0 |
| userfeedupdates | 7.0/s | 7.0 | 2010-07-17 11:00:42 (0:00:04 ago) | 8 | 1 |

Figure 2: The App Engine Admin Console shows your defined Task Queues.

If you click on the link for a given queue you can see the details for any tasks that are currently enqueued, as shown in Figure 3, and delete them if you like.

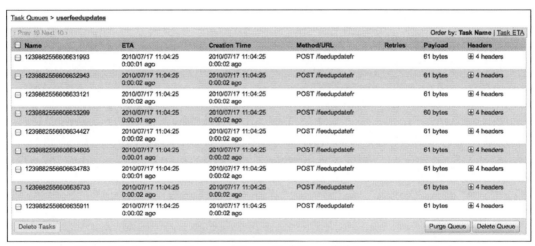

Figure 3: In the Admin Console, click on a Task Queue link to see its current tasks.

# Using application-defined Task Queues

To use a non-default Task Queue, pass its name to `QueueFactory.getQueue()`. The following example shows this construction, in code from `MessagesServiceImpl.initiateUserFeedUpdate()`.

```
import com.google.appengine.api.labs.taskqueue.QueueFactory;
import com.google.appengine.api.labs.taskqueue.Queue;
```

```
import static com.google.appengine.api.labs.taskqueue.TaskOptions.
Builder.*;
...
```

```
Queue queue = QueueFactory.getQueue("userfeedupdates");
queue.add(url("/feedupdateuser").param("uid",
 user.getUniqueId()));
```

Recall that, to obtain a handle to the default queue, you would instead call `QueueFactory.getDefaultQueue()`.

# Defining a task: TaskOptions

To define a task, pass a `com.google.appengine.api.labs.taskqueue.TaskOptions` object to the `add()` method of the `com.google.appengine.api.labs.taskqueue.Queue` instance. Calls to `TaskOptions` methods may be chained. So, as we have seen previously, the most straightforward way to define a task is to statically import `com.google.appengine.api.labs.taskqueue.TaskOptions.Builder.*` (which provides static creation methods). This allows you to use the following task definition idiom, where the chained calls instantiate a `TaskOptions` object:

```
queue.add(url("/yoururl").param("param1", val1).param("param2", val2).
param("param3", val3));
```

The `TaskOptions.Builder` methods include `param()`, `url()`, `method()`, `payload()`, and `taskName()`. Recall from *Chapter 9* that `server.FriendsServiceImpl` includes an example of how to construct a binary task payload. Be sure that the specified URL is mapped in `web.xml` as you would do with regular request handlers. Recall also that the Task Queue will run tasks as 'admin', so you can set the specified task URLs to require admin access.

These examples, and most examples in the *Connectr* code base, show examples of task parameter definition where the specific parameters used, such as `uid`, are 'hardwired' into the code. At times, you may need to specify the parameters dynamically. This arises, for instance, with the general-purpose `server.servlets.MigrationServlet` class introduced in *Chapter 7*. It passes any parameters returned from the migration invocation to the next task in the sequence. To accomplish this, we can use the `TaskOptions` object, and its `Builder` helper class, more explicitly.

```
import com.google.appengine.api.labs.taskqueue.Queue;
import com.google.appengine.api.labs.taskqueue.QueueFactory;
import com.google.appengine.api.labs.taskqueue.TaskOptions;
import static com.google.appengine.api.labs.taskqueue.TaskOptions.
Builder.*;
...
```

```
res = mg.migrate_up(cursor, range, params);
cursor = res.get("cursor");
...
Queue queue = QueueFactory.getDefaultQueue();
TaskOptions topt = TaskOptions.Builder.url("/migration");
for (String rkey : res.keySet()) {
  if (!rkey.equals("cursor")) {
    topt = topt.param(rkey, ""+ res.get(rkey));
  }
}
queue.add(topt.param("cursor", cursor)
.param("num",   ""+range)
.param("dir", direction).param("migration", migration));
```

The example above, from `server.servlets.MigrationServlet`, shows how this can be done. We explicitly create a new `TaskOptions` object `topt`, and for each migration key in the result hash `res` (except for the 'cursor', which is processed separately), we call the `TaskOptions param` method, updating `topt`. We can then add other parameters by passing `topt` to the `queue.add` method, and chaining further.

## Some Task Queue design considerations

In designing your application's tasks and Task Queues, it is useful to take a few things into consideration.

### Fanout and Task Names

Be sure to take advantage of parallelization by loading up a Task Queue with multiple tasks at once where possible. You can see this tactic used in *Connectr*, for example, with `server.servlets.FeedUpdateUserServlet`, which enqueues subtasks for all the user's Friends at once.

If multiple tasks can each spawn their own multiple tasks you can achieve a **fanout** effect that can be very efficient.

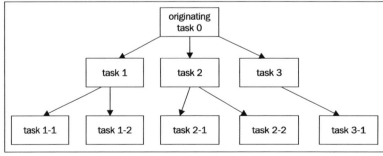

Figure 4: Task 'fanout'

Figure 4 illustrates the fanout effect. If each task adds multiple other descendant tasks to the queue, a 'task tree' similar to the figure may be produced, and multiple such tasks may potentially be running at the same time (depending upon queue configuration), which can be quite powerful.

In *Connectr*, we can see fanout with the /feedupdateloggedin task (described next).

With fanout, particular attention may need to be paid to error handling—recall that if a task fails, it will be retried until it succeeds, and if it has already spawned others, this may cause problems depending upon the nature of the tasks. For example, in Figure 4, if **task 2** were to fail, then when it was retried, additional instances of **task 2-1** and **task 2-2** would likely be added to the queue. For *Connectr's* task fanout, task repeats are not problematic, but in other contexts they could be.

If you have created a task 'fanout' pattern, and it is important to avoid enqueuing multiple instances of the 'same' task—which could occur if the task's parent task is retried on error—then one tactic is to create unique but reconstructable names for each task. It is possible to name tasks when you enqueue them, using the taskName method of Builder.

If there is already a task with a given name in the system—either in process as well as for a period of time after its successful completion (currently at least seven days) a task with the same name won't be enqueued. So, using task names can prevent duplicates if a node with descendants in a fanout is retried.

## Query cursors and next task creation

Of course, it is not always possible to parallelize your tasks. In particular, if you are using query cursors to step through a data series, each query gives you the cursor for the next. In this scenario, **enqueue the next task** *before* **processing the current set of results**. This will start the next task in the series running as quickly as possible.

You can see this tactic used in server.servlets.FeedUpdateServlet.

## Create many quick-running tasks

App Engine performance currently tends to be optimized towards tasks that run quickly and do not use much CPU. So, if it makes sense to split up a task into smaller ones, even if the overall computation required is approximately the same, you may see better performance than you would with a few longer-running tasks.

# Cron Jobs

App Engine allows tasks to be scheduled and run at specified times or time intervals. This is accomplished via Cron Jobs, which are defined in the `war/WEB-INF/cron.xml` file.

The `cron.xml` file consists of a `<cronentries>` element containing a number of `<cron>` elements. Each `<cron>` entry contains a `<url>` to run, a `<schedule>`, and an optional `<description>` and `<timezone>`.

The `<url>` is a URL from your application, typically mapped to a Servlet designed to run as a task. You can pass parameters to the handler by specifying them as part of the URL.

The format for the `<schedule>` element is "English-like". For example (from the App Engine documentation), schedule specifications can include the following phrases:

- every 5 minutes
- every 12 hours
- 2nd, third, mon, wed, thu of march 17:00
- every monday, 09:00
- 1st monday of sep, oct, nov 17:00
- every day 00:00

```xml
<?xml version="1.0" encoding="UTF-8"?>
<cronentries>
  <cron>
    <url>/feedupdateloggedin</url>
    <description>Update the feeds for active users; push notif. (when
enabled) if new content</description>
    <schedule>every 2 minutes</schedule>
  </cron>
  <cron>
    <url>/feedupdate?num=1&amp;max=100</url>
    <description>update the most recently requested feeds</
description>
    <schedule>every 10 minutes</schedule>
  </cron>
  <cron>
    <url>/migration?migration=packagepath.server.migrations.StreamItem
Purge&amp;dir=down&amp;num=10&amp;hours=168</url>
    <description>remove StreamItems older than a week</description>
    <schedule>every 58 minutes</schedule>
  </cron>
</cronentries>
```

The example above shows *Connectr's* `cron.xml` file (where you would replace `'packagepath'` with your path), specifying three Cron Jobs. Note that the `"&amp;"` must be used to specify an '&' in a URL; if this is not done, the XML will not validate.

The first Cron Job, defined to run every two minutes, initiates a task to update the feeds for those users who are logged in and active (that is, those currently generating client-side events), which in turn spawns subtasks for each such user. If use of the Channel API is enabled, as described in *Chapter 10*, a 'new content' notification is pushed to those users' clients.

The second Cron Job initiates a task to update the content of the most 'recently-used' feeds (as defined by the date a feed was last requested), and is defined to run every 10 minutes. It too spawns a series of tasks. Using query cursors, each task updates the given number of feeds (here, just `1`), then the query cursor spawns another task to continue the work, until the feed max (here, `100`) is reached. This Cron Job keeps the content fresh for the feeds most likely to be required. Recall that if a feed has just been updated, it will not be re-updated for a configurable latency period, thus the first and second Cron Jobs will not 'fight' with each other.

The third Cron Job runs about once an hour and removes from the Datastore those `StreamItem` objects older than the given number of hours (in the previous example `168`, or older than a week). This job also spawns a series of tasks—the deletions are done in small batches to ensure that each task runs relatively quickly and will not reach the 30-second task limit.

We will look at the Servlets that drive these tasks in *Regular background tasks*.

For jobs scheduled at an interval, such as the ones in the *Connectr* `cron.xml`, the interval until the upcoming job starts when the previous job is completed. If you want jobs to run at regular intervals, regardless of when they finished, you can add the keyword **synchronized** to the interval specification, for example, `every 7 minutes` synchronized.

**Cron Jobs are run against the default app version**, so Cron Jobs can fail if the default app code does not support the specified Cron actions. You will recall that all versions of an app share the same Datastore, so it is not necessarily a problem if a Cron Job runs against a different version—it depends upon the code.

 Some consider this a bug, or at least an "issue": see http://code.google.com/p/googleappengine/issues/detail?id=2725.

# Asynchronous server-side tasks in *Connectr*

Given the ability to define Cron Jobs and to specialize Task Queues, we now have the tools to support *Connectr's* asynchronous server-side feed updates, which will generate the series of StreamItem objects used by the client-facing code to build the displayed activity streams.

The tasks that we will use to accomplish this fall into two categories.

In the first category are tasks that **run regularly in the background**. These are the tasks, outlined previously, that are specified in the cron.xml file. The Servlets that support these background update tasks and their subtasks are discussed next in *Regular background tasks*.

In the second category are **tasks triggered by client activities**. Specifically, when a user logs in we want to trigger an asynchronous update of their Friend URLs right away so that the fresh content can be displayed very quickly. So, this task is not run on a Cron but instead it is triggered by a specific user login. The Servlet that supports this activity, and the details on how it is triggered, are described in *Context-Specific feed update tasks*.

# Regular background tasks

This section takes a look at the Servlets supporting *Connectr's* regularly-run background tasks, supported by the Cron service, and discusses some of the issues in defining the tasks and task parameters.

## Feed updates

Updates of *Connectr's* feeds are supported with two Cron Jobs, which run the /feedupdateloggedin and /feedupdate tasks.

## Updating feeds for active users

The /feedupdateloggedin task illustrates the use of *scheduled* tasks (the first such use in *Connectr*) and shows the use of the **Channel API**, introduced in *Chapter 10*. The purpose of this task is to keep feed content fresh and updated for those logged-in users actively using the site.

 As discussed in *Chapter 10*, at the time of writing, the Channel API is available only for local development and does not yet work for deployed applications. This is expected to change very soon.

/feedupdateloggedin **runs** server.servlets.FeedUpdateLoggedInServlet. The doPost() method of this Servlet, shown next, enqueues a /feedupdateuser task for each 'active' user (a 'lastActive' timestamp for each user is maintained, based on client-side events, which we use to filter on activity), setting a "notify" parameter to "true".

```
@SuppressWarnings("serial")
public class FeedUpdateLoggedInServlet extends HttpServlet {

   private static final int MINS = 20; // in minutes
   private static final int DELAY = 20; // in seconds
   private static Logger logger =
  Logger.getLogger(FeedUpdateLoggedInServlet.class.getName());
   ...


   // update all feeds
   public void doPost(HttpServletRequest req,
    HttpServletResponse resp)
   throws IOException {

      PersistenceManager pm = PMF.getNonTxnPm();
      try {
        List<UserAccount> results = getActiveUsers(pm);
        if (results == null) {
          return;
          }
        for (UserAccount user : results) {
        // For each active user, spawn tasks to update their feeds
        // and push an update notification as necessary
          Queue queue =
          QueueFactory.getQueue("userfeedupdates");
          queue.add(url("/feedupdateuser").param("uid",
           user.getUniqueId()).param("notify", "true"));
          logger.info("queueing feedupdateuser for " +
           user.getUniqueId());
        }
      }
      catch (Exception e) {
        logger.warning(e.getMessage());
      }
      finally {
        pm.close();
      }
   }

   ...
}
```

We have seen the /feedupdateuser task previously, in *Chapter 7*, it runs server.servlets.FeedUpdateUserServlet. Recall that this Servlet in turn spawns subtasks to update the feeds for the Friends of the given user. The subtasks, one for each Friend, are added to the Task Queue at once—generating a multi-level task fanout—and thus a number of update tasks may be run in parallel, which speeds processing.

We have modified FeedUpdateUserServlet from its previous incarnation in two respects. First, we have modified its subtasks to use a non-default queue, with a larger bucket size and throughput than the default. That's because we want these updates to be pushed through quickly.

Second, we have modified FeedUpdateUserServlet to take an additional "notify" parameter.

If the notify flag is set, then after all the Friend update subtasks are enqueued, an additional task, /usernotif (described shortly), may be enqueued to *run after a delay* (by default, of 20 seconds). We saw above that FeedUpdateLoggedInServlet sets this parameter. The /usernotif task is enqueued only if the Channel API is enabled for the app.

The code below shows the doPost() method of server.servlets.FeedUpdateUserServlet. Note the use of the countdownMillis() task builder method, which specifies the delay on running a task.

```
// update all feeds for friends of the given UserAccount
public void doPost(HttpServletRequest req,
  HttpServletResponse resp)
throws IOException {

  PersistenceManager pm =
   PMF.get().getPersistenceManager();
  String userId = req.getParameter("uid");
  String notify = req.getParameter("notify");
  UserAccount userPrefs = null;
  try {
    userPrefs = getUserAccount(userId, pm);
    if (userPrefs != null) {
      Set<Friend> friends = userPrefs.getFriends();
      // get the default queue
      Queue queue =
       QueueFactory.getQueue("userfeedupdates");
      for (Friend fr : friends ){
        // spawn off tasks to fetch the Friend-associated urls
        queue.add(url("/feedupdatefr").param("fkey",
        fr.getId()));
```

```
        }
        if (notify != null &&
         notify.equalsIgnoreCase("true") &&
         ChannelServer.channelAPIEnabled()) {
          // add task, to run later, to see if a notification needs
          // to be sent for that user.
          queue.add(url("/usernotif").param("uniqueid",
           userPrefs.getUniqueId()).countdownMillis(1000 *
           DELAY));
          logger.info("queueing usernotif for " +
          userPrefs.getUniqueId());
        }
      }
    }
    finally {
      pm.close();
    }
    resp.setContentType("text/plain");
    if (userPrefs != null) {
      resp.getWriter().println("queued up friend feed fetches");
    }
    else {
      resp.getWriter().println("no matching user found");
    }
  }
```

The /usernotif task runs `server.servlets.UserNotifServlet`. This Servlet (not shown) checks whether there has been any new content for the user since last checked, based on item date, and if so, pushes a notification of new content to the client via the Channel API, as follows:

```
ChannelServer.pushMessage(user, new ContentAvailableMessage());
```

As described in *Chapter 10*, receipt of this message by the client will trigger a client RPC request for the new content.

By delaying the launch of the /usernotif task, we allow a user's feed update tasks to finish running before checking for new content. There is no need to strictly coordinate with the feed updates to be sure that they have all finished. The use of `StreamItem` objects decouples the client display from the update process, and if there are any feeds that have not yet finished updating, we will just catch them next time around.

# Updating recently-accessed feeds

The /feedupdate task runs the server.servlets.FeedUpdateServlet, first introduced in *Chapter 7*. FeedUpdateServlet initiates a series of subtasks—each enqueuing the next by making use of the *query cursor*—that updates the N most recently-requested feeds over the set of all users, where N is configurable.

This task now runs on a specialized queue, with a slightly lower throughput and bucket size than the default. That way, if background feed updates are running a large part of the time—which may be desirable with a large user base—these tasks will not draw too large a percentage of the app resources.

The intent of updating the N most recently-requested feeds is that we don't need to proactively update feeds that have not been required lately. When a user logs in, the content of their Friend feeds will be updated at that time (as described in *Context-Specific feed update tasks*), and in the process, the dateRequested value for those feeds will be updated. Similarly, when a feed is added to a Friend object, the requested date of that feed will be set or updated. Recall that there is only one feed object for a given URL, so it may be 'shared' if multiple Friend objects point to the same feed. Conversely, if a user has not logged in for several months, then we might not update their feeds (unless those feeds are associated with other accounts as well) until they log in again.

The most useful value of N will depend upon the needs of a given site, how many feeds there are in total and the pattern of active users.

```
...
q = pm.newQuery(FeedInfo.class);
q.setOrdering("dateRequested desc");
if (cursorString != null) {
  Cursor cursor = Cursor.fromWebSafeString(cursorString);
  Map<String, Object> extensionMap = new HashMap<String, Object>();
  extensionMap.put(JDOCursorHelper.CURSOR_EXTENSION, cursor);
  q.setExtensions(extensionMap);
}
q.setRange(0, batch);
List<FeedInfo> results = (List<FeedInfo>) q.execute();
logger.info("performed query");
if (results.iterator().hasNext()) {

  batchcount++;
  Cursor cursor = JDOCursorHelper.getCursor(results);
  cursorString = cursor.toWebSafeString();
  Queue queue = QueueFactory.getQueue("frfeedupdates");
  queue.add(url("/feedupdate")
```

```
    .param("cursor", cursorString)
    .param("num", ""+batch).param("max", ""+max)
    .param("bc", ""+batchcount));

  for (FeedInfo f : results) {
    // update the feed if needed [if it has not just been updated]
    logger.info("working on feed: "+ f.getFeedTitle());
    f.updateIfNeeded(pm);
  }


}
    else {
     cursorString = null;
    }
  }
  ...
```

The code above shows the core of the `FeedUpdateServlet.doPost()` method. Once a result is returned and the query cursor is obtained, the task to process the next batch of feeds is *enqueued first*, before updating the current batch of feeds. Thus, the next task can be initiated while the current one is running. This allows higher throughput in the Task Queue.

## Purge of old data from the Datastore

A Cron Job is also used to periodically remove those `StreamItem` objects from the Datastore that are older than a given configurable interval. In contrast to the feed structures from which they are derived, which only hold the most recent items, the `StreamItem` objects may be maintained indefinitely, providing as extensive a record of the feed contents as desired.

App Engine is designed to scale well for large amounts of data. The appropriate removal date depends upon the application characteristics. If you—as the developer—are concerned about the size of your app Datastore, you may want to keep only a few days' worth of `StreamItem` objects. Conversely, if you have enough storage space—for example, if you have set up billing, as described in *Chapter 11*—then you may want to archive older `StreamItem` objects for a longer period of time. This would allow maintenance of a longer `Friend` history for each user. Here, for purposes of example, we decide that there is no particular reason to keep old `StreamItem` objects.

We have subclassed our `server.migrations.Migration` class, described in *Chapter 7*, to implement the purge of old `StreamItem` objects as a 'down' migration called `server.migrations.StreamItemPurge`. As in the examples in *Chapter 7*, the `Migration` class is invoked from `server.servlets.MigrationServlet`, as illustrated by the `cron.xml` example shown previously.

The `MigrationServlet` is passed an 'hours' parameter, which is in turn passed to the `StreamItemPurge` class, which indicates the hours in age before which the `StreamItems` should be removed. As shown in the `cron.xml` example, the regularly-run Cron Job sets `hours=168`, so a week's worth of `StreamItems` are maintained.

While we will not list the `StreamItemPurge` class here, it may be of interest in its use of a results hash, used in turn by the `MigrationServlet`, to pass information to the next migration task added to the queue.

# Context-Specific feed update tasks

In addition to regularly-run jobs, some server-side tasks are triggered by calls from the client side of the application, initiating background actions based on current usage of the application.

## Feed update on login

A user login triggers an update of all the feeds for the users' associated `Friends`. This update is triggered via the `MessagesService.initiateUserFeedUpdate()` method. `initiateUserFeedUpdate()` in turn launches `server.servlets.FeedUpdateUserServlet` as a task.

The code for the updated `FeedUpdateUserServlet.doPost()` method was shown previously. In this context, we will not launch this task with the 'notify' flag set, since the client already knows it needs to refresh. Not all of the update tasks may have finished by the time the **Latest Activity** panel is displayed originally upon login, but the client will refresh shortly, as was described in *Chapter 10*. Because of the regular update Crons, in general the content will be acceptably fresh already on initial display.

## Feed update on URL addition

On adding a new feed to `Friend` data, the feed content is pulled in right away. As was described in *Chapter 9*, the feed is added in a **transactional task** so the client does not need to synchronously wait on a response from the feed processing. As with `FeedUpdateUserServlet`, we place the transactional task on the `userfeedupdates` queue, which is configured to be more responsive than the default.

# Supporting synchronous content delivery: Datastore queries and caching

In addition to the asynchronously run background jobs, new methods are required to synchronously deliver stream content to the client on request. As introduced previously, the client might request content for all Friends of the user or only a selected subset. These methods reside in the `server.MessagesServiceImpl` class, which extends `RemoteServiceServlet`. This class ties together the use of a number of Datastore and cache-related design considerations and query constructions that we have introduced in previous chapters.

The `MessagesServiceImpl` class methods support the various modes in which the client might request activity StreamItems, for example, "give me the items since last request", "give me the most recent N items", or "give me the N items older than this date".

```
@RemoteServiceRelativePath("messagesService")
public interface MessagesService extends RemoteService {
  List<StreamItemSummaryDTO>
    getNLastMessages(Set<String> friendIds, int numMsgs);
  List<StreamItemSummaryDTO>
    getMessagesSince(Set<String> friendIds, Date since);
  List<StreamItemSummaryDTO>
    getMessagesPrior (Set<String> friendIds, Date prior,
    int numMsgs);
  Boolean initiateUserFeedUpdate();
  StreamItemDTO getStreamItemDetails(String id);

}
```

The previous code shows the `client.service.MessagesService` class which lists the client-facing methods of `MessagesServiceImpl` that implement those request modes.

These different request methods wrap a couple of 'core' methods: one used when querying over all `Friends` of the user (the default) called `MessagesServiceImpl.fetchBatch()`, and one for obtaining the stream items for just a subset of Friends, called `MessagesServiceImpl.fetchForFeeds()`. If the `friendIds` parameter is set to `null` when the methods above are called, `fetchBatch()` is used to fetch content from all feeds associated with all `Friend` objects of that user. Otherwise, the set of `friendIds` defines a subset of feeds from which `fetchForFeeds()` retrieves content. These query scenarios are treated differently, as described next.

Implementation of these methods has several interesting aspects: designing the data classes for efficient queries, use of DTOs to send results to the client, and use of caching. We will explore these aspects below by focusing on the core `MessagesServiceImpl` activities.

# Making StreamItem queries fast

The basic model behind the `MessagesServiceImpl` methods is straightforward: perform a query or queries that returns `StreamItem` *IDs only*, then obtain the associated summary DTOs for those IDs from Memcache—creating them from `StreamItem` objects only if there is a cache miss—and returning the DTOs to the client. Recall from *The StreamItem persistent class* that the summary DTOs are cached when the `StreamItem` objects are built, so cache misses should be few.

# Finding StreamItems for all Friends of a user: doing write-time work to make queries fast

To make it fast to find the `StreamItems` associated with a given user (that is, the items from the feed URLs listed for their `Friend` objects), we will do a bit of extra work at write time. This is similar to some of the strategies discussed in *Chapter 5*, where, by deriving a bit of extra information when we store objects, we can sidestep the lack of support for joins.

In the feed objects we will include a *multi-valued property* called ukeys holding the IDs of the associated `UserAccount` fields for that feed—that is, all users with `Friend` objects that list that feed. This list is updated whenever a feed object is created or its list of associated `Friend` keys updated. We push this same list to the `server. domain.StreamItem` entities as well, which are created when a feed is updated:

```
@Persistent
Set<Long> ukeys;
```

This field lets us query the `StreamItems` via a filter on the user ID, making it very efficient to find all `StreamItem` objects for a given user. Note that with this model, the ukeys of already-created `StreamItem` objects will not be retroactively updated. Because newer `StreamItem` objects are constantly being pushed into the top of the 'activity stream', we have decided that this potential inconsistency is acceptable given the speed tradeoff.

The `fetchBatch()` method of `server.MessagesServiceImpl` is the core method that fetches the appropriate `StreamItem` keys over all feeds for the `Friend` objects of the given user. It does this by filtering on the `ukeys` field of the `StreamItem` objects. The code that follows shows the portion of the `fetchBatch()` method that constructs and executes this query. The `sdate`, `prior`, and `range` parameters add date and range filters, and determine the exact query constructed. Note that the `StreamItem` query is a *keys-only* query. We describe shortly how its results are used.

```
private void fetchBatch(Date sdate, PersistenceManager pm, boolean
fetchEntries, boolean prior, int range) {

   ...
   // Construct and execute a query that fetches the StreamItems
   // based on the UserAccount id.
   UserAccount user = LoginHelper.getLoggedInUser(
    getThreadLocalRequest().getSession(), pm);
   Long userid = user.getId();
   String qstring = null;
   if (sdate == null) {
     qstring = " where ukeys == :u1";
   }
   else if (prior) {
     qstring = " where date < :d1 && ukeys == :u1";
   }
    else {
     qstring = " where date >= :d1 && ukeys == :u1";
   }
   Query q = pm.newQuery("select id from " +
    StreamItem.class.getName() + qstring);
   q.setOrdering("date desc");
   if (prior) {
     q.setRange(0, range);
   }
   q.addExtension("datanucleus.appengine.datastoreReadConsistency",
    "EVENTUAL");
   List<String> entryids;
   if (sdate != null) {
     entryids = (List<String>) q.execute(sdate, userid);
   }
   else {
     entryids = (List<String>) q.execute(userid);
   }
   ...
```

# Filtering the StreamItems on a subset of the user's Friends: Using key paths and contains()

If we are retrieving `StreamItem` objects based on the URLs associated with a *subset* of a user's `Friend`, the query construction process is different.

Instead of simply querying for all feeds associated with the given user, now we need to determine which feeds are associated with the selected `Friend` object, and then query on those feeds. This is done as a two-stage process.

In the first stage, we obtain the list of feed IDs associated with each `Friend`—that is, the IDs of the `FeedInfo` objects associated with the `Friend` IDs that we are filtering on. We cache these feed ID lists so we check the cache first against each `Friend` ID.

If we have a cache miss then it is an efficient query to obtain the feed ID list: we do a *keys-only* query for the `FeedIndex` IDs for a given `Friend` ID. From the `FeedIndex` IDs, we can derive the `FeedInfo` IDs *without performing another query*. This is because, as described in *Chapter 9*, we have defined the `FeedIndex` IDs to be the *children* of the keys of their associated `FeedInfo` objects.

Once obtained, we cache the list of feed IDs associated with that `Friend` ID, avoiding a Datastore query in future. In `server.FriendsServiceImpl`, we clear this cache if the `Friend` object's information is updated.

The following code shows the `MessagesServiceImpl.getFeedIds()` method, which checks the cache for a given `Friend` ID, and if there is a cache miss, queries to get the associated list of feed IDs. You may have noticed that an `'XMPP_FEED'` is also added to the list of feed IDs. This is a feed that provides optional content via XMPP push—its function is described next in *XMPP: Information push to the app*.

```
    private Set<String> getFeedIds(Set<String> friendIds,
      PersistenceManager pm) {

    HashSet<String> feedids = new HashSet<String>();

    if (friendIds != null) {
      // construct from set of friendIds
      Query q = pm.newQuery("select key from " +
        FeedIndex.class.getName() +
      " where friendKeys == :id");
      for (String friendid : friendIds) {
        // check for cached info
        Object finfo =
         CacheSupport.cacheGet(feedids_nmspce, friendid);
        if (finfo != null && finfo instanceof Set<?>) {
```

```
        feedids.addAll((Set)finfo);
    }
    else {
        List ids = (List) q.execute(friendid);
      HashSet<String> cachedURLs = new HashSet<String>();
      Key k;
      for (Object o : ids) {
        k = (Key) o;
        feedids.add(k.getParent().getName());
        cachedURLs.add(k.getParent().getName());
      }
      CacheSupport.cachePutExp(feedids_nmspce,
        friendid, cachedURLs, CACHE_EXPIR);
    }
  }
}

feedids.add(XMPP_FEED);
return feedids;
}
```

Note that we could alternatively have performed a **batch fetch**, as described in *Chapter 4*, over all Friend keys at once. That would be efficient too. Here we're using the heuristic that the user's set of filtered-over friends may change often but many individual friends are likely to remain a common factor in the filter sets, and thus, it is useful to cache feed ID lists for the Friend objects.

The second query stage uses this list of feed IDs to find the IDs of the StreamItem objects associated with those IDs. This is done in the server.MessagesServiceImpl.fetchForFeeds() method. To implement this query, we can use the contains() filter, as described in *Chapter 5*, which matches objects of the given 'kind' for which the indicated field holds one of the listed values.

The following code from MessagesServiceImpl.fetchForFeeds() shows the structure of this query. It returns the IDs of those StreamItem objects that have a feedUrl field that matches an element in the list of feed IDs.

```
List<String> fetchlist = new ArrayList<String>();
StreamItem entry = null;
Query dq = null, q2 = null;
String qstring = null;
if (sdate == null) {
```

```
      qstring = " where :f1.contains(feedUrl)";
}
else if (prior) {
   qstring = " where date < :d1 && :f1.contains(feedUrl)";
}
else {
   qstring = " where date >= :d1 && :f1.contains(feedUrl)";
}

// Partition feed id list into sublists
...

for (List<String> fsublist : partition) {
   dq = pm.newQuery("select id from " +
     StreamItem.class.getName() + qstring);
   dq.setOrdering("date desc");
   if (prior) {
     dq.setRange(0, range);
   }
   dq.addExtension(
   "datanucleus.appengine.datastoreReadConsistency",
     "EVENTUAL");

   List<String> entryids;
   if (sdate != null) {
     entryids = (List<String>) dq.execute(sdate, fsublist);
   }
   else {
    entryids = (List<String>) dq.execute(fsublist);
   }
   ...
```

However, we need to take some care in executing the contains query. As described in *Chapter 5*, a contains filter is implemented under the hood by performing a set of subqueries, one for each item in the contains list. In a sense, the contains construction is just an application-level convenience. Furthermore, at the time of writing, App Engine does not allow us to generate queries that **result in more than 30 subqueries**.

So, we will **partition** our list of feed IDs into sublists, ensuring that we do not hit the sub-query limit, and perform the keys-only query on each sublist (fsublist) separately.

For each sublist, the query gives us the StreamItem IDs (entryids), and we can then fetch the (likely cached) objects they correspond to.

We must then combine the resultant objects from the multiple sublist queries at the application level. We will do this by using a TreeSet to hold the results, and defining a Comparator for the TreeSet that sorts on the getDate() values of the set's objects (since we always want to return the results to the client chronologically-ordered). The following code, from server.MessagesServiceImpl.fetchStreamItems(), shows the TreeSet and Comparator defined for the StreamItemSummaryDTO objects.

```
...
summaries = new TreeSet<StreamItemSummaryDTO>(new
  Comparator<StreamItemSummaryDTO>() {
    public int compare(StreamItemSummaryDTO o1,
      StreamItemSummaryDTO o2) {
      if (o1.getDate() != null) {
        if (o2.getDate() != null) {
          return o2.getDate().compareTo(o1.getDate());
        } else {
          return -1;
        }}
      else {
        return 1;
      }
    }});
...
```

The TreeSet gives us a sorted set of the combined results from all the partition queries, which we can then convert to a list:

```
...
if (summaries.size() > range) {
  t2 = (new
    ArrayList<StreamItemSummaryDTO>(summaries)).subList(0,
    range - 1);
  // conversion to avoid generating serialization errors
  summaryList = new ArrayList<StreamItemSummaryDTO>(t2);
  }
else {
  summaryList = new
  ArrayList<StreamItemSummaryDTO>(summaries);
}
...
```

To return `range` results to the client, we perform each of our partition queries using that range, then use `List<E>.sublist()` to truncate the resultant combined list. This requires two steps, as the object that results from calling the `subList()` method is not serializable and will generate an error if we try to send it over RPC to the client. As shown in the previous code, we need to create a new `ArrayList` from the sublist, and send that via RPC instead.

# Stream cache management

With both of the query scenarios above, our `StreamItem` queries are keys-only queries, returning just the `StreamItem` keys. Such queries are much more efficient than returning an actual object from the Datastore.

We then use the keys to obtain the corresponding objects, first checking the cache. We are very likely to get a cache hit when we do this, since, as described previously, both the `StreamItem` objects and their corresponding `StreamItemSummaryDTO` are cached when the feeds are updated.

So, most of the time, we don't need to actually fetch the `StreamItem` objects themselves from the Datastore—we just use their keys to obtain the corresponding DTOs from the cache.

If there are any cache misses. then the `StreamItem` objects must be fetched from the Datastore. This is done efficiently by collecting a list of all `StreamItem` IDs that were a miss, then performing a batch fetch using the list of the 'missed' IDs (`fetchlist`). The next example, from `server.MessagesServiceImpl.fetchForFeeds()`, shows this process.

```
...
if (fetchlist.size() > 0) {
  // fetch the streamitem ids which weren't in the cache,
  // using their list of ids.
  q2 = pm.newQuery("select from " +
    StreamItem.class.getName() + " where id == :keys");
  q2.addExtension(
    "datanucleus.appengine.datastoreReadConsistency",
    "EVENTUAL");
  List<StreamItem> entries2 =
    (List<StreamItem>) q2.execute(fetchlist);
  // add the fetched entries to the cache, and to the
  // list of items we are building
  for (StreamItem e2 : entries2) {
    summaries.add(e2.addToCacheGetSumm());
    if (fetchEntries) {
```

```
        entries.add(e2);
      }
    }
  }
```

# XMPP: Information push to the app

The Extensible Messaging and Presence Protocol, or **XMPP** (http://xmpp.org/, sometimes referred to as *Jabber*) is an open, XML-based communication protocol, originally developed by *Jeremie Miller* and the Jabber open-source community. XMPP was originally motivated as an IM protocol and is often thought of in the context of 'chat' clients (including Google Talk) but its applicability and use is much broader. XMPP supports a push protocol so that a client does not have to explicitly poll for notifications and it can be used for many types of middleware messaging. For example, XMPP helps drive Google Wave.

 While Google Wave is being phased out in its current form, its XMPP-based protocol has been open-sourced for "Wave in a Box"; see http://waveprotocol.org/ and http://goo.gl/4Sqa for more information.

App Engine supports an XMPP Service and API. Using the XMPP Service, App Engine applications can send and receive messages to and from other XMPP-compatible services in a straightforward manner. App Engine apps are effectively XMPP clients, with the App Engine infrastructure providing XMPP server capabilities.

As we will see in more detail, what 'push' means with respect to App Engine apps is that each app has an XMPP address, and a special URL is requested each time a new XMPP notification is received at that address.

In *Connectr*, we will use App Engine's XMPP capabilities to receive a push stream of 'breaking news' items, as generated by an XMPP gateway application, which can be subscribed to by an App Engine app such as *Connectr*. If the subscription is enabled, breaking news items will be pushed to the app server from the gateway.

So, *Connectr* will not need to explicitly poll for new such breaking news items—it will not need to initiate a feed update task, as with its regular feeds. Instead, the breaking news notifications will be pushed to the app when the gateway generates them, allowing *Connectr* to simply process the notifications and add them to the series of StreamItems, thus including them in a user's activity display.

# The App Engine XMPP service and API

The App Engine XMPP service essentially allows any App Engine app to be an XMPP client, with the ability to both send and receive XMPP messages. Its API is straightforward to use and makes the use of XMPP easy.

 In development mode, your app cannot receive XMPP messages. It cannot, in actuality, send them either; if you have code that sends XMPP messages, they will not actually be dispatched; instead the message will just be printed to your console. So, *Connectr's* XMPP integration can only be used in a deployed version of the app.

## XMPP addresses

Each App Engine has an associated *default* XMPP address, that will be used when an XMPP message is sent, if the 'from' address is not otherwise specified.

This default address format is as follows. For the default app version, the address has this construction:

```
<app-id>@appspot.com
```

where `<app-id>` is replaced by your app ID.

For the app versions other than the default, the address has this construction:

```
<app-id>@<version>.latest.<app-id>.appspotchat.com
```

where again `<app-id>` is replaced by your app ID, and `<version>` is replaced by the app version string. Note the different domain name in the second example (**appspotchat**).

If in your code, you explicitly set the 'from' address as `<app-id>@appspot.com`, and the code is run by a non-default app version, the actual 'from' address will be converted to `<app-id>@<version>.latest.<app-id>.appspotchat.com`, with the version set appropriately. If you explicitly set the 'from' address to: `<app-id>@<version>.latest.<app-id>.appspotchat.com`, but the code is run by a version of the app that does not match the given version, an exception will be thrown. You can use the `<app-id>@version.latest.<app-id>.appspotchat.com` construction with the default app version as long as the given version is correct.

App Engine apps also support an alternate custom XMPP address format. With the custom format, a 'wildcard' component, which can be any string containing letters, numbers, and hyphens, can be included. This allows different addresses to be used for sending different types of messages.

For the default app version, custom address formats have the following construction:

```
<anything>@<app-id>.appspotchat.com
```

where `<anything>` can be any valid string as above. Note again the use of the `appspotchat` domain.

For non-default app versions, custom address formats have the following construction:

```
<anything>@<version>.latest.<app-id>.appspotchat.com
```

If in your code, you use the `<anything>@<app-id>.appspotchat.com` construction, but the code is run by an app that is not the default version of the app, then the address will be converted to: `<anything>@<version>.latest.<app-id>.appspotchat.com`, with the version set appropriately. Conversely, as with the non-custom example, specifying a version and then running the code with a different version of the app will cause an error.

The use of Google Apps domains in XMPP addresses is not yet supported for apps.

# Sending an XMPP message

To send an XMPP message from an App Engine app, you first need the XMPP or Jabber address of the recipient(s). For example, you can send a message to a Gmail or Google Talk user (using their Gmail address), any other Jabber account (such as one from `jabber.org`), or of course to another App Engine app, using the construction described in the previous section.

Use the `com.google.appengine.api.xmpp.JID` constructor to convert an address string to a `JID` (XMPP address) object. Then, construct a `com.google.appengine.api.xmpp.Message` via its associated `MessageBuilder`, indicating the message body (a `String`) and the recipient(s). Additionally, you can configure other features of the message, such as the 'from' address used (though, recall from the previous discussion that this address must be valid with respect to the sending app), and the message type. Create an `XMPPService` instance to send the message and check its delivery status.

```
import com.google.appengine.api.xmpp.JID;
import com.google.appengine.api.xmpp.Message;
import com.google.appengine.api.xmpp.MessageBuilder;
import com.google.appengine.api.xmpp.SendResponse;
import com.google.appengine.api.xmpp.XMPPService;
import com.google.appengine.api.xmpp.XMPPServiceFactory;

// ...
```

```
JID jid = new JID("app1@appspot.com");
String msgBody = "Breaking News....";
Message msg = new MessageBuilder()
    .withRecipientJids(jid)
    .withBody(msgBody)
    .build();

boolean messageSent = false;
XMPPService xmpp = XMPPServiceFactory.getXMPPService();
//use this check for addrs in the Google Talk network
if (xmpp.getPresence(jid).isAvailable()) {
    SendResponse status = xmpp.sendMessage(msg);
    messageSent = (status.getStatusMap().get(jid) ==
      SendResponse.Status.SUCCESS);
}

if (!messageSent) {
    // Send an email message instead...
}
```

The previous code shows the basic pattern of XMPP message construction and dispatch. The `xmpp.getPresence(jid).isAvailable()` test checks that the recipient is available before sending the message. At the time of writing, the `isAvailable()` test works only for Google Talk addresses, so do not use it, for example, with accounts from `jabber.org`. In addition, `isAvailable()` does not work to check other App Engine apps.

The `MessageBuilder` class allows its methods to be chained, in order to construct the message in a single statement. Its methods include:

- `withBody(String body)`: Sets the message body.
- `withFromJid(JID jid)`: Sets the sender JID.
- `withRecipientJids(JID jid1, ...)`: Adds one or more recipient JIDs.
- `withMessageType(MessageType type)`: Sets the message type.
- `build()`: Returns the finished Message.

To send a message to multiple recipients at once, you can either enumerate them directly, for example: `withRecipientJids(jid1, jid2, jid3)`, or pass an array of `JID`.

To set a message type, use one of the `MessageType` enum types: `MessageType.CHAT`, `MessageType.ERROR`, `MessageType.GROUPCHAT`, `MessageType.HEADLINE`, and `MessageType.NORMAL`. If a message type is not specified, the default is `CHAT`. An App Engine app can only receive messages of the types `CHAT` and `NORMAL`.

The sendMessage() method returns a SendResponse object. The response's getStatusMap() method returns a Map<JID, SendResponseStatus>. This contains a map of recipient JID to status codes. The possible status codes are SendResponse. Status.SUCCESS, SendResponse.Status.INVALID_ID, and SendResponse.Status. OTHER_ERROR.

Many chat servers will only accept messages for users that are "subscribed" to the sender. Typically a chat client will require a user to accept an invitation from or authorize the sender, if an unsubscribed sender tries to add the user to their contact or 'buddy' list or tries to send them a message. This holds for messages sent from App Engine apps, and an App Engine app can also send explicit chat invitations using the XMPP API. See the documentation for more information.

However, when communications are restricted between App Engine apps, invitation management is not necessary. An App Engine app accepts all chat invitations automatically and does not communicate invitations to the application-level code. Further, the App Engine XMPP service will route all chat messages to the application, regardless of whether the sender previously sent an invitation to the app. So, for the way in which we will use XMPP in *Connectr*, we do not need to deal with invitations—both an App Engine XMPP gateway app generating 'breaking news' notifications, and *Connectr*, which receives messages from that gateway, can communicate via XMPP in both directions without any formalities.

## Receiving an XMPP message

An App Engine app must be specifically configured to enable receipt of inbound XMPP notifications. Add the following entry to war/WEB-INF/appengine-web.xml:

```
<inbound-services>
  <service>xmpp_message</service>
</inbound-services>
```

Once the XMPP service is enabled, when App Engine receives a chat message for the app, it makes an HTTP POST request to the following URL path:

```
/_ah/xmpp/message/chat/
```

So, in web.xml, you must indicate the handler that will handle this request. For example, in *Connectr* the handler is a Servlet called server.servlets. XMPPAgentServlet, and our configuration is as follows:

```
<servlet>
  <servlet-name>xmppreceiver</servlet-name>
  <servlet-class>
    packagepath.server.servlets.XMPPAgentServlet
  </servlet-class>
```

```
    </servlet>
    <servlet-mapping>
      <servlet-name>xmppreceiver</servlet-name>
      <url-pattern>/_ah/xmpp/message/chat/</url-pattern>
    </servlet-mapping>
```

The `/_ah/xmpp/message/chat/` URL is restricted to admin access. The XMPP service (like the Task Queue service) runs with admin status automatically. The App Engine XMPP service knows how to route the App Engine address variants, as described in *XMPP addresses*, to their proper recipients. If a message is addressed to an app version that no longer exists, that message will not be delivered anywhere.

The final step, of course, is to write the handler itself, which must accept POST requests.

As mentioned in the previous section, an App Engine app will process messages of two XMPP types: CHAT and NORMAL. If the App Engine XMPP service receives an XMPP message with some other type, the request handler is not called. The default message type when sending a `com.google.appengine.api.xmpp.Message` is CHAT .

The incoming XMPP message is actually represented as a MIME multipart message under the hood, but there is a helper method for extracting the XMPP message information from the MIME data, given the `HttpServletRequest` object: the `XMPPService.parseMessage()` method takes the request as its argument, and returns a `com.google.appengine.api.xmpp.Message` instance.

```java
import java.io.IOException;
import javax.servlet.http.*;
import com.google.appengine.api.xmpp.JID;
import com.google.appengine.api.xmpp.Message;
import com.google.appengine.api.xmpp.XMPPService;
import com.google.appengine.api.xmpp.XMPPServiceFactory;

@SuppressWarnings("serial")
public class XMPPAgentServlet extends HttpServlet {
    public void doPost(HttpServletRequest req,
            HttpServletResponse res)
            throws IOException {
        XMPPService xmpp = XMPPServiceFactory.getXMPPService();
        Message message = xmpp.parseMessage(req);

        JID fromJid = message.getFromJid();
        String body = message.getBody();
        // ...
    }
}
```

The example above shows how the sender and message body (a `String`) can be extracted from the Servlet request object. That is essentially all there is to it. The Servlet can then process the message as appropriate for the app, and can check the sender's address in the case where different senders indicate different processing.

*Setting up Connectr as an XMPP client* will describe how the *Connectr* app can process XMPP 'breaking news' notifications, and incorporate them into its stream of feed items.

## XMPP-related quotas and limits

XMPP messages—both outgoing and incoming—have a size limit of 100KB, and the total size of an XMPP API call is limited to 1MB. Both outgoing and incoming messages count towards your bandwidth total. In addition, the XMPP API calls, amount of XMPP data sent, as well as the number of recipients messaged and the number of invitations sent, are all under quota control.

The quotas are different depending upon whether or not Billing is enabled, as described in *Chapter 11*—you can see the specifics by looking at the "Quota Details" page in your App Engine Admin Console.

## Setting up *Connectr* as an XMPP client

Now that we have seen how to both send and receive XMPP messages, we will look at how *Connectr* can use the XMPP service to receive news items from an XMPP gateway App Engine app (`http://connectr-xmppagent.appspot.com/`).

Our XMPP gateway app was built as a companion to *Connectr* in order to easily demonstrate the use of XMPP. The intent is that it will remain up and running indefinitely; however, if there should be any future issues accessing it, it is not key to the *Connectr* app's functionality.

A *Connectr* app is 'subscribed' to the gateway app to start receiving the XMPP news items by invoking a Servlet that performs the subscription. It then processes these news items (which have a known JSON-based structure) as they arrive, converts them to `StreamItem` objects, and persists them to the Datastore, in this manner injecting them into the series of `StreamItem` objects consumed by the `server.MessagesServiceImpl` methods.

So, this XMPP example also shows how multiple information sources may be processed independently in the background, and integrated into a common stream consumed by the client.

# Subscribing a *Connectr* app to the XMPP Breaking News Gateway App

The first step in using the XMPP service to receive messages is always to enable the incoming receipt of XMPP messages to the app. As described previously; this is done in the `appengine-web.xml` file:

```
<inbound-services>
  <service>xmpp_message</service>
</inbound-services>
```

We will then utilize a special-purpose Servlet, `server.servlets.XMPPRequestServlet`, which communicates subscribe or unsubscribe requests to the XMPP news gateway app. This Servlet has been configured in `web.xml` to require admin access, as shown in the following code:

```
<servlet>
  <servlet-name>XMPPRequest</servlet-name>
  <servlet-class>
    packagepath.server.servlets.XMPPRequestServlet
  </servlet-class>
</servlet>
<servlet-mapping>
  <servlet-name>XMPPRequest</servlet-name>
  <url-pattern>/xmpprequest</url-pattern>
</servlet-mapping>

<security-constraint>
  <web-resource-collection>
    <url-pattern>/xmpprequest</url-pattern>
  </web-resource-collection>
  <auth-constraint>
    <role-name>admin</role-name>
  </auth-constraint>
</security-constraint>
```

To subscribe the app to the news gateway agent's notifications, make the following request:

`http://<your-app-id>.appspot.com/xmpprequest?request=add`

To unsubscribe from the notifications, use:

`http://<your-app-id>.appspot.com/xmpprequest?request=remove`

Recall that this must be done for the deployed app, not your local development version.

The following code shows the `server.servlets.XMPPRequestServlet`, which sends the `add` or `remove` requests to the gateway agent. The default (automatically-generated) 'from' address is used when sending the request. When the message is received by the XMPP gateway app, the XMPP address or JID of the requesting app is added to a set of subscribers. So, the XMPP notifications will be sent to the version of the app with which you subscribed—for example, they will be sent to the default version of your app, if you used that version to perform the subscription.

```java
import com.google.appengine.api.xmpp.*;
import java.io.IOException;
import java.util.logging.Logger;
import javax.servlet.http.HttpServlet;
import javax.servlet.http.HttpServletRequest;
import javax.servlet.http.HttpServletResponse;

public class XMPPRequestServlet extends HttpServlet {

  private static final Logger logger =
  Logger.getLogger(XMPPRequestServlet.class.getName());
  public static final String XMPP_GATEWAY =
    "connectr-xmppagent@appspot.com";
  private static final String ADD = "add";
  private static final String REMOVE = "remove";
  ...

  public void doPost(HttpServletRequest req,
    HttpServletResponse resp) throws IOException  {

    String reqString = req.getParameter("request");
    if (reqString != null &&
      reqString.equalsIgnoreCase("add")) {
      sendRequest(ADD);
      resp.setContentType("text/plain");
      resp.getWriter().println(
      "The 'add' request was sent to " + XMPP_GATEWAY);
    }
    else if (reqString != null &&
      reqString.equalsIgnoreCase("remove")) {
      sendRequest(REMOVE);
      resp.setContentType("text/plain");
      resp.getWriter().println(
```

```
      "The 'remove' request was sent to " + XMPP_GATEWAY);
    }
    else {
      System.out.println(
      "in XMPPRequestServlet- did not understand request: " +
       reqString);
    }
  }


  public void sendRequest(String request) {

    JID jid = new JID(XMPP_GATEWAY);
    Message xMessage = new MessageBuilder()
      .withRecipientJids(jid)
      .withBody(request)
      .build();
    boolean result = sendMessage(xMessage, jid);
    logger.info("request: " + xMessage + " sent with result: "
      + result);
    // No constructive action is taken if there was a problem; this
could be added
  }

  private boolean sendMessage(Message xMessage, JID jid) {

    XMPPService xmpp = XMPPServiceFactory.getXMPPService();
    boolean messageSent = false;
    SendResponse status = xmpp.sendMessage(xMessage);
    messageSent = (status.getStatusMap().get(jid) ==
     SendResponse.Status.SUCCESS);

    return messageSent;
  }

}
```

For a remove request to work, the message must be sent from the same address as was the add message. This means that the remove will not be successful if in the interval between subscription and unsubscription, the app changes its default version status, since its automatically-generated XMPP address will then change as well.

# Processing the incoming XMPP notifications

Once a subscription is set up, and the breaking news XMPP app is sending XMPP notifications our way, we just need to hook up a Servlet, `server.servlets.XMPPAgentServlet`, which will handle and process the incoming XMPP notifications. We first configure the `web.xml` file so that the Servlet is associated with the special XMPP URL, `/_ah/xmpp/message/chat/`, as shown previously.

The following code shows `server.servlets.XMPPAgentServlet`. For simplification, this Servlet assumes that the only XMPP notifications that it will receive are from the breaking news gateway. If this were not true, further processing of the notifications might be required.

```
import com.google.appengine.api.xmpp.*;
import com.google.gson.Gson;
... Other imports...


@SuppressWarnings("serial")
public class XMPPAgentServlet extends HttpServlet {

  private static final Logger logger =
  Logger.getLogger(XMPPAgentServlet.class.getName());
  private static final String OK = "OK";
  private static final String ERROR = "ERROR";

  public void doPost(HttpServletRequest req, HttpServletResponse resp)
throws IOException  {

    PersistenceManager pm = PMF.getNonTxnPm();

    // We assume that only the 'XMPP news gateway' will be trying to
    // communicate with us.
    try {
      String strStatus = "";
      XMPPService xmpp = XMPPServiceFactory.getXMPPService();

      Message msg = xmpp.parseMessage(req);
      JID fromJid = msg.getFromJid();
      String body = msg.getBody();
      logger.info("Received a message from " + fromJid +
        " and body = " + body);

      if (body.startsWith(OK) || body.startsWith(ERROR)) {
        logger.info("Got ERROR or OK");
      }
```

```
        else {
          // process JSON data as an array of SimpleItems,
          // which is what we expect from the news app
          Gson gson = new Gson();
          StreamItem sitem;
          SimpleItem[] sitems =
            gson.fromJson(body, SimpleItem[].class);
          for (SimpleItem tw: sitems) {
            // create a streamitem
            logger.info("conversion: " + tw);
            sitem = new StreamItem(tw.getTtext(),
            tw.getTtext(), tw.getSource(), tw.getTdate(),
              "", "",  "http://twitter.com/" +tw.getTname() +
              "/status/"+ tw.getTid(), "xmpp", "", null);
            pm.makePersistent(sitem);
          }
        }

    } catch (Exception e) {
      logger.log(Level.SEVERE, Utils.stackTraceToString(e));
    }
    finally {
      pm.close();
    }
  }
}
```

The Servlet parses the incoming message. It expects the message to be either a response to the subscription request or an array of news items in JSON format. It tries to parse the news items as JSON against the expected format of an array of server.domain.SimpleItem objects (this class is used only to parse these XMPP messages). The Servlet uses the Google GSON library, which runs on App Engine, to do this (http://code.google.com/p/google-gson/). If there are any issues with the parsing, the Servlet takes no further action.

The result of a successful parse is a collection of SimpleItem objects. These objects are converted to StreamItem objects and persisted to the Datastore. The feed ID of these objects is set to a special string, "xmpp". Once stored, they may be accessed by the server.MessagesServiceImpl methods as any other StreamItem object.

After you enable the receipt of the breaking news items for a deployed version of your app, you should start to see regular requests to **/_ah/xmpp/message/chat/** in the Admin Console log for that app and see the news items in the streams for the app's users. The Servlet will log the sender's address, log the items it has received, and then store them as StreamItems.

Thus, via XMPP, multiple different sources of information may be pushed asynchronously into a common stream that can be accessed by the client.

# Summary

In this chapter, we've introduced the use of Cron Jobs, application-defined Task Queues, and the App Engine XMPP service. In addition to its focus on using tasks to perform asynchronous background work, the chapter also pulled together a number of concepts introduced in earlier chapters, including the use of caching, DTOs, query cursors, and several techniques for performing efficient Datastore queries.

These tools have allowed us to build a framework of server-side background jobs and tasks, running asynchronously from the client RPC methods, that support the generation of the 'activity stream' content—based on the content of the feeds associated with a user's Friends— that is displayed in the *Connectr* main panel.

Because *Connectr* background tasks don't require synchronization with the RPC methods or each other, and are designed to be rerun (if necessary) without causing problems, the server-side task framework is robust and mostly parallelizable, and lets us benefit from App Engine's ability to run a large number of tasks quickly. We make use of both regularly-run tasks and those triggered by client-side actions—such as a user login—in order to keep the stream content usefully updated.

We build `StreamItem` DTOs, and cache both the DTOs and their persistent counterparts, at the time the `StreamItem` objects are generated. So, we do proactive background work in order to make our RPC responses more efficient.

The `server.MessagesServiceImpl` RPC methods then simply tap into the Datastore and cache, and do not need to be concerned with which background tasks are running when. These methods execute keys-only queries to find the relevant `StreamItem` IDs to display, and then use the IDs to obtain the display objects from the cache.

Then, we described App Engine's XMPP service and used the app's ability to receive XMPP messages to add 'breaking news item' *push* to *Connectr* from a XMPP gateway. These news items are incorporated asynchronously into the activity stream as well.

# 13

# Conclusion and Final Thoughts

Most developers agree that building scalable AJAX apps is far from trivial. One goal of this book is to show how GWT combined with App Engine synergistically simplifies development and deployment in many ways.

App Engine provides automatic scalability and redundancy. As your user base grows, you don't need to add application or database server instances: scalability is automatic.

App Engine starts and stops additional instances of your app when needed, providing fully transparent load-balancing and fault-tolerant services.

With App Engine, you don't have to perform system administration. There are no systems to take care of per se, only your app needs to be managed. Activities such as hardware fulfillment, data backup, OS and database patching are all taken care of by the App Engine platform transparently.

The deployment of an app could not be easier: one click in Eclipse and you are done. Once deployed, you can choose in the Admin Console which version of your app is served to your users. You can have several versions running at the same time. This provides an easy way to test experimental features before making them available to your entire user base.

App Engine Admin Console provides an easy and powerful way to view all your apps' operations and statistics such as logs, quotas, and application errors, and browse the live data store.

App Engine also provides simple access to a powerful and growing range of *cloud services* such as the Task Queue and XMPP API, with others such as Map/Reduce, and OAuth on App Engine's roadmap. These services are themselves designed to be scalable, reliable, and they work well at high load.

Howewer, App Engine has some constraints and limitations. For example, there is currently a 30-second limit on all web requests, and so, long-running operations must be broken into smaller tasks and long-running file uploads are not supported.

While it is anticipated that some of these constraints will be relaxed in future, they ensure that apps developed on App Engine are highly scalable, both with respect to app servers and the distributed data store. So, you don't have to worry when your user base starts to grow.

As far as GWT is concerned, it is also an important tool in the developer's toolbox. The one thing that makes it different from all other AJAX framework is that GWT abstracts JavaScript completely: developers write their AJAX app entirely in Java and GWT compiles it into optimized JavaScript. While this could have been seen as a limitation because developers cannot generate and tweak their own JavaScript, this provides numerous advantages:

- First, GWT generates highly optimized browser-specific JavaScript. Therefore, developers don't have to know the specific problems and workarounds of each browser.

- Second, because GWT generates code for the browser, it is free to generate code in languages other than JavaScript as browsers evolve. For example, HTML 5 could be used by GWT to provide developers access to the latest advance of web technology.

- Finally, another advantage is that by using Java and not JavaScript as a software language for their app, developers have access to the rich suite of tools available for Java such as debugging, profiling, and project management.

Another goal of the book was to be a resource for a number of design patterns, approaches, and tips, illustrated by the *Connectr* app as a running example, so that code examples are readily to hand. As we introduced the various parts of the *Connectr* application, we developed these patterns both for GWT and App Engine as well as for communication between the client and server components of an app.

## Chapter 13

For GWT, these patterns and approaches included:

- Using UI Binder and resource bundles to declarative specify layout, images, and CSS specification of user interface elements.
- Design patterns for keeping code modular and manageable, including notably:
  - The MVP pattern and its related Display interface pattern
  - The use of the Event Bus pattern to allow application components to communicate between each other
  - The use of a centralized RPC class to centralize and harness Remote Procedure Call behavior

For App Engine, topics included:

- Approaches for data class design and querying including design to "get around" the lack of a relational database, instead leveraging the Datastore's features; and ways to design classes and queries so that we pull in and transmit only the data needed
- Use of migrations as an application's "soft schema" changes
- Use of query cursors to split time-consuming Datastore actions into manageable chunks
- Tuning Datastore query consistency/availability and latency settings
- Use of entity groups, transactions, and use of transactional tasks to tie together actions that span entity groups
- Use of JDO Lifecycle Listeners with Memcache to support caching
- Models for decoupled and asynchronous processing and task design to make an application more robust and scalable, including use of Task Queues and Cron Jobs to support background processing

*Connectr* also incorporated some patterns useful for client-server communication, including:

- Use of DTOs at multiple levels of detail
- Use of the Channel API for client-server push
- Use of OAuth and Google Accounts to support multiple login methods so that the app need not store user passwords

# What lies ahead for App Engine and GWT?

Google App Engine and GWT technology is already helping developers and companies to bring modern AJAX apps to the marketplace. However, the Web and the field of cloud computing is evolving rapidly and despite the technological marvels we see, we are still in the Internet stone age.

Many improvements are on App Engine's roadmap and expected soon. These include relaxed quota limitations, new enterprise features such as reserved instances to reduce spin-up time, additional integrated App Engine services and APIs, and a "Business App Engine" platform that offers an RDBMS.

When it comes to web applications it is clear that the meaning of hosting and system administration has already evolved: increasing numbers of developers have stopped buying or renting servers and instead have moved to more simplified and automated platform-as-service providers such as Google App Engine.

GWT, on the other end, has no lesser ambitions than to "clone traditional desktop UI onto the Web" according to the GWT website. There is still a long way to go but the show is already on the road and the journey promises to be exciting.

As rich internet apps become more powerful and complex, GWT combined with App Engine simplify their development and deployment—thus allowing developers to spend more time on building great user experiences for their audience.

# Index

# F

Facebook
  *Connectr*, integrating, with  284
  *Connectr*, registering with  284, 286
FeedIndex.addFeedURLs method  333
FeedIndex child  322
FeedIndex constructor  324
FeedIndex object  314, 315, 328
FeedIndex.updateFeedURLs method  333
FeedInfo classes  344
FeedInfo key  315, 325
FeedInfo methods  256
FeedInfo object  314
FeedInfo persistent class  315
FeedInfo.updateFeed() method  404
feed-related server-side processing
  asynchronous server-side tasks, in
          *Connectr*  416
  Cron Jobs  414, 415
  Task Queue  407
  tasks  407
  transactional tasks  407
FeedUpdateServlet.doPost() method  421
FeedUpdateUserServlet.doPost()
          method  422
fetchFriendSummaryDTO()  188
fetch group  122
Filter class  366
finally clause  99, 321
findOrCreate(user) method  306
firstName property  101
floating point number  102
Friend class  228
FriendDetails child object  90
FriendDetails class  114, 232
FriendDetails object  90, 137, 312
FriendDetails sub-object  115
FriendDTO class  90
FriendDTO object  125
FriendEditEventHandler class  193
FriendEditPresenter class  188
friendKeys list  328
FriendListPresenter  183
FriendListPresenter class  183, 184
Friend object  90
  about  124, 125

  creating  124, 125
  deleting  126
  list fetching, key list used  126
Friend objects  328
Friend persistent class  312
FriendPopupPresenter class  190
FriendPopupView.ui.xml  188
FriendSummaryDTO class  90
Friend.updateFromDTO()  132

# G

GAE
  about  8
  and GWT  7
  App Engine application hosting  11
  App Engine Datastore  9
  App Engines Datastore  9
  App Engine's scalable services  9, 10
  GWT with  14
GAE documentation, URL  20
GAE/Java documentation, URL  20
GAE/Java Google Group, URL  20
gae.pk-id field  109
gae.pk-name field  109
general GAE Google Group, URL  20
geographical point  103
getDefaultUser method  123
getExent() method  165
getFeedInfo()  344
getFriend method  131
getFriendSummaries() method  126
getFriendViaCache() method  347
getHeader method  222
getInputStream method  244
getKey() method  325
getLoggedInUser method  281
getObjectById method  120
getParent()  326
getParent() method  313, 326
getSession() method  225
getValue() method  406
Google account  102
Google App Engine (GAE)
  about  23
  for business  11
  surprises, for new developers  11, 12

**Thank you for buying**
# Google App Engine Java and GWT Application Development

## About Packt Publishing

Packt, pronounced 'packed', published its first book "*Mastering phpMyAdmin for Effective MySQL Management*" in April 2004 and subsequently continued to specialize in publishing highly focused books on specific technologies and solutions.

Our books and publications share the experiences of your fellow IT professionals in adapting and customizing today's systems, applications, and frameworks. Our solution based books give you the knowledge and power to customize the software and technologies you're using to get the job done. Packt books are more specific and less general than the IT books you have seen in the past. Our unique business model allows us to bring you more focused information, giving you more of what you need to know, and less of what you don't.

Packt is a modern, yet unique publishing company, which focuses on producing quality, cutting-edge books for communities of developers, administrators, and newbies alike. For more information, please visit our website: www.packtpub.com.

## Writing for Packt

We welcome all inquiries from people who are interested in authoring. Book proposals should be sent to author@packtpub.com. If your book idea is still at an early stage and you would like to discuss it first before writing a formal book proposal, contact us; one of our commissioning editors will get in touch with you.

We're not just looking for published authors; if you have strong technical skills but no writing experience, our experienced editors can help you develop a writing career, or simply get some additional reward for your expertise.

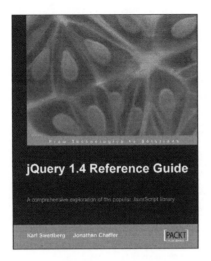

## jQuery 1.4 Reference Guide

ISBN: 978-1-849510-04-2      Paperback: 336 pages

A comprehensive exploration of the popular JavaScript library

1. Quickly look up features of the jQuery library

2. Step through each function, method, and selector expression in the jQuery library with an easy-to-follow approach

3. Understand the anatomy of a jQuery script

4. Write your own plug-ins using jQuery's powerful plug-in architecture

## Ext JS 3.0 Cookbook

ISBN: 978-1-847198-70-9      Paperback: 376 pages

Clear step-by-step recipes for building impressive rich internet applications using the Ext JS JavaScript library

1. Master the Ext JS widgets and learn to create custom components to suit your needs

2. Build striking native and custom layouts, forms, grids, listviews, treeviews, charts, tab panels, menus, toolbars and much more for your real-world user interfaces

3. Packed with easy-to-follow examples to exercise all of the features of the Ext JS library

Please check **www.PacktPub.com** for information on our titles

Made in the USA
Lexington, KY
17 March 2011